The Center for Chinese Studies
at the University of California, Berkeley, supported by
the East Asian Institute (University of California,
Berkeley) and the State of California, is the unifying
organization for social science and interdisciplinary
research on modern China

PEASANT CHINA
IN TRANSITION

This volume is sponsored by
the Center for Chinese Studies
University of California, Berkeley

PEASANT CHINA IN TRANSITION

*The Dynamics of Development
Toward Socialism, 1949–1956*

Vivienne Shue

University of California Press / Berkeley • Los Angeles • London

University of California Press
Berkeley and Los Angeles, California
University of California Press, Ltd.
London, England
© 1980 by
The Regents of the University of California
Printed in the United States of America

1 2 3 4 5 6 7 8 9

Library of Congress Cataloging in Publication Data

Shue, Vivienne.
   Peasant China in transition. The dynamics of
  development toward socialism, 1949–1956
  Bibliography: p.
  Includes index.
   1. Agriculture and state—China.   2. Land reform—
China. I. Title.
HD2098 1980.S55   338.1'851   80-13109
ISBN 0-520-03734-0

To my mother and my father

CONTENTS

TABLES

ACKNOWLEDGMENTS

Body clothed in a no-cloth robe,
Feet clad in turtle's fur boots,
I seize my bow of rabbit horn
And prepare to shoot the devil Ignorance.

HAN-SHAN, T'ang Dynasty

In this spirit, and not much more realistically armed for the battle, some years ago I began the research on which this book is based. Since that time, some of the deficiencies in my own weapons and armor have been made up by the help and support of many teachers, colleagues, and friends. And while we are, I suppose, still far from quelling the demon we have pursued, these people all have a share in what blows may be struck against him here.

Most especially, I wish to thank Ezra F. Vogel of Harvard University, where I did my doctoral work. It was during an unscheduled campus lunch discussion with him that the possibility of investigating a problem that later grew into this study first came to my mind. Through the months and years of research, he always expressed much confidence in the value of the work I proposed, never failing to offer encouragement and a sense of direction. And when I began to write the early drafts, he was my most faithful reader and critic. I have gained more than I can say from his generous spirit and his rare knowledge of Chinese society and politics.

Others at Harvard also helped, especially Benjamin I. Schwartz, who challenged me often to rethink my ideas and to find new vantage points from which to regard the data I was collecting.

During that time, Thomas P. Bernstein generously read through all the early drafts, offering many useful criticisms and suggestions. His special familiarity with the period made his comments most valuable to me. Martin K. Whyte also drew up knowledgeable and thought-provoking critiques of several chapters. And I received helpful comments from Roy M. Hofheinz, Kenneth Lieberthal, and Lynn White as well.

In 1976 I spent a very worthwhile semester at the Center for Chinese Studies at Berkeley. There Frederic Wakeman not only made the visitor feel welcome but also offered much good advice and encouragement on the work of revising the manuscript. At Berkeley I first came to know Marc J. Blecher, who was also there to write about rural Chinese politics. We spent so many remarkable afternoons trading ideas and thinking out loud together then that I cannot now be certain just how much I owe to his energetic creativity and insight—except that I know it is a very great deal.

As the revisions progressed, five scholars in particular gave me unusually fine and thoughtful criticisms and urged me to address new problems and topics. Although I know I have not been able to answer all their questions or follow all their suggestions in this work, I have learned a good deal in the effort, and am most grateful to James C. Scott, Edward Friedman, Mark Selden, Andrew J. Nathan, and Alfred Stepan for ideas and queries that have much enriched what I have thought and written. I wish to thank also Gordon Bennett, Benedict Stavis, Ying-mao Kau, and Angus McDonald for their help and encouragement along the way; and Thomas B. Wiens for one quite generous, and important, bit of bibliographical assistance.

My debt to Victor C. Falkenheim is a very special one. With an unerring sense for the development of the argument, he critically reviewed the entire manuscript just before its final revision and made numerous excellent suggestions for structural improvement. No one has helped me more to tighten the discussion and to clarify my own conclusions. The final product is much the better for the gift of his sure guidance.

An earlier version of part of Chapter 3 was published in *Peasant Studies,* and an earlier version of part of Chapter 5, in *Modern China.* I wish to thank both journals for permission to use this material. Burton Watson's brilliant translations of the poems by Han-shan are all taken from the collection entitled *Cold Mountain* and are used here with the kind permission of Columbia University Press.

My appreciation also goes to Eugene Wu of the Harvard-Yenching Library for making the acquisition and use of some of the provincial newspapers I required both quick and convenient. And I am grateful to John Dolfin and the staff of the Universities Service Centre in Hong Kong for doing the same while I was working there in 1973–74. Financial support under the Foreign Area Fellowship Program of the Social Science Research Council and the American Council of Learned Societies made possible the year of research in Hong Kong. Much appreciated research fellowships from the Harvard University East Asian Research Center and the Center for Chinese Studies at the University of California at Berkeley provided extra time for revision. My thanks also to Jonathan D. Spence and the Council on East Asian Studies at Yale University for financial assistance in preparing the manuscript.

To Henry, for good counsel, generous sacrifice, and for never once doubting the enterprise, I will always be most grateful of all.

V.B.S.

GUIDE TO THE FOOTNOTES

To save space, most titles have been eliminated from the footnotes. Full citations are given in the bibliography, which is divided into four sections. There each entry is numbered, and the relevant numbers appear in brackets in the footnotes. In the case of Chinese newspaper articles, the bracketed number in the footnote is accompanied by an abbreviation of the journal title and the date, so that readers may quickly recognize the source. (A list of title abbreviations follows.) References to books and articles with authors include in the footnote the surname—and in the case of Chinese names, the full name—of the author along with the bibliographic number. Titles are provided in the notes only for books without authors and in a few other cases that might otherwise be ambiguous.

ABBREVIATIONS USED IN
FOOTNOTES AND BIBLIOGRAPHY

CB	*Current Background*
CCJP	*Ch'ang Chiang Jih Pao*
CFJP	*Chieh Fang Jih Pao* (Shanghai)
CKCNP	*Chung Kuo Ch'ing Nien Pao* (Peking)
CKNP	*Chung Kuo Nung Pao*
FBIS	*Foreign Broadcast Information Service*
FKJP	*Fukien Jih Pao*
HHNP	*Hsin Hunan Pao* (Ch'angsha)
HHYP	*Hsin Hua Yüeh Pao*
HNCCP	*Hunan Ch'ün Chung Pao*
HNCNP	*Hunan Ch'ing Nien Pao*
HNCSP	*Hunan Chien She Pao*
HNNM	*Hsiang Nan Nung Min*
HPJP	*Hupei Jih Pao* (Hankow)
HTJP	*Hsing Tao Jih Pao*
HWJP	*Hsin Wen Jih Pao* (Shanghai)
HYHW	*Heng Yang Hsin Wen*
JMJP	*Jen Min Jih Pao*
JPRS	Joint Publications Research Service
KJP	*Kiangsi Jih Pao*
NCNA	New China News Agency
NFJP	*Nan Fang Jih Pao* (Canton)
SCMP	*Survey of the China Mainland Press*
SWB	*Summary of World Broadcasts* (Far East)
TKP	*Ta Kung Pao* (Tientsin)

INTRODUCTION

In China this century, the great experiment in rural transformation was born in war—the fury and determination of war against the Japanese invaders, and the agony and bitterness of brutal civil war. In the years before that terrifying time of violence engulfed the Chinese people, there had been many scattered attempts at rural reconstruction, improvement of peasant welfare, and agricultural development. Some of these experiments were subsidized by the national and provincial governments, some by missionaries and foreign foundations, some by Chinese universities and progressive private individuals, and some even by local warlords. A number of these efforts produced encouraging results, but the lessons and methods of the early experimental projects were never sufficiently distilled and systematized, nor were they widely proliferated in the countryside. During the war, however, in their revolutionary base areas near to and far from the fighting, the Chinese Communist Party (CCP) and its armed forces began evolving a comprehensive program for progress in China's villages. Their program rested first on the application of a fairly steeply progressive agricultural tax, and fixed ceilings on land rent and interest on loans to peasants. Second, it called for the expropriation of all land belonging to landlords and all or most of the land belonging to rich peasants, and the redistribution of this land to poor and landless peasants. Third, it advocated the organization of Mutual Aid Teams among poor peasants to improve their cultivation and increase their productivity, and it promoted the organization of presocialist Marketing Co-ops and Credit Co-ops for poor farmers. During the war years, in its northern bases, the Party had wide and diverse rural areas in which to experiment and to evaluate its programs, as well as time in which to refine its rural development policies and appeals to peasants.

By 1948, when the tide of war was turning in favor of the People's Liberation Army (PLA), enormous expanses of territory began falling extremely rapidly under Communist control. The Party brought its rural development policies with it as it conquered these territories, and this meant that over most of these later liberated areas the first sustained application of CCP reforms coincided with the arrival of military occupation forces. Thus the early moves against landlords and wealthier villagers in these areas, to balance more equitably the burden of taxation or to limit the worst excesses of tenancy and usury, were not, as in some other countries, simply legislated in the capital and left to the local functionaries of a sitting government to be implemented. The first steps in the CCP's rural reform effort were taken instead by the provisional military governors of a conquering army, holding territory and attempting to make improvements in the economic and social situation there, as it continued fighting.

With national liberation in 1949 and the rapid consolidation of peace in all parts of the country, the new government turned its full attention to implementing its rural reform programs. By the end of 1952 it had basically completed a radical land reform in all the new territories. And by the middle of 1956 it had moved the mass of China's rural population from its centuries-old patterns of private landholding and family farming into socialist cooperatives for production and marketing. This very rapid transition to socialism in the countryside was accomplished with minimal violence and disorder, without a disastrous drop in agricultural output or a terrible blow to existing productive capacity, and without an overall decline in rural standards of living.

The contrast between these swift CCP successes and the earlier halting attempts at rural reform in prerevolutionary China are striking indeed. Or if we compare China in this period with other developing countries in Asia where land reforms and a system of peasant cooperatives have been tried, such as India, the Chinese success is also outstanding. Or again, if we contrast the Chinese experience of socialist transformation with the more bloody and debilitating collectivizations in the USSR and elsewhere, we are struck with Chinese accomplishments. And finally, even if we compare the achievements of these brief years with later continuing efforts at rural reorganization and development in China itself, it seems that these early successes are again unusually clear and decisive. Progressive changes in China's agrarian order in the future proved harder to consolidate.

The research for this study was undertaken in an effort to understand better the dynamics of the CCP's early drive for rural reform and the reasons for its success. It was hoped also that this would shed some light on the general problems of transforming peasant societies and on the degree to which Chinese methods might be transferable to other societies suffering from similar problems of poverty, stagnation, and discontent.

Although there have already been some admirable attempts at analyzing the period from 1949 to 1956, most have concentrated on the great divides — on the land reform movement itself or on the "high tide" of collectivization. The intent of this study, however, has been to look in depth at the entire period with a view to understanding these changes in the countryside not as discrete convulsions but as process. An underlying motivation of this work has been the conviction that only a look at the total package and sequence of economic and political reforms introduced in the countryside can provide a sense of the flow of developments that drew peasants so quickly into conformity with the central plans for socialist transformation. Peasants tended to favor or oppose joining cooperatives depending on their perceptions of the political situation in the village and on their perceptions of their own economic alternatives, as independents operating within the evolving realities of labor supply, market and credit structures, tax incentive systems, and so on. To understand peasant options and perceptions, and therefore peasant choices in 1955–56 at the "high tide" of collectivization, we must understand the changes taking place in these surrounding systems in the immediately preceding period.

Thus Part One focuses on the situation in the villages immediately after liberation and on the conditions that pressed the leadership into deciding for a swift and all-inclusive land reform movement. Here, in the discussion of how land reform and the gigantic redistribution of wealth it entailed were administered, many of what were to become distinctive features of CCP rural political work are first examined. The victories of land reform, however, remained precarious and certainly not necessarily conducive to increasingly egalitarian distributions of wealth or to progress toward socialism. Therefore in Part Two we find the leadership administering a general progressive agricultural tax and a program for the establishment of farming Mutual Aid Teams for poor peasants—both important policies adopted to try to hold the line on the existing post-land-reform distribution of wealth in the villages. These were modest, interim policies intended to hem in, at least to some extent, the "rich peasant economy" and the "spontaneous capitalist tendencies" in the countryside that, in the postwar boom, could quickly have led to the reemergence of gross inequalities. But interim policies such as these were of limited effectiveness, and the difficulties they presented are explored here as background to the decision in late 1953 to press ahead with still more vigorous steps toward socialism in the countryside.

Thus in Part Three we find the central leadership determined to collectivize agricultural production, but moving first to restructure the economic environment of the peasantry—specifically moving to restructure the commodities markets and the rural credit market—to make collectivization materially more attractive to farmers. These comprehensive policies, when adequately implemented, constituted the directed demise of rural petty capitalism or the "rich peasant economy." They made the alternative of independent farming much less promising and feasible than before, and thus they paved the way for the rapid acceptance of collective organization. Therefore, when in Chapter 7 we finally consider the "high tide" itself, the background discussion of property, tax and marketing restrictions, credit and trade incentives, and so on helps make sense of the gradual process of change that had been building and of the quick, basically voluntary, decision so many peasants would make to try joining a cooperative.

The policies for development toward socialism examined here were indeed comprehensive, and by and large they were very successful. But they were not by any means designed and carried out without difficulty or without mistakes. The focus of this study is on policy implementation and on the actual problems encountered in the villages in getting planned reforms to work. What this focus reveals most clearly is that the Party did not approach peasants with an appeal that they forsake private interest and concern with personal welfare in favor of self-sacrificing love for the new collective or concern for the common good. Quite the contrary, Party leaders were unmistakably convinced that appeals on these grounds would be doomed to fail; the revolution could yet be stillborn if the people did not themselves give it life and recognize it as their child. The center chose instead precisely to try to use the indefatigable determination of peasants to improve their own private welfare as a motive force for change toward socialism. The challenge of policy making in the period, then, was to find ways in which peasant pursuit of private interest could be made to coincide with and even advance the revolutionary government's goals of socialist transformation. The programs examined here were introduced precisely in the effort to capture for the revolution the constructive, self-interested, entrepreneurial energies of peasants. In gross summary, this is probably how we can best account for the CCP's unusual successes in the countryside in these years.

But beyond this generalization, the body of this study suggests at least seven specific elements of the CCP's overall success. They and their implications for our analysis of the developing Chinese political process are discussed in the concluding chapter. They can be briefly outlined here, however, in order to suggest the kinds of conclusions to be drawn from the data presented.

First, it becomes clear that the new Chinese authorities achieved a high level of sophistication and specificity in policy planning for rural development. Guidelines issued to rural work personnel were almost always impressive in their detail, their provision for exceptional cases, and their clarity on the main goals and purposes to be kept at the forefront of the work. The contrast here with the Soviet workstyle at comparable periods is particularly great. Confusion about the principles of socialist transformation and lack of specificity about the organizational forms to be constructed hampered orderly collectivization in the Russian countryside.

Second, Chinese central planners remained cognizant of the limitations on their own ability to foresee problems and determine outcomes at the local level. They encouraged flexibility in basic-level policy implementation, and they were prepared for only partial fulfillment of goals. They were open to very irregular procedures, if they could be effective, and they did not expect or insist on perfect compliance with one program before launching the next.

Third, as this would suggest, they showed a marked preference for all-out bold attacks on rural problems, even when their own planning and administrative capacities were well below optimal levels for the tasks they faced. Although they had a conception of stage-by-stage revolutionary transformation and transition to socialism, they were concerned that drawing out the interim preparatory periods would give opposition forces the chance to become entrenched and more difficult to dislodge. Rather than delay action and lose an opportunity for progressive development, then, even when their own capabilities and the objective conditions in the villages were not altogether promising, they most often pushed ahead with reforms, doing as much as possible in the first thrust, and leaving until later the rectification of excesses committed in the heat of the struggle as well as the solution of more intractable problems. This gave the new government the appearance of always criticizing its own performance in administering a reform just attempted, but always simultaneously pressing ahead with even newer, more far-reaching plans for change. Although the still skeletal rural administrative apparatus clearly overextended itself repeatedly during these years, at the center they were convinced that their reforms would ultimately receive the support of the mass of peasants and that this in the end would ensure overall success. This confidence, which allowed them to risk so much change at once despite their undermanned and ill-trained rural cadre force, stands in marked contrast to the experiences of several other Asian countries, whose leaders have seemed to plan and prepare much better but have accomplished much less in the countryside.

Fourth, the Party recruited activists and cadres to carry out its rural reforms from among local villagers themselves. Although this by no means obviated all problems of communication and penetration, it did assist the new authorities considerably with difficulties of dialect, local custom, and peasant suspicion of outsiders. It also brought people with real knowledge of local history and conditions into the forming administrative apparatus in the new areas. These people were very green, without a sense of Party discipline, parochial in outlook, and almost wholly untutored in the concepts of Marxism-Leninism. Most were also illiterate. But in all these respects they resembled the mass of the peasantry to which the new government was intending to make its appeals for reform. It was to serve the Party well at this time to have such irreverent, unsophisticated, and practical people representing it at the base of its hierarchy in the villages. Their vantage point was very different from that of the old Party cadres and theorists. They could pose questions and find answers for them not conceived of at the Party center. The Party often blamed them for irregularities, but it also constantly relied on them and praised them for creative adaptation and for the day-to-day problem-solving energy that made the revolution workable in the villages.

Fifth, the Party's basic strategy for promoting rural change revolved around the management of village class struggle. The CCP employed a fairly elaborate class analysis for the interpretation of political conditions in the countryside, and it viewed its own task as being to *promote* the development of class struggle in the villages. To do this it not only carried out propaganda and education but it also directly intervened to manipulate the economic environment of peasants to make more plain and salient to them the convergence of their personal interests and their class interests, on the one hand, and the conflict of these with the interests of different classes in the village, on the other hand. The Party leadership was aware that a poor peasant's class interests, though real, could be complicated and camouflaged by other social factors; and among peasants the level of class consciousness was recognized to be low. That is why the CCP worked so doggedly, once in power, to restructure the real rural economic alternatives so that peasants' perceptions of their personal interests *would* clearly coincide with their assigned class interests. As a general approach to problems of rural political and economic transformation, this strategy proved extremely efficient, because once the leadership could establish genuinely conflicting interests along the lines intended, and could make them truly salient ones to peasants, then it could rely to a great extent on the natural energies of the people to effect the political changes that were desired. If these economic reforms alone were insufficient to mobilize peasants into a vigorous class struggle, then the Party could also carry out a strategic redrawing of the line that divided class enemies from class friends, and in this way it could tip the balance of village political forces in the direction of socialism. This combined strategy, more than anything else, accounts for the relatively rare resort to coercion in China to bring peasants toward socialism.

A sixth factor, closely related to the basic class strategy described above, was the new government's careful design and use of material incentives to draw peasants into cooperation with the planned steps toward village revolution and socialism. The many kinds of incentive systems employed stand out clearly in the narrative. They were the main means of reassuring peasants about their futures under socialism and the most graphic demonstrations to peasants that self-interest and class interest could indeed coincide for them. They created new constituencies for further reform, visibly isolating and making politically more vulnerable the village opposition to change. In all aspects of their work, central planners were attentive to the incentive systems they were setting up. While these systems did not always work as planned, peasants generally responded well, confirming the Party's conviction that peasants would make their choices for or against revolution and socialism on the basis of self-interested calculations.

Finally, throughout this period, central authorities cultivated a relationship with local communities that left a fair degree of discretion in the handling of local affairs to cadres on the scene. They also tolerated a degree of localist protectionism among basic-level cadres that kept the center somewhat less well informed of real conditions but permitted local communities a certain sense of independence from central demands. Rather than seek control over the disposition of everything down to the last catty of rice in the villages, central policy makers agreed to a certain looseness in the authority system that gave local cadres more room to maneuver between their obligations to their superiors and their obligations to their village constituents. This looseness was of course potentially very dangerous in what was soon to become a closely planned economy. But politically, in this period, it was healthy for the system, allowing the consolidation in many villages of a strongly supported, localist leadership peasants thought they could trust to protect them against the state center when it made unreasonable demands. This pattern of central-local relations was later to give rise to serious authority problems in the countryside, but at this period the center's preference for something less than total interference in local affairs proved invaluable in establishing the legitimacy of the new system in peasant eyes.

These are the seven elements of Chinese Communist success in rural work during these early years that emerge most prominently from this study. In the abstract they may seem to raise more questions than they answer. The chapters to follow, therefore, are designed to provide a more detailed understanding of the real obstacles and fears of the time and of how these seven factors, woven into the Chinese approach to rural change, reinforced one another and were decisive. As the narrative proceeds, the evidence mounts that in such mundane acts as squarely facing and accepting the complexities of the tasks set and learning to search out and utilize responsibly the small contributions of numberless undistinguished individuals lay the genius of the CCP in bringing about China's rural transformation.

SCOPE AND METHOD OF RESEARCH

This study focuses on the provinces of Hupei and Hunan, located in the Central South region of the country. There were several important considerations dictating the choice of these two provinces. First, they are part of the "later liberated areas," those areas of China not completely liberated from Kuomintang (KMT) control until 1949. A study of policies implemented in these areas reflects the most mature approach of the CCP to problems of early village revolution. In the Party's older revolutionary base areas of the north, rural policy was often characterized by trial and error. It was also frequently subject to the vicissitudes of the military situation and to the exigencies of strategic considerations. After 1949, to be sure, there were still security problems with KMT remnant forces and other armed counterrevolutionaries. And the war in Korea for a time threatened to bring on a foreign invasion. However, the CCP enjoyed much greater security after 1949 than it had known before, and it vigorously pursued its rural policies with a high degree of confidence and consistency. This is not to say that debates and disagreements over rural policy did not persist. But despite some uncertainties and the changes in pace, the overall policy line and the rationale behind it are extraordinarily clear and unambiguous for this period.

The choice of just two provinces out of the later liberated areas reflects the need to confine the relevant data base to a manageable size in a study such as this. And where provincial quantitative material is called for, I have, for the most part, chosen the data available for Hunan. Yet, I wished to avoid doing what might be considered a narrow case study. Even if generalizations about the whole of China are most often of little value, it should not be necessary to take refuge in a case study approach, denying all responsibility for the comparability of events outside the chosen area. If there is no such thing as a "typical" Chinese province, then we can at least choose to look at those provinces which, for the matter we wish to examine, seem to possess no peculiarities or special problems automatically tending to distort their experiences and to prejudice our findings.

Hunan and Hupei were selected in part because they appeared to fit this design. They were neither at the forefront of rural revolution in their area like Honan, nor did they lag behind like Kiangsi. They were neither as poor in agricultural resources as Fukien, nor as rich as Kwangtung. They each possessed some communities of national minority groups, but were inhabited overwhelmingly by Han people. Each enjoyed a reasonably well-developed rural economy with modest industrial and mining capacities, depressed by the war, to be sure, but still largely intact. And each could boast of a complex commercial network, as sophisticated as that of any province in China, linking its cities with the hinterland. In both cases, however, agriculture was indisputably the leading productive factor, and the population was overwhelmingly rural and peasant. If Hunan and Hupei cannot be called typical, they were not, at least in any very important way, greatly atypical or peculiar. Frequent checks on information flowing from other parts of the country during the period also confirm that most of the phenomena described here for these two provinces had close parallels in rural districts all over China.

For source material, I have relied heavily on the various provincial newspapers, the national press, journals, local handbooks, pamphlets, and the like. These sources, especially the provincial press, are excellent in many respects, not the least of which is the enormity of the material available in them. It is almost never necessary to rely on the statements made in one or two documents alone when trying to reconstruct important problems and issues using these materials. Hundreds, sometimes even thousands, of statements of a given policy or problem were printed, often with numerous examples and cases cited to illustrate them further. Because of the wealth of the material, I was able to make it a general rule not to include any phenomenon in this account unless I had found several separate reports of the kind in the sources; and most often there were scores to be found. The newspapers of this early period were far more lively and accessible than Chinese newspapers of the 1960's and 1970's. The stories are usually about real people, and they appear to address genuine and immediate problems of the times. Although many stories are primarily of propaganda or human interest value, many others are truly informative, including internal reports on conditions published for cadres' general information (often over authoritative signatures), reports of research units, blue ribbon committees, statistical offices, and the like. The resources of the Chinese daily provincial press in the 1950's have not been fully utilized in the West, and it has been a part of my purpose to demonstrate how much can be learned from these materials.

In addition to relaying information, however, the local press clearly also had didactic and inspirational roles to play at this period. The intended audience for most of the reports surveyed for this study was primarily the rural cadres and the cadres in cities or towns with responsibility for rural affairs. It was also hoped that the printed message might get through to a part of the illiterate peasantry by way of these cadres and activists in the villages. In the effort to educate and inspire these people about present policies and future prospects, there is no doubt that the newspapers persistently ignored the importance of certain kinds of issues and exaggerated others. Since, for example, the kinship or clan alliances of peasants did not fit well within the CCP's class struggle analysis of rural forces, there is little sustained discussion in the press of the interferences of family ties in the Party's political mobilization of the peasantry. Kinship-related problems are mentioned in a few sentences in many village reports, but there are no systematic analyses that would help us understand how widespread the problems were or what different forms they took. Likewise, reports of violence, especially violence against landlords and other class enemies, are incomplete in these newspapers. Beatings and killings are frequently alluded to, often criticized, but almost never counted up. The new authorities were engaged in mass mobilization to be sure, but they were also attempting to pacify the countryside. They did not wish to frighten people with their own reports, and in the case of violence at least they avoided dwelling on what ordinary people might consider the terroristic, uglier side of revolution. And there are other important issues like these that have only a sketchy existence in the provincial press of the period.

The newspapers also do not always offer the sort of comprehensive, well-documented figures on trends and developments that the researcher at this distance would like to find. By and large the authorities were very proud of the changes they could document, and they printed illustrative figures almost every day in the press. But the Chinese data collection and statistical systems at this period were still extremely weak. The significance of figures, their comparability with other statistics, even the data base used in arriving at figures are most often left unexplained. For illustrative purposes, to give a sense of trends and dimensions for Hunan and Hupei, I have chosen to include the results of many surveys and estimates made during the period. I have selected those which appeared most comprehensive and reliable, and I have for the most part been able to check them for comparability against reports from other provinces, counties, and so on, to determine that they are at least not wildly misleading. But every figure cited here, even those down to two and three decimal places, should be regarded skeptically. They are all roughly illustrative of the real situation, but they are probably not exact.

Thus there are certain limitations on the data in the provincial press, but it should be emphasized that their distortions do not by any means always serve to minimize problems or to augment the Party's victories. On the contrary, the difficulty with these sources comes in knowing how to compensate for exaggerations in the negative direction. Elated reports of astonishing successes and unparalleled enthusiasm among the peasant masses are relatively rare. But there are so many press reports of problems encountered in the Party's village work, of deviations and errors committed, misunderstandings perpetrated, faults uncovered, and general incompetence undeterred, that if we were to take seriously and record them all in proportion to the attention given to them in the sources, it would be hard to maintain a sense of the flow of generally satisfactory results in rural policy implementation during the period. These self-critical complaints, warnings, and exposés were often perhaps not so much news as they were teaching devices and illustrations of points that central and local leaders wished to make. Yet now they can be extremely valuable in trying to recapture the texture of events in those years, the issues animating village life, the fears, the hatreds, the dreams, and some of the realities determining village politics. They present us with quite a complex picture of rural affairs, not a simple or ideologically simplistic one. This study reflects both that complexity and the self-critical attitude of the CCP toward its own transitional achievements. The setbacks, disappointments, misapprehensions, and failures of a mixed record are woven throughout this story of overall success in the management of rural change.

PART 1

"CLASS STRUGGLE"

The Initial Redistribution
of Wealth in the Countryside

I used to be fairly poor, as poor goes;
Today I hit the bottom of poverty and cold.
Nothing I do seems to come out right;
Wherever I go I get pushed around.
I walk the muddy road and my footsteps falter;
I sit with the other villagers and my stomach
    aches with hunger.
Since I lost the brindle cat,
The rats come right up and peer into the pot.

HAN-SHAN, T'ang Dynasty

CHAPTER 1

Liberation, Pacification, and Preparation for Village Revolution

The Central South region of the country did not come under permanent Communist occupation until the middle of 1949. Wu-ch'ang and Han-kow were taken in May by the Fourth Field Army with Lin Piao in command. Ch'angsha fell in August. By this late stage of the revolutionary civil war, Communist forces were rapidly pursuing the collapsing KMT armies across the mainland, toward the sea. They were capturing one city after another, in quick succession, and under these circumstances the hard work of securing and pacifying the surrounding countryside could not keep pace with their victories in towns along the railway lines, rivers, and major highways. The countryside was alive with the confused and fearful activity that attends the collapse of one political order and its replacement by another.

Ragged bands of deserting KMT soldiers and officers roamed the land, resorting to highway robbery and making forays into villages to steal from peasants and merchants. Spies and informers moved back and forth and silently kept watch as others passed. Desperate people, displaced by the war, looked for relatives and tried to get back to their homes; others used the confusion of the times to flee from some personal misery, vengeance, or humiliation, daring to travel only at night, taking their chances of being set upon by bandits; landlords, tax farmers, petty KMT officials, conscription officers, opium runners, gamblers, and others who had reason to fear Communist expropriation and punishment concealed their wealth and property and tried to send it out of the country or even get themselves out of China. All these people moved like

15

shadows over the rural landscape, frightening the local peasants and giving rise to fantastic stories and superstitious prophecies told by firelight.

BANDIT SUPPRESSION

The new government's first task in rural village work, then, was to secure each area and protect the village and nearby roads from attack. Reports of the Party, People's Liberation Army (PLA), and public organs at the time all emphasized that the social revolution in the newly liberated countryside could not be expected to develop widely until more or less complete pacification and bandit suppression in the area had been accomplished.[1] The term "bandit" was used by the CCP at this period, as it had been used previously in Chinese history, to refer to all disaffected elements, both criminal and political, who would resort to violence against the government and the people. This broad definition allowed them to detain all sorts of people, from individual suspected saboteurs and counterrevolutionaries living in the villages, to whole bands of thieves and rebels hiding out in the hills. The bandit suppression campaign in the newly liberated areas continued throughout 1950 and into 1951, and thousands of people were arrested. The PLA launched a number of impressive expeditions into mountainous regions to round up bandits and destroy their camps.[2] And toward the end of 1950, it was announced that an estimated 210,000 bandits had already been killed or captured in the Central South region, with a suspected 100,000 bandits remaining at large.[3]

However, the necessity of protecting the villages from internal and external enemies dictated that there be more persistent and localized armed surveillance than the PLA could provide with its occasional round-up expeditions. Groups of PLA officers and men, therefore,

1. See, e.g., *CCJP,* 8 Dec. 49 [218]; *CCJP,* 25 Jan. 50 [185]; and also the report of Teng Tzu-hui at the first meeting of the CSMAC, *CCJP,* 7 Feb. 50 [50].

2. See, e.g., the report (NCNA, Hankow, 12 Dec. 50), *SCMP* 28 [522], p. 15. Here an expeditionary force of the Fourth Field Army is said to have killed and captured 12,721 bandits, and seized more than 7,300 firearms and 160,000 rounds of ammunition on a month-long foray into the mountains of western Hunan.

3. Tu Jun-sheng [521], p. 21. The total population of the Central South region at this time was estimated to be somewhere around 140 million persons, which makes the figures for bandits under discussion equivalent to less than one-quarter of 1 percent of the

traveled from village to village establishing, arming, and coaching local volunteers for people's militia units. Local peasants, youths, and other villagers were recruited into the militia, issued a firearm, and helped to work out a system of nightly guard duty and a plan for interrogation and investigation of the activities of suspected bandits and saboteurs. Their first act, very often, was to disarm the village population, at least those remnant *pao chia* functionaries and "local bullies" who were considered dangerous. Thus the People's Militia was often the first organized expression of the new political order to emerge on the village scene.

Because recruitment into local militia units was usually hasty and not based on careful investigation of individual backgrounds and motivations, the first village militiamen were not always suited for their jobs. Quite often they were themselves little more than "local bullies," attracted primarily by the guns and status of militia membership, knowing and caring little about the revolution. Other villagers were far from reassured when these types were mustered for local defense. There were even reports that many village militia branches had been infiltrated by bandit toughs, counterrevolutionaries, or landlords, who used their guns to silence and intimidate peasants rather than protect them. The new government nonetheless found it expedient to absorb questionable people temporarily, even into the militia, rather than to oppose them if they wanted to join. In the latter half of 1950 most village militia units were eventually to be subjected to rectification and reorganization in an effort to sift out the worst incompetents and "bad elements."[4]

---

total population. See also *CCJP*, 5 Feb. 50 [305]. It is not possible to determine from government accounts how many captured bandits were executed, jailed, or released without punishment. The official policy rule of thumb for the treatment of captured bandits that was propagandized, however, was to "punish principal offenders, pardon those who joined under coercion, and reward those who do meritorious service." This probably meant that only those persons against whom the government had a very compelling case were executed or jailed, while most were permitted to return to their homes, where they were kept under surveillance for a period. The captives who did "meritorious service" in informing on other bandits and leading the PLA to their hideouts were probably also rewarded with a guarantee of a relatively desirable class status assignment when the *ch'eng fen* for their village or town was done.

4. Early in 1950, Li Hsien-nien, chairman of the Hupei Provincial People's Government, had made the argument that the Party and the army could not help but rely at first on some landlords' agents, "dog's legs," *pao chia* chiefs and others in the villages who, from a class viewpoint, were not really trustworthy. These people, he maintained, did

Despite their imperfections, the majority of local People's Militia units did yeoman's service during the long antibandit campaign following liberation. They guarded the highways, kept records of the number of residents in each local household, and monitored the movements of suspicious persons. They made personal visits to the homes of families and friends of known bandits to pressure them to urge the outlaws to return home, turn themselves in to the authorities, and earn a reduced punishment. They also assisted peasants in crop watching and listened to peasant charges about the crimes of "local despots," compiling a file on such people to be used against them later or, in some cases, arresting them immediately. The net result, in the months following liberation, was that most rural areas of the Central South became gradually more secure, and the overall level of violence and fear declined somewhat.[5]

ANXIETIES, AGRICULTURAL CRISIS, AND RELIEF

Enhanced physical security alone, however, did not serve to eliminate all important fears or alleviate all anxieties in the villages. It was well known that the CCP was committed to making sweeping social and economic changes when it came to power, and the newly liberated territories were naturally alive with rumors about what the new government might do. A main cause of continuing unrest and apprehension was that there had not yet been time, in most villages, to carry out a thorough classification *(ch'eng fen)* assigning each person unequivocally to one class or another. Everyone was aware, because it had been well publicized, that the CCP intended ultimately to expropriate most of the property of landlords and possibly also of wealthy peasants, and to redistribute it among the poor. But exactly how and when this was to be done,

---

have some good points and could be of use to the revolution once they were reformed and educated. "But," he said, "if they continue to do despotic things, they should be disposed of *(ch'u-li)*." See *CCJP*, 6 Jan. 50 [341]. For reports on the rectification and further training of militiamen in Hupei in late 1950, see also *HPJP*, 29 Sep. 50 [55]; and *HPJP*, 23 Nov. 50 [82].

5. During this period, however, the potential for violent outbreaks provoked by unstable local and national conditions was never far below the surface. It was reported, for example, that during 1950 in the Central South region there were at least three separate periods during which banditry and sabotage became especially fierce. The first was during the spring food shortage; the second was immediately following the outbreak of war in Korea; and the third occurred after a spate of floods and droughts affecting several districts. See Tu Jun-sheng [521], p. 21.

who would and would not be counted as a landlord or as a rich peasant—these were the unsettled questions troubling almost everyone in the newly liberated territories.

In the meantime, evidently, almost all villagers were trying to minimize their apparent wealth so that they might be classified in the most favorable category possible. Peasants deceived work team cadres[6] as to their real standard of living, and also took deliberate action to decrease family food and sideline production for the coming season. Landlords and wealthier peasants, who had habitually made loans to poorer villagers during periods of scarcity, claimed not to have any surplus and refused requests for credit. Peasants who had usually hired farmhands during the busy season were afraid this might be declared illegal and that in any case it would be taken as a sign that they enjoyed surplus productivity and income. Many, therefore, declined to hire extra laborers, damaging output further and exacerbating the problem of rural underemployment. Similarly, many landlords refused to continue leasing land to their tenants, intending instead to transfer ownership of the land to relatives or friends temporarily, to evade classification as landlords. Peasants did not put fertilizer on fields they thought might soon be taken away from them. Creditors were demanding the immediate repayment of loans for fear that the provisional government might can-

6. The term "cadre" *(kan-pu)* was used loosely at this period to refer to anyone, high or low, in a responsible position in a government organ or a mass organization. Cadres were not necessarily Party members, nor did they necessarily have a long history of work for the revolutionary cause. The great majority in the Central South were recruited locally after liberation, and a large but unspecified proportion of them were of peasant background. Theoretically, most cadres received at least a portion of their maintenance needs in the form of a state salary. In this respect they can be distinguished from village "activists" *(chi-chi fen-tzu)*, pro-Communist peasants and other locals who did revolutionary work in their own villages but supported themselves without official salaries. In fact, the two categories were not clearly distinguishable, as peasant activists in almost all villages gradually took on more responsibilities and turned into cadres.

Work teams, small groups of cadres and activists usually organized at the county or subdistrict level, were briefed and then sent into the villages specifically to assist with almost every major political and economic reform carried out during the early 1950's. Depending on the complexity of the task and the severity of local difficulties, a work team might remain in a village for days, weeks, or sometimes months. Depending again on the task to be done, work teams might include educated youths, accountants, or other technically trained personnel. Work teams moved from village to village, enabling the new government to stretch its scant skilled administrative personnel far into the hinterland in this early period.

cel all debts and they would never be repaid. The rural economy was, for a time, in considerable disarray, as the people waited to see how hard and from which direction the wind was going to blow.

These trends in the new territories only compounded the depression in agricultural production already brought on by the war. As indicated by the figures in Tables 1 and 2 for Hunan and Hupei, the problem was serious. Except for rice in Hupei, which showed a modest increase in the period, production of almost all important crops in the two provinces was down compared with prewar levels.

Dangerous food shortages were expected in the winter and spring of 1949–50. Reports began coming in, soon after the harvest, that in parts of the area poor peasants were short one month's, three months', and even five months' worth of grain for the winter.[7] And early in January the new provincial governments began drawing up famine relief and supply plans as well as loan programs to tide over the poor.[8] Interest rates on these emergency loans were generally extremely low. In Hupei, for loan money distributed in February and March, no interest at all was charged until the end of July. From then until the end of October the rate applied was 0.5 percent per month, and all loans were to be fully repaid by the beginning of November. (This compares favorably with the approximately 1.8 percent per month interest charged by the People's Bank on ordinary loans for agricultural production during this period.) Emergency loans were, in principle, limited to those officially classified as poor, hired, and middle peasants physically capable of engaging in agricultural production. Even at this early date, however, preference in loan disbursement was given to members of Mutual Aid Teams and cooperatives where they existed, and people tentatively classified higher than middle peasant were only eligible for loans if they participated in or formed a Mutual Aid Team. These, as illustrated in later chapters, were to become firm patterns in government assistance programs over the years, intended to encourage the development of cooperative institutions while making available special support for the rural working poor.

In the Central South the various provincial governments issued a total of more than 200 million catties of grain in loans that winter. In addition were some 120 million catties in relief supplies and outright grants to famine victims.[9] Work-relief projects were also initiated in the region as

7. See, e.g., *CCJP,* 1 Jan. 50 [217].
8. See, e.g., *CCJP,* 17 Jan. 50 [342]; and also *CCJP,* 22 Jan. 50 [223].
9. Teng Tzu-hui [520], pp. 3–4.

TABLE 1. Hunan: Estimated Production of Major
Agricultural Crops
(In 10,000 *tan*)

Crop	Prewar	1949
Rice	14,146*	11,342
Wheat	600*	505
Sweet potatoes (grain equivalent)	785*	406
Cotton	38 (1933–37 average)	14
Ramie	16 (1937)	10

SOURCE: *Economic Geography of Central China* [459], p. 231.
*Average for 1931–36.

TABLE 2. Hupei:
Estimated Production of
Major Agricultural Crops
(In 10,000 *tan*)

Crop	Prewar	1949
Rice	7,013*	8,398
Wheat	2,588*	1,137
Barley	2,069*	814
Cotton	196	95
Ramie	25	5
Sesame	90	187

SOURCE: *Economic Geography of Central China* [459], p. 67.
*Average for 1931–37.

NOTE: The prewar figures in Tables 1 and 2 appear to be based on those published in *War-Time China* and on independent surveys by KMT provincial government offices and local banks.

a means of supplementing the incomes of some hungry farmers. It was reported that 200 million catties were given out in wages for work on water conservation and reforestation projects in the Central South, and 300 million more for road building, railroad, and bridge repair projects sponsored by the central government.[10] The regional government also made an effort to buy up unmarketed native products and handicrafts so as to put more grain into poor peasant hands. All these measures assisted in the effort to induce the famine refugees who were clogging urban centers to return to their villages and resume productive work. Humanitarian famine relief and work-relief programs naturally tended to enhance the new government's legitimacy in these areas. They also, however, assisted in economic recovery by getting many farmers back to their fields and by supporting basic capital construction and repairs for farm production.

High levels of emergency relief and subsidy to a crippled agricultural sector could not be long sustained, however. Removing obstacles to the postwar recovery of agriculture and ensuring that there would be rapid subsequent increases in output became top-priority matters, indeed obsessions, of China's new government. Pursuit of the planned rural economic and social reforms was not to be permitted to jeopardize or interfere with cultivation, and local cadres were specifically and repeatedly instructed to time their coming thrusts in village revolution to

10. *Ibid.*

coincide with the slack season, and to encourage peasants, in the meantime, to work to maximize their harvests.

The CCP was well aware that all hope for rapid national economic recovery and development depended on avoiding the kinds of catastrophic drops in agricultural production that, as the Soviet experience had shown, could be induced by reckless assaults on the villages. Whereas the USSR had possessed an agricultural surplus large enough to support much political disruption and economic mismanagement without immediately triggering urban food shortages and rural famine, the Chinese knew they would have no such margin for error. This awareness informed all government rural policy at this early period, and it dictated a decision to move slowly at first and to allow time for stabilization and for the preliminary establishment of the necessary political and administrative infrastructure at the local level before launching revolutionary programs. With deliberate speed, therefore, after liberation they began the organizational work in the villages that would lay the foundation for controlled revolutionary change.

LAYING THE INSTITUTIONAL FOUNDATIONS
FOR VILLAGE REVOLUTION: THE PEASANT ASSOCIATION

Of all the organizations and institutions set up in the villages as vehicles for involving local people in political struggle and for propagandizing government policy, by far the best developed and most responsible was the Peasant Association *(nung-min hsieh-hui)*. In most villages *(hsiang)*[11] a Peasant Association was formed as soon after liberation as possible, and higher administrative levels depended on these Associations, working under the guidance of basic-level cadres and special work teams, to carry out and oversee most of the local reform work.[12]

11. The *hsiang* or village (sometimes translated as "township") was the basic unit of administration in the Chinese countryside. A *hsiang* was usually made up of several hamlets or *ts'un*, divided geographically and by custom. The average population of a *hsiang* varied greatly across the country and changed also with administrative reorganizations. A rule-of-thumb population figure of 2,000 for Hunan and Hupei *hsiang* is convenient for the unit discussed in this study. But in many areas the real figure could be double this or half. A *hsiang* might contain one, several, or a great number of lineages. Most *hsiang* in Hunan and Hupei were mixed-lineage villages.

12. NCNA explained: "With farm hands and poor peasants as the main components, peasant associations unite middle peasants, handicraftsmen, and poor revolutionary intellectuals in rural districts and become the main force to combat feudalism, [they are] an

Peasant Associations were to consist primarily of poor and hired peasants, but were also to include sympathetic middle peasants and others in the villages. Rich peasants, landlords, and gentry were specifically barred from the organization, but the very acceptance of those classified as middle peasants distinguished these post-1949 Associations from the Poor Peasant Leagues employed in earlier, more radical land expropriations during the civil war. By 1949–50 the emphasis was definitely on minimizing the number of automatic class enemies, and on absorbing as many potentially revolutionary elements in the villages as possible, even if at the time they were recruited their opinions could not be called progressive. In fact, it was specifically asserted that peasants' groups consisting only of activists would necessarily become "divorced from the masses" in newly liberated areas and would not be able to carry out their tasks effectively.[13]

Village Peasant Associations were in 1950 officially declared to be the organ legally responsible for carrying out land reform in their area. But even before land reform, they assisted with many important village programs and reforms. They usually provided the forum for the local version of the "antidespot" movement,[14] aimed at the most hated collaborators, criminals, and bosses in the area. And they were an important tool in propagandizing and organizing the rent reduction and tax collection efforts discussed below. Through these early administrative and reform activities they first established their credibility and expanded their membership.[15]

---

ally of the people's government to destroy the old rule in new rural districts and aid in building the people's democratic dictatorship." (NCNA, Peking, 31 Dec. 50), *SCMP* 40 [509], pp. 17–18.

13. For a criticism of cadres wanting to rely only on "activists' associations" *(chi-chi fen-tzu hui)* and a full defense of the policy of admitting nonprogressives into the Peasant Associations, see *CCJP* editorial, 21 Mar. 50 [409].

14. See, e.g., *CCJP,* 27 Nov. 49 [410]; *CCJP,* 13 Dec. 49 [419]; and also *CCJP,* 15 Dec. 49 [396].

15. One district in Hunan, for example, reported a total Peasant Association membership of somewhat over 100,000 just before rent reduction in the area. Then, once the movement got underway, the membership quickly grew to surpass one million. (See *CCJP,* 23 Oct. 50 [83].) By the fall of 1950, Hunan province reported 6,396,307 members of Peasant Associations, which amounted to 23.1 percent of the total population at the time. See *CCJP,* 26 Sep. 50 [209]. This was slightly better than the showing for the Central South as a whole, which stood at about 25,250,000 or 21.3 percent of the entire population of the region. See *CCJP,* 19 Sep. 50 [426].

Most *hsiang* Peasant Associations quickly chose an executive committee, called the Peasants' Deputies Committee *(Nung Tai Hui)*, to take on general responsibility to act for the full membership. Once these deputies were operating satisfactorily, a further selection was to be held to establish Peasant Association committees at higher administrative levels, specifically at subdistrict and county levels.[16] These higher organs eventually would come to oversee the work of *hsiang* Associations, and a full Peasant Association chain of command would gradually be brought into being. In the early days before land reform, it was not recommended that general elections be held to choose the peasants' deputies at various levels, but rather for local government and Party cadres to select some promising activists and to invite them to serve on the committees.[17] Election by the full membership was said to be the best method, but it was only considered reliable after there had been ample time for propaganda, education and "ferment"—which might not come about until the land reform movement was well underway, or even until it was over.

Since the Peasant Associations were responsible for a broad range of programs, many upper-level cadres in charge of rural work displayed a marked reluctance to rely on or hand over meaningful authority to the local *Nung Tai Hui*. They knew that the class status of many peasant deputies was not favorable and that their understanding of policy was quite superficial. A good many cadres adopted the attitude that it was preferable to delay some village work for several months until they could tend to it themselves, or else send a solid work team to manage it, than to turn the work over to local peasants' deputies for completion. Time and again these cadres were criticized for failing to delegate responsibility to the *Nung Tai Hui*, trying instead to do all the work themselves *(pao pan tai t'i)*.[18]

Although cadres who hesitated to rely on the *Nung Tai Hui* were se-

16. *HPJP*, 17 Nov. 50 [323]. Note that here a provincial Peasant Association already existed before the wide establishment of county and subdistrict organs, which casts doubt on whether the Association's hierarchy was in fact created "from bottom to top."

17. *CCJP*, 11 Feb. 50 [304]. Here it is also mentioned that in the early stages the selection of peasants' deputies was sometimes left to *pao chia* functionaries in the villages, but that this frequently led to poor choices and deputies whose *ch'eng fen* was impure.

18. See, e.g., *CCJP*, 24 Feb. 50 [369]; also *HPJP*, 5 Dec. 50 [303]; and *HPJP*, 5 Dec. 50 [153].

verely criticized for divorcing themselves from the masses, many of the faults and inadequacies they complained of were soon to be recognized as real and of a serious nature. Toward the end of 1950, many reports began to appear about the poor overall quality and ambiguous class composition of local Peasant Associations. It was repeatedly asserted, at this time, that during the earliest village reform movements, when the Associations had been experiencing dramatic growth, many undesirable villagers and people of questionable class background had been absorbed into the organizations and were now responsible for holding back and distorting their operations. This was also said to be true of the *Nung Tai Hui*. One critical analysis of Peasant Association work, originally appearing in *Hsin Hunan Pao* in the fall of 1950, estimated that only 20 percent of all Peasant Associations could be considered reliable in terms of leadership and the class backgrounds of the membership, and well over half the total were judged to have serious shortcomings.[19]

In view of such poor overall assessments as this, a general purification of Peasant Associations was called for to expel those who should not have been permitted to join. This purification, and an accompanying rectification of local cadres' workstyle, occupied the summer and fall of 1950.

In December of that year, the GAC (Governmental Affairs Commission) approved a set of regulations to govern the election and the functions and powers of a *hsiang* people's government.[20] The *Hsiang* Committee of People's Deputies was, in effect, to take over the role of the Peasant Association's *Nung Tai Hui* and become the basic-level government organ in the countryside. The *Nung Tai Hui* would have to be replaced after land reform, because technically it represented only the peasants in a village, and although it was the ideal organizational form for leading land reform and other early revolutionary village programs primarily affecting the peasants, it could not claim to represent the other classes of people living in villages who would have to be given a say in the structure of a permanent *hsiang* government. Each *hsiang* was eventually to be divided into electoral districts for purposes of choosing members of the new committee (Article IV). And, if necessary, national minorities and small surname groups were to be given proportional representation so as to ensure a voice for all residents, except for landlords,

19. *CCJP*, 24 Sep. 50 [84].   20. *CB* 144 (12 Dec. 51) [500], pp. 11–12.

counterrevolutionaries, and other class enemies who were to be deprived of their political rights.

The *Hsiang* Committee of People's Deputies would finally establish itself as the basic administrative organ in the rural areas, eventually developing departments of public security, finance and economics, health and education, and so on. But by and large the election of deputies in the Central South did not actually take place until about 1953, after land reform had been completed everywhere. Thus, the original Peasant Association *Nung Tai Hui,* following their initial purifications in 1950, still had some years of important work ahead of them.

THE PARTY, WOMEN, AND YOUTH

There were a few other institutions taking root in the villages immediately after liberation, most notably the Party, the Youth League, and the Women's Association. Although the Communist Party was never intended to become a mass organization, vigorous recruitment was carried out in new territories coming under Communist control, and through 1949 the total number of Party members in the country did increase rapidly.[21] After national liberation, however, the recruitment drive slowed down and became concentrated in the urban areas.[22] All through the land reform years, a rectification and purification of Party ranks kept the total number between 5 and 6 million. Although finding and organizing local activists was the revolutionary government's most basic technique for beginning village revolution, these activists did not by any means automatically become Party members. On the contrary, there was a desire that they first be "steeled in struggle" before being considered for membership. Most of them went through a period of proving themselves during land reform and were later admitted to the Party ranks or else advised to wait a while longer before making an application.

Throughout the early 1950's, in most villages, the number of CCP

21. In mid-1950 it was reported that the Party had a total membership of just over 5 million and that 2 million of those had joined during the previous eighteen months. See NCNA, 1 Jul. 50, *SWB* 64 [501], p. 47.

22. See Schurmann [481], pp. 128–131. In mid-1950 the Party Central Committee was reported to have "decided that no more members should be accepted in the rural old liberated areas and that there should be no enlistment in the Party in newly liberated areas pending the completion of land reform." See NCNA, 1 Jul. 50, *SWB* 64 [505], p. 48.

members was small. In many *hsiang* there were no local Party members at all. Even in villages with several members, the Party group exerted its influence through other institutions, such as the Peasant Association, and did not generally act independently for or by itself. The Chinese Communist Party, the prime mover behind both policy and strategy for the restructuring of village life, was usually not terribly impressive in its size or demeanor in the villages at this time.

The Youth League in these early days was far more effective as a revolutionary mass organization in the urban areas than in most rural villages.[23] In fact, in the countryside there seems to have been rather widespread misunderstanding about exactly what the Youth League was meant to be, how it was to operate, who were to be its members, and what was to be its relation to the Party.[24]

It may have been intended that the League should open its doors to practically all youths in the vast newly liberated areas at this time and concentrate on giving them a basic introduction to government policies and Communist principles. But this proved difficult since many long-time Youth League members and cadres preferred to keep the organization more selective and were reluctant to recruit widely in the countryside. When they were officially criticized for their "closed-door" attitudes, they frequently overcompensated. Youthful villagers then sometimes found themselves "impressed into service" *(la fu)*. They were made to sign the register of League membership, whether or not they wanted to join, so that the organizers would have evidence that they were indeed making up for their former "closed-door deviation."[25]

23. See *CCJP*, 13 Mar. 50 [121].

24. For a report of a Youth League branch that refused to obey Party policies or to submit to decisions of the local Peasant Association, and that even arrogated to itself powers to judge and punish in village civil and criminal cases such as those involving adultery and theft, see *CCJP*, 15 Oct. 50 [158].

25. See *CCJP*, 13 Dec. 49 [299]; and *CCJP*, 23 Dec. 49 [248]. Compare with *CCJP*, 26 Apr. 50 [71]. The term "deviation" *(p'ien-ch'a)*, used throughout this study, is part of CCP administrative jargon. It was used by the Party center to characterize negatively all kinds of situations in which local cadres failed to adhere to ideal guidelines for policy implementation. The term is preserved in the narrative here not to suggest how these local cadres' actions should be judged by us, but to convey a sense of the Party's official attitude toward what they saw as avoidable "errors," "mistakes," and "policy distortions." Many of the so-called "deviations" discussed here were not cadre failures as much as reflections of cadre values, priorities, and perspectives that differed from those at the Party center.

The result of all this maneuvering was to dissipate the potential of the Youth League movement in the countryside, at least temporarily, and generally to prevent it from becoming a very helpful force in village reform work before land reform.[26]

The Women's Association was another mass mobilization organization typically established in a village soon after liberation but, like the Youth League, not accorded very high priority; it therefore did not generally live up to its revolutionary potential at this time. In addition to acting as a vehicle for involving women in the general class struggle to take place in the village, the Women's Association was largely intended to awaken its members to a realization of the especially heavy oppression suffered by women in traditional society and to the better life options that were to be open to them in the newly liberated Chinese society. The Women's Association was used to propagandize the 1950 Marriage Law and its fundamental concepts of equality of the sexes, freedom of marriage, and divorce. As expected, these notions were greeted with hostility by many men since they threatened previously unchallenged male prerogatives. There was also considerable tension between older and younger women over these questions, since a young woman, inspired to leave home to find a job or a husband on her own, not only defied the men in her family, but also the older women to whom she traditionally also owed obedience.[27] There tended to be a generational split as well on the question of divorce — younger women favoring divorce in cases of unhappy arranged marriages, and older women taking a more conservative stand on the matter. In fact, cadres were often afraid to propagandize the Marriage Law because they thought it could raise familial and social tensions in the village to such an extent that agricultural production might be adversely affected and the more important class struggle issues overshadowed.

Another reason for slow progress before land reform was that Women's Association work in the villages was usually left to female cadres who were few in number. Male cadres avoided becoming deeply involved in women's work because they often felt embarrassed and un-

26. There were exceptions to this generalization. In many villages, activist Youth League members played as important or even more important a role in the early reform movements than the scarce local Party cadres. See *CCJP*, 5 Feb. 50 [127].

27. For a description of the tensions between older and younger women engendered by Women's Association work, see *CCJP*, 24 Sep. 50 [377].

comfortable with women,[28] and because they regarded the women as backward and thought their other tasks of revolutionary mobilization were more promising and more important.

Thus a number of new institutions were established in the villages within a matter of months after liberation to mobilize and channel peasants into the drive for rural social revolution. But the Party itself was deliberately kept very small, and women's work and youth work were downplayed somewhat to avoid stirring up generational or family conflicts that could divert attention from the issues of local class struggle. This left the Peasant Association in the position of chief importance. It was the one, of all the new mass institutions, that took its membership primarily on the basis of economic class status, as opposed to other distinguishing social characteristics or patterns present in the villages.

As the following chapters will illustrate, the deliberate effort to highlight, exacerbate, and then manage class-based struggles in the villages was to be the new leadership's chief method of achieving social reform and political change. The intention to set aside for later resolution other, non-class-based village struggles in order to concentrate on class relations was present from these earliest days and remained basic strategy throughout the transition period. The other new institutions performed supportive roles, while the Peasant Associations took in the greatest numbers and began to propagandize the principles and policies of class struggle. All the new institutions, however, were set up so hastily that they were destined to undergo repeated purifications and rectifications even as they were used to promote social revolution.

THE FIRST REFORMS: TAXATION
AND REDUCTION OF RENT AND INTEREST

With this variety of mass mobilization institutions just taking shape in the new territories, the leadership moved ahead with a few relatively mild economic reforms, putting off for a while the launching of its programs of revolutionary seizure and redistribution of land and other prop-

28. For some Hunan and Hupei examples, see *HPJP*, 17 Nov. 50 [161]; and *HHNP*, 28 Dec. 50 [368]. Of course, part of the initial purpose of establishing a separate organization for women was first to sidestep and then to help overcome some of the same cultural attitudes about proper public behavior and male-female roles that made male cadres feel ill at ease at village women's meetings.

erty. These earliest reforms involved an initial rough classification of villagers into poor and rich, landlords and tenants, exploiters and exploited. And since the great majority of villagers would receive favorable designations, it was expected that they would overcome much of their earlier anxiety and return wholeheartedly to farm production. Since, also, those given unfavorable classifications were to find that they were nevertheless not in immediate danger of all-out expropriation, it was hoped they too would be reassured and would adopt a more conciliatory demeanor and return to normal economic activity, hiring labor, marketing their surpluses, and so on. Thus, while these reforms were important first steps in demarcating the lines of village class struggle and in redistributing wealth from the better-off to the worse-off households in the villages, they balanced concern for equality and justice with concern for keeping up and expanding overall farm output. More disruptive revolutionary struggles and land seizures were delayed for a year or more while the new authorities completed the pacification of the countryside and the initial recruitment of village activists. Those activists, who would later take the lead in the land reform movement itself, often first came to the attention of work team cadres sent into the villages in pursuit of these earlier interim reforms.

The new government's first reform, in the area of taxation, certainly won the early active support of many. The high priority given to economic recovery and to increasing farm output could not keep the state from the unavoidable necessity of immediately taxing agriculture in the new areas. But while intended primarily to generate revenue, the early approach to taxation in the countryside proved in many respects to resemble a further form of relief to the poor.

The first tax collection in 1949–50 was, by the government's own admission, rather a crude affair; no official tax regulations were yet in effect for these areas. The army did much of the work, however, and the general principle observed by PLA details and tax collection work team cadres was apparent enough. They seized as much as they could from the obviously wealthy, resorting, when they had to, to coercion. They always tried to give the most poverty-stricken and destitute households total exemptions. And for the majority of households falling somewhere between these two extremes, they set a figure significantly below the previous KMT levies and granted many petitions for special consideration. This tax program was assuredly not administered with an even hand all over the Central South. In some places it was clearly applied inequitably, and in others it was badly distorted. Still, the overall effect was to reduce the tax burden on the poor and to raise the exactions made from wealthier villagers.

None of this was lost on the peasants. The first tax collection pointed toward a general redistribution of wealth in the countryside, but it did so while also allaying the immediate fears of many peasant families about their futures under Communist rule. Many who had worried that they might be treated like landlords were relieved to find that they were not; and most were gratified at the prospect of a tax break.

A second tone-setting reform, which was moderate yet definitely challenging to the landlord class in that it signaled a beginning to the redistribution of wealth in the countryside, was the policy of rent and interest reduction. The main thrust of this program, adapted from earlier second United Front policies, was that the rent paid by tenant farmers to landlords and the interest rates charged by creditors be reduced by 25 percent. In addition, all back rent owed by tenants at the time of liberation was to be forgiven. This was to apply to all individual landlords, as well as to religious institutions, schools, societies, and other corporate landlords.[29]

The 25 percent reduction in interest on loans was good only for private debts contracted after liberation, although all debts *owed to landlords* prior to liberation were cancelled. Credit obligations between other villagers dating back before liberation were not supposed to be affected. The rent charged on oxen when they were loaned out was also specifically exempt from the 25 percent reduction (Article IV). In an effort to ensure that animals not be destroyed by their owners, and to encourage their wider use in cultivation, this was one rental relationship officially permitted to continue at the preliberation rates of exchange.

It was hoped again that the implementation of rent and interest reduction would serve to calm those peasants who were needlessly agitated by the fear that their property would be confiscated. For rent reduction to be carried out in a village, a greatly simplified determination of class status

29. Also prohibited were all other special exactions made by landlords, such as the obligatory donation of free labor by tenants and the presentation of ceremonial gifts or parts of the harvest to landlords. The revised rent reduction regulations are contained in a directive signed by Lin Piao, *NFJP,* 21 Sep. 50 [172]. See also the rent reduction regulations in *Collection of Important Land Reform Documents* [8], pp. 103–106. The earlier rent reduction regulations and the way they were implemented in two different old base areas are contained in Ch'i Wu [4], pp. 116–131; and Selden [482], pp. 229–237.

for each family would have to be made. All those renting land would be called tenants; and all those renting out land would be classified as land-lords.[30] Other villagers, especially the relatively comfortable peasants, who had feared the outcome of the classification process, were expected to breathe a sigh of relief at this and to return to their fields secure in the knowledge that they were neither to be lumped together with the land-lords nor subjected to immediate expropriation.

Although its goals were moderate and its means peaceful, rent reduction still involved an element of class struggle. Work teams of cadres were sent into the villages, and with the help of local activists they collected information on the extent of tenancy, on the landlord households, and on the prevailing rates of rent and interest. They then called mass meetings of tenant households to propagandize the policy and to induce all tenants to report exactly how much rent they were paying and to get each one to agree to work for a reduction. Conferences with individual landlords followed during which the CSMAC[31] order was explained to them by cadres, and they were advised to comply. Sometimes general public meetings were also employed to persuade, cajole, or shame land-lord households into agreeing to the rent cut.[32] Then, in cases where advance deposits had already been made by the tenants, landlords would (usually publicly) return the agreed portion of the deposit.

Except for the provinces of Kwangtung and Kwangsi, this process was said to have been completed across 80 percent of the entire newly liberated Central South region by mid-1950.[33] These initial attempts at

30. Handicapped people, widows, teachers, and small traders who were actually quite poor but who relied on renting out land for all or part of their income were to be permitted to petition for exemption from the rent reduction regulations at this time. See *NFJP*, 21 Sep. 50 [172], Article IX. Land use patterns in the Central South were extremely complex. Many families rented some land and rented out other land, thus falling into both of these oversimplified categories. A much more sophisticated set of classifications came into use with the land reform movement; these are discussed in Chapter 2. See also Tables 4–12 for illustrations of the real distribution of families in Hunan into land-lord and poor peasant categories.

31. Central South Military Affairs Committee, the top organ of the regional provisional government immediately following liberation.

32. For early accounts of how rent reduction was to be carried out in the villages, see *CCJP*, 23 Dec. 49 [274]; and also *CCJP*, 24 Dec. 49 [267]. For some interesting fine points on the implementation of rent and interest reduction in Hupei, see also *CCJP*, 6 Jan. 50 [126].

33. NCNA, Peking, 20 Jun. 50, *SWB* 62 [512], p. 57. See also *CCJP*, 12 Apr. 50 [226]. For a comment on the importance of carrying out rent reduction in the early part of the year, see also *CCJP* editorial, 1 Mar. 50 [292].

rent reduction were not always very successful, however. Reports came from all over Hunan and Hupei, for example, that in villages where rent reduction had been "carried out" it had nonetheless not achieved its goals because the tenants had not been well mobilized and were not determined to see it through. Most commonly, tenant farmers either refused to take back the rent money that landlords had been pressured into returning to them; or else they accepted the money or grain in public but took it back to their landlords secretly, with disavowals of any desire to inconvenience the landlord or change the terms of their previous agreement. Poor tenants often went through the motions of rent reduction to please local activists and the work team cadres, but they actually continued paying rent at the old rates to preserve the goodwill of their landlords.[34]

Frightened of the risks involved in pressing the landlords and doubtful that reformist or revolutionary enthusiasm in their villages would ever become strong enough to overrule landlord influence and protect them from reprisals, these peasants were a long way from militancy. And other tenants, who did accept and keep returned rent payments, expressed their own misgivings about future stability and protection by spending their extra cash unwisely and wasting it on frivolous consumables.[35] To invest it in the land and in production, as the government had intended they should do, seemed to them to be risky, even foolhardy, in view of the continuing uncertainties of the near future.

THE PROBLEM OF PROPER SEQUENCE IN BEGINNING VILLAGE REVOLUTION

Vacillating, irresolute behavior on the part of peasants was always officially explained as the result of a failure to carry out sufficient propaganda, education, and mass mobilization before the implementation of rent reduction. Work team cadres and local activists were continually being told to make sure that they had achieved a high level of mass mobilization and determination among tenants before attempting to carry out the program in a given village. By the same token, however, they were warned against wasting too much time on merely marshaling popular sentiment against landlords and were urged to get on with the

34. *CCJP,* 23 Dec. 49 [274]. See also *CCJP,* 26 Feb. 50 [407].

35. See the reported instances of peasants wasting the fruits of rent reduction on "eating big plates of food," "drinking wine," and "in houses of ill repute," in *CCJP,* 15 Apr. 50 [164]; and also *CCJP,* 15 Apr. 50 [244].

actual implementation of the provisions of the rent reduction order, so that peasants could quickly have the use of the returned grain and cash. Peasants were frequently heard to complain that "speaking bitterness" and punishing offenders during the long mass mobilization phase was fine, but that these activities alone were not going to fill their bellies.[36]

The difficulties associated with making the transition from mass mobilization to the implementation of rent reduction were clearly exacerbated by the preconceptions many former base area cadres brought to their work. These men and women, accustomed to the more advanced political situation of the older liberated areas, were evidently appalled by what they necessarily regarded as the backwardness and low level of political consciousness of the poor peasants in newly liberated villages. They saw a need for extended mass mobilization work and political education among peasants. They tended to emphasize class struggle rather than the orderly implementation of rent and interest reduction when talking to local peasant activists, and they feared the consequences of rent reduction if it were carried out essentially as a means of easing a temporary food shortage, without the dimension of revolutionary class struggle being made clear in the minds of poor peasants.

Some of these cadres, consequently, appeared to hesitate in moving ahead with the rent reduction program. They were caustically criticized for acting as if they were "bound hand and foot" (shu shou shu chiao), a deviation linked to "empiricism"—knowing how to proceed only when circumstances closely resembled one's previous experience. But, at the same time, cadres who decided to press for quick implementation of rent reduction despite the prevailing low level of political consciousness, and who then came up with unsatisfactory results because of peasant vacillation, deception, and collusion with landlords, were liable to be criticized and blamed for deviations of "commandism" and "formalism."[37]

36. For conflicting demands made on cadres in this regard, compare CCJP, 29 Sep. 49 [193]; and CCJP, 1 Dec. 49 [425]. For complaints that some cadres pursued antidespot mobilization work to the detriment of rent and interest reduction, see CCJP editorial, 10 Mar. 50 [405]; and CCJP, 15 Mar. 50 [175].

37. See, e.g., CCJP, 22 Apr. 50 [102]. There were innumerable reports at this time on the various deviations of which rural leaders had been found guilty and the ways of rectifying them. For an interesting discussion of "commandism" (misapplied force or

The dilemma facing rural cadres at this time was merely a reflection of a more basic problem involved in beginning village revolution. To lead most of China's peasants to make demands on landlords and the rest of the established village elite at this point generally seems to have required convincing them of at least three things: first, that to make such demands was justifiable and fair; second, that there was a reasonable chance the movement could be carried off and their demands met; and third, that there would not be some other occurrence or unforeseen factor that would intervene to deprive them of the fruits of the struggle. The usual techniques of propaganda and education, the "speak bitterness" and accusation sessions, seem generally to have been quite effective in giving most peasants the conviction that they ought to take action against local landlords. But the other two propositions were far more difficult to prove to peasants' satisfaction without more concrete evidence or results. Concrete results, however, could only be displayed *after* the movement had gotten under way; but with the CCP's insistence on the importance of mass participation, to get the movement properly under way it was first considered essential to convince peasants to participate. Work team and village cadres were thus caught in a vicious circle, needing to demonstrate that they would be able to start the village revolution before they could in fact start the revolution.

There is, perhaps inevitably, a problem of proper sequence in beginning a new mass movement such as the one the CCP brought to its later liberated rural villages. In the face of the natural reticence of peasants, it was necessary for cadres to be resourceful and to take their own calculated risks. Most often what they had to do was make a start at policy implementation, even when the majority of peasants were clearly not yet fully convinced that it was safe or sensible to go along. Then, with luck,

coercion), see *CCJP,* 1 Dec. 49 [286]; *CCJP,* 17 Jun. 50 [337]; and *CCJP,* 17 Jun. 50 [101]. The deviation of "bureaucratism" (the inflexible or unimaginative application of rules and regulations or the invention of unnecessary forms and procedures) is examined in *CCJP,* 17 Jun. 50 [358]; and *CCJP,* 17 Jun. 50 [101]. "Empiricism," as already mentioned, referred to an excessive reliance on experience gained before national liberation and a consequent failure to adapt to new policies and situations. It is discussed in *CCJP,* 31 Dec. 49 [150]; and in *CCJP,* 22 Feb. 50 [415]. "Tailism" (following the masses instead of organizing and leading them, resulting in a breakdown of revolutionary discipline) was less common but also criticized at this time, as in *CCJP,* 9 Dec. 49 [72]; and *CCJP,* 17 Jun. 50 [358]. Rural cadres were also occasionally reprimanded for instances of ordinary corruption such as accepting and soliciting bribes and dispensing special favors.

the preliminary results would be sufficiently encouraging to influence peasant attitudes and to raise their determination and their enthusiasm for participation.

ON RECTIFICATION

Quite often, of course, the attempt failed. For one reason or another, the earliest results did not inspire confidence, and wavering peasants would begin backing down, failing to attend meetings, and refusing to take rent reductions from their landlords. It was, indeed, commonplace to read in the local press that rent reduction had been a failure, to one degree or another, in 50, 60, or 70 percent of the villages in a given area. And time and again it was reported that in villages where the work had originally been declared successful, it had later turned out to have many shortcomings. In these cases there was nothing to do but begin again, devoting more time to intensified propaganda and preparation, and doing what could be done to change the conditions giving rise to peasant vacillation.

Special investigative work teams were sent from the county into the villages, to assess the progress made and to correct deviations from official policy. These work teams heard reports from local cadres, carried out their own inspections, and usually called a series of small group meetings in which responsible peasants were encouraged to ask questions, raise problems, and voice complaints. While these means alone were frequently insufficient, they generally elicited a first critique of the current situation in the village that called for remedial action.

Investigative reviews and rectification of errors and deviations were eventually to come to follow all major campaigns and initiatives in rural transformation work. The rent reduction movement was merely the first in a long series of rural programs, initially implemented quickly, achieving only a modest degree of success, and later improved through repeated investigation and rectification drives in the villages. The repetition of campaigns in villages where they had been abortive and the rectification of work where it had proved to be unsatisfactory became, in fact, fixtures of the rural transformation process in China. For many years, rural cadres found it necessary to begin the implementation of one or another policy in conditions that, as they were well aware, were far from mature and more than likely to produce disappointing results. Sometimes, of course, they did this primarily in response to demands from upper administrative levels for faster and faster progress. But also quite often they consciously adopted this strategy themselves in the realization that only by beginning the movement could they produce any concrete results and benefits, however modest and imperfect at first, that might be utilized to build peasant enthusiasm and strengthen the resolve to carry on.

As an approach to local politics and administration, this cadre inclination to press on with a particular policy despite recognized "immaturity" in the village situation is quite significant. It stands in marked contrast to the lack of resolution and resourcefulness that had been characteristic, with few exceptions, of rural local administration in China earlier in the century. It also suggests that rural work cadres possessed considerable (if not always unbounded) faith that the centrally determined policies they were being asked to press would, even without much preparation and propaganda, appeal to a large enough number of villagers that they would ultimately meet with success.

Village investigations and rectifications generally entailed a good deal of criticism and self-criticism. Cadres and activists, along with ordinary peasants whose failure of nerve or whose otherwise nonmilitant behavior had in one way or another endangered the chances of success for all the rest, were commonly treated with open scorn and ridicule and were called upon to explain themselves. The process of rectifying village work was far from being the imposition of undifferentiated, authoritarian patterns and strictures, as it is sometimes viewed. Local behavioral and ethical norms were brought to bear in the course of investigation and criticism, and the sessions tended in fact to be very lively, marked by bawdy and bitter humor, desperate threats, and poignant excuses. For local leaders who had failed to face up to the complexities of their situation and who had attempted to use high-handed, short-cut, simplistic approaches to local problems, the rectification of village work often constituted something of a political education and a lesson in the potential for either healthy progress or reinforced stagnation resting in their own leadership roles.

The open give-and-take characteristic of the investigation and rectification process in rural communities played an important part in redefining the nature and the terms of village politics. In fact, the reason why the rectification device was so important in the village transformation process and why it will be alluded to so often in this study is that it stood at the juncture between the simple (or mechanical) implementation of

central directives and the acting out of real local politics. Indeed, rectification meetings frequently provided the very forum in which the local
political process could be staged and best observed.

Rectification was a two-way process. On the one hand it allowed for
lower-level cadres and administrative personnel to try to bring the situation in their area more in line with central models. But it also called for
activists and ordinary villagers to express their views on the prevailing
state of affairs, what was wrong, and how and whether things might be
improved. At some stage during a typical follow-up investigation and
rectification, the people themselves had to be questioned and consulted,
and their perceptions and preoccupations had to be taken into account in
making corrections and revisions. This process of popular consultation
in village rectification was an element of what the CCP has referred to as
the "mass line" style of work. It provided an effective means by which
to achieve the much touted goal of adapting central policy, derived from
CCP experience in the old base areas, to local realities in the new territories. The whole process thus imparted a degree of resilience and
flexibility to the new government's early rural work that was crucial in
the effort to produce revolutionary changes in reality and not merely on
paper.

But periodic rectifications of village work and of cadres' workstyle
were not only useful tools for more efficient rural administration; they
also symbolized the passing of many traditional notions about
"politics-as-usual." Central laws and directives providing for popular
reforms were not to be disregarded routinely whenever it was inconvenient to carry them out; local officials were to be made accountable for
their actions; and above all, the ability of poor and ordinary people to
have some say in the way their village affairs were handled, and their
right to speak out, were to be upheld. A credible system of periodic
rectifications thus stood as a safeguard that such new principles of revolutionary politics as these would be maintained. Or, more accurately,
the rectification system was a partial guarantee that when these principles were violated, some action would be taken to help restore them.
And for many new cadres who went through one or two early rectifications of their work and workstyle, it did not take long to catch on to what
were likely to be the rewards and the pains of their positions. There
would be supervision from above and from below. The personal power
wielding of the new village leaders was brought under scrutiny, and in
the course of such sessions it was hoped that a new definition of the

political sphere and of the proper uses of power in the village would evolve. Under the watchful eye of the investigative work team sent down to the village for the rectification phase, these meetings may well have provided some of the most effective new means of political expression and participation actually available to ordinary peasants.

Still, the democratic aspect of rectification should not be overemphasized. After all, the Party and the government wanted local cadres to *lead* the villagers toward socialism, not just to reflect peasant opinions. For most of the time, their central task was to be to raise peasant political consciousness from its prevailing low level to the higher level they themselves had presumably already achieved. Thus it was Party policy that in cultivating a core group of village revolutionary leaders all but the very worst of them be allowed to come through rectification without losing their self-respect or much of the respect of others.

It also proved to be in the interest of peasants that their local leaders and representatives not be thoroughly humiliated before the visiting work team cadres, and not be singled out for censure by upper administrative levels. After all, these local cadres were the very individuals who would be in a position to serve as intermediaries between the peasants and the newly forming bureaucracy. It was important both that they appear as credible spokesmen for the village and that their own natural sense of belonging and obligation to the community not be shattered by complaints and accusations against them. Thus, mass criticism was usually restrained even during rectification. Cadres, of course, were aware of these various restraints on the process, and it helped both to make the criticism/self-criticism more acceptable to them and to clarify their responsibilities to the community.

As local cadres with localist sentiments and local obligations worked out their relations with the local masses, it naturally affected their relations with their administrative superiors. It seems fairly apparent that, at the center, these cadres were regarded at once as advisors and as adversaries. They were trusted with enormous responsibility, on the one hand, and held to be indispensable in carrying out all manner of programs at the basic level. On the other hand, however, they were expected to be prejudiced in their assessments of "the needs of the masses." Indeed they were even expected to misrepresent the facts as they knew them—something the following chapters show they regularly did—in their efforts to promote local interests. Their middle-level superiors had somehow to learn to discount and weigh their opinions accurately, without falling prey to their designs and without needlessly disappointing, alienating, or berating them. The drama of rectification was clearly one important component in this complex process of establishing and refining a working relationship between central and local authority within the new system.

Inasmuch as vigorous investigation and rectification drives were regarded as part of the normal and healthy functioning of the newly forming system, any routinization or perfunctory performance of the process was to be condemned. Although the drives were certainly not quickly reduced to empty ritual, there was a tendency toward evasiveness, avoidance of real confrontation, mechanical, formalistic, or perfunctory behavior on the part of cadres and other responsible individuals even at this early period, which often required that the investigations and rectifications be repeated several times before they were considered successful. With rent reduction, in many villages it was necessary to repeat the sequence of quick policy implementation followed by investigation and rectification at least two or three times before the outcome was judged good enough. It the course of this kind of spotty development in the first year or more after liberation, the rent reduction movement served the purpose not only of bringing some material relief to hard-pressed tenants, but also of sketching out a new mode of political activity and a new model for the distribution of political power in the villages. In these respects, as well as in the more obvious ones, rent and interest reduction prepared the way for the revolutionary upheaval of land reform.

Still, while pointing the way toward the future and putting to rest certain immediate anxieties, tax policy, rent reduction, and the subsequent rectifications could not eliminate all the fears of peasants concerning what was to come. After all, in most villages there had still not been a definitive classification of each household. Considerable tension and uncertainty continued to pervade the villages. The machinations of peasants who persisted in trying to reduce their apparent wealth were copiously reported in the press, and the schemes of those who hoped to get themselves on friendly terms with activists or to bribe cadres so that they might be afforded favorable treatment continued to mark the local scene. Even with all the new government's early organizational efforts, which have been sketched here, this situation in the villages was to persist until the upheaval of land reform finally provided a definite response to many of the doubts and questions that remained.

CHAPTER 2

Land to the Tiller

Without any doubt, agrarian reform was the keystone of the CCP's program for rural revolution and development. In the revolutionary base areas, the Party had already had years of experience in carrying out agrarian reform and was therefore well aware of its political and economic potential. Seizing land from the rich and redistributing it among the poor was an idea with a long and honorable pedigree in Chinese political thought and a centuries-old peasant insurrectionary tradition to support it. The idea had become still more current in the twentieth century after Sun Yat-sen popularized it. And a land reform program was even embraced in theory by the KMT under Chiang Kai-shek, although little was ever done to make it a reality. By dispossessing the landlord class and giving grants of land to poor peasants, the Communists knew they would be making good on an old promise to the peasantry. Peasant support for the Party would certainly rise, other things being equal; and consequently the legitimacy of the new government would be much enhanced among the great majority of villagers.

Buying immediate peasant support with land, then, was one aim of the CCP's agrarian reform in the new territories—one it frankly acknowledged. But earlier years of experience in land reform work had taught that if the movement were handled properly it could bring much more permanent systemic changes than a mere upsurge in the CCP's popularity. Land reform could be used to emasculate the traditional village elite, the entire old rural power structure; it could become the spearhead of a genuine social revolution to change the fundamental relations of power in the countryside. The Party had found earlier that it was possible to get peasant support for land reform in areas where tenancy itself was not a serious problem, where land concentration was not especially severe, and even where extreme population concentration made the amounts of land available so small that poor peasant family income was hardly improved at all by redistribution. It could get this peasant support, however, only if it broadened the scope of the land reform movement to address all the major grievances of the poor against the local elite, including taxation, usury, forced conscription, theft, coercion, or other forms of exploitation. The point, they had learned, was to transform the land reform, which might have been confined to the mere tactical redistribution of goods, into a village revolution to overthrow the local establishment in all its manifestations.[1]

Earlier revolutionary experience had made the Party leadership realize that land reform should not be regarded only, or even primarily, as a means of raising the standard of living and enhancing general peasant welfare. Without the continued burden of landlords' excess consumption and inefficient investment, it was indeed expected that the rural economy would be able to recover and grow more rapidly. CCP leaders spoke in terms of liberating the rural productive forces from the bonds of feudalism and they predicted a great upsurge in agricultural output. Still, from the Party's point of view the greatest significance of land reform lay not in its potential for economic growth but in its role in redefining the village polity, putting power in the hands of groups who had previously been nearly silent in the day-to-day political decision making affecting their villages, and establishing new patterns and new modes of participation in local political affairs. "Land reform" was to be more than economic reform; it was to be a revolutionary class struggle.

If land reform could be used to smash the socioeconomic struts and braces of the *ancien régime* in the countryside, it could also serve to lay the foundations in the villages for the new order. The Party would use the land reform movement to find village activists and future cadres— reliable people to be trained for local leadership in the place of those members of the old elite who were "knocked down." The development of a reliable indigenous force of local cadres in the newly liberated rural areas was regarded as a matter of first priority, and it was assumed that the best way to accomplish this end was to put activist peasants and

1. This argument is developed by Pepper [476], pp. 229–330. See especially p. 311.

sundry volunteers to work immediately on the administration of the early agrarian reform, giving them what amounted to on-the-job training. Land reform struggles would themselves provide the backdrop against which these people would emerge, gain experience, and be observed. Later there would be time for some weeding out and further training by the Party. Eventually, as the economic situation improved after the reform, and as their local political leadership roles were consolidated, the Party expected that these tried and respected village leaders could be called upon to administer a gradual transition to socialism in the countryside.

Thus, the CCP had four main objectives in land reform. First, it would enhance its own legitimacy in the eyes of numberless peasants who would benefit directly from the reform. Second, it would spur economic growth by eliminating much luxury consumption and make more peasant families solvent by curbing exploitation, thus cutting down on central government welfare and relief obligations and allowing greater national investment for growth. Third, it would bring to their knees its own natural political rivals in the villages, the lower remnants of the old elite, and in so doing demolish the old patterns of local politics and the old assumptions about the origins and the uses of power in the countryside. And finally, it would take the opportunity to replace that old elite with its own locally recruited and consciously cultivated activists from the lower peasant classes, making them into a new leading force in village affairs, a force they could later rely on for the administration of further reforms.

For all of this to come about, the Party insisted that the crucial point was to turn land reform into village class struggle. The discussion in this chapter, therefore, begins with the CCP's class policy in 1950. It is clear that the Party designed these classifications and the Agrarian Reform Law together to make a material appeal to the broadest possible rural constituency, leaving in isolated opposition to the reform only a very small percentage of village inhabitants. In particular this meant relaxing its pre-1949 policy on the treatment of rich peasants and taking other steps to reduce the potential dissension among different subgroups of "the broad peasant masses." Thus, in contrast to the rural reform programs of some other Asian countries, CCP policies avoided giving benefits to some types of tenants and not others or to some types of villages and not others. The CCP's class policy and Agrarian Reform Law defined the potential beneficiaries, the "revolutionary peasant masses," to include almost everyone in the villages except the very wealthiest families, a few criminal or marginal elements, and hardcore counterrevolutionaries such as Japanese sympathizers and some KMT operatives.

In effect, the Party tried thereby to deactivate many existing lines of cleavage in village society in an effort to create greater solidarity and unity of purpose among peasants. For reform purposes it deliberately ignored clan and surname groupings; small neighborhoods; religious divisions; differentiations between young and old, women and men, cotton farmers and rice farmers, and so on; and it applied a fairly simple set of economic class distinctions to almost all villages. In very rough terms, the CCP divided villagers into landlords, on the one hand, and rich, middle, poor, and destitute peasants, on the other. Landlords were to be the target of reform, which they of course would oppose. Rich peasants were to be relatively unaffected, and they were expected to be neutral. Everyone else, they wanted it made clear, was a probable beneficiary of reform, and with this interest in common all were enjoined to unite and work together for change.

As indicated below, the Party was not always successful in papering over the other non-class-conscious points of cleavage among the peasantry. Many people resisted the new categories; others who generally accepted them still found them not suitable for all facets of life and continued to identify themselves partly along more traditional lines. And very often such persistent allegiances brought on fragmentation of the new polity that the Party labored to shape and much trouble in implementing village reforms. Still, as a formula for mass mobilization, it was employed with considerable success not only in land reform but also in the later stages of rural transformation, when the groupings of relevant class categories were to change somewhat; but the tactic of isolating a very small minority of reform opponents for attack remained effective.

But the village class struggle demanded more than a mere judicious classification of the population. It called for the great majority of peasants, once classified, to take part in the overthrow of the landlords and the seizure and redistribution of their possessions. A genuine class struggle, the Party held, could not be mechanically administered by a few activists or outsiders. Real class struggle would take more than general mass acquiescence in the reform: it would take a high level of active mass participation. And for this it was necessary that at least a rudimentary class consciousness be a part of the peasants' own motivations and explanations for their actions. Therefore, this chapter examines the Party's much-admired methods of mass mobilization and education in land reform and indicates how difficult it often was to attain these basic preconditions of successful village revolution.

Peasants clearly responded well to the economic benefits of the reform. But they were fearful and hesitant in grasping political power. Peasants and peasant cadres continued to perceive political possibilities in the old terms. They did not yet share the Party's vision of a political system in which power could remain for long in the hands of the poor. They expected that after the reforms had run their course, it would be back to politics-as-usual. Convincing them to act, to take the risks of direct political participation, therefore, often took patience and skill and much time.

Recognizing the time this process would require, the Party originally had intended to carry out land reform in the new territories gradually, on a relaxed timetable that would allow careful control by experienced cadres and thorough mass mobilization. But as already explained, the longer the actual implementation of land reform was delayed, the longer the apprehension, the rumors, the tension, and the drag on production in the new territories seemed likely to persist. For it made no sense to feed an ox all winter if the animal was going to be given to someone else for ploughing before spring. It made no sense to put down scarce fertilizer on fields that could well be transferred to another family. And it made no sense to hire hands or extend loans to neighbors if the new authorities would regard these as serious types of exploitation placing the villager in a category with landlords and evil despots. So, at least, reasoned most of China's peasants, and the impact this reasoning could have on the government's number-one priority—the rehabilitation and expansion of agricultural production—was a continued cause for alarm.

The center was under pressure, therefore, to push ahead with land reform on a very great scale in 1950.[2] (See Table 3.) It could not pursue

2. In Hupei, for example, it was originally planned that land reform be begun in villages scattered over twenty-three counties, containing about 8,065,000 people. But by mid-November, villages in eighteen more counties with a population of about 6,000,000 were added to the list, bringing the total affected population to approximately 14,210,000—an estimated 58.3 percent of all people living in the province. In Hunan the figures were comparable: an original plan to begin land reform in some thirty-three counties with affected villages containing about 17,000,000 people was later revised to

TABLE 3. Hunan: Progress in Completing Land
Reform, 1950–52

Time	Hsiang Completed	Population* of Hsiang
July 1950	214	—
Oct. 1950–Apr. 1951	5,479	13,880,933
Jun. 1951–Sep. 1951	2,108	4,124,673
Oct. 1951–Apr. 1952	4,892	10,451,210
Total	12,693	28,456,816

SOURCE: *Hunan Villages before and after Land Reform* [16],
p. 116.
 NOTE: For some similar progress reports on Hupei, see *CCJP*,
17 Apr. 51 [222]; and *CCJP*, 31 May 51 [224].
 *The total province population in 1952 was estimated as
29,112,407; the total number of *hsiang* was 13,274. This left 581
hsiang, with a population of 655,591, still to complete land
reform.

the movement slowly, in the orderly, well-organized fashion it had
hoped for. This chapter therefore examines the organizational methods it
employed to supervise and regularize the work of local activists and to
provide central guidance and general policy education for them. Organizational techniques used in this period, such as the keypoint-to-area
method of reform planning, the deployment of special work teams, the
issuance of propaganda about model experiences, and the establishment
of a far-flung village reporting network, are often assigned the credit for
the success of China's land reform. The CCP has a deserved reputation
for grassroots organizational strength in the countryside that sets it apart
from other revolutionary Marxist parties. But in the newly liberated
areas discussed here, it is clear that during land reform the central supervisory and training effort, although impressive, was nonetheless inadequate to the scale and the speed of change in the villages. New cadres
and activists unavoidably committed all manner of tactical mistakes and
deviations from the Party's own desired policies and procedures, as they

thirty-five counties and about 19,000,000 people. This involved about 40 percent of the
total area of the province and more than 60 percent of the total population. The 1950
autumn speed-up in land reform goals was felt throughout the Central South. For these
figures, see *HPJP*, 17 Nov. 50 [319]; *CCJP*, 12 Nov. 50 [219]; and *SWB* 85 [506], p. 56.
Compare the report of Li Hsueh-feng to the CSMAC delivered on 25 Sep. 50 in *CCJP*, 12
Oct. 50 [395] with the NCNA report of 29 Nov. 50 in *SWB* 86 [497], p. 61. See also
CCJP, 16 Apr. 51 [207] and *FBIS* (Wuhan) 29 Nov. 50 [496] and *SWB* 87 [498], p. 27.

were urged by their superiors to press on with reforms regardless of the obstacles they might encounter.

The general success of land reform in these areas can be attributed more to the repeated, *post hoc* rectifications of errors along the lines outlined in the first chapter than to the initial organizational strength or depth of the Party. Land reform marked only the beginning of the formation of a rural cadre infrastructure in these new areas; the force remained thin and inexperienced for some time. In these circumstances, the Party was understandably not too fussy about procedure. If rural workers could get a job done acting at least roughly in accord with policy intentions, then this was clearly considered good enough, and there would always be time afterward for seeing to the fine points and the formalities.

Thus, while the Party encountered many difficulties first in eliciting and then in controlling the popular forces of class struggle during land reform, its initially flexible approach to local administration, coupled with its attention to the longer-term education and training of village-level cadres, were key elements in the movement's overall success. In the space of about two years, the Party's four main objectives in land reform were decisively achieved throughout almost all the newly liberated territories.

AGRARIAN REFORM: CLASS POLICY

The proper implementation of land reform in China depended, first and foremost, on the accurate classification of each household in each village. As already indicated, several crude, *ad hoc* classifications had already been made in most villages for tax purposes during rent reduction, in forming the Peasant Associations and so on. But in redistributing land ownership rights, so much depended on class status that a careful and methodical classification of each household was imperative if legal and policy demands were to be observed. In attempting to evaluate the Chinese land reform, since class distinctions were so subtle and yet so important, it is essential to know something of what the standard class labels signified.[3]

3. The following discussion is based primarily on four important documents: "Decisions Concerning the Differentiation of Class Status in the Countryside," *CB* 52 [494], pp. 2–20; "CSMAC Supplementary Regulations Concerning the Differentiation of Class Status in the Countryside," *CCJP,* 29 Oct. 51 [120]; *The Agrarian Reform Law of the People's Republic of China, CB* 42 [489], pp. 2–9; and "Some Regulations of the

Landlords

By definition, landlords owned land but did not work on it. They relied for income on renting out the land or using hired laborers to work it. They might also sometimes make loans and engage in some industrial or commercial enterprises, but if their major source of income was from land rent, they belonged in the landlord class. And this included their income from any so-called "public land," school land, or clan land they managed. An important part of this definition is the stipulation about not engaging in labor. In order to qualify as a laboring household, it was only necessary for one member of the household to be doing "essential labor" for four months a year. Essential labor referred to ploughing, planting, reaping, and the other major farming tasks. Other auxiliary jobs, such as weeding, growing vegetables, and looking after draught animals and yard animals, were regarded as "nonessential." A family was considered to be engaged in nonessential labor if one member either did essential labor for under four months of the year, or if one member did nonessential labor for at least four months of the year. Many families relying primarily on income from rent did also have at least one member who participated in farm labor, essential or nonessential or both. A little work, however, was not enough to exempt such a family from classification as landlords in the Central South or other later liberated territories. If the amount of land rented out by the family was three times greater than the amount worked by family members plus hired hands, the family members would still be classified as landlords regardless of their labor on the land. And if the family happened to own a comparatively large amount of land, the standard criterion might be reduced to two times as much land rented out as worked by members of the family and hired hands.

Under the land reform law, all the land, all the draught animals, all the farm implements, and most of the grain the family did not actually require to eat, as well as any extra rooms or houses not needed for living space, were to be confiscated from households classified as landlords. In confiscating their land, all crop land, fallow land, mountain land, ponds, dams, dykes, groves, and trees were included. Graveyards, however, were not to be touched. The animals taken included cattle, horses, don-

CSMAC Concerning Actual Procedures for the Agrarian Reform Law," *CCJP,* 2 Nov. 50 [381]. Useful explanations of most of the points of law and policy discussed here can also be found in *Study Questions and Answers on Land Reform* [30].

keys, and mules, but not pigs, sheep, ducks, chickens, or other yard animals. Agricultural implements to be confiscated included all basic tools such as ploughs, seeders, hoes, stone rollers, shovels, carts, sickles, scythes, water wheels, winnowing machines, sieves, flour mills, huskers, grain storage vats, and harnesses. For the time being, however, certain tools and implements such as water pumps and cotton gins, considered to be technologically advanced, were left in the landlords' hands, presumably so that they would not be ripped out or ruined by peasants who did not know how to operate them properly. In taking over landlords' houses, all brick, tile, wood, and stone being used by landlords to build new buildings were included, as well as barns and animal pens, crop watching shelters, and summer homes and hunting cabins in the mountains. When houses were confiscated, furniture and bedding were to be included, and although there is nothing in the law about it, common practice in the Central South seems to have been to collect most of the extra clothing of landlord families as well.

According to the Agrarian Reform Law, all industrial and commercial enterprises located in the countryside were to be protected against confiscation and redistribution, and this included enterprises owned or operated by landlords. Therefore, all buildings, shops, factories, storehouses, sun drying areas, and warehouses, as well as draught animals that were used in such enterprises were *not* taken over. The capital, machines, tools, raw materials, and all the products and goods of these enterprises were also protected. Agrarian reform was regarded rather strictly as a means of eradicating the various forms of "feudal exploitation," that is, exploitation of the labor of others by means of tenantry, sharecropping and, to a certain extent, the hiring of farm labor. The land reform movement as such was not intended to extend into the sphere of "bourgeois capitalist exploitation," and landlords who happened also to run small businesses on the side were not supposed to be deprived of their assets and investments or of their opportunities for future entrepreneurial activity, simply because of their classification as landlords. Nevertheless, land owned by landlords and used to grow raw materials for a commercial or industrial enterprise was not protected and could be confiscated along with other land. Landlord merchants and industrialists would thenceforward have to purchase raw materials for their businesses on the market. Furthermore, any machinery or technologically advanced equipment in use in such enterprises, although not actually confiscated, was nationalized. Owners, therefore, could not sell it or use it as collateral for loans; they were expected to continue operating it for productive purposes.

Generally speaking, all the regulations that applied to individual landlords also applied to corporate landlords, such as churches, temples, monasteries, and clan associations. Where this referred to schools, hospitals, old age homes, orphanages, or other institutions performing approved public services but depending on income from rent to support their operations, the local government issued a promise to substitute funds from public revenue.

To qualify for landlord classification a family must have lived in landlord fashion for at least three years before liberation. Any landlord family that had not enjoyed that standard of living for three years and could honestly claim the title *nouveau riche* was fortunate, since a less onerous classification would have to be found for it. However, any arrangements made since liberation expressly for the purpose of evading the consequences of agrarian reform, such as those involving the mortgage, sale, or gift of landlords' land that should have been liable to confiscation, were declared null and void. Where peasants had bought or taken mortgages on such land and suffered a considerable loss through its subsequent confiscation, however, arrangements for compensating the peasants were to be made.

Absentee landlords were required, in the winter of 1950, to report to the local authorities and make a detailed declaration of their financial assets.[4] Any landlords who were suspected or accused of having committed crimes or counterrevolutionary activities were to be arrested and sent to the county seat for trial before the new people's tribunals, then in the process of being established and staffed. A special set of regulations was promulgated for handling the cases of lawbreaking landlords.[5] However, landlords were not supposed to be subjected to physical violence by cadres or villagers simply by virtue of their class status.

Rich Peasants

The main criterion for differentiating landlords and rich peasants was that of labor on the land. Rich peasants engaged in essential labor for at

4. *SWB* 83 [488], p. 36.
5. *NFJP,* 21 Nov. 50 [118]. See also *CCJP,* 18 Jan. 51 [115]; and *CCJP,* 29 Jul. 51 [119]. The Central People's Government (CPG) regulations for people's tribunals and the accompanying *JMJP* editorial can be found in a most useful anthology, *Collection of Important Land Reform Documents* [8], pp. 118–127. They are also reproduced in a local handbook, *Land Reform Handbook* [21], pp. 101–110.

least four months out of the year, although in other respects their wealth and standard of living might have been comparable (even superior) to some landlord families. Rich peasants generally owned their own land, although many both owned and rented land for cultivation. It was even possible for a rich peasant household to be in the position of renting all the land it cultivated from others. By and large, however, rich peasants owned both land and a more than sufficient supply of tools and oxen, and although they definitely worked the land themselves, they were also dependent on some sort of exploitative relationship for a significant portion of their total income. The form of exploitation associated with rich peasant status was the hiring of long-term farm laborers to work their land.

Rich peasants might also, of course, make loans, rent out a part of their land, or engage in commerce. But those classified as rich peasants derived 25 percent or more of their total income from exploiting others in one way or another. In order to facilitate the calculations, it was said that a family that regularly hired two long-term laborers should be classified as a rich peasant household. If the household hired only one long-term laborer but engaged in other forms of exploitation as well, careful figuring was required to determine if the income derived through exploitation amounted to 25 percent of the total family income. If it came to 25 percent or more, the family was to be classified as rich peasants; if not, they might be called middle peasants or well-to-do middle peasants. A rich peasant family renting out land exceeding (in size) the amount of land that family members and their hired laborers together cultivated was to be classified as "rich peasants of the semi-landlord type."

To be valid, the rich peasant classification could only be applied to families who had derived at least 25 percent of their total income from some sort of exploitation for at least three consecutive years, counting backward from the date of liberation of their locality. If it could not be proven to be three years, or if they were three nonconsecutive years, the family was to be classified as well-to-do middle peasants, despite their present level of exploitation.

Under the Agrarian Reform Law, all the land owned and cultivated by a rich peasant family and its hired hands remained the property of the family. Even the land rich peasants rented out was not to be confiscated in ordinary circumstances, although there was a provision that after all other confiscated land was divided up, if the most basic needs of the poorest peasants had not yet been satisfied, then some or all of the land the rich peasants rented out could also be confiscated and redistributed.

But this required provincial government approval, since it was regarded as an exceptional measure; and even when it had to be done, it was stipulated that rich peasants were under no circumstances to be allowed to fall below the standard of living of the middle peasants in their area. The land rented out by the so-called rich peasants of a semi-landlord type was, by contrast, to be routinely confiscated along with landlords' land. The mortgaging, selling, or giving away of land by rich peasants was not prohibited, as it was for landlords, and therefore all such arrangements made after liberation remained binding. However, if some of the land involved in these transfers would actually have been liable to confiscation, the case was to be handled in the same way as described above for landlords' land. The houses, oxen, implements, and surplus grain and capital of rich peasants were, in general, not to be touched.[6] Naturally, also, any commercial enterprises owned or run by rich peasants were not subject to confiscation.

It is important to note here two things about the nature of official policy toward rich peasants. First, the careful delineation between landlords and rich peasants, the protection of rich peasants' property, and the preservation of what was called "the rich peasant economy" were all certainly quite different from the harsher attitudes and policies toward rich peasants that had prevailed during land reform in the old liberated areas. Then rich peasants had been lumped together with landlords as a class to be eliminated; they were as much the objects of struggle as landlords, and all their assets were to be seized and redistributed.[7]

Second, the stipulation that for a family to qualify as rich peasants at

6. The Agrarian Reform Law itself makes no specific mention of these rich peasant possessions. For elucidation and explanation of the policy of protecting these assets from confiscation, see *Simple Land Reform Policy Propaganda Materials* [29], pp. 18–21.

7. For a discussion of the old policies and assumptions regarding rich peasants, see the report of Jen Pi-wu in *Typical Experiences in Land Reform and Party Rectification* [35], especially pp. 51–53. And for an example of how gradually the change in thinking on the question of how much to leave in rich peasants' hands during land reform came about, see Liao Yüan [25], pp. 23–24. Liao says, in explaining a new draft of the Agrarian Reform Law, "With regard to rich peasants, in addition to dividing up their land more equally, only their excess animals, implements, and houses are to be seized. That is, seize only their possessions that are in excess of those of most middle peasants, and do not seize their entire holdings. (We cannot seize their entire assets, all their houses, and so on, because rich peasants themselves participate in labor, and their assets are in part the fruit of their own labor.)" These words were obviously written during the time of policy transition.

least 25 percent of its income should be the fruit of exploiting others was a recent change from 15 percent. This had the effect of significantly reducing the number of households that could potentially be classified as rich peasants. Both these moves were intended to assist in achieving the general policy line for land reform summed up in the slogan "rely on the poor and hired peasants; unite with middle peasants; neutralize the rich peasants." This policy line reflected a standard CCP tactic of reducing to a minimum the number of people that a given program would undeniably affect adversely, so as to maximize the number who could favor it or at least not oppose it. The rise in the allowable degree of exploitation from 15 percent to 25 percent created more middle peasants where before there would have been rich peasants. And the increased respect for and protection of rich peasants' property rights gave those who were ultimately classed as rich peasants far less to fear from land reform. It was hoped that this would indeed "neutralize" the rich peasants by first making them a very small minority in the villages, and second by inclining them, if not to support land reform, at least not to fight it, since most of the threat to their self-interest had been removed.

Despite the government's clear and well-reasoned intentions, however, the classification of rich peasants in the villages remained a very tricky issue. It certainly was the cause of grief and concern far out of proportion to the size or wealth of the rich peasant class. Despite all the seemingly complex rules and regulations, there remained considerable flexibility in the matter of who was and was not a rich peasant and, once that was decided, what could and could not be taken from a rich peasant. These rules were often interpreted simplistically, inconsistently, even cavalierly, and almost always to the detriment of the rich peasants in question. As it was to turn out, the actual treatment of rich peasants during land reform and the real future of "the rich peasant economy" were not as favorable as official policy in 1950 had made it seem.[8]

Middle Peasants

Middle peasant families generally owned land and worked it themselves, although they might also rent some land to cultivate, rent out some of their own land to others, or hire hands to help with the work.

8. For a full discussion of the official attitude toward rich peasants and the desirability of preserving the rich peasant economy in 1950, see *Reference Materials on Problems of Land Reform* [28], Vol. 1, pp. 1–32.

These households usually possessed adequate farm implements and perhaps an ox. They had a better overall standard of living than most peasants in their village and they might occasionally (but not regularly) engage in some mild form of exploitation such as making loans or hiring long-term laborers. If this sort of exploitation was fairly regular and if its fruits approached but did not exceed 25 percent of the family's total income, they had to be classed as well-to-do middle peasants. There were also sometimes cases in which the family's level of exploitation slightly exceeded 25 percent of its income, but because it was faced with some special difficulties such as sickness or flood damage, it was still to be allowed the classification of well-to-do middle peasants. During land reform no middle peasants were to have any of their property expropriated, and in certain circumstances middle peasants might even receive some of the "fruits of struggle" in the redistribution phase of the movement.

Poor Peasants and Hired Hands

Poor peasant households might own a part of the land they cultivated and rent the rest, or they might own none and rent it all from others in the village. They generally did not possess all the tools they needed, and they were often the ones exploited by the other classes discussed so far, since they were frequently tenants and debtors. They also generally had to hire themselves out as farm laborers for extra income, and where there was difficulty in distinguishing middle peasants from poor peasants, an important criterion was that middle peasants did not as a rule have to sell their own labor power (that is, hire themselves out), while poor peasants did. Hired hands and their families, in contrast, were generally (though not necessarily) even poorer than poor peasants. They owned no land or only a tiny amount, and depended for the most part on odd jobs or longer-term contracts to work for other farmers in order to support themselves. Poor peasants and hired hands were the classes primarily intended to receive land and other goods as a result of land reform.

Small Rentiers

People who depended heavily on renting out land for income, but who did this either because they were physically unable to work their land or because they spent most of their time in some other occupation such as teaching or commerce, were not considered to be landlords despite their exploitation of others. As long as the land they rented out did not exceed

200 percent of the average local per capita landholding, they were called small rentiers, and their land was not to be expropriated. If the land did exceed this limit, they might still be called small rentiers, especially if they were none too wealthy, and only the part of their land over the 200 percent mark would be taken. But this rule was occasionally waived if the small rentier in question was a member of the family of a PLA soldier or a "revolutionary martyr." If, on the other hand, there were no such extenuating circumstances, and the small rentier's income from other occupations besides land rental was comparatively good, then he or she might be requested by the Peasant Association to allow part or all of the land rented out to be confiscated and redistributed. Small rentiers did not generally receive more land in the land reform, but they often were given other confiscated items for which they had a special need.

These five were by no means the only classes of people in the countryside who were affected by land reform. There were numerous other classifications, such as bankrupt landlord, poor odd-jobber, idler, intellectual, religious practitioner, enlightened gentry, merchant, small land-manager (the same as small rentiers except that they employed hired hands instead of renting out land), handicraftsman, handicrafts capitalist, peddler, professional person, sublandlord (person who leased and subleased land), local despot, feudal mountain lord, forest enterprise manager, fisherman, herdsman, KMT functionary, convicted criminal, and so on. Then there were also the problems connected with marriages across class lines. Some of these classes of people were supposed to be accorded special treatment during land reform, and others were not.[9] In fact, what finally happened to them probably depended more on how the local people and cadres judged their character, their personal connections, and their past behavior than on the special considerations recommended in government policy papers.

Nor was all land to be treated in the same way during confiscation and redistribution. All great forests, large water conservation works, large expanses of wasteland, salt fields, mines, lakes, marshes, rivers, and ports were nationalized and were to be administered by the government. Many large specialty farms and nurseries were also nationalized and

---

9. For some special Central South regulations referring to feudal mountain lords, fishermen, and criminals see *HTJP*, 30 Jun. 51 [108]; *CCJP*, 18 Aug. 51[225]; and *CCJP*, 6 Apr. 52 [109].

turned into state farms, but this accounted for only a tiny percentage of the total land cultivated. And then there were special regulations governing the disposition of sand flats and tidal land; empty or fallow land within villages; land owned by overseas Chinese; mortgaged land; land adjacent to railways, highways, ferry points, and bridges; famous and scenic spots; the sites of ancient remains and cultural relics; and also for wasteland reclaimed by individual peasants since liberation.[10] Thus it is only the more central and basic laws and policies pertaining to China's land reform that are discussed here.

LAND TENURE PATTERNS
AND THE PRINCIPLES FOR REDISTRIBUTION

The conventional wisdom of the day indicated that in central and southern China the peasants were richer and the landlords poorer than in the Party's old revolutionary base areas of the north. As soon as they were in a position to do so, therefore, the new provincial officials conducted their own sample surveys and were at some pains to demonstrate that, while land concentration may not have been as extreme as in the north, land was certainly not equitably distributed in the new areas and that a thorough-going land reform in the new areas would unquestionably be justified and necessary. Reproduced here are some of the findings of these early surveys, first for the entire Central South and then for Hunan province alone.

First, in carrying out their investigations the government survey teams recognized tremendous local differences, and therefore they divided the villages in the region into three categories: A, the areas with the greatest dispersion of landownership; B, the areas with standard dispersion of landownership; and C, the areas with concentrated landownership. (See Table 4.)

The CSMAC Land Committee, which did the survey, conceded that according to their information this indicated that land had become somewhat less concentrated in landlords' hands in this area during the years since 1911. But doing the calculations in *mou*, the traditional

10. Wasteland reclaimed since liberation was not to be confiscated and redistributed. This was important, as will be clarified in the next chapter, in order to keep some promises made in the agricultural tax laws. Many of the regulations governing special types of land can be found in the sources cited in note 3.

TABLE 4. Central South Land Tenure Patterns

	Class	% of Population	% of Land Owned
Type A: Contains	Landlords	3	15+ [a]
Approximately 15%	Rich peasants	5	15 (approx.)
of Rural	Middle, poor, hired, and other	92	60 (approx.)
Population of			
Central South[b]			
Type B: Contains	Landlords	3	30+ [a]
Approximately 40%	Rich peasants	5–6	15
of Rural	Middle, poor, hired, and other	90+	50
Population of			
Central South[c]			
Type C: Contains	Landlords	3–4	50[a]
Approximately 45%	Rich peasants	5	15
of Rural	Middle, poor, hired, and other	90+	20–30
Population of			
Central South[d]			

SOURCE: *HHYP* 3 (Nov. 50) [264], pp. 45–47.
NOTE: This survey was based on about seventy *ts'un* scattered throughout the region.
[a]Including public land, school, clan, and club land managed by landlords.
[b]Approximately 15 million people.
[c]Approximately 50 million people.
[d]Approximately 60 million people.

Chinese measure for land area equal to one-sixth of an acre, they emphasized that for the entire region there were only about 1.5–2.0 *mou* of farm land per capita, and that landlords owned an average of 10–20 *mou* while poor peasants owned generally no more than 0.50 *mou*.

If these early findings approached reality, then a later survey for Hunan province alone suggests that landlords owned a somewhat greater proportion of farmland in Hunan than they did in the Central South region as a whole.[11] (See Table 5.)

But generalized figures such as these obviously obscured the great differences among *hsiang* within Hunan of which the government was aware. To reflect these differences most accurately, they judged, the province could be best analyzed and understood in terms of a geographical or regional categorization that permitted comparisons among

11. Confirmation of the greater degree of concentration of landownership in Hunan than in other Central South villages can also be found in *Investigation of Rural Village Conditions in Hunan* [17], pp. 3–12.

TABLE 5. Landownership by Class in Hunan before
Land Reform

Class	% of Population	% of Land Owned
Landlords	4	55*
Rich peasants	5	13
Middle peasants	30	25
Poor peasants	39	6
Hired hands	10	none
Others	12	1

SOURCE: *Hunan Villages before and after Land Reform* [16],
pp. 17–18.
*Includes 9% public land managed by landlords.

villages near lakes, among those in hilly areas, and among those in
mountainous regions.[12] (See Tables 6–8.)

To underscore even more firmly the considerable variation prevailing
among villages in Hunan, the findings of a few individual village surveys can be included here. (See Tables 9–11.)

Of the four *pao* (wards) included in this last survey, Table 12 provides
the details on the one with the greatest degree of land concentration.
While in the same group of four West River *pao*, the one with the
greatest dispersion of land ownership, by contrast, claimed landlords as
representing only 1.8 percent of the population and owning only 5.45
percent of the land. Poor peasants in that *pao* constituted nearly 32 percent of the population and owned 25 percent of the land.[13]

It should be clear from the diverse findings of surveys such as these
that even if exactly the same rules were applied for confiscating and

12. An almost identical series of findings for lakeshore, hilly, and mountainous areas
of Hunan is reported in *CCJP,* 26 Apr. 51 [207]. A survey conducted in the mid-1950's
reported that mountainous areas comprised 64.64 percent of the land area in Hunan
province; hilly areas, 29.5 percent; and lakeshore areas, 5.86 percent. See *Hunan
Nung-yeh* [15], p. 266.

13. Relatively fewer comparable surveys for Hupei villages were found. Some are
available in *Investigations of the Rural Condition* [18], pp. 17–26. Here is one example
for fourteen administrative *ts'un* in Huang-p'i county's Fang-mei district in 1950. The
source is Yen Chung-p'ing [39], p. 278.

	Landlords	Rich peasants	Middle peasants	Poor and landless	Others
percentage of population	3.9	3.1	24.1	61.5	7.5
percentage of households	3.6	2.7	21.8	62.7	9.2
percentage of land owned	31.9	7.7	26.6	28.3	2.1

TABLE 6. Hunan: Landownership by Class in
Lakeshore Areas before Land Reform

Class	% of Population	% of Land Owned
Landlords	3	60
Rich peasants	4	7
Middle peasants	34	26
Poor peasants	42	4
Hired hands	9	none
Others	8	1
Public land	—	2

SOURCE: *Hunan Villages before and after Land Reform* [16], pp. 17–18.

NOTE: Public land—originally intended to be owned and used jointly to produce income for village public welfare services—was customarily managed by local landlords or other members of the village gentry. In CCP rural surveys, therefore, and because of the scope this arrangement afforded for corruption, public land was regarded as effectively belonging to village landlords. See also Tables 7, 8, and 10.

TABLE 7. Hunan: Landownership by Class in Hilly
Areas before Land Reform

Class	% of Population	% of Land Owned
Landlords	4	33
Rich peasants	7	20
Middle peasants	28	26
Poor peasants	36	8
Hired hands	5	none
Others	20	1
Public land	—	12

SOURCE: *Hunan Villages before and after Land Reform* [16], pp. 17–18.

TABLE 8. Hunan: Landownership by Class in
Mountainous Areas before Land Reform

Class	% of Population	% of Land Owned
Landlords	3	27
Rich peasants	5	14
Middle peasants	23	26
Poor peasants	44	18
Hired hands	16	none
Others	9	1
Public land	—	14

SOURCE: *Hunan Villages before and after Land Reform* [16], pp. 17–18.

TABLE 9. Investigation of Villages in Heng-Yang Municipality, Sixth District, Sixth Pao

		Landlords	Rich Peasants	Middle Peasants	Tenant Middle Peasants	Poor Peasants	Hired Peasants	Part Peasant, Part Traders	Peddlers	Others	Total
	Number of households	6	4	28	27	125	3	5	20	12	230
	% of households	2.6	1.8	12	11.5	54.5	1.3	2.3	8.7	5.5	100
	Population	33	16	115	107	491	14	24	65	50	915
	% of population	3.5	1.6	12.5	11.8	53.5	1.5	2.8	7.1	5.7	100
Land use (mou)	Total land cultivated	81	48	258.2	368.9	754.9	0	33.5	0	2.5	1547
Land use (mou)	Self-owned and cultivated	81	16	115	27.9	82.9	0	10.5	0	2.5	335.8
Land use (mou)	Rented in	0	32	143.2	341	672	0	23	0	0	1211.2
Land use (mou)	Fallow	0	8	68.5	64.5	94.5	0	0	0	3.5	239
Land ownership (mou)	Total	546	61.7	161	28.9	113.4	0	10.5	0	8	929.5
Land ownership (mou)	%	59	6.5	19.3	3.1	12.2	0	1.1	0	0	100
Land ownership (mou)	Self-cultivated	81	16	115	27.9	82.9	0	10.5	0	2.5	335.8
Land ownership (mou)	Rented out	465	45.7	46	1	30.5	0	0	0	5.5	593.7
Land ownership (mou)	Average per capita land owned	16.5	3.8	1.4	0.2	0.2	0	0.04	0	0.06	

SOURCE: *Investigation of Rural Village Conditions in Hunan* [17], pp. 94–95.

NOTES: Included in this table is some land lying outside the *pao*.

There were also 22 landlords living outside the *pao* who owned and rented out 389.6 *mou* within it; 96 other households outside the jurisdiction renting out 440.5 *mou*; 3 fields of "school land" rented out amounting to 16.5 *mou*; and 6 "public land" fields rented out, amounting to 69.1 *mou*.

redistributing land in all these villages, the ultimate outcomes and new patterns of landownership would still be quite different from place to place.

What principles, then, had central authorities decided to follow in redistributing land and other assets confiscated in villages like these? According to the rules, after having all their land confiscated, landlords were to be given back an amount equal at least to that of poor peasants so that they might earn their own living. Landlords and idlers who received land and who had no actual experience in farming might have wanted to sell, mortgage, or rent it out and use some of the money for investment in another occupation or business. But in the Central South and other later-liberated areas they were forbidden to do this and, for practical purposes, were left with no alternative but to work the land, however ineptly at the beginning. This was to be the means by which they could "reform themselves through labor."

Rich peasants and middle peasants did not usually receive land during redistribution. However, in those cases where redistribution left middle peasants actually below the new average household landholding, they might also be given some land and other means of production to improve their standard of living.

Naturally it was the landless, the poor peasants, and the hired hands who were to have first priority in the redistribution. Their needs were to be met first, insofar as possible. An important factor in dividing up the available land among the many poor peasant households was the number of dependents in each family. Families with more mouths to feed were to be given more land. But special consideration was also ordered for one-person and two-person households with one or both members capable of farm work. These were to receive more than the normal allotment for one or two people, other village conditions permitting, so as to make it more feasible for them to support themselves solely by working their own land.

Handicraftsmen and peddlers were also to be given a share of land and other means of production, according to their individual circumstances. But if their regular occupations supported them and their families well enough, this was not necessarily done. Monks, nuns, and priests, as well as other religious practitioners, were also to be given a share of land and other means of production equivalent to that held by the local average peasant household, if they were able and willing to work the land. Cadres, PLA wounded, demobilized servicemen, and men currently

TABLE 10. Investigation of the Eighth Pao of Ning-Hsiang County, Fourth District, Yang-Ch'uan Village

	Land-lords	Rich Peasants	Middle Peasants	Poor Peasants	Hired Peasants	Handi-crafts-men	Small Traders
Number of households	20	30	132	228	60	44	12
%	3.7	5.5	24.5	43	11	8	2.2
Population	136	203	917	1305	226	196	33
% of population	4.5	6.7	30.2	43	7.4	6.5	1.1
Land owned	7880	3098	7329.18	2591.1			
%	35.2	13.2	32.54	11.5			
Self-cultivated	1070	2165	5836.2	1797.8			
%	9.9	20	53.5	16.6			
Rented out	6895	933	1492.96	793.5			
%	59	8	12.4	6.8			
Rented in	—	900	4708.56	6079.7			
%	—	7.8	41.2	51.1			

SOURCE: *Investigation of Rural Village Conditions in Hunan* [17], p. 68.
NOTE: Measurements of land in this table are not given in *mou* but in *tan* (equal to 10 catties or 110.23 pounds) according to its average annual yield in grain. In this *pao* landlords and rich peasants (together 11.2% of the population) owned 48.4% of the land area—56% if the so-called public land is included. Poor peasants (43% of the population) held 11.5% of the

TABLE 11. Survey of Four West River Pao in Ch'angsha County, First District, Lang-Li Village

	Land-lords	Rich Peasants		Middle Peasants	
		Ordinary	Tenant	Ordinary	Tenant
Number of households	65	84	33	257	155
% of households	5.55	4.62	1.81	14.07	8.48
Population	409	619	198	1,741	1,080
% of population	4.603	6.966	2.229	19.595	12.155
Land use (*tan*) Total land cultivated	4,557.5	11,037	4,527.3	16,888.1	13,517.5
Self-owned and cultivated	4,208.5	8,445.3	656.2	11,803.5	1,879.2
Rented in	349	2,591.7	3,871.1	5,084.6	11,638.3
Land ownership (*tan*) Total	21,051.6	11,176.3	868.2	14,302.5	2,116.2
%	38.98	20.695	1.607	26.48	3.919
Self-cultivated	4,208.5	8,445.3	656.2	11,803.5	1,879.2
Rented out	16,843.1	2,731	212	2,499	237
Average per capita land owned	51.42	18.05	4.38	8.21	1.96

SOURCE: *Investigation of Rural Village Conditions in Hunan* [17], pp. 18–19.
NOTE: As in Table 10, land measurements are here given in *tan* of grain.

	Self-employed	Itin-erants	Religious People	Transients	Public Land	Total
Soldiers						
4	4	1	2	1		538
0.7	0.7	0.18	0.55	0.18		
11	9	1	4	4		3045
0.36	0.3	0.03	0.13	0.13		
					1663.5	22561.78
					7.56	
						10868.8
					1663.5	11777.96
					14.2	
						11777.96

land area. Figuring again in terms of *tan*, 81.2% of all the land rented out belonged to landlords and rich peasants (including the public land). 51.1% of this was leased by poor peasants; 41.2% by middle peasants. But for various reasons of convenience even poor peasants chose to rent out some land—an estimated 30.5% of the total they owned.

Poor and Hired	Dirt Poor	Ordinary Tenants	Others	Total
414	256	422	111	1,797
22.68	14.02	23.11	6.07	—
1,308	1,497	1,669	364	8,885
14.711	16.848	18.784	4.097	—
8,430.1	10,806.9	8	88	69,860.4
3,440.5	105.8	1	12.7	30,552.7
4,989.6	10,701.1	7	75.3	39,307.7
3,847.8	268.7	1	373.1	54,006
7.125	0.497	0.002	0.69	—
3,440.5	105.8	1	12.7	30,552.7
407.3	162.9	—	361	23,453.3
2.94	0.18	.0006	1.03	—

TABLE 12. Survey of the Tenth West River Pao in Lang-Li Village

	Land-lords	Rich Peasants	Tenant Rich Peasants	Middle Peasants	Tenant Middle Peasants	Poor Peasants	Tenant Poor Peasants	Others	Total
Number of households	18	24	10	48	41	71	65	96	373
Population	100	176	57	318	272	323	350	298	1894
% of population	5.28	9.23	3.02	16.79	14.33	17.05	18.75	15.73	100
Land use (tan)									
Total land cultivated	1168	3309	1725	2789.4	3602.5	794.5	1686.8	78.5	15153.7
Self-owned and cultivated	1076	2587	42	1944.4	178.5	458.7	33.8	5.2	6325.6
Rented in	92	722	1683	845	3424	335.8	1653	73.3	8792.1 (sic.)
Land ownership (tan)									
Total	8702.2	4046.5	42	2325.4	172.5	458.2	33.8	5.2	15792.3 (sic.)
%	55.09	25.6	0.21	14.7	1.09	2.9	0.21	0.03	100
Self-cultivated	1076	2587	42	1944.4	128.5	458.7	33.8	5.2	6325.6 (sic.)
Rented out	7644.8	1459.5	—	381	—	—	—	—	9425.3 (sic.)
Average per capita land owned	87.02	22.99	0.75	7.51	0.625	1.42	0.421	0.121	8.33

SOURCE: *Investigation of Rural Village Conditions in Hunan* [17], pp. 19–20.
NOTE: As in Tables 10 and 11, land measurements are here given in *tan* of grain.

serving in the army and their families were also to be given a share equal to the average peasants' new holdings. But if cadres were receiving government salaries or had other means of supporting their families adequately, the amount granted to them could be reduced appropriately or eliminated.

The right of women to own land independently was newly guaranteed, and therefore single women, divorced women, and widows were also to receive an equal share of land. Unemployed people in the cities who had originally lived in the countryside could obtain permission from the authorities to return to their villages and be given a share of land if they wanted to farm. The same was to be true for runaway landlords who returned and for hired hands and servants who had lived outside their villages for a long time but who wanted to return. In most villages a small amount of land was retained for possible distribution to other families who had left the village under various circumstances and whose whereabouts were not known but who might be expected to return. The *hsiang* government, in the meantime, was to rent the land out for cultivation. Once the redistribution was settled, title deeds were to be made out for each household and rights of inheritance by legitimate heirs were to be reaffirmed.

In connection with the guidelines and methods of redistributing land, there are two special points that should be mentioned. First, the *hsiang* was to be taken as the unit in making class divisions, confiscating, and redistributing land. In solving some particular dilemmas the relevant locale was occasionally to be extended to the county, but there was never any attempt, as there has been in other Asian countries implementing agrarian reforms, to set a provincial or national standard for the wealth of classes or for land per household. This meant that within villages the greater inequities were to be eliminated, but that the often much more significant inequities across villages and across counties were not even to be addressed. This state of affairs seems to have been accepted by everyone as quite normal, and except for natural disasters and the like, when emergency aid was naturally offered to the stricken, the notion that wealthier *hsiang* should share with poorer ones was never given serious consideration.

Second, in distributing land among the poor villagers, the principle behind the slogan "land to the tiller" was to be observed. This meant that the actual tenant or hired hand who had worked a piece of land for a landlord was to be the one to receive that piece of land in the redistribution. It was not only the symbolic value of this policy that appealed to the Party. It was hoped that this procedure would help to avoid quarrels within the villages concerning who would receive some more and some less desirable bits of land. Also, the less moving around of people and their work places the better from the point of view of keeping land reform as smooth and nondisruptive as possible. Peasants who felt confident that they would not be moved off their land and over to the other side of the village were more likely to plant and fertilize their fields as usual, thus offsetting some of the production backlash brought on by the uncertainties of land reform.

This principle, like all the principles, definitions, and regulations sketched here, could not always be applied literally or perfectly rigorously. The Party continually stressed the need for flexible policy application in the villages so as to avoid creating new injustices while trying to rectify old ones. In the end, all these guidelines for official fairness and retribution were subject to revision in accordance with the village consensus on individual cases.

ORGANIZATION AND ADMINISTRATION OF THE MOVEMENT

As explained in Chapter 1, the local branch of the Peasant Association was charged with managing the entire land reform campaign in the villages and with implementing all the important policies outlined here. However, most Central South villages did not yet possess a stable, reliable, or representative Peasant Association capable of undertaking the task. Even after land reform had been completed, a survey of 8,602 villages in Hunan province indicated that Peasant Associations still only encompassed 39.8 percent of the rural population.[14] And in the early stages of land reform membership was even lower than this. To help organize and lead the Peasant Associations, therefore, some new governmental institutions were created, some new methods of utilizing cadres were tried, and some old ones were strengthened and expanded.

First, a Land Committee *(t'u-ti wei-yüan-hui)* was established for each county, special district, and province in the Central South[15] and given responsibility for coordinating the reform movement in its area.

14. *Hunan Villages before and after Land Reform* [16], p. 143.
15. *CCJP,* 22 Jun. 50 [114].

These committees, standing in hierarchical relationship with one another, were responsible for all aspects of land reform, including cadre training, the publication of propaganda materials, investigation and research concerning local conditions, and subsequent adjustments and modifications in plans and procedures. The provincial land committees were to be comprised of thirty to forty-five persons; the special district committees, of fifteen to twenty-five; and the county committees, of seven to fifteen. (There is no information on the size of the committees' staffs.) It was the members of these committees, in consultation with the Central South regional authorities, who actually set targets and timetables for the movement in the region. And the Land Committees appear to have had the final word on which villages in their area were to undergo land reform, and in what approximate sequence.

A most important tool for carrying out the plans of the Land Committees was the land reform work team. These small groups ranged from three to thirty members, depending on the size of their assigned villages and on the stage of the movement. They generally moved from village to village, propagandizing, organizing, and attempting to make local situations conform to policy guidelines. The extremely large number of villages beginning land reform almost simultaneously demanded a correspondingly large number of work teams staffed with capable and knowledgeable cadres. This was the first great challenge of the movement for local authorities in the newly liberated areas, one they exerted tremendous efforts to meet. Just as land reform was beginning in earnest, it was announced that 103,000 land reform cadres had already been trained and were on hand for work in the Central South region.[16] But it was quickly conceded that over 90 percent of these were "new cadres," whose training for land reform work was very sketchy indeed. Although some of them had participated in the preliminary experimental land reform work in the region, under 10 percent of the total were old cadres with true experience of land reform.[17] In December 1950 there were said to be about 22,000 cadres taking part in land reform in Hunan province. Of these, 93 percent had been participating in "revolutionary work" for under a year, and some for only ten or fifteen days. "Old cadres" accounted for only 7 or 8 percent, and not all of them had experience in

16. NCNA, 29 Nov. 50, *SWB* 86 [497], p. 61.
17. See the report of Tu Jun-sheng at the third meeting of the CSMAC in *CCJP,* 18 Apr. 51 [318].

land reform work. Furthermore, of the 22,000 total, 70 to 80 percent were "intellectuals from landlord and rich peasant families," probably because unlike peasants they were both literate and able to leave their homes for unspecified periods to travel around with the work teams; only 20 to 30 percent were peasants.[18] Toward the end of the movement, Hunan reported 74,941 cadres participating in land reform work and broke them down into the following four categories:[19]

10,708	newly raised up nonworker/peasant long-term cadres
18,077	temporary peasant support brigade members
19,007	land reform work team members
27,149	on-duty cadres

Although these category designations are rather vague, it would appear that nearly all members of the first three groups were "new cadres" and only a very small proportion of those in the fourth group had any experience in land reform work before 1950. (The great majority of those making up the difference between the 22,000 originally reported and the now nearly 75,000, however, were evidently from peasant backgrounds.)

A common saying of the time reflects something of the probable distribution of experienced cadres in the hierarchy: *shang hao, chung shao, hsia tsao* ("the upper ranks [of cadres] are good, the middle ranks are few, and the lower ranks are awful"). Certainly local government offices put a great deal of effort into special training classes for newly recruited cadres, and this produced some good results.[20] But the fact of the matter was that in order to create the number of land reform work teams needed, all sorts of people had to be absorbed as cadres, and there was little time to educate them for their work. Even city middle school children were sometimes given time off to help with land reform work,[21] and members of other "democratic parties" were specifically accepted

18. *CCJP,* 26 Apr. 51 [207]. A similar figure for cadres from landlord and rich peasant background is given in L. P. Deliusin, *Bor' ba Kompartii Kitaia za razreshenie agrarnogo voprosa [The struggle of the Communist Party of China to resolve the agrarian problem]* (Moscow, 1964).

19. *Hunan Villages before and after Land Reform* [16], p. 117.

20. For some reports of early cadre training classes and other special facilities see, e.g., *CCJP,* 4 Jan. 51 [167]. This is a rather pessimistic overview of the work to date. Even in more localized and optimistic reports, however, numerous shortcomings of the training are noted. See, e.g., *HPJP,* 12 Nov. 50 [215].

21. *HPJP,* 12 Nov. 50 [74].

as members of land reform work teams.[22] After all, the CCP had not been the only organized force favoring agrarian reform in China, and the voluntary assistance of all sympathizers was quite actively solicited. Members of the intelligentsia naturally brought some especially valuable skills to the task, and they were evidently absorbed into land reform work teams and land reform administration by the thousands. This influx of the educated, urbanized elite into the ranks of the cadres was to have certain undesirable repercussions, from the Party's point of view, but during land reform these people, by their sheer presence, made a tremendous contribution toward giving the movement life and depth.

Keypoints

Once the land reform work teams were drawn up and ready to go, they were deployed on what was known as a "keypoint" basis. The use of keypoints was to be one of the standard devices of the Party and the government for implementing important rural policies. As the term suggests, certain key villages were selected to receive special work teams and to be the first to begin land reform in their area. Their experiences, both good and bad, would serve as models for the surrounding villages, and their development would provide a testing ground and a demonstration platform for work teams and local cadres.[23] If the strategy worked as planned, new peasant activists would be discovered in the keypoint village and brought into revolutionary work there. Both work teams and local cadres would gain valuable experience while carrying out land reform in what was intended to be a carefully controlled situation. After the work in the keypoint village was well under way or almost complete, work team cadres would be reassigned and some of the newly recruited local activists would also be sent on to work in villages in the surrounding area. This was called "going from point to area" or "combining point and area," and by this means it was hoped that the land reform movement would grow and spread more or less naturally over all the newly liberated territories, maintaining a steady pace and not snowballing out of control.

Peasants in surrounding villages would naturally hear the gossip about

22. *CCJP*, 10 Nov. 50 [111].

23. The purpose of the keypoint system and the experiences of land reform in various keypoint villages were given a great deal of coverage in the contemporary press. A few of the more informative reports are *CCJP*, 15 Feb. 51 [70]; *CCJP*, 17 Feb. 51 [345]; and *CCJP*, 1 Mar. 51 [335].

how land reform was progressing in the keypoint village. Peasants and cadres from outlying villages would also be brought into the keypoints to observe and participate in the process, especially during the stages of confiscation and redistribution of land. The keypoint cadres were, likewise, to visit surrounding villages periodically to make official reports to the village leaders, keeping them abreast of progress and setbacks along the way. But however close relations between the keypoint and surrounding village cadres were supposed to be, work teams were warned against neglecting their keypoint work in order to assist and supervise mass mobilization in the outlying villages. Their most important task was to make sure a good job was done in the keypoint village so that it might serve as a model. They were cautioned that it would not do to rush off in response to requests for help from the surrounding villages, allowing those villages to catch up with or even jump ahead of developments in the keypoint. This, it was pointed out, would definitely lead to chaos since then there would be no nearby models to emulate and virtually no cadres who had participated in a complete and proper village land reform.[24]

The emulation of keypoint models as a means of ordering village politics during land reform had a number of interesting consequences for the later development of the movement and for subsequent trends in the administration of rural transformation. The experiences in keypoint villages provided local cadres and activists in the surrounding communities with concrete examples, in readily recognizable form, of the application of official principles, guidelines, and theoretical assertions to real and familiar situations. However painstaking and precise official pronouncements on the differentiation of classes and their treatment in land reform may appear to us now, to local activists, who were as yet unaccustomed to their roles as political opinion makers and unused to looking beyond their more immediate environments to make abstract comparisons between their own villages and others, these guidelines must often have seemed puzzling or inappropriate. The work in keypoints brought revolutionary theory and legal principles down to cases and, for local Party and non-Party workers, made comparisons with their own villages easier and more meaningful. The activities in keypoints, then, served a largely didactic purpose, with regard to the lower-level rural leadership personnel who observed them. The "keypoint-to-area" strategy was an

24. On the finer points of moving from point to area see *CCJP,* 20 Feb. 51 [375]; and Jao Shu-shih [504], pp. 43–45.

important one in beginning the training of local people and in quickly bringing into being a capable leadership group at the village level, ready to implement present and future central policies for rural development.

Activists in surrounding villages were told to emulate the experiences of the keypoints but definitely not to imitate them mechanically. The very multiplicity of situations and problems encountered and reported in the keypoints themselves ruled out the propagation of any one strict pattern to be followed and alerted activists to the fact that conditions in their own villages were unlikely to mirror exactly the conditions of any one keypoint village. The work in keypoints was not to be standardized or rigid. On the contrary, it was to put a premium on flexibility in dealing with diverse situations. The keypoint strategy was important, then, in demonstrating to rising rural cadres the real intended content of policy statements and slogans but also in impressing them with the need for good preparatory investigation, flexibility, intelligence, and imagination in the process of bringing rural policy designs to fruition in their own villages.

When land reform or some other work was finally accomplished satisfactorily in a keypoint village, after difficulties of one sort or another had been surmounted, it gave courage and hope to those who had worried that the policy might never be made to succeed, and it simultaneously gave pause to those who had foreseen nothing but easy victories. Both tendencies existed among those who backed reforms and who worked for them in the villages; and the keypoint method helped in bringing a certain maturity to the political work of those people, restraining somewhat their impulses toward ''adventurism,'' on the one hand, and ''immobilism,'' on the other. In all these ways, the keypoint method was a contributory factor in what was to be a protracted process of creating a resourceful and reliable network of committed political operatives in the countryside, on whom the central authorities were to have to rely heavily for future progress in village transformation.

There is a question about the criteria by which the keypoint villages were chosen. The public documents of the period are inconclusive on this issue, sometimes seeming to imply that only villages where land reform had a good chance of proceeding smoothly and successfully were chosen; and at other times implying that the goal was to select a fair cross section of all kinds of villages for keypoint work.

A number of factors must have played a role in the selections. Reasonably good communication and transportation links with the keypoint villages were, for example, an important qualification in the early period. The emphasis was on careful control of work teams by the county office, frequent reports, consultations, and meetings to iron out difficulties. The close liaison desired demanded that there be some telephone or telegraph connection to the village and easily passable roads linking it with the subdistrict headquarters. This automatically eliminated the most backward and isolated villages and tended to create a concentration of keypoint villages in suburban areas, since in the early phase the land reform movement was largely directed from urban centers. The same kinds of considerations also encouraged the choice of market towns as keypoint villages. Peasants in surrounding villages took a natural personal interest in market town developments, and frequently wealthier landlords who rented out land in the surrounding villages resided in the market towns. If these towns became keypoints, such landlords came under attack immediately, and this served to break the ice for their tenants living in the smaller villages scattered around the keypoint.[25]

There seems to have been a tendency to choose as keypoints villages that had been Communist-controlled at some time before 1949, and especially villages where CCP land reform policies had been implemented years earlier. Although in some cases this may have reflected a belief that success was more certain in those villages, in many other cases the choice appears to have been prompted by a concern that the old-style, more violent and radical land reform might spontaneously reemerge there and endanger the orderly development of the movement along the more moderate lines now envisioned. On the principle that outdated familiarity breeds confusion, the old CCP base areas of the Central South seem to have been especially carefully monitored during land reform.

MOBILIZATION PROCEDURES, PROBLEMS, AND DEVIATIONS

When a work team arrived to carry out land reform in a village, the first steps involved investigation of local conditions, the rectification and purification of the village's Peasant Association and the other mass

25. Ting Ling, in her novel *The Sun Shines over the Sankan River* [485], illustrates the difficulty of persuading peasants to begin the struggle against a landlord living in another village where land reform had not yet gotten underway. The overlapping interrelationships that bound China's rural villages into a complex social network created con-

organizations, propagandizing the basic land reform policies, and carrying out a new and thorough classification of villagers.²⁶ These tasks inevitably overlapped one another and consumed different amounts of time and energy in different places. There were some rules about the timing and the order of the classification procedure, however, which it was important to follow faithfully. It was necessary that the entire classification of all village households (not just of the landlords) be completed before the expropriation began.²⁷ If the confiscation were carried out first and villagers came to know exactly how much property was going to be available for redistribution, the greatness or smallness of the amount was likely to have an unfair influence on the classifications assigned to many village households.²⁸ It was preferable, therefore, that class categories be assigned while ignorance of the exact benefits to be obtained still prevailed. In doing the classification itself, however, it was recommended that landlords be classified first, then rich peasants and so on.²⁹ This was to enable cadres and masses to eliminate the landlords from the discussions as early as possible so that they would not be able to "cause confusion" and disrupt the process. In villages where the classification did not conform to these guidelines the outcome of land reform was generally badly distorted, and the eventual rectification that followed was especially complex.

Once these early steps were complete, or almost complete, the work of mobilizing the poor peasants to take revolutionary action against the landlords was to begin in earnest. The main methods used to mobilize peasants for land reform have been described many times and there is, therefore, no need to dwell on them here.³⁰ *Su k'u* (speak bitterness) meetings were probably the most common of the techniques employed.³¹ At these public meetings, poor peasants were led to air their

---

ditions in which the "point-to-area" method could be extremely effective. However, this same complex network sometimes made it impossible to isolate a keypoint village and treat it separately from its surroundings during land reform.

26. *CCJP,* 16 Oct. 50 [155]. See also *HPJP,* 1 Dec. 50 [287]; and *HPJP,* 24 Nov. 50 [200].

27. See *CCJP,* 13 Jan. 51 [378]; and *CCJP,* 17 Jan. 51 [314].

28. An example of this, working to the detriment of middle peasants, is reported in *CCJP,* 15 Jan. 51 [282].

29. *HPJP,* 22 Nov. 50 [87]. See also *CCJP,* 17 Jan. 51 [314].

30. Good descriptions can be found in Hinton [460], *passim,* and Pepper [476], pp. 229–330.

31. *CCJP,* 8 Jan. 51 [221]. See also *CCJP,* 6 Jan. 51 [370].

old grievances against landlords and other wealthy villagers and to describe the misery of their own lives directly or indirectly attributable to
their exploitation by the landlords. The purpose of the meetings was
essentially twofold: to convince peasants that they had indeed suffered
enough under the feudal system that they were justified in seizing landlords' property and to build their courage for actually carrying out the
deed. Of course, most of the stories told at *su k' u* meetings were already
common knowledge in the villages, although sometimes peasants were
moved to reveal instances of suffering and humiliation long concealed
from their neighbors. The repetition and reminder of old acts of cruelty
and the tales of deprivation not only served to enflame peasant hatred but
also frequently constituted something of an education for the work team
cadres, especially those from "enlightened gentry" families and from
the cities.[32]

Sometimes, to make landlords' exploitation even more graphic for
vacillating peasants, a ritual "settling accounts" *(suan chang)* was carried out during which peasants estimated the cost to them of things lost,
opportunities lost, and lives lost through landlords' exploitation. An
actual bill was sometimes drawn up and used against landlords during
the later accusation phase of the movement. But *suan chang* was primarily another vivid symbolic device employed during the mass mobilization stage, to convince tenants and peasants of the justice of land reform
and to strengthen their determination to confront the landlords.

It was a fundamental principle of the Party's rural work at this time
that, despite the fact that poor peasants and hired hands were often the
most difficult to mobilize into the revolution, it was only they who could
be depended on to demand a thorough land reform movement without
compromise, since it was they who stood to gain the most from the
effort. That is why it was insisted that local cadres "rely" on the poor
and hired and merely "unite with" the middle peasants. Middle peasants were not by any means to be the prime beneficiaries of the struggle
ahead, and the Party fully expected that when they realized this they
would slacken off in revolutionary agitation and turn their attention to
things more immediately in their own interest, such as tending their own
farms. The CCP officially regarded middle peasants as too willing to
compromise in land reform. Relying on them would mean not seeing the
struggle through to the end.

32. *CCJP*, 11 Jan. 51 [56].

Land reform struggle meeting in the suburbs of Peking, 1950. (Hsinhua News Agency)

The problem, however, was in convincing the poor and hired that ultimate victory in the struggle was sure enough to make it reasonable for them to take the risk of leading it. To accomplish this, the special work teams often had to conduct separate mobilization sessions for poor peasants, and it was even recommended at times that a distinct Poor Peasants' Association be set up for the purpose.[33] These new Poor Peasants' Associations were not to be given the extensive powers to run the land reform movement held by Poor Peasant Leagues in the north before 1949. The regular Peasant Associations, with their heavily middle peasant membership, were simply to be by-passed temporarily, and the Poor

33. *CCJP,* 17 Jan. 51 [314].

Peasants' Associations became the center for village propaganda and organizational work for a time. But the chairman of the Poor Peasants' Association was supposed to be one of the members of the original *Nung Tai Hui*. And once poor peasants had been mobilized and a number of them were prepared to take leading roles in the land reform struggle, the two organizations were to be merged to make a new peasant association with "the poor and hired as the core." Sometimes even efforts such as these proved inadequate, however, and it was necessary to take steps to recruit more poor peasants into leadership roles during the rectification phase that followed the initial completion of land reform in the village.

Although generally very effective, this array of mass mobilization techniques did not always produce immediate satisfactory results because many peasants, however miserable their own lives, could not be convinced that it was right for them to take other people's property. Others apparently exercised such scruples only in cases of landlord families from their own clan,[34] but their inability to give up "clan sentiment" for "class consciousness" inhibited the overall village movement nonetheless. Superstitious beliefs, unwillingness to challenge what they feared might be their own preordained "fate," and persistent rumors of a possible "change of sky" and consequent punishments for those who had been rash and disrespectful prevented many poor peasants from joining the movement wholeheartedly. The Party's own reports admitted a notable lack of peasant confidence that the challenge to landlords could ultimately be successful. There were ample precedents in Chinese history for a half-hearted reform that would tread only lightly on the dominant classes, leaving them bruised but in a position to recoup their former prerogatives before much time elapsed. And the revenge and retribution that could be expected to accompany such a potential landlord resurgence were also clearly predictable and readily foreseen by poor peasants. A great deal was at stake for every individual involved in land reform, and the undeniably widespread anxiety as to whether the reform would actually be seen through to the end must account in part for both the furtive timidity of many villagers and the spirited determination of many others.

In the more commercialized rural areas of the Central South, one complication was that peasants often failed to appreciate the distinction

34. *CCJP,* 17 Jan. 51 [100].

between a landlord's land rent and the landlord's business enterprises as sources of income and types of exploitative activity. When work team cadres insisted on protecting the manufactory and commercial enterprises of landlords, local peasants feared that the landlords would not really be "knocked down"—that they would retain enough power and prestige to stay in control of village affairs and eventually take revenge on their attackers.[35]

The single greatest fear afflicting peasants at this stage, however, was that land reform would somehow get out of control and that they would not be able to stop it once it had started. After the landlords' land had been taken, then rich peasants might come under attack, and after them, middle peasants. Even some poor peasants who had not yet been pressed to reveal all their assets to the cadres were afraid that the time might come when these things would be found out and taken away from them, to be given to people even poorer than themselves. At this stage the fear of appearing to be wealthy became more intense than ever before. Some rich and middle peasants reportedly tried to make gifts of some of their land to their village, no doubt in an effort to head off total expropriation.[36] Households actually in need of extra hands for production delayed hiring anyone, even if they had already been assigned a desirable classification. Peasants still stayed away from their fields. The following season's production continued to be endangered.[37] The mass mobilization phase of the movement may have prepared many poor peasants to take revolutionary action, but it left many others simply in a state of great agitation and uncertainty.

Meanwhile, those classified as landlords were realizing the immediate threat to their own livelihood and their sometimes frantic actions during these days further augmented the tension. Some landlords were to give in quite meekly to the demands of cadres and peasants, when they were finally made. But most tried to take what action they could to reduce the impending personal disaster, or at least to make the ultimate victory for their opponents less sweet. They resorted to all kinds of sabotage and evasion, some crude, and others rather clever.

Landlords usually first attempted to sell or transfer to loyal friends and relatives those pieces of property they knew were liable to confisca-

---

35. *CCJP,* 15 Oct. 50 [408].   36. *CCJP,* 7 Apr. 51 [214].
37. See, e.g., *CCJP,* 9 Jan. 51 [140].

tion.[38] Since such transfers were officially outlawed, many landlords began to search for loopholes in the law that might permit them to keep control over some of their assets. In some villages, when landlords understood the meaning of the principle of "land to the tiller," they began dismissing their past tenants and leasing the land to others whom they wanted to have it after the reform. In some cases, the new "tenants" made secret payments to the landlord for this consideration; in others, the landlord simply parceled out holdings among family members and friends and depended on them to reciprocate with support after land reform had run its course.[39] If these maneuvers did not succeed, threatened landlords often turned to destruction of their own property while it was still theirs, rather than allow it to fall into the hands of peasants and cadres. In their own eyes perhaps there was more dignity and defiance in these acts than hatred or revenge. The government, however, condemned them as saboteurs and counterrevolutionaries. They were subject to detention or arrest, trial, and imprisonment.[40]

Reports of sabotage and violent crimes by landlords filled the local press during the early stages of the movement, and there were continual reminders of the need for reliable militia units in the villages to prevent counterrevolutionary acts and to apprehend criminals.[41] All the alarming reports notwithstanding, however, actual losses due to sabotage by landlords do not appear to have been very severe. After the first thrust of land reform in Hunan, when over 2,000 *hsiang* were said to have completed the process, the government released these statistics on "landlords' sabotage": houses burned, 5,000+ rooms; forest fires, 284 instances; animals slaughtered, 998 head; cadres murdered, 93 persons. To help put these figures in perspective, it was also reported at the same time that 441,531 rooms, 18,786 head of draught animals, over

38. *HPJP*, 20 Nov. 50 [336]. The proscription against the sale or transfer of assets by landlords had been in effect since early 1950. At that time rich peasants were included, but this was later changed, leaving only landlords subject to the restriction. See *CCJP*, 5 Mar. 50 [208].

39. *CCJP*, 24 Aug. 51 [254].

40. In addition to the provisional regulations for dealing with lawbreaking landlords (see note 5 above), several supplementary rules for handling landlords and landlord criminals were published. See, e.g., *CCJP*, 20 Aug. 52 [81]. When landlords were sent away to prison or labor gangs, their land and houses were supposed to be kept by the *hsiang* government for their return. See *JMJP*, 22 Aug. 51 [110].

41. See, e.g., *CCJP*, 26 Feb. 51 [90]; and also *CCJP*, 16 May 51 [62].

772,000 pieces of farm equipment, and over 3,161,600 *mou* of land had been confiscated from landlords in these same villages.[42]

Looking more particularly at some statistics on the population of draught oxen in Hunan, it would appear that an increase in deaths not due to disease did cause the annual rate of increase in the population to fall, but that the province nevertheless managed to produce a net gain in live oxen during land reform.[43] (See Table 13.)

Similarly, dislocations attributable to the reform were not serious enough to interfere with the natural postwar recovery of agricultural production in the province.[44] (See Table 14.)

Figures such as these tend to confirm the impression that actual losses due to landlords' sabotage were not too serious, despite all the publicity about their crimes and "wrecking activities." And even though rich peasants and other anxious poorer peasants sometimes also committed acts of sabotage to try to protect themselves, the real losses of means of production were kept to a gratifyingly low level during the whole of China's agrarian reform movement.

As the phase of propagandizing and mobilizing the peasantry continued and as village tension mounted, however, there frequently occurred something of an overreaction among the formerly reluctant poor peasants—an outbreak of pent-up emotions in the form of violence and even brutality against local landlords. Angry scenes, the storming of landlords' houses, the dragging out and beating of victims—these and other violent reprisals were often triggered at the moment by the discovery of cases of sabotage or other counterrevolutionary maneuvers perpetrated by landlords. There is no way to estimate the numbers of people beaten and killed. Instances of "unrestrained violence" were frequently reported and condemned in the official press, but no comprehensive figures were printed. Other estimates are highly speculative

42. *CCJP,* 20 Apr. 51 [253].

43. For some reports of needless deaths of oxen in Hupei and other provinces, see *CCJP,* 21 Feb. 51 [355]; and *CCJP,* 24 Apr. 51[69].

44. Theorists of development frequently conclude that land reforms should be expected to have short-term adverse effects on agricultural production. Huntington, for example, writes, "The immediate impact of land reform, particularly land reform by revolution, is usually to reduce agricultural productivity and production. In the longer run, however, both usually tend to increase." Huntington [464], pp. 378–379. The evidence for China's land reform does not fit this pattern: production and productivity rose steadily, if not always dramatically, from 1949 through the early 1950's.

TABLE 13. Estimated Population of Draught Oxen in Hunan, 1948–52

	Total Number Animals (approx.)	Number Deaths from Disease	% of Total Dead from Disease	Number Surviving Animals (approx.)	% of Increase in Number Surviving Animals (approx.)
1948	2,390,000	239,000	10.0	2,151,000	—
1950	2,392,971	83,754	3.5	2,309,217	7
1951	2,555,032	79,206	3.1	2,475,826	7
1952	2,595,200	51,904*	2.0	2,543,296	3

SOURCE: Adapted from some figures given in *Hunan Villages before and after Land Reform* [16], p. 178.

NOTE: It is not known exactly when the first estimate of the total population was made, nor at what time of year the three later estimates were compiled. Therefore these figures must be regarded with caution and are offered here as merely suggestive of the possible dimensions of fluctuations in the ox population around the time of land reform. It may also be noted that a later estimate made in *Hunan Nung-yeh* [15], p. 88, put the total for 1952 at 2,694,573, a figure not very far from those given here.

*Projected from figures for the first half of the year, assuming the same death rate over the entire year. The excellent decline in deaths from disease was the result of an impressive program of vaccination and treatment mounted by the province.

and often suspect.[45] Nor are there any adequate means of gauging to what extent corporal punishment for these people could be said to be justified (in view of their own past behavior)—either by Western standards of morality and justice or by Chinese standards. Official policy did not condone mob violence or other physical attacks on landlords. Lawbreakers were to be sent to the courts for trial and punishment. And yet, the deliberately great speed of the movement in combination with the almost total lack of a trained and neutral police force in the countryside practically guaranteed that mobs would form and have their way. The precautions that would have been necessary to put a stop to all violent outbreaks simply were not taken. There seems to have been a certain repugnance among Chinese leaders at the thought of tightly reining in

45. Stavis has made the best review of the evidence on deaths during land reform and offers this tentative conclusion: "It would appear that somewhere between 400,000 and 800,000 people were killed officially after 1949 . . . . The Chinese Communist leadership had estimated that landlords and their families constituted 4–5 percent of the rural population—about 20 million people. This would imply that 1 to 4 percent of landlords' families met death. If a half-million people were killed in land reform, this would be 0.1 percent of the rural population or 2.5 percent of the landlord class and would represent roughly one death in six landlord families." Elsewhere Stavis considers it reasonable to assume that as many people were killed "unofficially" as officially, and so if he is correct, the total for the land reform period (1949–52), including nonlandlords, may be somewhere over one million deaths in the entire country. Stavis [484], pp. 29–30.

TABLE 14. Growth of Total Value of Agricultural Output in Hunan, 1949–52

(In 10,000 yüan)

	1949	1950	1951	1952	1952 as % of 1949	Average Rate of Increase as %
All agriculture and sidelines	158,422.00	191,752.45	219,078.68	265,725.49	167.73	10.89
Agriculture only	120,455.06	140,846.27	156,527.65	187,229.87	155.43	9.22
Forestry	2,455.54	2,970.50	3,625.80	4,715.06	192.01	13.94
Cattle breeding	14,199.56	17,040.20	23,686.26	31,117.73	219.41	17.02
Fishing	316.84	414.65	414.05	671.80	212.03	16.22
Other sidelines	20,995.00	30,480.83	34,824.22	41,991.03	200.00	14.87

SOURCE: *Hunan Nung-yeh* [15], p. 85.

NOTE: These figures are interesting because they indicate the absolute changes over the period of the land reform movement itself. But since they take 1949 as the base year, alone they would be misleading for comparisons with prewar productivity and growth rate. (See Table 15.)

the revolutionary masses during land reform, and also a certain faith that genuine mass mobilization itself would prevent any too terrible mood from sweeping the land. As Tu Jun-sheng said:

It is unavoidable that among the masses there will be some actions that are too heated. We must be good at educating them to reform, but we must not pour cold water on them. If the masses are truly mobilized, there cannot be any very great mistake.[46]

PEACEFUL LAND REFORM

At any rate, central and provincial authorities did not consider violence in land reform to be their worst problem. On the contrary, from the beginning they devoted their most concentrated efforts to combatting the deviation they referred to as "peaceful land reform."[47] This meant land reform without struggle, that is, without class struggle.

According to Party and government policy, land reform was not simply a matter of changing the land tenure pattern in the countryside; it was also a matter of destroying the old assumptions about status and power that underlay traditional village life. In short, it was to be a revolution. If the seizure of the land were not preceded by a thorough discrediting of the landlords, their exploitation, and the old social system supporting them, then, it was believed, the mass of peasants could not undergo a revolution in their own way of thinking. Some would take the land feeling that it had been stolen from its rightful owners; others would regard it as having fallen into their laps by pure good luck alone.[48] Determined, self-righteous mass participation in the struggle and seizure was believed to be essential if the process were ultimately to be viewed as legitimate by the mass of peasants. This was the goal of all the "speak bitterness" sessions and of all the other efforts at mass mobilization.

To quote Tu Jun-sheng again, this time in criticizing the proponents of a peaceful land reform:

They do not understand that land reform is a revolution to revolutionize the social system. It is a whole series of political, economic, and cultural

46. Tu Jun-sheng [413].
47. The press and official pronouncements began to inveigh against peaceful land reform almost as soon as the movement had begun, and complaints and warnings about the bad effects of peaceful land reform persisted throughout the entire campaign and subsequent rectification period. *HPJP,* 27 Nov. 50 [130].
48. *CCJP* editorial, 8 Jan. 51 [96].

revolutions, with dividing up the land as the core, in order to destroy the old and build the new. Land reform involves the peasants' using revolutionary means to struggle and seize the land. It is definitely not a case of landlords giving up the land as a favor. First we do battle and then we seize the fruits. Now we have not yet fought, yet we think of taking our enemies prisoner. This is not possible.[49]

The raising of peasants' class consciousness and their personal struggle against landlords were held to be vital aspects of land reform. If poor peasants were to receive land without first having to mount a revolutionary struggle for it, the consequence would be a serious distortion of the movement. Land reform without the assertion of power by the broad masses of people would merely be a façade behind which the old evils—the personal power of landlords and the non-class-conscious submissiveness of peasants—could and would necessarily continue to prevail. Only with the legitimacy that angry mass participation would provide could the real distribution of power and the fundamental nature of village politics be truly altered. Only then would the old elite be truly ousted.

It was usually the land reform work team cadres who took the blame if a trend toward "peaceful land reform" grew to serious proportions. Some of them, it was said, were old cadres who had once been criticized for excessive leftism during the more violently radical land reform implemented in some of the old revolutionary base areas. Now they were determined not to be criticized again for the same mistake, and they tried to carry out land reform as peacefully as possible, emphasizing orderliness and avoiding what they regarded as the potentially disruptive mobilization and involvement of the masses of poor peasants.[50]

Other cadres were themselves from landlord, rich peasant, or intellectual backgrounds and, feeling a certain affinity with those villagers under attack, did their best to avert unpleasant scenes. It was charged that these cadres often argued that landlords, like backward peasants, were merely unfortunate products of the old society who could not be blamed personally for what they had done in the past. They maintained that once the land was divided equitably everything would right itself, and there would be no need to resort to angry struggle. To those who advocated *su k'u* for the poor peasant mobilization, they responded with

49. Tu Jun-sheng [413]. For further discussion of the necessity of struggle in land reform, see also *CCJP*, 8 Jan. 51 [422].

50. *HHNP*, 18 Dec. 50 [162].

the suggestion that landlords should be given their own opportunities to "speak bitterness" against other villagers so that all opinions could be heard.[51] Views such as these were considered dangerous to the movement.

Although local cadres took the blame for instances of "peaceful land reform," much of the evidence indicates that they were having to deal with many peasants who did not initially want to take part in overt struggles against other villagers. Whether it was out of fear or friendship, moral commitment or political apathy, these peasants much preferred to allow land reform to happen to them without any very deliberate participation on their part. They hoped it could be carried out by the government cadres in the manner of a tax collection. But it was precisely this sometime tendency of peasants to rely on government gift giving that was to be avoided.

> [It is incorrect to think] that if the peasants want land, that is enough, without considering from whom they want the land. If they want the land from the government and are holding out their hands toward the government, that proves they are not ready to carry out the Agrarian Reform Law. If, on the other hand, they want the land from the landlords, then they have truly stood up. Giving them land when they merely want it from the government will provide the landlords with opportunities to ruin everything.[52]

If peasants had accepted the land as a gift from the government, it was feared (perhaps somewhat unnecessarily) that they would clamor for more such gifts in later hard times. In any case, it was important for the central leadership's intended policies of village transformation that peasants realize there was no more wealth to be captured and handed out after land reform; greater wealth would have to be created by their own work.

Even with the best of intentions and a full understanding of the dangers of peaceful land reform, work team cadres who faced unwilling or apathetic peasants and tried to mobilize them were not always successful. To complete their assignments and keep pace with directives from above, they often resorted to managing the whole affair themselves with the assistance of only a few local activists. In some villages work team cadres went so far as to accept election as chairmen of the local Peasant

51. *HHNP,* 20 Dec. 50 [315]. See also *CCJP,* 11 Jan. 51 [56].
52. Tu Jun-sheng [413].

Association or to take on other local government posts.[53] When they were subsequently transferred to other stations, the revolutionary work in these villages naturally collapsed since peasants and even local activists had not been prepared to carry on. For not achieving the proper degree of mass mobilization and responsibility, these cadres were later charged with the deviation of *pao pan tai t'i* (taking over and running everything themselves) and for falling into a pattern of peaceful land reform. In villages where this occurred, the rectification of village work following land reform concentrated heavily on mass mobilization after the fact.

MORE ON DEVIATIONS

Besides peaceful deviations and violent deviations, a number of other serious types of distortions appeared in the rapid evolution of land reform.

Probably the most common sort of deviation reported was the "infringement" of the interests of rich peasants and middle peasants and people engaged in commerce. Very often some of their property, contrary to the letter and the spirit of the Agrarian Reform Law, was confiscated and redistributed along with that of landlords. There were many different circumstances under which this unlawful infringement occurred. In some villages there simply were no landlords to be expropriated, and cadres and peasants (deliberately or misguidedly) mistook the wealthiest villagers for landlords and treated them accordingly. Sometimes rich and middle peasants were wrongly classified as landlords from the start; at other times they were given a proper classification, but in the heat of the struggle, perhaps in anger over an act of sabotage they were found to have committed or suspected of having committed, they were lumped together with landlords and treated to the same punishments. In still other cases, the economic conditions and relationships in the villages were truly so complex and difficult to untangle that honest mistakes in classification were made, and it was often quite some time before a revised village classification righted the wrongs that had been done. During the long rectification period following land reform, the reimbursement of rich peasants and middle peasants who had suffered unjustly was a prominent feature on the agenda. The rapid

53. *CCJP*, 20 Apr. 51 [397]. See also *CCJP*, 8 Nov. 51 [148].

change in official attitude toward rich peasants that, as explained below, followed on the heels of land reform makes it doubtful, however, that most rich peasants were in fact ever adequately recompensed.

If the mobilization and confiscation stages in a village proceeded reasonably well, there still might be problems or deviations when it came to the redistribution of the fruits. The approved method of redistribution involved establishing several different grades of neediness among those families entitled to receive something. Then, with the households assigned to these different grades, small group discussions were to be held in the *ts'un* so that the peasants could express their wishes, and then preliminary lists of which items were to go to which families were drafted. After more discussion, reconciliation of conflicting requests, and compromise, a final list would be compiled and approved by the *Nung Tai Hui*. In this process, especially in large *hsiang,* it appears that the *ts'un* was taken as the unit for redistribution.[54] In practice, this may well have meant that poor peasants could only request land, tools, and oxen confiscated from households in their own *ts'un*. It is apparent how this approach—another instance of the local area principle in action—worked to perpetuate certain old inequalities.

This rather sedate and scrupulous redistribution procedure was not always observed, however. Sometimes all the movable objects to be redistributed were spread out inside a large enclosure and those entitled to receive something were allowed in, on a rotation basis, to choose and carry home whatever they fancied.[55] In other villages there was a strong feeling among cadres and peasants that everyone who had helped with land reform ought after all to receive something. In practice, this approach probably worked to the advantage of middle peasants and to the disadvantage of poor and landless peasants. A variant of the view involved the notion that all who were to receive some of the fruits of struggle ought to receive an equal amount. These non-class-conscious tendencies, typical of peasant movements, were denounced by the Party as "egalitarian deviations" when they were discovered.[56] Although equal land divisions would help raise the standard of living of all villagers, they would also tend to preserve the same wealth differentials between classes, leaving the poor and hired as badly off relative to the middle and rich peasants as they had been before land reform. Where

54. *CCJP,* 15 Feb. 51 [382].   55. *CCJP,* 14 Mar. 51 [154].
56. *CCJP,* 15 Feb. 51 [382]. See also *CCJP,* 21 Mar. 51 [230].

these strains of "egalitarian" thinking emerged in the villages, the higher-level land committees tried to take immediate action to reassert the prior rights of the poorest.

Even when work team cadres had a clear grasp of the approved principles for redistributing the wealth, they frequently encountered difficulty in finding a reasonable disposition of certain assets. The first rule to be followed was that the redistribution should in no way lessen the potential productivity of the assets and, if possible, it should enhance it. Farmland *(t'ien)* itself posed some vexing problems in this regard, but rationally dividing up the *t'ien* was evidently simplicity itself compared to finding an equitable pattern of distribution for fish ponds, streams, lakes, reservoirs, orchards, and *t'ung,* tea, and bamboo groves.[57] Unsure how they were going to manage these things, work team cadres sometimes postponed their confiscation for an abnormally long time. Rumors then spread to the effect that these assets were not going to be redistributed for private ownership by the villagers after all, but were to be taken over by the government for public use. Responding to such rumors, some villagers determined to make use of these things while they still had them and began cutting down trees and catching all their fish to eat or sell.[58] This problem was made worse by the fact that cadres who came down from the north and were basically unfamiliar with some of these peculiarly southern resources were often in the higher-level decision making positions when questions about their disposition arose—positions to which, ironically, they had been assigned because of their greater experience in land reform work.

All delays in land reform, once the campaign had begun, tended to give rise to still more anxieties. Quite often it was necessary, for example, to suspend land reform activity temporarily with the onset of the agricultural busy season.[59] Most peasants would then once again become uncertain whether to plant as usual. Some of them desperately insisted that if the work team would not go ahead with land reform, they would do it themselves without any official sanction. After all, many had taken grave risks in accusing the landlords and helping to mobilize sentiment against them. They were understandably nervous about giv-

57. *CCJP* editorial, 6 Jul. 51 [231].

58. Compare this with a similar episode of tree felling at a later stage of village transformation as described by Chou Li-po in his novel *Great Changes in a Mountain Village* [455].

59. *CCJP,* 14 Apr. 51 [234].

ing the landlords respite and a chance to regroup, only as a concession to the inevitable rotation of the seasons. Landlords were, furthermore, quite likely to use the hiatus to hide or destroy more of their own property and therefore to make confiscation and redistribution, when they finally came, more meager. But official policy demanded a suspension of most land reform work (although not of mass mobilization work) during the busy season, to make sure that the political struggle would not interfere with production and output. This, disappointed villagers were told, could not be helped.

These were by no means the only difficulties and deviations that sprang up in the course of land reform. For example, the main element of implementation strategy, the keypoint method, sometimes became inoperable. Some cases where work teams had altogether failed to establish keypoints were reported.[60] In Hunan, a variation on the keypoint method called the "one-three-nine system" received official praise. The idea was that from one keypoint village the movement would spread to three surrounding villages; and from each of those three to three more, and so on. But soon there were reports that this systematic approach had been abandoned by the local cadres in some counties and they were trying instead to move from one *hsiang* to ten surrounding *hsiang* in one step. In other places the surrounding villages were, with evidently disturbing frequency, developing land reform more quickly than the keypoint.[61] The CCP's vaunted rural organizational capability thus showed some of its limitations in the vast newly liberated countryside.

The tendency of local cadres to move ahead in accord with their own perceptions of local political possibilities and their disregard of the plans for orderly implementation coming down from above were impressive early instances of so-called radical "adventurism" at the basic level. This was criticized as undisciplined and dangerous, and the importance of keypoint organization for controlled policy implementation was reasserted in the rural campaigns that followed. Yet the tendency toward more radical timetables and more abrupt measures was to reappear again at future moments of intense political work. Despite official disapproval and dogged rectifications, it clearly was understood at this time that centrally devised organizational methods like the keypoint system could not be applied well by cadres everywhere. The frequent disjunction between organizational plan and village reality during land reform was

60. *CCJP,* 13 Jan. 51 [205].   61. *CCJP,* 17 Jan. 51 [314].

stoically accepted as inevitable, and in the circumstances considerable leeway and discretion had to be left to local cadres. A pattern of lower-level ''adventurism'' and higher-level tolerance for it during land reform merely prefigured what was to come in the complex relationship then developing between local cadres and central planners.

Still, there were other early problems with local cadres. For example, there were reports of simple cadre corruption, of cadres who were co-opted by landlord families and counterrevolutionaries, and of cadres who failed utterly to make contact with the peasant masses.[62] These and all other cadre deviations were subject to investigation and correction during the rectification following land reform in each village. This rectification, intended like almost all rural village work rectifications during the early years to correct errors due to inadequate time and preparation in the first thrust of the movement, was even more than usually institutionalized as a full stage of the campaign.[63] This was so, perhaps, in recognition of both the extraordinary complexity of the task and the extreme quickness of the movement, conditions that made a period of review and assessment all the more necessary. It seems that almost as soon as a village reported its land reform was completed a special investigation team was sent down to look for shortcomings in the work.[64] In addition to searching out cadres' deviations and possible faults in the degree and scope of local mass mobilization efforts, the visiting investigation teams took a special interest in the activities of landlords.[65] They searched out secret plots and cases of sabotage. Where they found continued landlord resistance to the new political order, they took steps against it, meanwhile authorizing expropriation of any families incorrectly spared and changing the classification of persons where there had been previous errors.

Investigation teams eventually visited every village, and usually they discovered so many mistakes and made so many changes that it would be accurate to say that land reform was carried out all over again in the majority of villages. A village's first announcement of its completion of land reform was almost always premature, and the reform process could

---

62. A few of the more interesting reports on cadres' corruption and failure to relate to the peasants are *CCJP,* 29 Jan. 51 [243]; *CCJP,* 25 Feb. 51 [78]; *CCJP,* 8 Jan. 51 [447]; and *CCJP,* 13 Mar. 51 [41].

63. *CCJP,* 31 May 51 [224].

64. *CCJP,* 12 Feb. 51 [288].

65. *CCJP,* 4 Mar. 51 [233].

not actually be said to be complete until investigation and rectification had cleaned out the worst impurities and put the local situation into greater conformity with central policies.[66] It was then that time was taken to try to bring peasant consciousness more in line with Party hopes and straighten out all the local cadres' deviations from the various central policies discussed here.

HOW TO ASSESS LAND REFORM

The Chinese land reform movement touched nearly everyone living in the countryside. Considering the numbers of people, the vastness of the territory, and the newness of the government, the almost universal penetration of the movement was indeed remarkable. A glance at some aggregate figures for just one province may provide a sense of the enormity of the project. In Hunan, when 12,085 out of 13,274 *hsiang* had completed land reform, it was estimated that the following amounts of wealth had been confiscated and redistributed:[67]

land	24,874,819	*mou*
draught animals	281,461	head
farm implements	2,092,618	pieces
grain	1,838,186,400	catties
houses	4,512,676	rooms

In the entire Central South, about 40 percent of all the cultivated land was confiscated, and approximately 60 percent of the population received some land in the redistribution.[68] In Hunan and Hupei this came to somewhere between 1.0 and 2.5 *mou* per person. That is, a family of five might receive between one and two acres to add to the land, if any, that it already possessed. Even in Chinese peasant farming terms, this was not a lot. Land reform made a relatively few people poorer, and a great many people somewhat better off. But it made no one rich.

---

66. By the time 3,751 Hunan *hsiang* completed their land reform follow-up investigations and rectifications, for example, they had added considerably to the land and goods requisitioned during the first thrust of the movement. According to *Hunan Nung-yeh* [15], p. 67, these villages expropriated an additional 286,263 *mou,* 197,792 rooms, 9,431 head of oxen, 1,428,327 agricultural tools and household implements, and 938,788 catties of food grain.

67. *Hunan Villages before and after Land Reform* [16], p. 119.

68. *CCJP,* 12 Jul. 51 [347].

Although the total amounts of wealth transferred are impressive, and although the new land and tools received certainly gave new hope to millions of subsistence farmers, the real significance of land reform seems not so much that it marked the beginning of a new economic order as that it brought about the demise of an old political order. Economic, social, and political relations in rural villages were revolutionized by land reform. Old forms of political power were, if not eliminated, severely crippled. Landlords and those branded as "despots" were, for the moment, allowed to stand for everything that was oppressive, exploitative, rotten, and corrupt in the old system. Even if the peasants had to be mobilized to "speak bitterness" *after* the division of the land, during the rectification phase of the movement, insofar as possible the Party saw to it that landlords did not merely fall in the villages, but that they came down humiliated and excoriated by the rest of the community. They represented a political order in which the poor could only accept suffering and could never legitimately stand up for themselves. Now outcasts, deprived of their material possessions, they bleakly stalked the villages, visible reminders of the changed political order, of the new powers of the poor. Obviously, on the plane of personal relations and of individual convictions, the pace of change was not always so rapid; but so many fundamental assumptions were undercut by land reform, and so many seemingly immutable facts of life were tossed away like broken sandals, that it was evident to everyone that there could be no wholesale return to the way things used to be.

More than anything else, the land reform movement had been a process of articulating and clarifying the nature and the terms of class struggle in the countryside. It was the main means of dismantling prevailing village power relations and of establishing new ones. In this sense, the reform was more profoundly a political and social reform than an economic one.[69]

69. This is not to deny that the impact of agrarian reform was tremendous, from the point of view of the Chinese economy as a whole and of subsequent national economic growth. As both Lippit and Riskin have shown, China's land reform was instrumental in directing more of her agricultural surplus—some of it only potential and some of it lost to unproductive uses—into savings and investment so as to achieve an improved economic growth rate and a more balanced and steady pattern of development. However, as Riskin has also suggested, it was only the thoroughgoing social and political revolutionary aspects of the CCP reform that made it possible to reap these economic benefits. See Riskin [513], pp. 49–84; and Lippit [468], *passim*.

In Marxist theoretical terms, land reform was to revolutionize not only the distribution of ownership of the means of production but also the social relations of production. Although it was not intended that the renting out of land and the hiring of farm laborers be prohibited after land reform, it was intended that a landlord class (or a class of individuals living primarily on the product of the labor of others and not themselves contributing to production) be totally eradicated. Such a radical reform, seeking not merely to limit the exploitation of the landlord class but instead denying its very right to exist, brought forth profoundly emotional responses from nearly all classes of rural people, since nearly all stood either to be hurt or helped by a reorganization of village life that took as its starting point the invalidation of the legal and moral basis of "landlordism."

As explained, the excitement and apprehension elicited by the anticipation of such a radical restructuring of long-accepted values and facts of life in the villages created an aura of anxiety that threatened the maintenance of a reasonable level of agricultural output. In recognition of this threat, the Chinese leadership opted for faster and faster implementation of the movement, in an effort to preempt potential sabotage by landlords and others, and also to restore as quickly as possible a sense of normalcy in the countryside that would induce the peasantry to return to regular farming. On the whole they were successful in averting further drops in output. Even with the unprecedented transfers of property, the mass mobilization, and the other interruptions of normal routine associated with the land reform movement, the natural postwar trend toward agricultural recovery was not reversed. (See, for example, Table 15.)

The Party's shrewd class policy had made it possible for the great majority to unite in the demand for land against a small number who were declared enemies in the villages. This was a necessary condition of the manageability of the mass movement, helping to keep it from fragmenting, turning in on itself, and ultimately frightening all farmers away from production. Yet all these tendencies did persist to some extent in the villages, still endangering the movement's success in places. A reasonable class policy was not in itself sufficient for the reform's success. The mass movement also required knowledgeable and skillful local leadership if it were to follow the designs of the center.

To provide this kind of leadership, with the still skeletal rural administrative network at their command, it was imperative that central authorities find local activists immediately and delegate to them responsibilities for which they clearly were hardly prepared. This was in

TABLE 15. Index of Agricultural Crop Recovery in Hunan, 1949–52

Crop	Highest Prewar Level	1949	1952
All grains	100	64.7	164.19
Wet rice	100	67.2	108.46
Wheat	100	84.2	47.07
Other grains	100	38.1	44.71
Potatoes	100	51.8	168.07
Cotton	100	36.8	140.13
Ramie	100	62.5	101.65
Tea	100	24.4	45.19
Peanuts	100	27.9	53.74
Tobacco	100	97.5	267.34
Sugar cane	100	20.8	107.80

SOURCE: *Hunan Nung-yeh* [15], p. 85.

NOTE: Although agriculture's overall share of the gross value of provincial output declined over the period from about 83 percent in 1949 to about 79 percent in 1951, as compared to a rise in industry's share from about 17 percent to about 21 percent, the change in the structure of the value of agricultural output showed an abrupt turn away from subsistence grain cultivation and toward expanded production of cash crops and growth in livestock breeding and other sidelines. See Table 14 and *Hunan Nung-yeh* [15], p. 85. This suggests that the natural peacetime restoration of the domestic marketing network, over the province as a whole, was not impeded by the implementation of the land reform movement.

accord with a mode of operations, sketched in the previous chapter, of launching all-out, complex policy implementation efforts despite a readily apparent immaturity in the general political situation and despite the lack of a fully trained and prepared cadre staff on the local scene. Even with the use of keypoints and special training courses to upgrade and regularize the administration of the campaign, it is evident that the enormous speed of the movement frequently outstripped its capacity to organize properly.

This speed thus gave rise to many of the deviations and problems in the land reform movement discussed here. An examination of these problems and deviations provides a more vivid sense of the content of struggle and the texture of events in the period. In evaluating them, however, it is important to bear in mind that all these difficulties and deviations from official policy were recognized and confronted at the time by the leadership. They were viewed precisely as deviations, sometimes merely unfortunate, sometimes dangerous. They were addressed directly, and eventually—through repeated investigations and rectifications if necessary—they were either solved or at least brought into closer conformity with the desired range of outcomes.

The *post hoc* rectification procedure was thus extremely important to the center in consolidating and improving its most valuable legacy of land reform—the network of local peasant activists who had stepped forward and could now be tapped for future village leadership roles. Most had acted without much understanding of Party theory or long-term policy. During the period of rectification, in the course of analyzing and criticizing their own fears and weaknesses, it was intended that they would learn some important lessons in Party theory and village policy. During rectification, local activists were held accountable for their own deviations from desired policy and for their failures to mobilize and lead reluctant peasants beyond the bounds of their previous life strictures and into the revolutionary surge. Those who would be cadres were constrained to realize and correct what in the Party's terms were errors; to take seriously the model political roles and methods put forward by higher levels; and to exert themselves to communicate newly learned political and moral attitudes to their peasant constituents. At this time of greatest political upheaval in the Chinese countryside, local cadres and activists were simultaneously gaining important information about the standards of behavior that would be expected of them in the future.

But even a long and arduous rectification could not solve many of the problems of the local cadres. In fact, the very protractedness of the period before the final resolution of land reform in many villages may have contributed to some new problems with local cadres. During the long and often painful rectification of land reform, political agitation continued but the achievements of the movement remained indefinite. Meanwhile, villagers were being promised that once the political struggle was finally over they would be able to settle down to production and the hard business of making their own fortunes *(fa chia chih fu)*. With the eventual completion of land reform investigation, review, and rectification, it seems that most villagers were more than glad to return to their normal production routine and their own affairs.[70] There was, in fact, something of a mass retreat from political problems and a collective sigh of relief that it was at last possible to return to work. This new atmosphere swept the villages and naturally also touched village cadres and activists, many of whom began to think and talk about giving up their political and government roles and returning to their farms.[71] Some of them, no doubt with considerable justification, felt that they at last

70. There were some exceptions to this general rule—landlords who refused to work the land left to them and old or sick people who were not themselves able to work. See *CCJP,* 19 Jul. 51 [354].

71. Thomas P. Bernstein has explored this phenomenon in [492].

deserved a rest, that the revolution was now "over," and that there was no need for them to continue sacrificing their personal lives for political work.[72] Especially some of those who had been criticized during land reform and rectification decided that the cares and responsibilities of a cadre's life were more than they wished to continue to carry.[73] Some simply abandoned their posts and left for home. Others began neglecting their official work, skipping meetings, failing to file reports, and generally betraying their apathy and disinterestedness in political mobilization and administrative work. The Party had to devote some effort to remobilizing these rural political dropouts in the months after the completion of land reform.

There were other lingering problems in consolidating the new cadre force. During land reform rectification, for example, a limited reclassification of the village population was made to take account of the changes in family welfare produced by the reform. Landlords retained their old classifications, despite their losses in real wealth. But many formerly classed as poor peasants or hired hands, now in possession of some land and other fruits of struggle, had to be reclassified as "new middle peasants." Many village activists fell into this group, and although they may well have resented being handed a less favorable class status as a reward for all their efforts, the Party for its part still expressed unease at having to rely on so many "new middle peasants" for village political work.[74] Middle peasants, even new ones, and even those who had been activists, were still considered unreliable for promoting the transition to socialism. They were to be "united with"; but it was poor

72. *CCJP,* 2 Aug. 51 [424]. See also *CCJP,* 27 May 51 [374].

73. *CCJP,* 8 Nov. 51 [148]. There were other cadre morale problems at this time too. Many work team cadres, who had regarded their participation in land reform as part of a tremendous national effort and a chance to prove themselves, now were expecting promotions and hoping for transfers to cities or mining towns. The officially articulated government policies put renewed emphasis on the continuing importance of rural village work, however, and if they were not immediately transferred and promoted, these ambitious cadres quickly came to resent what they saw as a condemnation by the Party to serve out their lives in uninteresting surroundings inhabited by dull and politically backward peasants. See *CCJP,* 16 Aug. 51 [416].

74. *CCJP,* 6 Mar. 51 [301]; and *CCJP,* 22 Apr. 51 [73]. This second article states that the tendency for middle peasants to take the lead and seize control of village affairs early on, during rent reduction, is incorrect and should be avoided. While Bernstein [493], p. 23, asserts that "almost all" the activists recruited during land reform were poor peasants, many of whom were later reclassified as middle peasants because of their good fortune in land reform, these and other sources for Hunan and Hupei indicate clearly that

peasants who were to be "relied on," because they were going to have the most to gain from socialist cooperation and could therefore be expected to pursue socialism most vigorously. Hence the Party continued observing and weeding out the network of local activists that land reform had produced. Since the center was not content to rely only on those who had already stepped forward, the years following land reform saw a renewed effort to recruit more people from the ranks of the still-poor peasants.

Thus China's radical and reasonably well-administered land reform must be seen as the indispensable first step in village revolution, most importantly because it displaced the old village elite and upset the traditional expectations and values that had determined village politics, but also because it brought into being a large body of local political activists and operatives who would serve as the core of the government's rural administrative infrastructure in the years ahead. Yet at the center it was recognized that much more political organizational work and mass mobilization work remained to be done. Even by many who had themselves joined in the thick of the crisis, land reform had been rather naively perceived as a once-for-all scramble for control that would produce a permanent solution to their problems. Very few who were present at the beginning seem to have realized that, as far as class struggle in the countryside was concerned, land reform was but the initial battle of a protracted war. Thus, while the completion of land reform did settle many issues and did dramatically reduce the tension and anxiety that had gripped the countryside, it left many other questions about the future unsettled. And for many of those who had confidently viewed land reform as the joyful culmination of rural class struggle and the revolution, the events of the next few years were to be both painful and instructive.

---

people classed as middle peasants tended to enter village political struggles in disproportionate numbers from the very earliest days following liberation. See, e.g., *CCJP,* 17 Jun. 51 [314]. The Party was familiar with this phenomenon. Pepper [476], p. 257, reports that in the old revolutionary base areas the leadership of the pre-land-reform village struggles against corruption, land tax evasion, and local despots "tended to be quickly monopolized by middle peasants." In the Central South later liberated areas the problem was not so extreme as to suggest a middle peasant monopoly, but it did reappear despite deliberate Party efforts to find poor and hired peasants for leadership roles. Along with the "new middle peasants" weeded out of the ranks of local leadership during land reform follow-up rectification, therefore, there were probably many activists who had always been middle peasants.

PART 2

"TO SETTLE DOWN AND GET RICH"

Problems in Maintaining a More Equitable Distribution of Wealth

In the house east of here lives an old woman.
Three or four years ago, she got rich.
In the old days she was poorer than I;
Now she laughs at me for not having a penny.
She laughs at me for being behind;
I laugh at her for getting ahead.
We laugh as though we'd never stop:
She from the east and I from the west!

HAN-SHAN, T'ang Dynasty

CHAPTER 3

Tax Reform

Chinese peasants had been given to understand that after the completion of the land reform movement every household would be able to settle down with whatever new land and tools it had been allotted, and would be left alone to make its living in the fields and in the marketplace. *Fa chia chih fu* was the phrase used to sum up this vision of the future, and it served both to mobilize peasants to participate in the reform movement and to reassure them that the movement's impact would be halted short of disaster. This phrase, often translated "to settle down and get rich," more literally means "to set up a household and make one's fortune." It definitely conjured up an image of a continuation of the private small peasant mode of production, of a village economy basically unchanged except for the elimination of arbitrary exactions by bandits, soldiers, and "local bullies," and the virtual elimination of rent payments to land-lords. China's land reform had done nothing to challenge private owner-ship or the small-holder system of cultivation.

Most peasants clearly responded enthusiastically to what they saw as new opportunities in a familiar economic environment, setting out inde-pendently after the convulsion of land reform to secure and expand their personal and family livelihoods. The radical impulse to wipe out rich peasants as well as landlords had been quelled, by and large, and now many farmers aspired to become rich peasants themselves. Within the Chinese leadership at this period there was clearly much debate about the most desirable pace of progress toward socialism in the countryside. In 1952 and 1953, there were occasional leftward thrusts in some parts of the country, including advocacy of the rapid establishment of semi-socialist agricultural production cooperatives. But in later liberated Hunan and Hupei only a very small number of production co-ops were formed, and these functioned only on an experimental basis. The supporting institutional infrastructure of marketing co-ops and credit co-ops that would be required for semi-socialist production units to take root was not yet in place in the region.

Yet, land reform had left an unstable class situation in the villages in which the comparatively better-off households—rich and middle peasants—might well find opportunities on the free market, in extending short-term loans or in other ventures, to improve their positions even further at the expense of the comparatively less well-off. The possible, even predictable, tendency toward repolarization in the distribution of wealth in the villages that this would mean was a development the revolutionary government was committed to prevent.

This chapter and the next, therefore, examine two important programs—agricultural taxation and promotion of Mutual Aid Teams for farming—administered in this interim period as part of the effort to impede village economic repolarization while not yet pressing for socialist transformation of the rural economy. In its graduated impact, the tax worked first as a primary restraint on income growth for the rich and upper-middle peasant classes. In its many incentive provisions described below, however, it worked also to spur expanded agricultural production and to promote peasant entrepreneurship. The new government used appeals to peasants' self-interest to motivate participation in the land reform movement and, as these two chapters illustrate, it continued to build private incentives for peasant compliance into all its major rural policies thereafter.

Chinese tax work at this period is interesting because it incorporated so many old, even ancient, concepts and devices, yet generally achieved with them a much greater thoroughness and equity over large areas than had seemed possible for Chinese rulers during most of the previous two or three centuries. The "normal annual yield" concept, the quotas, and the problems of peasant tax evasion described here had all been part of the paraphernalia of Chinese tax administrators for generations. If this government was able to enforce its tax demands and administer its tax concessions so much more readily than its predecessors, much of the explanation lies in the existence of its new local cadre force and in the generally higher levels of popular participation in public affairs, both of which were legacies of the land reform campaign. But penetration of the

Peasants after land reform redistribution. (Hsinhua News Agency)

villages had its limits as far as tax matters were concerned, as described here; and the considerable successes in rural tax administration that were achieved during this period were attributable not only to the efforts of the village cadres but in part also to the assignment of extra middle-level personnel in charge of investigation and record-keeping. The central authorities were anxious to eliminate arbitrariness in taxation because it was a source of misinformation and mistrust between peasants and officials. They were also anxious that revenue collections be effective, however, to provide adequate grain to the cities during the Korean conflict and to assist in making realistic plans for national investment over the next few years.

In its capacity to tax agriculture in the later liberated areas, the new government obviously possessed not only the major means to assure its own solvency but also an important weapon to be used in support of its broader plans for rural transformation. In this chapter some data are presented to show that the tax weapon was indeed utilized skillfully by the new leadership, to generate revenue to finance its activities, to further the redistribution of wealth from rich to poor in the countryside, to enhance its own legitimacy in the eyes of the majority of peasants, to rejuvenate the rural economy and improve the supply of commodities, and to allay the persistent fears of peasants about their own probable economic opportunities in the immediate post-land-reform period. To do this it is necessary first to step backward and review the evolution of agricultural tax policies before and after liberation and through the completion of land reform.

EARLY CCP TAX METHODS

By 1949 the Chinese Communist Party had already had twenty years' experience in taxing the peasantry. During that time it had evolved a variety of methods and strategies for gathering revenue that could be applied successfully in the dissimilar socioeconomic environments it encountered as it moved across China and in the new rural conditions it created with its own policies of reform and revolution. It had begun experimenting in Ching-Kang-Shan with a straight proportional 15 percent tax on agricultural income to be reduced to 10 percent or even to 5 percent under special conditions, including natural disaster.[1] By 1930, however, the CCP was already moving in the direction of a more subtle graduated tax system later tested and used widely in the base areas of the Anti-Japanese War.

During the period of the second United Front, the CCP was not in a position to pursue land reform or a radical redistribution of wealth in the villages to soften the harsh lines of rural economic stratification in the areas under its control. By employing a steeply progressive tax schedule, however, it was able to keep the burden on the shoulders of the greatest number of peasants at a tolerable level, in that way helping to preserve peasant goodwill and building confidence for future struggles. At this time too the CCP clearly came to realize the potential in tax law and tax collection policy for furthering some of its goals besides the mere collection of revenue. The new tax provisions included incentives designed to encourage peasants to increase production, for example, and other provisions intended to demonstrate to peasants that the government would be magnanimous in relieving disaster victims and the most miserably poor of their tax obligations. It was also recognized that tax law and tax policy held considerable propaganda and education value for the CCP; they were widely used to spur both patriotism and class consciousness during the war years. These years gave the revolutionaries

1. These provisions are part of the 1928 Hunan-Kiangsi Border Area Soviet Land Law. An outline history of CCP agricultural taxation policy before 1949 is available in Li Ch'eng-jui [22], pp. 59–93. For an interesting but incomplete commentary on the period, see also Wu Tan-ko [36], *passim*.

time to become somewhat more shrewd and sophisticated in the field of agricultural taxation. Systems and techniques were developed that would have been the envy of many an established, stable government—if not for their efficiency, then for their responsiveness and applicability to the actual conditions with which they had to cope.[2]

But the CCP was nothing if not flexible, and when the Japanese were finally driven out and reform of the landholding system once again became the first priority of the social-revolutionary movement, there was no hesitation in abandoning the tax systems that had been painstakingly constructed under the United Front and in choosing other methods better suited to the newly emerging social conditions. The CCP returned to a proportional tax system in 1946, this time usually employing a standard deduction to be taken by each taxpaying household. This arrangement preserved the basic element of the progressive tax in that the wealthy paid higher taxes than the poor, but it also shifted the burden somewhat toward the middle-income households, the rationale being that as a result of land reform both the poorest and the richest households had been pushed sharply toward the middle.[3] From 1946 through 1949 the Party and the PLA administered this proportional tax system in its post-land-reform areas.

All the CCP's years of experience, however, could not make the tax collection of 1949 orderly and careful. When the PLA liberated Hunan and Hupei in 1949, along with most of the rest of Central China, it was also the PLA that collected the taxes, giving peasants in most of the area their first experience with taxation under the revolutionary government. The swiftness of the advancing front, the hazards of securing newly won territory against bandits and remnant KMT troops, and the impossibility of sparing enough men from the front to administer civil affairs in the new liberated areas all made it necessary to collect taxes on the run in 1949, without the niceties of graduated tax schedules and standard deductions. Once liberation of the mainland had been completed, it was generally admitted by the Chinese leadership that the 1949 tax collection in the later liberated areas had been a crude affair that had needlessly frightened some peasants and made a bad impression on others.[4] PLA

2. For an examination of the taxation systems in two different old base areas, see Lindsay [508], pp. 1–15; and Selden [482], *passim*.

3. Li Ch'eng-jui [22], p. 85.

4. For a criticism of the 1949 tax collection with special reference to the Central South, see the directive signed by Lin Piao in *CCJP,* 12 Sep. 50 [117]; and also the draft

officers and Party cadres had neither the time nor the personnel to enforce a detailed tax code, and so they simply demanded high payments from the obviously well-to-do and took little or nothing from the poor.[5]

Once the new government had been officially proclaimed and the situation had been calmed to some extent, a belated attempt was made to assure richer peasants and landlords that they were under no immediate threat of financial ruin through heavy taxation. The State Council issued its "Directive on Land Reform and Tax Collection in the Newly Liberated Areas"[6] on February 28, 1950. This directive stipulated: (a) that no less than 90 percent of the rural population should be taxed. This was meant to spread the tax burden more evenly over the rural population, exempting from taxation only the poorest 10 percent; (b) that no more than 17 percent of the total produce of any newly liberated area should be collected as tax; (c) that for any given household the surtax imposed by the local government must not exceed 15 percent of the amount that household paid as tax to the central government. This was probably intended to discourage corruption among local cadres as well as to correct their tendency to impose local surtaxes selectively, perhaps even punitively, on rich peasants and landlords; and (d) that the tax burden on any one household should not, as a rule, exceed 60 percent of the total real income of the household, although this could be raised as high as 80 percent in certain circumstances.

These general guidelines were evidently small comfort for the rich and the well-to-do in the villages. Throughout the first half of 1950 they continued to try to conceal their real wealth by selling, mortgaging, or giving away their possessions. There was no mass slaughter of stock and draught animals in Hunan and Hupei, but some animals were slaughtered and disposed of in order to diminish the apparent wealth (and tax liability) of their owners. In many areas storehouses holding the recently collected tax grain were burned by disgruntled villagers, landlords, and their agents to underscore their dissatisfaction with the tax procedures and to frighten the poorer peasants.

By far the most dangerous form of tax evasion resorted to by the landlords and better-off peasants at this time, however, was the decision by hundreds of thousands deliberately to lower their own incomes, at least temporarily, by cultivating less of the land they owned themselves and by renting out less of it to tenants for cultivation. If left unchecked,

---

report of Yang Shao-ch'iao, vice-chief of the Finance Department of the CSMAC, *CCJP,* 22 Jul. 52 [399].

5. Li Ch'eng-jui [22], pp. 138–139.   6. *JMJP,* 1 Mar. 50 [136].

this trend would have resulted not only in reduced public revenue but possibly also in widespread unemployment and a serious food shortage, which would inevitably have struck the poor much harder than the wealthy villagers who had precipitated it. To meet this threat in the newly liberated areas, the government needed a comprehensive and finely graded tax law to provide incentives for increasing production, disincentives for failing to produce, and effective sanctions against all types of tax evasion. On September 5, 1950, drawing heavily on the experience and the lessons of the Anti-Japanese War years, the Central People's Government Committee issued the "Provisional Regulations on Agricultural Tax in the Newly Liberated Areas."[7] This was the first fully detailed statement of tax policy for the newly liberated areas, and it contained most of the elements that were to be important in tax work for the next several years.

BASIC FEATURES OF AGRICULTURAL TAX POLICY

The 1950 Provisional Regulations called for a fairly steeply progressive tax, as was most appropriate in a socioeconomic environment still marked by widely separated extremes of wealth and poverty. The schedule table (Article XII) begins with a 3 percent levy on all households with a per capita annual income between 151 and 190 catties of rice; and it rises by graduated increments ranging from 39 catties to 139 catties, each incremental rise corresponding to 1 percent of tax increase, to a maximum tax of 42 percent on households with a per capita annual income of 3,411 catties or more. (See Table 16.) Households near to starvation levels where the per capita income fell below 150 catties were tax-exempt, except in areas where this would have resulted in over 10 percent of the total number of households being granted an exemption. Where that would have happened, the minimum taxable income was to be lowered to 120 catties (Article XI), and it was taxed at the lowest rate of 3 percent.

The Taxable Unit

The basic taxable unit was ruled to be the household *(hu)* (Article II). To determine the average per capita income of members of the house-

---

7. *Collected Laws and Decrees of the Central People's Government* 1 [329], pp. 269–274. The regulations are also reproduced in *HHYP,* 1950, pp. 1358 ff. They are summarized in Li Ch'eng-jui [22], pp. 140–146, and are discussed in Li Shu-te [507].

TABLE 16. 1950 Agricultural Tax Schedule

Tax Grade	Annual Average per Capita Agricultural Income of Household	Tax Rate %	Tax Grade	Annual Average per Capita Agricultural Income of Household	Tax Rate %
	Under 150 catties	Exempt	20	1151–1230	22
1	151–190	3	21	1231–1310	23
2	191–230	4	22	1311–1390	24
3	231–270	5	23	1391–1490	25
4	271–310	6	24	1491–1590	26
5	311–350	7	25	1591–1690	27
6	351–390	8	26	1691–1790	28
7	391–430	9	27	1791–1890	29
8	431–470	10	28	1891–1990	30
9	471–510	11	29	1991–2110	31
10	511–550	12	30	2111–2230	32
11	551–610	13	31	2231–2350	33
12	611–670	14	32	2351–2470	34
13	671–730	15	33	2471–2590	35
14	731–790	16	34	2591–2710	36
15	791–850	17	35	2711–2850	37
16	851–910	18	36	2851–2990	38
17	911–990	19	37	2991–3130	39
18	991–1070	20	38	3131–3270	40
19	1071–1150	21	39	3271–3410	41
			40	over 3411	42

SOURCE: Li Ch'eng-jui [22], p. 142.
NOTE: For these calculations, the original grain of the household is converted into a catty equivalent of the primary grain of the area.

hold, the total household income derived from agricultural production[8] was divided by the number of members of the household who were dependent primarily on agricultural production for their livelihood. Such persons were referred to as *nung-yeh jen-k'ou* (agricultural population or agricultural dependents). Thus any portion of a peasant household's yearly income earned through commerce, transport, labor in a factory or shop, or the like was not liable to taxation under these regula-

8. This included "the *entire proceeds* of income yielding land (for example, farms for both food and industrial crops, fish ponds, woods, orchards, vegetable gardens, mulberry fields, bamboo groves) with the exception of a few minor items like stalks and fodder." But the tax did not apply to income from nonagricultural sideline occupations or from livestock raising. See Chao Kuo-chun [451], p. 154. Although subject to great variation from place to place, rural family income from nonagricultural sidelines probably ranged between 20 and 30 percent of total income. See, e.g., Chen Nai-ruenn [454], p. 431, for a 1955 nationwide estimate.

tions. By the same token, any household member who relied mainly on his or her income from nonfarm work could not qualify as a dependent to be averaged in for purposes of agricultural tax computation. Naturally, reckoning the relative degrees of dependence on nonfarming employment for each villager was not a matter easily settled, especially in villages near urban areas where opportunities for diverse sorts of work were more numerous, and where peasants regularly divided their time between their fields and day labor or contract labor in the city. Nevertheless, for the ordinary peasant household in which most work was either directly or indirectly related to farming and most income was derived from farming, this method of calculating the average per capita income to be taxed amounted to giving a modest deduction for nonproductive household members—the very young, the very old, and the infirm.

This effect can be illustrated briefly by comparing two hypothetical households. A household of four—man, woman, aged mother, and small child—with an agricultural income of 3,000 catties has an average per capita income of 750 catties for the year. Consulting the schedule table, it can be determined that this puts them in tax bracket number 14, for which the rate is 16 percent. 16 percent of 3,000 is 480, and they are therefore left with 2,520 catties after taxes or 630 catties each. A second household consisting of two unmarried brothers, also bringing in a total of 3,000 catties, would have an average per capita income of 1,500. According to the schedule, it would be in tax bracket number 24, paying at a rate of 26 percent. 26 percent of 3,000 is 780 catties, and the brothers are therefore left with 2,220 catties after taxes, or 1,110 catties each. If the average per capita income method were not applied and the total amount extracted by the government from these two households together (1,260 catties) were to remain constant, both households would have to pay at a rate of 21 percent of total income. This would leave the family of four with only 2,370 catties, or 592.5 catties each, which represents a 37.5 catty reduction for each of them for the year. The two brothers, on the other hand, would also retain 2,370 catties, or 1,185 catties each, a 75 catty gain for each of them for the year. Using the average per capita income of a household as the basis, then, clearly worked to the advantage of families with either nonproductive dependents or with members too numerous to be supported on the land available to them. This advantage, although real, was certainly not overwhelming. It was, as the example illustrates, only partially compensatory, leaving the overall distribution of wealth still far from equalized.

The revolutionary government's choice of the farming household as the basic taxable unit is itself interesting in view of the frequent use, earlier in Chinese history, of much larger socioeconomic groupings such as clan, hamlet, and village for this purpose.[9] But since it was the CCP's express desire to engender class struggle within hamlets and villages, to divide these residential units, as it were, into economic segments, and to highlight and encourage conflicts among some of the segments, it was far more sensible to avoid treating hamlets and villages as single economic units for tax purposes. In the adversary relationship between government and citizens that tends to develop over tax matters (and that certainly existed in rural China at this time), to apply the tax to a large residential unit would have been to invite alliance among the different groups in the unit to attempt, both openly and covertly, to resist government demands. Taxing the individual household assisted the revolutionary government in averting such misalliances among the masses, thereby not only making it easier to apply the tax law rigorously and bring in the required revenue but also making it less likely that the revolutionary class struggle would be hampered by the government's own tax policy.

The Party appears never to have seriously considered the alternative of applying the agricultural tax to the individual. To understand why, it should first be noted that the Chinese tax did not apply to the value of the land an individual owned: it was the harvest or income derived from the land that served as the tax base.[10] The Chinese tax was a tax on output or production, not on possessions or property. In such a system it is reasonable that the tax should be applied to the production unit rather than to the individual peasant, landowner, or proprietor as such. And in China in 1950 the basic agricultural production unit was indisputably the farming household. The production process generally involved all able-bodied members of the household, to one extent or another, the skills and strengths of the several members being combined to achieve the harvest. Later, when Mutual Aid Teams and Agricultural Production Cooperatives were established and succeeded the *hu* as the basic production organization in the village, Chinese tax law was modified and these organizations then also replaced the *hu* as the basic taxable unit. For the time being, however, the household was the unit most consistent with

9. Li Ch'eng-jui [22], p. 73. In fact, the CCP itself appears to have experimented with using the hamlet *(ts'un)* as the basic tax unit in 1930.
10. Ecklund [458], p. 44.

the theory of CCP tax reform policy and with the nature of farming in China.

The Normal Annual Yield

So far the discussion has proceeded as if the agricultural tax were based on each household's actual annual income—in fact it was not. This small complication was one of the most important aspects of the government's approach to taxing the peasantry. The tax was based on a hypothetical figure referred to as the "normal annual yield" *(ch'ang-nien ying-ch'an liang)* (Article VI). This figure represented the harvest (calculated in terms of the primary grain of the area) that could reasonably be expected from the land owned and rented by the household, given the natural qualities of the land, the usual management and cultivation practices of the farmers, and a normal growing year—a year neither of bumper crop nor of natural disaster. The number of *mou* owned and rented by each household, the productivity of the land, and the number of *nung-yeh jen-k'ou* in the household were all to be determined by a *hsiang* (or *ts'un*) Agricultural Tax Investigation and Determination Committee consisting of representatives of the various classes in the village. In their calculations, the phrase "natural conditions of the land" was to refer to its quality, irrigation, topography (highland, lowland, level, or hilly), and weather conditions (temperature, rainfall, wind, and sunlight). The "management of the land" was to refer to the usual amount of labor power expended on comparable land in the area, animal power, fertilizer, the usual cultivation techniques, and so on. And "cultivation customs" was to refer to the number of harvests usually reaped by local farmers in one year and the crops they usually raised.[11]

Once the normal annual yield figure was determined for each individual household, the household was required to pay the tax on it, regardless of what its *actual* income from the land might be for the year. That is to say that if, by hard work and innovation, they were able to raise their actual income above the normal annual yield estimate, they were permitted to retain the portion of their crop in excess of the normal annual yield figure, tax-free. If, on the other hand, they were not industrious and permitted their harvest to fall below the normal annual yield

11. "Stipulations of the Finance Department . . ." in *Collected Laws and Decrees of the Central People's Government* 1 [389], p. 277.

figure, they were nonetheless required to pay the full tax as if they had attained the normal yield (Article VII).

Furthermore, when irrigation or other improvements were made on the land, raising its productivity and therefore its expected annual yield, the official normal annual yield figure used for tax purposes was *not* to be raised in consequence. The official normal annual yield would remain in force and unchanged for five years if the peasant financed these improvements or for three years if they were government-financed (Article VIII). Table 17 illustrates how, on this system, the central agricultural tax revenue broke down as a proportion of actual and of normal yields for Hunan province between 1949 and 1957.

This scheme for calculating the agricultural tax clearly set in motion a number of overlapping incentive systems affecting peasants. First, it provided them with an incentive at least to meet the target of their declared normal annual yield, or else pay the penalty in extra taxes. This was of use to the government in turning back a tendency among conspiring landlords, rich peasants, and other villagers to withdraw some of their land from cultivation at this time, so as to reduce their income temporarily. All reasonable hope for a tax benefit to be derived from a deliberate decrease in production was removed by this provision, reinforcing the central government's plans to avoid rural unemployment, avert a food shortage, and raise overall agricultural output.

Second, this scheme provided an incentive for farming households to exert themselves to squeeze a larger crop from their land than they were normally able, since all the extra produce they could harvest was to be theirs free of tax. The familiar fear of being driven into a higher tax bracket was meant to be canceled out by this provision in favor of the central government's desire to encourage a speedy increase in total agricultural output.

The third incentive provided by this scheme encouraged peasants to invest in large-scale improvements to their land without fear that they would be heavily taxed on their increased productivity. Not yet able to make large-scale state investments in agriculture, the new government could at least manipulate its tax laws so as to encourage individual capital investment.

Finally, the normal annual yield tax assessment system, with its use of the primary grain as the standard for calculating the productivity of a given piece of land, created an incentive for peasants to expand their

TABLE 17. Agricultural Tax as a Proportion of Normal Annual Yield and of Actual Yield: Hunan, 1949–57

| | Taxable Farmland (mou) | Normal Annual Yield (catties) | | | Annual Yield (as catties of grain) | Tax as % of Yield | |
		Total (as grain)	Average per capita	Average per mou		Actual Grain Collections As % of Normal Yield	As % of Actual Yield
1949	41,695,686	12,655,909,492	539	304	—	—	—
1950	42,921,840	15,095,172,900	589	352	—	—	—
1951	44,210,534	17,725,700,400	635	401	—	—	—
1952	53,230,490	20,208,292,416	675	379	23,054,770,000	14.83	13.00
1953	53,665,193	20,241,347,635	660	377	23,986,380,000	14.83	12.51
1954	53,695,208	20,243,871,004	650	377	20,791,760,000	12.03	11.71
1955	53,217,688	19,885,787,699	628	374	24,396,840,000	14.12	11.51
1956	52,810,094	19,809,104,257	624	375	22,960,370,000	12.60	10.87
1957	53,501,274	20,043,197,452	621	375	—	14.16	—

SOURCE: *Hunan Nung-yeh* [15], p. 105.
NOTE: Actual annual yield is computed in this table in constant 1952 prices converted to unhulled rice equivalent.

cultivation of cash crops relative to grain.[12] By this move central planners hoped to supply and rejuvenate the industrial sector of the economy and to aid its postwar recovery. For this incentive mechanism in the tax law to become operative, however, it had to be implemented in conjunction with careful government control of the marketing of some specific crops. Since a peasant household's income was calculated, for tax purposes, in terms of the grain the family members could produce on their land, and since that figure was fixed, it was possible for them to come out ahead if they planted a crop they could market at a higher price than they would have received for grain. They might then purchase grain for their own use and pay their tax in cash, in purchased grain, or in their own crop (Article XIX). No matter which they chose, they would be paying tax on a hypothetical income from grain production considerably lower than their actual income from the cotton or other cash crop harvested. For wary peasants to be motivated by this incentive, they had to be assured of a favorable marketing situation for their alternative crop after the harvest. And to create this necessary condition, the government used its state trading companies to set market prices on cash crops that would be attractive to farmers.[13] The more attractive prices offered for cash crops alone might have been sufficient to influence peasant households to plant them, but the farmers' knowledge that the tax on their crop would not be raised even if their income rose must have added considerable weight to the argument.

Some provincial governments made even more attractive provisions. In Hunan in 1950, for example, all farmland in cotton, ramie, tobacco, sugarcane, peanuts, and painting and dying materials was automatically taxed as only middle-grade rice land, regardless of its actual quality.

12. Li Ch'eng-jui [22], p. 141. See also *Thirty Questions and Answers on Agricultural Tax Policy* [33], pp. 5–6.

13. In reality, as Perkins has pointed out, in 1950 the state trading companies were not yet sufficiently well-entrenched to set prices singlehandedly. Using cotton as his example, since it was one of the economic crops the government was most anxious to support, he observes, "Since there was still substantial inflation and state purchasing organs were too new and weak to fix a particular set of prices, directives of 1950 and 1951 were worded in terms of minimum cotton grain price ratios to be guaranteed to cotton farmers. These regulations then were supplemented by a list of official state-set absolute prices for major cotton-producing areas." Perkins [477], p. 34. The 1951 minimum cotton grain price ratio for middle-grade cotton in Hunan was 1:10. (*Hunan Nung-yeh* [15], p. 220.) For some figures on the volume of trade handled by state trading companies nationally in this early period, see Ch'u Ch'ing et al. [7], pp. 12, 18–19.

And all income from production of *t'ung* oil, tea oil, bamboo, and tea was not taxed at all, except where such income was particularly great (that is, equivalent to more than about 2,000 catties of the primary grain), in which cases, unlike other agricultural taxes that were based on yield, a levy equivalent to 6 percent of the market value of the cultivated land itself would be made.[14]

In any event, the possibilities involved here were not lost on the peasants. In the short space of two years the government had apparently attained the level of certain cash crop production that it desired through this incentive system, and it began to move to reverse the trend back toward grain production.[15] The joint application of price incentives and tax breaks on certain crops had worked efficiently, and it would be used again by central planners in the future to achieve desired rearrangements in the structure of the agricultural economy. The quick nationalization of the major industries of China and the greatly expanded revenues this brought to the state were making it possible for the government to enter the rural market and absorb the costs of holding certain commodity prices down and others up, as incentives to farmers to change their patterns of production.

Unrelated to the normal annual yield system but also designed as an incentive for peasants to increase total output was another set of stipulations in the Provisional Regulations (Article V) offering certain tax exemptions. There were exemptions of from three to five years on all income from virgin land opened to cultivation for the first time by a farmer. An exemption from taxation for one to three years could be had on income from land once cultivated but recently left barren. To encourage conservationist cultivation practices, the central government granted a total tax exemption on crop rotation land during the year it

14. *Hunan Nung-yeh* [15], p. 101. But in 1951 these provisions were revised and made tighter. For example, for *t'ung* oil, tea oil, tea, and so on the tax-exempt ceiling was lowered to 1,000 catties of grain equivalent.

15. In June 1952 a *People's Daily* editorial explained: "During the past two years, economic crops and grain were taxed similarly, which means much lighter tax on economic crops. This measure did play an active role in the restoration and development of economic crops in some cases and relative curtailment of output of . . . grain. The sowing area of economic crops has developed to a certain extent and the emphasis of agricultural production increase now is to raise per hectare yield and to guard against blind expansion of sowing areas of economic crops. Hence, where economic crops have been too lightly taxed, the tariff should be properly raised in order to balance the peasants' burden." *SCMP* 359, 20 Jun. 52 [518]. See also Perkins [477], p. 37.

had to lie fallow. And again, provincial authorities often added their own incentive provisions to promote certain aspects of production. In Hunan in 1950, any household collecting with its own labor mountain, forest, or water products (wild medicinal herbs, lumber, fruits, water plants, and so on) or any household turning out sideline products (such as woven bamboo articles) was not taxed on income from this work.[16] And in 1951, to encourage cattle breeding, each head of cattle owned by a household entitled it to a tax reduction of fifteen catties of rice.[17]

In addition to these incentives for increasing output, the 1950 regulations also contained provisions for tax relief to peasants who failed to attain their normal annual yield due to natural disasters or other calamities (Article XXIV).[18] And there were other authorized forms of tax relief, sometimes referred to as "social reductions." For example, dependents of revolutionary martyrs[19] were privileged to count all their martyred dead as members of the household *(nung-yeh jen-k'ou)* as a special compensation for their loss (Article X). And they, as well as army dependents, families of work personnel on the supply system,[20] the aged, weak, orphaned, widowed, crippled, and other especially poor people might all be granted exemptions by recommendation of the *hsiang* Tax Investigation and Assessment Committee and with approval of the county government (Article XXV).[21] It is difficult to gauge how much potential revenue was left uncollected as a result of these sorts of

16. *Hunan Nung-yeh* [15], p. 101. But if the forests or lakes were rented out and the household's own labor power was not employed while it was receiving income from them, that income was to be converted into a rice equivalent and taxed as if it were income from land rented out.

17. *Ibid*.

18. The real formula for tax relief for disaster victims is not stipulated in either the 1950 or the 1951 Provisional Regulations, but in Hunan in 1951 the reported guidelines were:

> 20% tax reduction for a 20–30% crop loss
> 30% tax reduction for a 30–40% crop loss
> 40% tax reduction for a 40–50% crop loss
> 60% tax reduction for a 50–60% crop loss
> 80% tax reduction for a 60–70% crop loss
> cancellation of all tax for over 70% crop loss

See *Hunan Nung-yeh* [15], p. 102, where there are also guidelines for the tax relief provided after the 1954 floods.

19. People killed while fighting for the Communist cause.

20. Cadres and other civilians receiving some payment from the government.

21. In 1951 in Hunan, these categories of people were entitled to tax reductions of from 10 percent to 30 percent, and they might petition the county government for more.

tax relief, but it is evident from the discussion devoted to these provisions over the years that a great many people applied for and were granted such exemptions, at least for a time. Table 18 provides the most detailed information available on the extent of tax reductions made in Hunan during the period 1949–57.

DISCRIMINATION AGAINST LANDLORDS AND IN FAVOR OF TENANTS

Despite all the attention to tax reductions and to the provision of various incentives, however, the primary purpose of the tax law was the generation of revenue, and especially the extraction of revenue from those segments of rural society best able to pay. Therefore, having taken care that agricultural production as a whole should not be adversely influenced by a vigorous implementation of tax policy, the central government included in its regulations stipulations designed to enhance both total revenue collections and the progressive nature of the tax system, by adding to the burden on landlords, rich peasants, and other wealthier villagers.

The most significant of these stipulations is contained in Article XV of the Provisional regulations, which authorizes different standards for calculating income from land, depending on whether the land is owned by its cultivator, rented out by its owner, or rented by its cultivator. Income from land cultivated by its owner was to be reckoned as 100 catties for every 100 catties harvested; while income from land rented out by its owner was to be reckoned as 120 catties for every 100 catties received by the landlord; and income from land rented by its cultivator was to be reckoned as 80 catties for every 100 catties received by the tenant. This arrangement meant a 20 percent increase in taxable income for income derived from renting out land, since this income originated in the exploitation of the labor of others. It also represented a 20 percent reduction in taxable income for tenant farmers, as a kind of compensation for the fact that their labor was being exploited. Li provides Table 19 as an example of how this system would work, with the corresponding desired class distinctions.

Also that year, members of national minority groups were given a 50 percent reduction, but in 1954 this was reduced to 10–30 percent (or more if they successfully petitioned the county government). This last stipulation was also said to apply to people of Han nationality who were living in national minority areas of the province, if they were just as poor as the local minorities. See *Hunan Nung-yeh* [15], pp. 102–103.

TABLE 18. Hunan Agricultural Tax Levies and Collections, 1949–57

(In catties)

		Lawful Tax Reductions						Actual Collections		
	Planned Rate-Based Tax Levy	Natural Disaster Reductions	Social Reductions	Other Reductions	Subtotal	As % of Planned Levy	Adjusted Tax Levy	Catties	As % of Adjusted Levy	Local Surtax
1949	—	—	—	—	—	—	—	1,264,705,882	—	864,931,479
1950	—	—	—	—	—	—	—	1,705,460,000	—	577,690,026
1951	—	—	—	—	—	—	—	2,454,836,424	—	553,124,386
1952	3,364,747,816	—	—	—	353,809,019	10.52	3,010,938,797	2,997,814,584	99.56	—
1953	3,339,654,849	201,832,679	97,168,027	—	299,300,706	8.96	3,040,354,143	3,002,177,783	98.74	38,536,954
1954	3,353,015,400	784,096,457	98,459,381	—	882,555,838	26.32	2,470,459,562	2,436,472,534	98.62	131,114,975
1955	3,266,798,808	—	—	—	408,433,481	12.50	2,858,365,327	2,808,823,958	98.27	137,010,017
1956	3,231,289,640	457,742,685	242,184,039	—	714,838,015	23.50	2,516,451,625	2,497,205,905	99.24	120,441,362
1957	3,278,887,441	241,731,205	158,871,115	32,958,743	433,561,123	13.22	2,845,326,318	2,838,758,838	99.76	310,585,478

SOURCE: *Hunan Nung-yeh* [15], p. 104.

NOTES: Some of the figures in this table have been adjusted from the reporting series of various special districts and municipalities. Totals therefore do not always precisely coincide.

Other Reductions for 1957 includes national minority reductions.

Starting in 1955 a *hsiang* ordinary expenditure surtax was levied but the statistics are not included here. Local Surtax refers only to the provincial surtax.

TABLE 19. Adjusted Income Tax Effects

Class	Actual Income	Adjusted Income*	Tax Rate	Tax per 100 Catties
Landlord	Income from rent: 100 catties	120	42%	50.4
Rich peasant	Income from rent: 50 catties; Income from self-cultivation: 50 catties	60 / 50 → 110	25%	27.5
Middle peasant	Income from self-cultivation: 100 catties	100	13%	13.0
Poor peasant	Income from tenancy: 100 catties	80	7%	5.6

SOURCE: Li Ch'eng-jui [22], p. 144.
*Income from rent plus 20%; income of tenant minus 20%.

This table represents an ideal arrangement, of course, but it illustrates several interesting points. First, it should be noted that in this example, if there were no adjusted income system and all taxpayers were still paying at these same rates,[22] the government would have collected 87 catties, or 21.75 percent of the 400 catties total income. But with the adjusted income system in force, the government actually collected 96.5 catties or 24.13 percent of the 400 catties total income. This is an increase of 9.5 catties, a gain of over 10 percent in real revenue. The adjusted income system, therefore, was not merely another veiled mechanism for redistributing wealth from rich to poor by penalizing exploiters. Since landlords generally would be paying at higher rates than tenants, the government itself stood to gain significant quantities of revenue by this arrangement.

Second, this system worked like a double-edged sword against landlords, because as it was adding to their taxable income it could simultaneously be pressing them into a higher tax bracket. As the landlord was impelled up the tax schedule, the tenant dropped into a lower bracket, and since the income increments at the tenant's end of the scale were much smaller than at the landlord's end (see Table 16), the tenant might

22. This second assumption would almost certainly not hold where considerable rent payments were involved, as explained below. And if the assumption does not hold, revenue would generally be reduced even below the 87 catties suggested for this example.

well drop several percentage points before the landlord would be raised by one. The system provided considerable real benefit to tenant farmers, therefore, while the government collected expanded revenue entirely at the landlords' expense.

The 1950 Provisional Regulations also had to take into account the effects of the rent reduction campaign then being enforced in the later liberated areas on the mutual tax obligations of landlords and tenants. Article XVI therefore contained a set of regulations to keep the pressure on landlords. Where the rent reduction campaign had succeeded in bringing a 25 percent reduction of rents on leased land, in accordance with the law, the landlord and the tenant were each to pay tax on their own portion of the income from the land, subject to the adjusted income system just described. Where rents had not yet been reduced according to law, landlords were to pay the tax on their portion of the income from the land (again applying the adjusted income system), and in addition they were also required to pay the tax on the tenant's portion of the income, at the rate of 9 percent.[23]

The real impact of these regulations on individual landlords and tenants must have varied greatly, of course, depending on the local terms of leasing land, the productivity of the land involved, and other factors. Generally speaking, however, when taken in conjunction with the enforced rent reduction these regulations put the landlord in a squeeze. And there were still other regulations intended to force landlords to shoulder more of the tax burden. For example, in taxing land that transcended administrative boundaries (Article XIV), there was further discrimination against landlords. Land owned and cultivated or rented for cultivation by a peasant that happened to be across a province, county, subdistrict, or village boundary from the place where the peasant resided was simply to be combined with other land owned or rented by that farming household for calculating the tax. But by contrast, any land outside a landlord's province that the family rented out was to be taxed separately as if there were another household there and as if the household had only one member. This usually raised the landlords' taxes ap-

---

23. If however, the rent reduction campaign were implemented in that locality after the landlord had paid the tax but in the same fiscal year, the amount of tax paid for the tenant would be deducted from what the landlord was judged to owe the tenant in returned rent. A corresponding ruling was included for cases in which the tax was paid before any rent was collected by the landlord: the tenant paid the tax for both parties, but was credited with the landlord's tax when later paying rent to the landlord (Article XVI).

preciably, since it barred them from claiming other household members as dependents on the income from that land.

Land owned and rented out by a landlord family in the same province but in a different county, subdistrict, or village might either be combined with their other holdings or treated separately, as deemed most convenient by the province or county government concerned. From this it appears that the discrimination was aimed primarily at large landlords with holdings in two or more provinces. For the smaller but still important landlords whose holdings were extensively scattered in a particular area, local officials had discretion in determining how their taxes should be paid. The combined rather than split calculation of the family's income may well have been a favor to be earned by landlords from local cadres.

Corporate landlords, like individual landlords, were also subject to more strict taxation. Schools, orphanages, old age homes, and hospitals supporting themselves in part or completely by farming were to pay a 7 percent tax on income derived from land they worked themselves or cultivated with hired hands; but the rate was 10 percent on land they rented out.[24] Ancestral halls, private associations, monasteries, and missionary societies were to pay 14 percent on income from land they cultivated themselves, 25 percent on income from land worked by hired hands — a milder form of exploitation — and 40 percent on income from land they rented out (Article XIII).

The fineness of stipulations like these may tend to give the false impression that tax work in the newly liberated areas was carried out with a remarkable degree of precision. In fact, before, during, and even well after the land reform movement it is clear that the official investigative, data-gathering, and statistical networks in the countryside were only embryonic and certainly much too weak to have executed these regulations to the letter. Also, as illustrated in the latter half of this chapter, there were widespread problems with tax evasion and corruption that made real local revenue collection a much more crude and motley affair than these carefully refined provisions suggest. Nevertheless, cadres were able to make a good approximation of the intended pattern of revenue collection in many individual villages, and where they managed this,

24. Schools, orphanages, old age homes, and hospitals, however, were also entitled to apply to the county government for a total or partial tax exemption on all agricultural income to encourage the continuation of their services (Article IV).

word of its effects, especially its effects on landlords, naturally spread throughout the surrounding area.

In the months immediately following liberation the agricultural tax acted, in much the same way as the rent reduction and interest reduction campaign in the villages, to align and mobilize forces for the coming upheaval. There were a series of public meetings in each village at which every family declared its own tax liability in what was called a "self-report." These tax meetings gave the mass of poor peasants and tenant farmers a legal reformist vehicle for challenging landlords and experiencing a gain at their expense before land reform, without requiring them to take up arms or even to defy the landlords face to face. They gave landlords and other wealthier villagers a cause to disobey the government either openly or covertly, and this in turn afforded activists and cadres an early opportunity to interfere with them and mobilize sentiment against them. In this way, tax work helped to mobilize the poor and middle peasants, plunging them into the task of drawing out and exposing the full extent of the landlords' possessions—a form of political action that was to be important again later during land reform. The early propaganda on behalf of the tax program, even if it was not always completely believed, made it plain to poorer villagers whose side the government intended to take. And the marked shift in the burden of taxation from the poor to the rich was clear to all, even if it was not always rigorously achieved.

Thus the message conveyed before land reform was unambiguous: although the new government was not yet seizing landlords' land and giving it away, it was nonetheless intent on making life difficult for them while noticeably easing the burden on the poor. The message of official tax policy after land reform, when the position of landlords was radically changed, would of course be somewhat different.

MODIFICATIONS AFTER LAND REFORM

Several important alterations in tax policy were called for once land reform had been accomplished. As pointed out in Chapter 2, land reform was executed comparatively quickly in the Central South; but however rapid, it could not be instantaneous. And this necessarily left the central authorities in the position of simultaneously taxing some areas where land reform had been accomplished, other areas where it was in progress, and others where it had not yet begun. To cope with this, two different sets of agricultural tax regulations were issued and applied each year as the reform progressed; one for the pre-land-reform areas and one for the post-land-reform areas.[25] The differences between them were considerable.

The first and clearly most appropriate modification for post-land-reform areas was to soften and flatten the slope of the graduated tax rates. Instead of beginning at 3 percent and rising to 42 percent as before land reform, the new schedule started at 6 percent for average per capita incomes between 150 and 200 catties and rose to a 25 percent tax on average per capita incomes exceeding 1,450 catties (1951 regulations, Article XII; and 1952 regulations, Article XIII). The less steeply progressive tax rate corresponded with the elimination of the greatest disparities in wealth through reform of the landholding system. Nevertheless, post-land-reform taxation had not been handled this way in the older liberated areas, where a proportional tax had been implemented instead. But then the land reform process in the old liberated areas had been quite different from the later post-1949 land reform. Rich peasants (as well as landlords) had then had their property expropriated and redistributed, and the subsequent distributions of wealth and income were more deliberately and pointedly equalized. In the newly liberated areas, by contrast, rich peasants had been protected under the Agrarian Reform Law. Only their "feudal tail" of renting out land had been "cut off." It was estimated that on the average their assets after land reform were still one and a half to two times as great as those of poor peasants. Thus, with wealth still far from equalized, it was appropriate to preserve a modified progressive tax system. Indeed, it was argued, it was necessary to continue to apply a progressive tax in order to "limit the rich peasant economy"—to prevent the reemergence of a wealthy class in the villages, a harmful class of capitalist exploiters.[26]

Of course, under this post-land-reform system, poor peasants at the lower end of the tax schedule were going to have to pay higher rates than before. But this was justified, they were told, since following land reform their financial position had improved markedly, and after taxes

25. For the 1951 sets of regulations see *CCJP,* 23 Jun. 51 [134]; and *CCJP,* 19 Aug. 51 [326]. For 1952, both sets of Central South regulations were first printed in *NFJP,* 25 Sep. 52 and later reprinted together in *Handbook for 1952 Agricultural Tax Work* [11], pp. 2–22.

26. This explanation is given fairly clearly in Li Ch'eng-jui [22], p. 148; and in Li Shu-te [507], pp. 7–8. For a comparison of the tax formulas in old and new liberated areas in 1952, see the directive signed by Chou En-lai in *SCMP* 359, 20 Jun. 52 [499]. It is also interesting to note that in 1952 plans were already being made to replace the *pro*

they would still be left with more grain for consumption than before.[27] They were also reminded that due to an across-the-board increase in agricultural output after land reform, the total percentage of output taken by the government in taxes was to drop from somewhere near 17 percent in 1949 to about 13.2 percent in 1952.[28] And this, of course, would mean more grain and cash left in peasant hands.

A second important modification after land reform was to cease adjusting taxable income on the basis of whether it originated from land leased by the cultivator, land owned by the cultivator, or land rented out by the owner. This system was abandoned altogether, and each 100 catties income was to be counted as just 100 catties for tax computations (1951 regulations, Article XVIII).[29] This, it was explained, was because before land reform it was primarily landlords and rich peasants who rented out land, while after land reform those renting out land were in the main poor households lacking labor power, martyrs' dependents, PLA dependents, widows, and some poor peasants who had received land during the redistribution but who still lacked animals or implements to cultivate it all themselves.[30] These households, it was indicated, plainly ought not to be discriminated against for renting out land, since their aim was not to exploit their tenants but innocently to make use of what they had received in the land reform.[31]

---

rata system in the old liberated areas with a progressive system in 1953. In explaining the need for this change, the *People's Daily* said: "It was correct at that time to apply the *pro rata* tax system. But at present, many changes have taken place in rural economy in a general upward trend in the old liberated areas. In order to meet the tax-bearing capacities of the various strata of peasants it is entirely necessary and proper that we make preparations to introduce a progressive tax system next year . . . . Since the landlord class no longer exists the progression of tariff can be comparatively gradual. Therefore, when the system of progressive tax is applied, the peasants' burden in old liberated areas will be rendered more equitable and reasonable." *SCMP* 385, 30 Jul. 52 [511], p. 13. Clearly, the natural erosion of equality after land reform was recognized and understood even at this early date; and there can be little doubt that this understanding of conditions in north China informed the Party's plans for future development of the later liberated areas as well.

27. *Thirty Questions and Answers on Agricultural Tax Policy* [33], p. 7.

28. Li Shu-te [507], pp. 13–15. See also the advance estimate by Chou En-lai of revenue as a percentage of total output in "Directive of the State Council . . ." in *Collected Laws and Decrees of the Central People's Government* 1 [133], pp. 275–276.

29. For an explanation of this in a clearer context, see also *CCJP,* 23 Jun. 51 [134].

30. Li Ch'eng-jui [22], pp. 148–149.

31. This obviously made a certain amount of sense. But just as obviously there must

As pointed out already, the adjusted income system had worked not only to help tenants and hinder landlords but also to expand the government's total revenue from agriculture. In abandoning the adjusted income system, then, did the central government stand to lose significant amounts of revenue? Evidently not. If the official analysis of the situation was correct, practically all land rented out after land reform was owned by households with a generally small or only average total income. Such households, unlike the stereotypical landlord households before land reform, were paying their taxes at rates comparable to (or even lower than) those of their own tenants. Enlarging the taxable income of such poor landlords (now more aptly referred to as small rentiers) would have been a burden on them while adding little to total government revenue. This reform, therefore, both simplified tax administration and corresponded to the altered conditions in the villages.

A third significant modification was the abandonment in 1952 of discrimination against income from rented-out land that lay across administrative boundaries (1952 regulations, Article XVI).[32] Income from all land cultivated by household members or rented out, even that which lay across province boundaries, was now to be taken together and taxed at the same rate. This change corresponds with the view that households renting out land after land reform were not the sort of exploiters who should be specially limited and regulated by the tax laws.

Furthermore, while this sort of landlord was no longer subject to any

---

have been many poor households of similar description that received some income from renting out land before the land reform and were penalized for it, along with regular landlords, where the old tax regulations had been correctly implemented. If it was not equitable to penalize these poor households after land reform, then surely it could not have been equitable to penalize them before land reform. This in fact appears to have been recognized in 1952, when the adjusted income system ceased to apply to households renting out land because they lacked labor power in the non-land-reform areas as well as in the land reform areas. (1952 Regulations for Non-Land-Reform Areas, Article XVII). This was done on the condition that the income of such households did not exceed 200 percent of the local average income, a provision included to accord with Article V of the Agrarian Reform Law dealing with the classification of small rentiers. (See the discussion of small rentiers in the section of Chapter 2 entitled "Agrarian Reform: Class Policy.")

32. There seems to be no good reason why this was not changed in the 1951 regulations along with the cessation of the adjusted income system. But strangely, the relevant Article XVI in the 1951 regulations retained exactly the same wording as the analogous article in the 1950 regulations.

extraordinary tax, the tenant in the case was still given a tax break on the income derived from leasing the land in question. This income was to be taxed at the rate that would have been charged if the tenant's only income had been the amount actually earned from the land owned by the tenant household: that is, income from tenancy was not to be included in taxable income for the purpose of determining the tax rate for the household (1952 regulations, Article XVII). This measure of tax relief to tenants obviously had a greater beneficial impact on a tenant household, the greater the proportion of total income that was derived from tenancy. It is not certain whether this measure was intended as a compensation to peasants who still had to resort to part-time tenancy after land reform, or as a small incentive to prospective tenants to cultivate tracts of land owned by small rentiers in inconvenient locations, or both.

Several other significant changes in the tax law were made at the time of land reform. One of the most interesting was a special provision to relieve the distress of one- and two-person households (1951 regulations, Article X, section 4; 1952 regulations, Article XI, section 4). It was determined that all households with only one member should be taxed as if there were actually two agricultural dependents *(nung-yeh jen-k'ou)*, and all households with only two members should be taxed as if there were three. This was evidently contrived in recognition of the fact that after the expropriation of land reform very small households were often not viable without exceptional assistance.

Another interesting type of tax relief was that offered to the families of refugees who had fled their homes because of famine or other disaster (1951 regulations, Article X, section 10; 1952 regulations, Article XI, section 10). This clause allowed such families to claim their missing relatives as dependents. (But if three years elapsed without their receiving a letter from the refugees, the household would have to forfeit its claim to them as dependents.) In a similar addition, it was stipulated that increases or decreases in each household's population should be noted annually, and that all legal transfers of land and changes in land renting relationships between households should also be noted each year and appropriate revisions should be made in the tax status of the affected households (1951 regulations, Article XIX, section 1; 1952 regulations, Article XIX, section 1).

The tax regulations for post-land-reform areas included a number of new rules for dealing with special exceptions and particular cases such as land abutting the national railways and land in yards and threshing floors traditionally left uncultivated. Also added were incentive provisions designed to encourage afforestation, mechanization of agriculture, and the adoption of other advanced cultivation techniques, as well as the successful operation and growth of Agricultural Production Cooperatives, where they had already been formed.

As should be evident from this summary, tax policy and the tax regulations themselves both before and after land reform were carefully drawn up to promote certain important economic and political goals. They reached a high degree of specificity and responsiveness to existing conditions in the later liberated areas. After land reform, with its homogenizing effect on society, it became possible to streamline and simplify the law to a certain extent. And essentially in the form it took at this time it remained in effect for several years. Not until 1958, and the nationwide formation of people's communes, were rural incomes considered sufficiently leveled to allow abandonment of the progressive tax and adoption of a standard proportional levy.

Yet, the progressive schedule retained after land reform was hardly severe. If the agricultural tax had been the only redistributive demand made on village incomes at this time, considerable disparities in wealth would surely have remained and just as surely would have widened. With the landlords beaten, the tax burden had to fall squarely on the mass of ordinary peasants. It was, for this reason alone, no longer desirable that it appear to have a punitive effect. Although these tax provisions were propagandized as safeguards against the reemergence of a rural wealthy class of exploiters and although they clearly served this function to an appreciable extent, their most pertinent aspects often seemed to be the attention they gave to ensuring that there would be rises (not necessarily equitably distributed) in farm family incomes, as well as their marked incentive appeals to the entrepreneurial instincts of peasants. With their three-year fixed assessments and with the normal yield tax base set comfortably below the actual output for most households, these provisions, in effect throughout the mid-1950's, are more striking for their encouragements to peasants to "settle down and get rich" through individual, private efforts in a state-ordered, benevolent economic environment than for their contribution to socialist transformation.

In designing the agricultural tax laws in this way, the new authorities were attempting to demonstrate their solidarity with the legitimate aspirations of the mass of peasants and their willingness to see peasants take personal advantage of the new economic opportunities now potentially available to them after their little land reform windfalls. Of course, the tax was by no means the only redistributive demand on better-off peasants' incomes in this period. The formation of cooperatives and other pressures toward socialist reorganization, as discussed below, would soon become irresistible. But after the initial, pre-land-reform thrust against the landlords and other wealthier villagers, the role of the agricultural tax in pressing rural transformation was not a central one. CCP tax policy even seemed in some ways to promote the small peasant private economic orientation against the larger trend toward collectivism. Without much doubt this was a deliberate move to stabilize what was traditionally a volatile flashpoint of hostility between Chinese peasants and Chinese governments. If it became necessary to apply more pressure on the agricultural sector, the revolutionary government would prefer to find other means than straight taxation.

But however sensitive and well-constructed the laws examined here might have been, their real impact on peasants could only be as good as their actual implementation from village to village. As already illustrated, peasants had remained skeptical, throughout the early reforms, of their long-term durability. If the central authorities now expected peasants to respond as if they really thought there might be a chance for them to "settle down and get rich," this response would have to be in part a product of their confidence that the cadres would keep their word about future tax demands. Creating this confidence in the complex village conditions of 1950–52 was not always easy for tax officials or local cadres. But since future peasant-official relations on tax questions were strongly affected by the experiences of these early years, it is important to turn back to them again now to look for the most common types of problems encountered in rural tax policy implementation and the methods employed to deal with them.

HIDDEN LAND

From the beginning, the single most serious and persistent problem the government faced in taxing the peasantry was known as the problem of "hidden land" *(man t'ien)* or, as the peasants sometimes called it, "black land" *(hei t'ien)*. Under this general heading fell a great variety of tax evasion techniques, typically involving concealment of the existence of certain tracts of land or misrepresentation to the authorities of the productivity of land. Tax evasion by peasants was an old problem in China. Through generations under the authoritarian central and weak local government that characterized imperial and republican China, peasants had learned to play the tax evasion game, sometimes with the humorless joy that comes of outwitting an inept opponent and sometimes with the deadly seriousness of a struggle for survival.

The revolutionary government inherited this problem when it came to power. Although the authorities liked to say that landlords and rich peasants were the ones primarily guilty of concealing land and that the great majority of poorer peasants were eager to pay their taxes to support the revolutionary government, they were in fact well aware that tax evasion was extremely widespread, even of epidemic proportions, and that it crossed all class lines. Estimates that 30 percent or more of the productive land had been concealed were common in the Central South.[33]

Peasant Fears
and the Scope of Tax Evasion

Profound distrust of government was part of the peasants' cultural heritage. They had not in the past survived by being candid about their tax liability. Peasants automatically disbelieved government promises about low taxation. They expected taxes to rise sharply in the coming years, despite government assurances to the contrary, and they concealed land for immediate benefit and as a hedge against the future.[34] Another motivation for concealing land was the fear and uncertainty many peasants felt about the coming land reform. To avoid expropriation it was important to seem to be among the poorest when compared to other villagers. Concealing property—especially land and its full

33. See *CCJP* editorial, 19 Jan. 50 [246]; and *CCJP*, 6 Feb. 50 [212]. This source also asserts that in Ch'ang-te special district concealed land varied between 25 percent and 40 percent of the total productive land. For another early estimate and examples of the extent of concealed land, see *CCJP* editorial, 6 Oct. 50 [94]. See also the report by Yang Shao-ch'iao, *CCJP*, 9 Aug. 52 [346]. Yang relates that after the first stage of land investigation in Ling-ling special district (Hunan), the number of *mou* rose 48.7 percent over what had originally been reported to the government and that revised figure exceeded the highest KMT estimates for the area by 35.5 percent. For a Russian estimate of hidden land in 1950 see Chekhutov [453], p. 90, where landlords and rich peasants are said to have concealed 30–40 percent of their land.

34. There are innumerable reports in the Chinese press that explore the motivations of peasants for concealing land. Two of the more interesting and complete ones are *CCJP*, 28 Mar. 51 [156]; and *CCJP*, 11 Oct. 51 [266].

productivity—seemed the most promising way to feign extreme poverty.

In preparing for land reform, therefore, peasants tried to deceive the tax collection officials about their income and their holdings. The knowledge that other villagers would be doing the same, and for the same reasons, naturally inspired them to attempt to conceal more and more of their land to ensure that they would come out near the bottom when compared with the others, their fraudulence notwithstanding. Inevitably then, villagers often reported only a fraction of their actual production to the tax cadres.

Similarly, knowing as yet little about the new government's tax methods, peasants feared that people in other villages and hamlets would somehow manage to conceal even more of their land and would in consequence pay less, leaving their village to shoulder a disproportionately large part of the final tax burden for the area.[35]

While most peasants who concealed land immediately after liberation probably did so on the basis of their own self-interested calculations, quite a few were more heavily influenced by fear of what other villagers might do to them if they did not lie than by hopes of what they personally might gain if they did. In the closely circumscribed socioeconomic environment of the village, peasants were certainly not always able to consider the welfare of their own households as distinct from that of other households, larger kinship groups, or other overlapping permanent and temporary alliances of villagers. If a landlord family was trying to conceal some of its land, for example, it might well offer all its tenants a material reward for helping to deceive the cadres about the true productivity of the land each tenant cultivated. Such a reward would come to the tenant in addition to the tax money that could be saved by misrepresenting the land's real output. But the reward might well be accompanied also with an explicit or implicit threat from the landlord to punish the tenant, by violent means or simply by refusal of a continued lease on the land, if the tenant failed to lie to the cadres.

Before land reform, in land-scarce areas of the Central South, landlords maintained considerable leverage over peasants in this way and they benefited proportionately to a much greater extent than their tenants and other villagers from this tax evasion. A report of the situation in one Hupei county claimed that landlords routinely concealed half their land; rich peasants concealed three-tenths, and middle and poor peasants

35. *Ibid.*

concealed two-tenths. In areas where there were numerous landlords, the report went on, the concealment was quite apparent. Nevertheless, "it was not easy to investigate the facts" because of the reluctance of villagers to say anything to a cadre that might jeopardize a landlord's position.[36]

Where clan or other kinship relationships cutting across class lines were involved, peasant protection of landlords was even more stubborn. There are numerous reports in the local press of cases where the existence of even quite distant family relationships induced otherwise law-abiding peasants to shield tax evaders. Sometimes, where the force of clan relationships was still very powerful in the life of the individual, counterrevolutionary or simply tax-evading clan members were able to confuse peasants completely about the nature of the government's tax policy and convince all members to conceal land collectively. Peasants were misled into thinking that taxes would be levied on the clan as a whole, rather than on individual households, and that therefore it was in their own interest to do what they could to help conceal the land of other members, so as to lower the tax on all.[37]

It appears to have been relatively easy to conceal land and the true productivity of land in these early years because of the general confusion and uncertainty that marks a transition period and because of the skeletal nature of the rural administrative structure in the later liberated areas. Cadres who had come down from the old liberated areas were generally unfamiliar with the rice-based economy of the south and therefore at a loss to estimate productivity. Locally recruited cadres were more familiar with general agricultural conditions, but they were by and large illiterate, unable to handle much mathematical calculation, and uncertain about the particulars of government tax policy. Furthermore, since they had been drawn from among the people, they tended to reflect many of the same anxieties in their own attitudes and behavior. Village cadres and activists themselves quite often concealed land and conspired with others to evade taxation. They too had fears that their village would have to pay more than other villages and, feeling responsible for the welfare of their villagers, they were not above lying about local output to

36. *CCJP*, 21 Oct. 50 [196].

37. *CCJP*, 15 Dec. 49 [159]. It is also mentioned here that clan sentiment was interfering with antidespot and antibandit work, and with the rent and interest reduction campaign.

higher-level officials.[38] Nor were village cadres automatically immune to special pressures from friends and relatives.

To guide and supplement the tax work of village cadres, tax collection work teams were sent down from the county, subdistrict, and other levels of government where they were organized on an *ad hoc* basis. They moved from village to village explaining the basic aspects of tax policy to the local cadres and helping them to organize the investigation of harvest conditions, make assessments on each household, and collect and transport the tax grain to government granaries. A great many literate office workers, students, and former tax collection officials were pressed into service on the work teams.[39] By and large they had only received a few days of specialized training for the work, but their ability to read and handle figures and their relative familiarity with the basic principles of taxation made them a valuable resource. As in the land reform movement, the deployment of mobile work teams was an important device for utilizing to the greatest possible extent scarce trained personnel and political workers with special skills.

The members of the intelligentsia on these work teams, like their counterparts on the land reform work teams, did sometimes come under fire for being too lenient with landlords, since they themselves often came from landlord or other unfavorable class backgrounds. Still, the rapid movement of these work teams from village to village generally enabled them to view particular problems with detachment and to avoid the personal entanglements that hampered the objectivity and effectiveness of local cadres. It was, however, this very mobility that in the end put limits on their effectiveness by depriving them of the sort of detailed knowledge of local affairs needed to "pull out" concealed land. In a few villages, the presence of the work team may have been decisive in attaining complete and honest tax reporting. But, from the anxious attention given to the problem of concealed land by the central and provincial

38. *CCJP,* 21 Oct. 50 [196]. Here it is wryly suggested to village and subdistrict cadres that one way they could induce peasants to reveal hidden land if they were having difficulty was to "take the lead" and reveal their *own* hidden land. This, it says, would initiate a "chain reaction." See also *CCJP,* 12 Sep. 52 [237].

39. Immediately after liberation, in fact, it was reported that *all* Party and government personnel at province level and below, except for a very small number left on the job, had been thrown into the struggle for grain tax collection. In addition, in Hunan alone, 10,000 "worker/peasant activists and members of the intelligentsia" were said to have taken part in the movement that year. *CCJP,* 6 Feb. 50 [212].

governments, it is apparent that tax evasion was persistent and widespread even during and after land reform.

In the meantime, tax collection units simply had to do the best they could. In practice this meant relying heavily on the "self-reports" or personal income estimates made by the peasants themselves. This method was officially called "self-report, public discussion, and democratic determination of yield" *(tzu-pao, kung-i, min-chu p'ing-ch'an)*. It generally involved convening a *ts'un* general meeting at which all heads of households estimated their taxable income and declared their eligible dependents. These estimates and declarations were then subject to public discussion, scrutiny, and challenge, the final decision on each household's tax liability then supposedly being made in conformity with the consensus of the meeting as to its true income. It is easy enough to see how reliance on this system alone would allow fear, uncertainty, jealousy, and misapprehension to distort the facts and create numerous imbalances in tax assessment.

The inadequacy of the "self-report" method was clear to all. But it continued to be employed as the only viable alternative to leaving taxes uncollected or to collecting them totally arbitrarily. Tax collection work, like other efforts at policy implementation conducted in this period in unpromising environments, was subject to later review and rectification. Often the follow-up investigations and rectifications of tax work revealed much taxable land unreported, even after land reform had been carried out in a village. An October 1951 survey of thirteen villages in one area of Hunan where land reform had already been completed revealed that 10–20 percent of real productivity was still being concealed.[40] Even in Ch'ang-sha county, where land reform had begun early and where the masses had been declared to be comparatively thoroughly mobilized, the voluntarily reported output of land was found to be "extremely inaccurate" in post-land-reform villages.[41]

Sustained efforts were made to explain the official tax policy to peasants in villages with suspected hidden land in the hope that once they understood that the system would be reasonably fair if it were honored, they would voluntarily give up tax evasion. Appeals were also made, especially during the Korean conflict, to their patriotic sentiments in the

40. *CCJP,* 30 Oct. 51 [239]. For further evidence that hidden land remained a serious problem even after land reform, see the decision signed by Lin Piao in *CCJP,* 9 Aug. 52 [123].

41. *CCJP,* 30 Oct. 51 [239].

hope of inspiring them to fulfill their tax obligations honestly.[42] But such appeals to reason, to a sense of justice, and to nationalistic sentiment were evidently known from the beginning to carry insufficient weight with tax-evading villagers.

Other appeals, in the form of material incentives for compliance with the law, had to be made to peasants as well. In the summer of 1951, for instance, the CSMAC offered an immunity from prosecution and a bonus to self-confessed tax evaders.[43] The offer was this: poor and middle peasants who voluntarily revealed black land in response to the government's call would not be required to pay back taxes on the income from the black land, and furthermore, their income from it for the current year would not be taxed. The income from voluntarily reported black land would not be added to the household's original normal annual yield estimate, and the tax rate applied would consequently not be revised upward. On the other hand, black land not voluntarily reported by the peasant, but found out by investigation, was to be taxed according to the regular tax schedule.

Even landlords and rich peasants were offered an incentive to make a clean breast of their affairs at this time, although the offer was not quite so generous for them. They were to be relieved of having to pay back taxes on black land revealed voluntarily, but they were required to pay the tax for the current year. The revealed income would be added in calculations of their normal annual yield, and if that were to put them into a higher tax bracket they would be taxed at the higher rate.

Even local cadres were offered incentives to uncover hidden land. As early as March 1950, the State Council announced that all local areas that exceeded the tax quota sent down from above and that had not violated tax policy or tax law in the process would be permitted to retain 80 percent of the surplus tax grain, 20 percent to be remitted to the central government.[44] This, it said, would be a reward *(chiang-li)*. Such an increase in funds available to local cadres must surely have encouraged them to shake down suspected tax evaders. There is no way to estimate how much hidden land may have come to light thanks to these early incentives to cadres and peasants, but the programs must have been considered productive on the whole, because rewards for activism and

42. *Ibid*. See also *CCJP,* 12 Sep. 52 [237].
43. *CCJP,* 26 Jul. 51 [113].
44. "Decision of the State Council . . . " in *Collected Laws and Decrees of the Central People's Government* 1 [124], p. 254.

honesty in tax work were retained in the 1951 and 1952 regulations for land reform areas (Articles XXVII and XXXI, respectively).

Quotas

This example of incentives for cadres raises for the first time here the matter of tax quotas. Tax collection quotas, sent down from the upper levels of government to be met by village cadres, were an enduring feature of tax work in the countryside. The quotas were based at first on very rough estimates and old provincial tax records. The use of quotas was certainly significant for several reasons, but especially for its impact on the hidden land problem. The use of the self-report system and the calculation of the normal annual yield encouraged independent treatment for each household, despite peasants' original fears that they would be lumped together with others. How much tax any given household would have to pay was to have nothing in particular to do with how much tax any other household would be paying, according to this system. The individual peasant had no direct interest in what tax rate was assigned to other households or in how much land others were managing to conceal. Likewise, the neighbors of any given peasant family had nothing to gain or lose by its concealing land. The simultaneous introduction of *hsiang* or *ts'un* quotas, however, cast the entire situation in a different light.

If there was a village quota to fulfill, then it was after all in each household's interest to expose the hidden land of other households, so that all others would pay more tax and at a higher rate. If others paid more, the target could be reached without making any special extra levies on the general population. It was especially in the interest of peasants hiding comparatively small amounts of land to inform on those hiding comparatively large amounts because they had much more to gain than to lose in the trade-off. The government was perfectly well aware of the effect tax quotas would have on peasants and their plots to conceal land. And lest there be any misunderstanding, they made it quite clear as early as 1950:

> In order to open up the movement [to draw out concealed land], once the tax quota for a hamlet has come down, [the peasants] should be given to understand that the hamlet quota will absolutely not be raised or lowered if they reveal concealed land so as to permit appropriate readjustment of the burden among villagers and to enhance the peasants' enthusiasm for revealing hidden land.[45]

45. *CCJP,* 12 Sep. 50 [117].

The application of tax quotas to hamlets and villages was clearly a divisive mechanism. It gave tax-collection cadres a trump card to play in the black land game. And it must often have offered them their first opportunity to break into a phalanx of villagers trying to deceive them. A quota for an entire hamlet set peasants against each other by giving each an interest in making sure that the others all paid their just proportion of the total. It may seem that this contradicts what was said earlier about the central government consciously choosing to tax the household rather than the hamlet, since a tax applied to a larger residential unit would tend to unify the population in tax evasion. In fact there was no contradiction, for while a quota was to be issued for a hamlet or village, the household, not the village, remained the basic taxable unit. Peasants were aware that the amount of the quota each household would have to pay would at least roughly correspond to whatever determination could be made of its real income. This would not have been the case if the hamlet itself were taken as the taxable unit. It was, therefore, the combined effect of issuing hamlet quotas while taxing each household separately that gave individual peasants an incentive to inform on their neighbors and to assist tax cadres in exposing concealed land.

The quota system, in this respect, promoted intravillage conflict, although it was not necessarily conflict that fell out along class lines. And while class conflict was what the revolutionary government desired to promote, generalized interpersonal conflict in the village, which could act to fragment the unity of the masses and turn the revolutionary struggle into pointless factional infighting, was just what it wanted to avoid.

Tax quotas were therefore applied rather loosely, with considerable flexibility exercised by local officials before land reform, when it was extremely important for the Party to attain unity and cooperation among the peasant meases. It was only after land reform had been achieved over a large area of the Central South, and when better production data had been collected, that there was a move to design and apply quotas more rigorously and to put them more closely under central control.[46] The more determined use of quotas, then, came at a time when the non-class hostilities they could potentially ignite in the villages would not endanger the more crucial class struggle involved in land reform, and when

46. See *CCJP*, 13 Jul. 51 [75]. Lax application of quotas in the pre-land-reform areas was not necessarily the result of conscious policy, of course. It was often due more to administrative inadequacy and a general lack of hard tax data in the newly liberated areas.

more stringent measures may very well have been desired to deal with villages persisting in tax evasion even after land reform.

It is true that if the elaborate tax regulations and rate schedules described earlier had been working properly, all households would have been assigned a proper normal annual yield figure, would have paid their taxes at the appropriate rate, and there would have been no place at all for a quota in the process. Some rural administrators objected to the use of quotas and other crude tax assessment measures on these grounds. They admitted that rough quotas might be necessary in the turbulence of the pre-land-reform situation, when there was insufficient survey data on normal yields, but they hoped to abandon them in favor of a more sensitive and discriminating tax according to the rate schedule, in the much more favorable conditions prevailing after land reform.[47] Others in rural administration, however, defended the continued use of tax quotas.[48] They admitted that some cadres had completely surrendered to "quota thinking." The slogan of these cadres was said to be: "The first thing is the quota; the second thing is also the quota; and the third thing also is the quota."[49] They even conceded that this simplistic "quota thinking" was a great obstacle in doing good tax work. Nevertheless, they thought quotas were absolutely necessary if higher governmental levels were to know how much revenue they could expect and be able to make even short-range plans. The quota system, they argued, not only should not be abolished but should be refined as more accurate data became available, and applied as carefully as possible.

The quota system did allow central planners to do one very important thing that taxation according to rates alone would not have allowed them to do, namely, to adjust and balance, at least partially, the amounts of revenue extracted across *hsiang* and across counties. The tax regulations and the system of rates were concerned with fairly balancing the tax collected across households. But they could do little to ensure that the total taxes collected from village to village or county to county were fairly distributed. The differing amount of hidden land from place to place was not the only factor involved where there were imbalances. Villages where most peasants had to process their crop before it could be marketed or where it was necessary to transport the goods long distances

47. See *CCJP*, 4 Apr. 52 [149].

48. See Wu Tan-ko [36], Chapter 6, "The Problem of Contradiction between Tax Assessment by Rates and by Quotas," pp. 52–61.

49. *Ibid.*, p. 54.

to market them naturally had considerably higher production costs than others. Likewise, there were great variations from village to village and county to county in the irrigation, fertilizer, labor power, and animal power investments needed to produce a crop of the same market value. If compensation were not to be made for villages with higher production and marketing costs and peasants were to be taxed solely on their output according to the rates, there would be many inequities. Much was written about the need to even out gross imbalances across geographic areas, and the application of quotas based on careful consultation with and supervision of local cadres was taken to be the most effective way to accomplish that end.[50]

The quota system was consolidated after land reform and has remained in use ever since. It proved a useful tool in drawing out hidden land. All tax evasion was not eliminated even after land reform, however, and although the absorption of peasants into Mutual Aid Teams and later into Agricultural Production Co-ops made tax evasion more difficult, the phenomenon even then was not unknown.[51] Still, central planners were sufficiently satisfied with tax reporting after land reform to announce a tax freeze in 1953. The peasant's burden was stabilized at its 1952 level. The freeze lasted through 1955. In theory, as peasant production increased after land reform, the tax on each household would remain the same, leaving it with a small amount of surplus capital to be reinvested in agriculture. In reality, a good deal of what the average peasant saved in taxes must have gone to investment in the Credit Co-ops and Supply and Marketing Co-ops that were established everywhere in the next few years. Any extra cash on hand that peasant families enjoyed thanks to the stabilization of taxes after 1952 made it somewhat easier for them to accept and participate in these new socialist organizations intended to restructure the production and marketing of agricultural crops.

CORRUPTION, LOCALISM, AND OTHER PROBLEMS

Hidden land may have been the problem with the most serious implications for central planning and control, but it was by no means the only stumbling block in local tax work. Ensuring the security of grain

---

50. For a description of how this was to be done by means of discussions "from bottom to top and from top to bottom," see *CCJP*, 28 Aug. 52 [112]. See also the lengthy discussion by Li Ch'eng-jui in *TKP*, 25 Mar. 53 [191].

51. See, e.g., *Ts'ai-cheng* no. 3 (1957) [356]; and *Ts'ai-cheng* no. 8 (1957) [64].

storehouses was another serious concern in the new territories. The burning of public granaries was particularly prevalent in the months immediately following liberation, but it continued sporadically at least throughout 1951. Counterrevolutionaries and other disgruntled villagers, bandits, and vandals robbed and burned local storehouses to steal supplies and frighten peasants who were cooperating with the revolutionary government. In the Central South, the provincial governments announced stiff penalties for saboteurs:

> Any person or persons who dare to lead the masses in a refusal of payment in kind, in the theft of public grain, destroying foodstuffs or disrupting communications, shall be sentenced to death without exception. Those who circulate rumors, stir up the people, disturb the social order, or violate the state's laws will be severely punished. Those who pillage or steal public grain, or adulterate it with sand or water or any other means, as well as those who intentionally employ delaying tactics in the payment in kind due, will be prosecuted in accordance with the law.[52]

People's Militia units were organized to protect local granaries and law-abiding villagers. Buildings chosen as storehouses were supposed to be easily defensible and have specially posted guards. In fact, however, there seems to have been a good deal of laxity in security precautions, leading to unnecessary losses. The authorities complained that some activists assigned to guard granaries thought there was no personal glory and no future in the work and failed to take it seriously. Some reportedly did not even know where their assigned granaries were located. And others, once they discovered a theft, were too frightened to inform their comrades that they had allowed it to happen, and therefore no better security measures were ever adopted.[53]

There was a general lack of attention to the problems of storage and accounting of public grain on the part of local cadres. Also, the close central supervision of local grain supplies was not necessarily a goal rural cadres were anxious to facilitate. The central leadership attempted to institute thorough and orderly reporting systems so that they could keep abreast of the situation regarding public grain.[54] But there simply

52. *SWB* 84 [514], p. 58 (also *FBIS* Wuhan, 17 Nov. 50). For reports of local acts of sabotage, see also *CCJP,* 6 Feb. 50 [61]; and *CCJP,* 14 Sep. 51 [357].

53. *CCJP,* 15 Feb. 51 [104].

54. *CCJP,* 14 Oct. 50 [76]. Here local cadres are ordered to make a report on the grain collection situation in their area to the special district level every ten days. The report is supposed to be written, but in case of special problems or difficulties they are urged to telephone or telegraph.

were not enough local cadres who could use an abacus, make calculations correctly, and keep the accounts straight. Winter investigations inevitably showed that the public granaries held quite different amounts of grain from the amounts originally reported.[55] Many of these cadres were also apparently inexperienced in inspecting and evaluating grain. Most peasants did not automatically send their best grain to the government tax collectors. Quite often, whether deliberately or inadvertently, the grain had not been dried properly or was infested with insects and molds. Cadres at the granaries failed to detect grain of poor quality and it was accepted and stored with good grain.[56]

Provincial governments ordered local grain storage cadres to take measures designed to mollify suspicious or angry tax-paying peasants. Cadres were to give peasants tea when they brought their grain to the storehouse, and also to help them find a place to stay overnight and make arrangements to feed their animals.[57] And by law peasants were to be reimbursed if it was necessary for them to travel over 100 *li* (about 31 miles) roundtrip to deliver their tax grain (1951 regulations, Article XXII). Despite the demonstrated concern of upper-level authorities, there continued to be sporadic reports of lower-level confusion and inefficiency that inconvenienced and annoyed tax-paying peasants. There were even cases of cadres at the granaries beating up peasants,[58] and there were some indications of conflicts between local cadres who were reluctant to hand over their village's grain and the cadres at the storehouses who were supposed to collect it.[59]

Added to these problems was a certain amount of plain corruption in the ranks of new local cadres. Some accepted bribes from villagers to lower their tax assessments. They also appropriated public grain to their own use or used it to make private loans at high interest rates.[60] The most common transgression, however, seems not to have been the acts of

55. *CCJP*, 14 Jan. 51 [116].

56. *CCJP*, 19 Aug. 51 [132], where it is reported: "This spring the protection of public grain work met with many difficulties. Everywhere the grain rotted and was infested with insects, largely because when it went into the storehouses it was not completely dry and the quality was low. Not enough attention was paid to investigating the quality of grain, and at the various levels of administration there was insufficient mass mobilization to get [peasants] to send in good grain."

57. *Ibid*.

58. See *CCJP*, 14 Sep. 51 [357].

59. *HPJP*, 16 Nov. 50 [392].

60. *CCJP*, 19 Aug. 50 [137].

selfish and corrupt individual cadres but rather an attitude of unthinking wastefulness and easy authorization of expenditures from public funds. Local cadres were admonished for using public money for building new office buildings when they might well have converted existing structures to their use; for buying more stationery and ink than they needed; for purchasing lamp oil to be used during nighttime meetings, when they might just as well have gathered in the daytime; and for employing a full-time cook at headquarters and giving themselves a diet superior to that of the local peasants, when they should have cooked for themselves and made do with the common fare.

The public money and grain wasted by cadres was usually not from the national granaries. It was collected as part of a surtax intended to finance local government operations. In 1949 cadres were authorized to collect a surtax of about 20 percent (see Table 18). That is, a surtax was to be levied on each household, not to exceed 20 percent of the household's total tax payment to the central government, the extra revenue to be used to cover local government expenditures. In 1950 the maximum allowable local surtax was reduced to 15 percent; it was raised to 20 percent again in 1951, and finally, in 1952, lower-level surtaxes were officially abolished altogether, although this apparently did not affect surtax collection by province-level governments. Until an efficient finance system could be strung from province to counties to subdistricts to villages, the use of a local surtax was probably the only realistic method of sustaining county, subdistrict, and *hsiang* government. As soon as the device could be dispensed with, it was abolished, to strengthen more centralized control over the disbursement of revenue and at the same time to diminish opportunities for petty corruption and misappropriation of funds.[61]

Cadres' corruption was an embarrassing problem for the revolutionary government. But far more grievous a problem was cadres' complicity in concealing land and evading taxes. It has already been noted that village cadres were not above concealing their own land, and many were also quite prepared to help other villagers conceal land. Some hoped to gain the goodwill of villagers by helping them to deceive the government.[62] Others did not want their village or hamlet to appear to be more

61. For discussions of the abolition of local surtaxes, see *CCJP*, 9 Aug. 52 [346]; and *CCJP*, 9 Aug. 52 [123]. For a report on attempts to eliminate the *ts'un* granaries in Hupei as early as 1951, see *CCJP*, 13 Jun. 51 [363].

62. *CCJP* editorial, 24 Oct. 52 [423]; and *CCJP*, 10 Oct. 52 [98].

wealthy than others for fear that this would bring suffering to their people.[63] This attitude among cadres was called by many names: "departmentalism" (*pen-wei chu-i*), "localism" (*ti-fang chu-i*), and "one-sidedly taking the mass viewpoint" (*p'ien-mien ti ch'ün-chung kuan-tien*). "Localist" cadres underestimated yields, made conservative production plans for the coming year, made sure that output did not appear to rise greatly from year to year, and applied for disaster relief for their villages whenever they could find an excuse. (This last they probably did less in the hope of actually receiving aid than of forestalling increases in their assigned tax quotas.) The deviation of "localism" was particularly difficult for upper-level cadres to isolate and eliminate in tax matters, because cadres and peasants tended to present a thoroughly united front against outside investigators. By the same token, county and district cadres were not entirely free of "localist" sentiment themselves. They hoped to keep their areas free of excessive taxation so as to have more local capital for investment and to earn the gratitude of their subordinates. This, in turn, did not make them the most enthusiastic of investigators. The middle and lower levels of the newly forming bureaucracy seem to have shared complicity in much early tax evasion.

Although "localism" was the more heavily criticized deviation, it was paired with an opposing tendency called "quota thinking."[64] Thinking only about fulfilling the quota that was handed down and not taking account of local conditions and peculiarities was judged to be just as mistaken as thinking that dwelt only on local peculiarities. "Quota thinking," unlike "localism," however, might result in either overly favorable or unfavorable treatment for the area concerned. Yet at the root of both deviations lay still another, which the authorities called "careerism." If some "quota thinking" cadres were merely lazy and trying to take the easiest way of doing a job, most seem to have been attempting to please their superiors by doing exactly what they were asked to do. "Localist" cadres, in contrast, apparently were hoping to build their careers by catering more to their constituency, the peasants, than to their superiors.

None of the government's tax-related problems described here were the sort to be solved in a matter of months or even years. Central authorities seem to have been well aware of this, and they had to be satisfied with only a gradual amelioration in the local-level tax collection

63. *Ibid.*   64. *SCMP* 213, 9–10 Nov. 51 [503], pp. 39–41.

capability, following on repeated training sessions, propaganda, education, and rectification efforts. There was a certain tolerance of the milder forms of localism, but sabotage, corruption, and dishonesty, in particular, were combatted with the usual mix of stiff penalties for serious offenders and education and rectification for the rest. The worst problems and deviations were recognized and brought under control in the early 1950's, but similar tendencies would reappear sporadically at times of strain in the future.

TAXATION AND THE CONSOLIDATION OF THE REVOLUTION

As this survey of agricultural tax policy and problems suggests, the revolutionary government's approach to taxing the peasantry proved to be not only an effective means of obtaining revenue to support itself but also a significant factor in the process of rural village transformation and the early consolidation of the revolution. Agricultural taxation was used before land reform to begin the redistribution of wealth, and it was used during and after land reform to assist in rejuvenating the rural economy, and to create a favorable environment for small peasant farming, trade, and investment.[65] The relative success of early tax policy implementation and of the elimination of tax evasion both considerably narrowed the credibility gap between peasants and government on tax matters for the first time in several generations, and also visibly reduced the opportunities for squeeze and corruption by local-level officials. In addition, however, it exposed peasants somewhat more directly than before to potential central demands, and made them therefore more sensitive than

---

65. The discussion here has been confined solely to the agricultural tax, but there were of course other forms of taxation to which peasants were often liable. Sales taxes levied on the marketing of goods and produce were probably the most significant of these. They had proliferated to such a degree under KMT and warlord governments that the CCP when it came to power regarded them as serious contributing factors in the rural economic depression and the constricted state of the domestic trade network. Efforts similar to those discussed here, to eliminate many of these extra taxes and to rationalize and build incentive systems around others, were made by the new central and provincial governments, apparently with a fair degree of success. But since many of these taxes fell within the purview of county and subcounty authorities, and since they were sometimes important local revenue sources and sometimes desirable tariff protections for local peasant traders, there were occasional reports of difficulty in enforcing these central reforms of subsidiary taxation in the very early years.

ever to tax cues as indicators of governmental intentions either to limit or to support improvements in family income. This is one reason why some fairly sustained and careful attention to implementation of the various tax incentive programs discussed here was to pay off in the short run in enhanced peasant confidence and ease of mind in responding to government assurances that they might truly "settle down and get rich" in the post-land-reform era.

But, as explained, central agricultural tax policy also made a contribution to the emergence of open class conflict in the villages. It emphasized class divisions within the community and involved a preliminary classification process placing each villager into one group or another. Then it prescribed measures for penalizing some groups and assisting others. While the tax regulations themselves never in any way justified open conflict or even hostility between classes, they accentuated class differences and the adversary relationship between rich and poor. Furthermore, the preeminent position given to the individual household in the implementation of tax policy contributed, as has been pointed out already, to the emphasis on class and class conflict by reducing somewhat the financial importance of larger kinship groups and other associations that might have tended to camouflage or even smother class hostility. And insofar as agricultural tax policy highlighted and promoted class conflict in the villages, it helped to create a revolutionary situation amenable to CCP organization and leadership.

The meetings, plans, and arrangements surrounding the assessment, collection, and delivery of tax grain also gave peasants some of their earliest opportunities to try to trust and rely on village cadres and the work team cadres. Not infrequently, of course, the corruption or incompetence of local cadres made villagers doubtful about their reliability. Generally, however, their tax work seems to have cast them in a reasonably good light. Only on the issue of drawing out concealed land was there a serious point of tension between cadres and peasants. But the concentration first on drawing out the hidden land of landlords and rich peasants only, and then the cadres' own "localist" deviation, did much in the early years to defuse that potential conflict. The tentative relationship of trust and interdependence that was to develop between cadres and peasants, partly as a result of their collaboration on tax matters, often actually became more robust than the central authorities would have wished.

In taxing agriculture, as in rent and interest reduction and in land reform, the Chinese leadership needed the cooperation of the mass of the peasantry, and it therefore designed its tax incentive programs to make it possible for peasants to pursue their own self-interest while working in concert with the government. The creation of this possibility did much to make rural tax work, even with all the qualifications mentioned here, reasonably successful. It also did much to legitimize the new government, to win support among peasants for more radical village transformation policies, to help consolidate the political as well as the economic gains of land reform, and to restore an atmosphere of normalcy and predictability in the villages consistent with the natural desire of peasants at that time to settle back to work.

As outlined in the next chapter, the revolutionary government went on to use similar material incentives and appeals to peasant self-interest to promote Mutual Aid Teams among the poor to further consolidate their economic and political gains from land reform. As with taxation, peasant and local cadre response was generally good. But before long, both programs were judged inadequate to the tasks of restraining the resurgent capitalist "rich peasant economy" and of preserving the *status quo* in rural wealth distribution patterns. A central decision would be made at the end of 1953 to supersede moderate policies like these with more vigorous and deliberate promotion of a transition to socialism in the countryside.

CHAPTER 4

Mutual Aid

The reform of the landholding system and of the rural taxation system accomplished a basic redistribution of the existing wealth and put an end to certain chronic forms of exploitation in peasant villages. These reforms did not, however, put an end to poverty. The small additional piece of land, the rake, or the part-interest in an ox a peasant household received in land reform was welcome and useful; but these things alone simply could not create prosperity where before there had been scarcity and suffering. The expropriation of landlords and the wider distribution of the ownership of the means of production sometimes even temporarily diminished the peasant's economic security rather than enhancing it. As a tenant farmer or hired hand, a peasant had generally enjoyed the use of the landlord's oxen and full complement of tools. During land reform, tools and oxen were dispersed, divided, and reallocated along with the landlords' land, many times leaving poor peasant households with more than they had owned before, but less directly available to their use. Similarly, the more equal distribution of investment capital made producers extraordinarily vulnerable. In times of natural disaster or calamity, for example, a rich peasant or wealthy landlord family with enough residual capital to make loans was in a position to rescue stricken neighbors, albeit at high rates of interest. But where no household had sufficient accumulated capital to survive the disaster and advance a loan, all were victimized and those who were hardest hit had no recourse.

As land reform was completed, the Chinese government's embryonic rural credit and loan apparatus and ambitious disaster relief programs were still inadequate. The industrial and handicrafts sectors of the economy were still disorganized and incapable of quick and cheap mass production and distribution of farm tools. And the total number of oxen and other draught animals was still far from sufficient. It was to cope with these continuing peasant difficulties that after land reform the central leadership immediately began to propagandize and to press for the establishment of Mutual Aid Teams (MATs) among poor and middle peasants.

The Mutual Aid Teams, as they were advocated by the central government, were to be extremely small and relatively informal groupings of peasant households, organized to make up for some of their deficiencies in means of production by exchanging labor and sharing tools and oxen.[1] Above all, Mutual Aid Teams were expected to help their members increase total agricultural production through sharing and more rationally utilizing their available resources. A rise in the actual crop yield of poor peasants would constitute the most direct and natural form of relief from poverty, raising members' incomes enough, it was hoped, to keep the gap between them and the richer villagers from widening rapidly. In addition, better crop yields would improve the supply of raw materials for industry and expand the purchasing power of the peasantry, thus creating a wider market for industrial products.

In spite of all the disorganization and the backwardness of Chinese agriculture, there was at this time an ebullient sense of optimism at the center about what could and would be accomplished in improving agricultural production technique and expanding total output. Many members of the leadership were encouraged and excited by the Soviet industrialization example, and there was much talk of tractors, chemical fertilizers, mechanization of agriculture, and electrification of the countryside in the official literature of the period. Occasionally in this literature there was also a tendency to speak grandiosely about the importance of rapid industrialization. Yet on the whole, the leadership, in comparing Chinese realities with Soviet experiences, realized that with no sizable agricultural surplus and with the population-land density so close to the subsistence margin in China, any industrialization strategy that ignored or depressed agricultural growth would be out of the question. Thus, while the CCP did wish to see China industrialize quickly and during the First Five-Year Plan period did pursue a

---

1. See *Mutual Aid and Cooperation in Agricultural Production* [26], pp. 21–32.

lopsided sectoral investment strategy, it did not consider enforcing a violently unpopular and precipitate agricultural collectivization drive like that of the Soviet Union earlier in the century.[2]

In the period right after land reform, the Party still regarded industrialization as the precondition of agricultural collectivization.[3] This conviction was reflected in First Five-Year Plan budget priorities. In a few years' time, when performance in agriculture clearly failed to meet their expectations, they were to reverse this view, then coming to see collectivization as the best route to turning out the agricultural surplus needed to spur industrialization and in turn, still further agricultural development. But in all their thinking, industrialization was always directly linked with continuous growth in agriculture and with improved standards of living for peasants. At no time did they entertain the possibility of squeezing the rural sector to the point where productivity and peasant incomes stagnated or fell, as had been the method of forced collectivization in the USSR. Collectivization would therefore have to be gradual so as to avoid alienation of the peasantry and the potential economic losses that would bring. The transition to socialism in the countryside was to proceed slowly, through several phases, and each step forward was to be predicated not only on an accomplished increase in productivity but also on an improvement in peasant welfare. As for the Mutual Aid Teams, they were to be the first modest step in organizing peasant farming, the first link in the chain of development toward socialism in the countryside.[4] Teng Tzu-hui explained it this way:

> The industrialization of the country demands a correspondingly swift development of agriculture. The swift advance of the development of agriculture demands that the existing scattered small farms, which use draught animals, are irrigated by manpower and use only natural fertilizers should step by step be replaced by large farms using machines for cultivation and irrigation and using chemical fertilizers. If we say that the existing small-scale commodity economy of individual peasants is

2. As Lippit [468], pp. 112–113, points out, although the state budget during the First Five Year Plan heavily favored industry over agriculture, the redistribution of land reform enabled peasants to make greater self-investments in their farms; thus gross investment in agriculture at this period was probably somewhat less markedly inferior compared to investment in industry than the Plan alone would indicate. Stavis [484], Ch. 3, provides a good discussion of Chinese thinking in the period on the relationship between agricultural collectivization and industrialization.

3. See Meisner [471], pp. 142 ff.

4. "Decisions on Mutual Aid and Cooperation . . . " [495], p. 3.

adapted to the use of draught animals, irrigation by manpower, and use of natural fertilizers, then the future big farms employing machines in cultivation and irrigation and using chemical fertilizers will naturally demand replacement of the present system of private peasant ownership by the system of collective peasant ownership, that is, the system of collective farm ownership.

The systematic carrying out of the socialist transformation of agriculture, as directed by Comrade Mao Tse-tung, means to gradually transform the present system of private peasant ownership of land and replace it, on a voluntary basis, by means of mutual aid teams and cooperatives, by collective peasant ownership of land.[5]

What were the advantages of Mutual Aid Teams expected to be, and how would they tend toward socialism? First, by sharing oxen and implements, peasants lacking some of the means of production would gain the benefits of their use, and total production would be increased. Poor peasants would be enabled to provide for themselves through cooperation with others and become productive taxpayers instead of a burden on the government's resources. Mutual aid was, in reality, a bootstrap operation intended to prevent poor peasants from going under. By keeping the poor afloat, mutual aid would help slow down the reemergence of what the Party regarded as capitalist class relationships in the villages. If a poor peasant family failed to make a go of it with what they were allotted during land reform, they might have to sell their land to someone with enough capital to buy it—probably a rich peasant; they would certainly have to take a personal loan at high interest from someone with enough capital to make loans—probably a rich peasant; and they might well need to hire one or more of themselves out to a family with more land than they could (or would) work themselves—probably a rich peasant family. The greater impoverishment of the poor would result in the further enrichment of the comparatively wealthy, and such a trend, if unchecked, would tend to recreate a rural class configuration that the government had taken pains to destroy, and the reemergence of which it was not prepared to tolerate.[6] The Mutual Aid Teams, it was hoped and expected, would bring poor peasants closer to self-sufficiency and solvency, and thus make them less dependent on the services of rich peasants and other potential capitalist exploiters.

5. "Basic Tasks and Policies in Rural Areas," in *Mutual Aid* . . . [474], pp. 29–30.

6. There was considerable disagreement and debate at the upper levels of Party and government, at this time, about the degree to which the emergence and development of a rural capitalist class could be tolerated if the transition to socialism were eventually to be

Second, even the limited and modest use of collective labor that could be expected in the Mutual Aid Teams was regarded as a means of improving labor discipline and cultivation techniques. Team members, since their livelihood depended at least to some extent on each other, would demand diligence and hard work from their fellows and be vigilant against slackers, incompetents, and shoddy work. All this would have its effect in increasing production and in demonstrating and propagandizing the benefits to be gained through collective labor. Able and experienced team members also would find it worth their while and in their own interests to teach the younger and less clever members special techniques likely to increase production. This greater dissemination of skills, along with a limited degree of division of labor, was confidently expected to result in more efficient and better trained farmers.

Third, the Mutual Aid Team, as it bought out members' implements and oxen and purchased new tools jointly, would be taking a step toward collective ownership of the means of production and the socialization of agriculture. And fourth, the very functioning of a Mutual Aid Team necessarily involved a certain amount of overall planning and coordination among households and individual members. This was expected to bring a new dimension to the organization of Chinese agriculture, and to help eventually in integrating the producers' tasks and needs with the requirements of state and cooperative distributors (particularly the growing network of Supply and Marketing Cooperatives). Production planning and organization in the Mutual Aid Teams would give team leaders practice and experience that would prepare them for the more elaborate organizational demands that would come with collectivization.[7] And with that experience, they could be brought somewhat more readily into conformity with government economic and agricultural policy than could scattered individual peasant households.

This, then, is essentially what was expected from the Mutual Aid

---

successfully carried out. Many high officials were convinced that a limited capitalist class would have to be tolerated if economic growth were to be maintained, until the broad masses could be thoroughly persuaded of the benefits of collectivism and socialism—a process they estimated might take several years. Even they, however, regarded any expansion of rural capitalism as basically reactionary, potentially very dangerous, and most assuredly temporary.

7. These four constitute by no means a complete list of the advantages claimed for and expected from Mutual Aid Teams. See also *CCJP*, 8 Apr. 52 [240]. Other interesting advantages claimed for MATs can be found, e.g., in *HHNP*, 16 Apr. 54 [256], in which large-scale mechanized farming is emphasized; and also *HHNP*, 19 Apr. 54 [255], which emphasizes expanded opportunities for credit arrangements within MATs.

Teams: a modest expansion of agricultural production; a certain (limited) resistance to capitalism and the "rich peasant economy"; and a generally more manageable, more easily led peasantry. The projected life span of the teams was a matter of considerable debate and disagreement within the Party. During land reform it had been widely held that once established, Mutual Aid Teams would stay in operation for several years—maturing, expanding, and gradually creating conditions for the transition to cooperatives and collectives. In the event, Mao Tse-tung and other top-level leaders soon came out in favor of stricter and speedier limitation of capitalist tendencies in the countryside and much more rapid collectivization. The Mutual Aid Teams were, by and large, superseded by co-ops after only a few seasons in operation. Despite their short official life span, however, these teams were a vital part of the early rural transformation and transition to socialism.

TRADITIONAL CHINESE FORMS OF MUTUAL AID

Mutual aid, exchanging labor, and sharing oxen and farm implements were ancient, not novel, ideas in peasant China. The development of mutual aid practices in traditional China could hardly be chronicled here, therefore, but it is possible to sketch some of the main features. These practices were the familiar ones with which the Party had to work. In mutual aid, as in taxation, the leadership adapted many old concepts to its purposes, consciously aiming to broaden and systematize them.

One of the most prevalent traditional forms of mutual aid was labor exchange. Trading work between households took several forms. The simplest of these was probably the arrangement in which Chang San worked one day on Li Ssu's land and was compensated by Li Ssu working one day on Chang San's land. In this straightforward trade, there was generally no adjustment made for any variation in strength or technical skill between the two farmers.[8] If one of the farming households requested more labor from the other than it could usefully return, it would frequently reimburse the other at the local rate for hired labor. Sometimes the repayment in labor or in kind was immediate; at other times accounts were squared three times a year, just before each of the primary festivals—the Dragon Boat Festival, the Mid-Autumn Festival, and the Spring Festival.[9]

Another sort of simple labor exchange took place between farmers

8. *HHNP,* 14 Apr. 54 [250].   9. *Ibid.*

and handicraftsmen in which the peasant helped cultivate the crafts-man's land in exchange for some goods, some carpentry work, or the like. There was also a system, however, according to which two days of agricultural labor were counted as equivalent to one day of handicraft work.[10] Accounts, again, were usually settled before the three festivals.

Still another type of labor exchange was frequently reserved for larger-scale or joint agricultural projects such as carrying mud for em-bankments, repairing dykes and roads, or repairing and operating water wheels. All the members of several households would pitch in on one project with less attention given to balancing the contribution of each against the others. If the project, when completed, would primarily ben-efit one of the households, then that family might provide food for all the helpers. If it was a project of benefit to all, then it was more likely that every helper would bring his or her own food and whatever tools they had that might be useful. In such projects, obviously, the labor power and tools contributed by different families could not always bal-ance out; yet the gain in speed or efficiency in completing the job might make the trade a reasonable one nonetheless. This group project ap-proach was sometimes employed during the busy seasons for planting and harvesting, especially perhaps when the weather was threatening, in an effort to save time. When the busy season was over or when the emergency passed, these labor exchange groups characteristically dispersed.[11]

The second important type of mutual aid involved the exchange of draught animal power. Probably the most common form of exchange occurred when a peasant family without an ox offered their own labor power as reimbursement to an ox-owner for temporary use of the ani-mal. Usually one day of work by an ox was considered to be equivalent to two days or one and a half days of work by a man. An ox-owning household would generally not rent out the ox to another until they them-

10. *Ibid.* See also *CCJP,* 11 Jun. 51 [379].
11. *Ibid.* See also *KJP,* 9 Oct. 54 [353]. Another form of mutual aid, which may be regarded as a variant of labor exchange, was *ta pao kung* — work for widows, the el-derly, the sick, orphans, and the very poor who were friends or neighbors. This basically charitable work was done voluntarily for a day or half-day, after the farmers had com-pleted their own work. The work was done without pay; usually but not always the laborers were given a meal in the recipient household. This type of mutual aid, like all the other forms of labor exchange mentioned here, was usually concentrated in planting, watering, and repairing irrigation dykes. See *HHNP,* 14 Apr. 54 [250].

selves had completed whatever task at hand required ox-power. Most often, apparently, the borrowers were responsible for feeding and caring for the ox while they employed it; the ox-owners, likewise, had to provide food for the borrowers when they came to work off the debt.[12]

Another common solution to the ox-shortage problem was referred to as "buying a share in an ox." The precise terms depended on the number and the means of the peasants involved, and on the going price of an ox. In one type of arrangement, Chang San would give Li Ssu one-quarter of the price of an ox, making it possible to make the purchase. This was called "buying one leg of an ox." Li would then take the full responsibility for feeding and sheltering the animal, allowing Chang the use of it only for ploughing, and perhaps also in emergencies. But Li, as the greater shareholder, was entitled to all the other uses of the ox-power, and would retain all the ox manure. Where no one peasant family could produce three-quarters of the price of an ox, several households would frequently pool their resources to make the purchase. Then, commonly, all the owning households would share the responsibilities of feeding and caring for the animal; and each would likewise have an equal claim on its use and to the manure. Sometimes, however, where contributions to the purchase price were not all equal, each household would provide fodder for the ox only in proportion to how large a share it had; and if one household were charged with sheltering the animal, it alone could collect and use the manure. There were several variations.[13]

As far as the loan of tools and implements was concerned, the exchanges seem to have been generally somewhat less formalized than the exchange of labor and oxen. Most farm implements could be borrowed and used without repayment. If a borrowed tool were damaged or broken, however, it was a matter of considerable embarrassment. In the borrowing and lending of some tools, small repayment or consideration of some sort was often expected. For instance, when using a water wheel owned by someone else, the borrower typically gave some *t'ung* oil to the owner afterward to oil the wheel.[14] Failure to make such a present to

---

12. *CCJP,* 11 Jun. 51 [379], and *ibid.*

13. *Ibid.* See also the report of the Huang-kang [Hupei] CCP Land Committee in *JMJP,* 11 Feb. 54 [310]. Sometimes, also, as with *ta pao kung* involving human labor power, ox-owners would allow poor households the use of the ox for ploughing *(ta niu hui),* as an act of charity and neighborliness.

14. *HHNP,* 14 Apr. 54 [250].

the lending household, while not strictly speaking a breach of faith, might well impair personal relations between the families.

All the foremost traditional modes of mutual aid were generally of a seasonal nature. They concentrated on planting, transplanting, harvesting, and fighting drought or other natural disasters. Except where there was joint ownership of oxen, mutual aid obligations were generally both contracted and fulfilled in a matter of days or weeks. The farmers evidently preferred it this way. After all, there were unwelcome risks involved in longer-term commitments. One family's ox might sicken and die, or a farmer's land might be flooded, washing away fertilizer and leaving the fields littered with debris. As long as the basic unit of production was the individual household, it was altogether safer and more prudent to make mutual aid arrangements when the relevant conditions were clear to all, and to conclude them before there was an opportunity for compromising situations to develop.

Similarly, traditional mutual aid arrangements were nearly always made between friends, close neighbors, or relatives; the trustworthiness and commitment of each participant in the arrangement was thus reinforced by already existing bonds of family relationship and friendship. In most cases mutual aid was carried out between farmers with adjoining fields and common dykes and irrigation ditches.[15] In many places an exchange of meals was almost always part of the agreement, and in this way a certain amount of social pressure was put on individual households; there was as a result some ostentation and unnecessary waste. But mutual aid was essentially voluntary, and except for irrigation projects and dyke repairs the agreements usually involved only two to five individuals. The scope for serious social pressures surrounding mutual aid was therefore rather limited. There was also no group leader or overseer in traditional mutual aid undertakings, and little elaborate planning. Each household evaluated and passed judgment for itself on the work accomplished by others, but there was little opportunity and no special mechanism for appeal in cases of dissatisfaction with their performance.

It should also be noted that by and large mutual aid was practiced by the poor and the relatively poor in the villages.[16] It was generally an *ad hoc* solution to some of their problems of selective deprivation. This is not to say that rich peasants and landlords did not participate in and sometimes even initiate similar sorts of exchanges. But if these arrangements involved a richer and a poorer household, quite often the

15. *Ibid.*   16. See Korkunov et al. [466], p. 14.

labor or the loan of the ox would be contributed by one side only and the debt would not be repaid immediately. Over time, these more unequal relationships could come to resemble the cultivation of patron-client ties rather than mutual aid deals between equals. It was poorer peasants who relied on the genuine mutual aid arrangements most heavily and used them most frequently.

MUTUAL AID TEAMS AS OFFICIALLY ADVOCATED

Even a brief survey of the types of Mutual Aid Teams promoted by the revolutionary government in the early 1950's reveals a deliberate Party effort to assimilate and adapt traditional modes of mutual aid.[17] For example, Party planners insisted that the teams be kept small, resisting the tendency in some areas to enlarge them to anywhere from thirty to sixty individuals. Such overblown organizations were said to be too hard to manage efficiently or equitably.[18] And if a team were to outgrow its management capacity, attempting too many projects simultaneously, it risked disillusionment, failure, and ultimately collapse. The varying conditions in different areas of China evidently precluded any hard and fast limits on team size, but in the beginning for the Central South at least the recommendation was from three to five households per team.[19] In this respect, rural planners were certainly not overly ambitious.

The Party and government were likewise, as a matter of policy, content to allow Mutual Aid Teams to form around kinship groups, as they had in the past.[20] Friends and neighbors, households that had agreed to labor exchange relations in the past, and most particularly peasants who shared embankments and irrigation ditches and who labored in adjoining fields were encouraged to form Mutual Aid Teams together. In droughts and heavy rains, farmers with shared irrigation systems would not be tempted to run off to tend to their own fields as were team members whose fields were far apart. And the hope was that if people already knew and trusted one another, they would be more apt to cooperate successfully. Such existing relationships may just as well have been flawed by old resentments and hostilities, but it was thought better to

17. *JMJP,* 11 Feb. 54 [310]; and *HHNP,* 14 Apr. 54 [250].
18. *CCJP,* 11 Jul. 51 [372].
19. *CCJP,* 11 Jun. 51 [379]. See also *CCJP,* 13 Jun. 51 [187].
20. *CCJP,* 11 Jul. 51 [380]. For some evidence that teams in the Central South were frequently organized "with the well as the unit" see also *JMJP,* 5 Jul. 52 [92].

begin by relying on them than to try to create other artificial groupings. Also the leadership was prepared, at least for the time being, to allow mutual aid to retain its traditional seasonal nature. Although their goal from the start was for Mutual Aid Teams ultimately to function all year round, official policy maintained that team members should not be forced to cooperate every day or in every task. Although the seasonal Mutual Aid Team was only step one in a long and difficult transition process, leading officials scolded the impatient ones who wanted to skip over it without regard to the peasants' sentiments. They advocated temporary concessions to the peasants' reluctance to overcommit themselves.

> It is wrong to belittle this elementary form of mutual aid, which has the possibility of being accepted at the present time by the broad masses of the peasants, or to refuse to give active leadership in its promotion on the ground that such temporary, seasonal exchange of labor cannot be regarded as mutual aid and that only year-round mutual aid teams can be regarded as such.[21]

The announced goal of the central authorities, however, was to establish the year-round type of Mutual Aid Team everywhere, as soon as peasants would agree to them. During the slack seasons these teams, unlike the seasonal teams, would cooperate in sideline production ventures. Most sideline production, or small cottage industries, had traditionally been confined to individual households in rural China. By joining together in teams, it was hoped, production, efficiency, and peasant income might all rise, as the availability of sideline products in the countryside also generally improved. There were some sideline occupations the government did not wish to promote, such as the making of joss sticks and other articles of a religious or superstitious nature. But there were many cottage industries that commerce and trade authorities were anxious to see enlarged, such as weaving fishnets, baskets, and mats; processing tea and sugar cane; brick making; and incubating and candling chicken and duck eggs.[22]

Year-round Mutual Aid Teams were also desirable because their more

21. "Decisions on Mutual Aid and Cooperation . . . , " [495], pp. 7–8. See also *CCJP,* 11 Jun. 51 [379].

22. There were some full-time hatcheries in operation in rural areas, but for an account of the incubation method involving fishnets and barrels of warm rice that could be practiced by individual peasant households, see Phillips et al. [478], pp. 151–153 and p. 158.

varied and longer-term undertakings would necessitate some simple but joint household production planning, as well as a certain degree of division of labor, both steps tending toward agricultural collectivization. Technical improvements were considered more probable under these conditions, and the greater accumulation of capital expected in year-round teams would make possible more joint purchases of farm tools and oxen. The accumulation of commonly owned property was regarded as one of the important steps leading to full collective ownership of all the means of production. For all these reasons, therefore, year-round Mutual Aid Teams were deemed more efficient and progressive than seasonal teams. After only one or two years of seasonal cooperation, propaganda, preferential financing, and the successes of model year-round teams were expected to induce seasonal teams to make the transition to full-time cooperation and more systematic coordination.

In official policy on Mutual Aid Teams, there were other similar concessions to the conservatism and the reservations of the peasants in order to get at least some elementary teams established and functioning. One of the more conspicuous temporary concessions came on the issue of female participation in team work. The Party openly favored women's full participation in agricultural labor and equal compensation for equal work. But traditionally, in some parts of China, women's participation in agricultural work was the exception rather than the rule. In many of these places women undeniably made a significant contribution to the family income through sideline occupations. But in the original seasonal Mutual Aid Teams, as noted, sideline production was left outside the realm of cooperation. It follows, therefore, that women were generally denied membership in the teams, at least in the beginning.[23] The decision not to press for women's assimilation immediately was a conscious policy designed to keep the Mutual Aid Teams as similar as possible to the old forms of mutual aid. The leadership had every intention of fully integrating women into the rural labor force, both as a matter of social equality and as part of the effort to increase agricultural output. But, since it touched on very deep-seated emotions and beliefs, the principle was not forced for the time being, in the interest of avoiding unnecessary friction.

From these examples it should be clear that, as a matter of policy, Party leaders were intent on building the new Mutual Aid Teams on the

23. See *CCJP*, 13 Jun. 51 [187].

existing, customary foundations. Nevertheless, they did not hesitate to introduce some modifications if they judged most peasants would accept them. One such innovation was to emphasize that each team should have a leader *(tsu-chang)* chosen from among its members. The team leader was ultimately responsible for all the activities of the team, for arranging its work, for seeing that it met its obligations to the government, the People's Bank, or the Supply and Marketing Cooperative, as well as for keeping track of the labor exchange situation among members. The *tsu-chang* did not necessarily have to be a cadre or even an activist, but he was supposed to have good political consciousness and be responsive to the leadership of cadres and activists. Even more important than this, however, he was supposed to possess good production skills and personal qualities. It was imperative for the success of the Mutual Aid Team that he be respected as a man and as a worker. The quality of the leadership of the *tsu-chang* was evidently considered to be the most critical factor in the success or failure of a Mutual Aid Team.[24] It appears that no Mutual Aid Teams were officially formed without designating a team leader, and teams were generally distinguished and referred to by the name of the *tsu-chang*. Later, when Agricultural Production Cooperatives were formed, they received names like "Red Star Co-op" and "Eternal Prosperity Co-op." But at the time of mutual aid, the references were more prosaically and personalistically to "Li Ching-ho's Team" and "Wang Ch'eng-ming's Team."

A second important CCP modification of traditional mutual aid practices was the introduction of a simple workpoint system for measuring and keeping track of work done and compensation due within each team. In traditional forms of mutual aid, informal labor-day trade-off systems had, as explained, already been in use. But government policy required more sensitive, more flexible systems, and conscientious record keeping. The concept of a point system seems in itself to have been generally acceptable to peasants.[25] But as shown below, considerable confusion

24. *CCJP,* 14 Apr. 52 [376]. See also *CCJP,* 11 Jul. 51 [380].

25. There were naturally exceptions to this generalization. The *Yangtze Daily* reported that occasionally when a team was organized around a core of households with family relationships, they would be hesitant to adopt a point system. If their relations were good to begin with, they felt that they could work out exchanges and compensation informally among themselves, without the explicit and potentially conflict-laden application of a regularized system. In such cases, it was reported that local cadres had to exert themselves in persuading the team members to adopt a workpoint system, and once

and resistance were often still encountered in implementing detailed team workpoint systems. Nevertheless, government policy was firm on the matter of a fair and comprehensive labor calculation system designed to keep exchanges balanced and equitable and to prevent the serious exploitation of some team members by others. And this carried with it a certain routinization and regularization and a certain explicitness and publicity that were not characteristic of traditional peasant mutual aid and labor exchange arrangements.

Central policy on Mutual Aid Teams advocated several other innovations and modifications, although these were less vigorously pursued. Each team was encouraged, for example, to draw up an overall seasonal production plan with estimates of the work time required for the various tasks and the amount of seed and fertilizer needed. All internal questions were supposed to be submitted for open and democratic discussion and decision by team members, with regular times set aside for raising grievances. As for joint purchases or other responsibilities undertaken by the team as a whole, it was urged that the contributions of member households toward purchase and maintenance be assessed in proportion to the grain yield of the land they owned. This principle in particular was probably honored more in the breach, since members often preferred more flexible arrangements. Poorer households were frequently willing to put more than their share toward the purchase price of an ox if the other members would allow it all the manure rights, and so on.

As already indicated, government policy did call for gradual expansion of the scale and the scope of mutual aid. It was to be extended to include sideline production as well as agriculture, and the teams were to become permanent, year-round, and gradually larger, both through merger and through the assimilation of more and more independent farm-

---

they had adopted it, to abide by it. See *CCJP,* 11 Jul. 51 [380]. An interesting further complication sometimes developed when teams adopted a workpoint system for some tasks but not for others. An amusing report from Hunan describes a team, complete with workpoint system, that decided to build some new houses by joint effort. At first they declared they would not keep any account of which members chipped in on the work, saying that they could depend on good feelings *(kan-ch'ing)* and that it would not be friendly to keep records. But then some families started sending only women and children to do the house building because they earned relatively few workpoints on regular tasks. Finally relations became so bad within the team over this issue that they decided to assign workpoints for house building as for other tasks. Thus, the adoption of workpoint systems may sometimes have injured friendly relations among members and other times have helped to preserve them. See *CCJP,* 10 Oct. 51 [129].

ers. Furthermore, with very few exceptions,[26] every village in the later liberated areas was supposed to have several Mutual Aid Teams functioning within a year or two after the completion of land reform. The struggle and mutual suspicion, as well as the expropriation and reallocation of property during land reform, had undermined, disrupted, or made obsolete a great many existing mutual aid arrangements. Quick reestablishment and development of peasant mutual aid patterns was, therefore, not only important for furthering the revolution but also for the basic recovery and growth of agricultural production.

However rapid and all-encompassing the mutual aid movement was meant to be, there were some people in the villages who were not supposed to be eligible for team membership, and others who were to be permitted to join but not to enjoy the full rights and privileges of membership. The Party had developed a distinct class policy regarding Mutual Aid Teams, although it was neither so strict nor so subtle as the class policy enunciated for the land reform movement. This class policy proved very difficult to carry out, but it sheds considerable light on the way in which the CCP viewed the purposes and functions of the Mutual Aid Teams in the transition period. In particular it demonstrates the sensitivity of the Chinese leadership to the possibility that traditional hierarchical or dependency relationships could reemerge in the guise of mutual aid.

Former landlords were totally barred from team membership. Since most landlords were living in the villages, in reduced circumstances, under close "supervision" by their government, denied their citizens' rights, and under notice that they should earn their own living by farming, it was at least arguable that admission to Mutual Aid Teams might have assisted them in their "reform through labor." But this suggestion was brushed aside with the assertion that the reform of landlords and

26. National minority areas and mountainous Han areas were often exceptions. In national minority areas, the slower development seems to have been largely attributable to an insufficient number of local cadres and to cultural differences and communication problems. In mountainous areas, on the other hand, difficulties in pressing for mutual aid involved the backwardness in the mode of agricultural production. Where there were fewer irrigation ditches, embankments, and water wheels, and where farming families lived at greater distances from one another, it was definitely more difficult for MATs to take root. See, e.g., *HHNP*, 2 Jun. 54 [171]. In describing one mountain village in Hunan it is here explained that until a few months previously there was only one MAT in the entire *hsiang*. At the time the report was written, 51 percent of the families were said to be organized into teams. See also *JMJP*, 27 Oct. 53 [445].

other bad elements was simply not the function of Mutual Aid Teams, which were organizations for increasing the productive power of laboring peasants. Furthermore, Mutual Aid Teams were to have some powers—to grant loans and awards and to manage their affairs by democratic discussion and equal participation—that were not powers legally available to landlords. Former landlords were still officially blamed for sabotage and continuing instances of agitation against the government. Under these circumstances it was held to be possibly extremely harmful to the consolidation of teams to allow landlord elements to join.

Rich peasants also were barred from joining Mutual Aid Teams, as a further step in maintaining and broadening the village class struggle. The teams were viewed as labor organizations based on the principle of voluntarism and mutual benefit. Within such organizations, the exploitation of hired labor, which was associated with the rich peasant class and which was deemed neither voluntary nor mutually beneficial, could not be permitted. Even the Mutual Aid Team, as an organization, was itself not permitted to hire long-term labor for cultivating its land; this was intended as a precaution against development of the team along capitalist lines rather than along socialist lines, and against the possibility that team members could become a new exploiting class in the villages rather than standard bearers in the march toward cooperatives.

There is implied here an undeniably marked change in the official attitude and policy toward rich peasants. As recorded in Chapter 2, throughout land reform the official policy toward rich peasants had been to "neutralize" them in the struggle against the landlords by guaranteeing them a certain amount of protection against expropriation. At that time the "rich peasant economy" was to be encouraged—the term became quite respectable. And there was even a strain in the propaganda of the period indicating that after the land had been redistributed, all peasants would have the opportunity to "settle down and get rich," that is, to become rich peasants themselves. If the change in policy toward rich peasants after land reform was not unexpected, it was certainly abrupt. Now when Teng Tzu-hui spoke of the rich peasant economy, he expressed the new line in these words: "permitting the existence of the rich peasant economy but restricting its development."[27]

Rich peasants were excluded from mutual aid since they represented

27. "Basic Tasks and Policies in Rural Areas," in *Mutual Aid* . . . [474], p. 34.

the spontaneous capitalist tendencies in the villages; the "rich peasant economy" was a petty capitalist economy, and it ran counter to the thrust toward rural socialism. Rich peasants themselves were clearly under no immediate threat of expropriation; the government did not even express any desire to destroy them as a class. On the contrary, until the cooperative economy could be fully developed, there were certain useful economic functions that, for practical purposes, only rich peasants could perform in the villages. It was becoming clear, however, that rich peasants were not officially going to be permitted to make any significant personal financial progress. This was just the beginning of a period during which the possibilities for economic advancement open to rich peasants were to be severely circumscribed. The promise of a chance to "settle down and get rich," it was becoming apparent, was to be extended only to poor and middle peasants. For rich peasants getting richer was not yet impossible, but it was going to become more and more difficult.

Rich peasants were not even supposed to organize Mutual Aid Teams among themselves. They were permitted to join together for production, but as a matter of policy they could not apply the name "Mutual Aid Team" to their organizations since this would "sow confusion" about the true nature of the teams. In reality, it was said, rich peasants' teams were partnerships for the exploitation of hired labor and not mutual aid organizations at all. Because the relationship between the rich peasant and the hired peasant was that of employer and employee, or exploiter and exploited, it was fundamentally not a relationship of mutual aid and cooperation, and it would not do to call it that.

It was allowable for a rich peasant to hire a Mutual Aid Team member, if all members of the team had discussed the matter and agreed to it. But since the rich peasant employer might well try to persuade the employee to leave the Mutual Aid Team by raising his wages, letting him have the use of an ox, or by some other personal promise, a close watch was to be kept on the economic relationships between rich peasants and team members.

This aspect of the mutual aid class policy, not surprisingly, raised a number of interesting difficulties. First, poor and middle peasants were often anxious to have rich peasants join their team so that they would have the opportunity to share their tools and oxen. Team members were generally quite prepared to overlook the rich peasant's uncongenial habit of employing hired hands. This phenomenon was so frequent, in fact, that the government was forced to make an uncomfortable compromise on the matter. If the other team members really wanted rich peasants to remain so that they would have the use of their tools and animals, it could be allowed; but these teams must, in other respects, be quite strong and purposeful, and the rich peasants must not be permitted to serve in any team leadership capacity. Such an arrangement, although certainly not wholly satisfactory, was apparently considered preferable to other methods of bending the rules that were in use. Sometimes, for example, rich peasants had ceased hiring labor in order to qualify for Mutual Aid Team membership. Their larger farms and comparative wealth almost guaranteed them a dominant position, once in the teams, and it was feared that they would use this power to distort the team's workpoint system in their favor. It is easy to imagine how one or two rich peasants, without determined opposition, might convert a Mutual Aid Team into a cheap source of labor for the cultivation of their own surplus land. To put limits on this, the government preferred to authorize rich peasant team members to keep their outside hired hands while instructing other team members to prevent rich peasant leadership or domination of the group. This, it was hoped, would give to poorer peasants the use of rich peasant property that they wanted, without exposing them to easy capitalist exploitation.[28]

Despite all these official restraints, many rich peasants were still able to prosper, for a time, through good fortune, the reluctance of local cadres to enforce some of the rules, or their own private credit and loan activities. It was not until 1956 and the countrywide whirlwind establishment of higher-level Agricultural Production Cooperatives that the "rich peasant economy" was actually decapitated.

Rich peasants and landlords were not alone in being officially excluded from Mutual Aid Teams. All small rentiers, whether capable of work or not, who lived on rents and did not engage in labor were not

28. It may be wondered what would induce a rich peasant to join a Mutual Aid Team under such terms. The government-sponsored favorable credit and marketing arrangements (most often available to teams and not to independent farmers) must at least partly explain why rich peasants were sometimes willing. Also, there is no doubt that many rich peasants feared that unless they voluntarily shared some of their property with poor peasants, it would be taken from them by force, as with the landlords before them. During and after land reform there were constant rumors of a coming second great struggle and redistribution. Many rich peasants hoped that a helpful and cooperative attitude toward government policy and their poorer neighbors, even if not in their immediate interest, might serve to spare them from a worse future.

permitted to participate. It was held that the collecting of rent or the paying of wages by small rentiers within the Mutual Aid Teams would not have been consistent with the mutually benefiting principle of exchange of equal value *(teng-chia chiao-huan)* that underlay team membership. Simply relying on rent and not doing labor would distort the nature of the teams. As for army and martyrs' dependents, orphans, widows, and other special categories of people who were classed as small rentiers, their difficulties were considered to be ultimately a matter for the socialized economy to settle. It was simply not held to be rational to put the burden of these people onto the Mutual Aid Teams, which were to be profit-making organizations of peasant agricultural labor, not organizations of socialized economy. Small rentiers who were lacking labor power would, as a rule, have to continue renting their land or hiring laborers to till it for a while longer. Individual tenant farmers working the land of a small rentier, however, if they were joining a Mutual Aid Team, were generally allowed to carry the rented land in with them. Thus, some of the land of a small rentier might be worked collectively by the members of a team. Similarly, a year-round team (but not a seasonal or temporary one) was officially permitted to rent land to be cultivated collectively by team members from a small rentier. This was especially useful to teams with a surplus labor problem, and it provided another way in which the difficulties of small rentiers might sometimes be alleviated by Mutual Aid Teams, even without their own direct participation in them.[29]

This then was the Mutual Aid Team as the Party wished it to be. Resembling traditional forms of mutual aid very closely in the beginning, the teams were to become gradually more responsive to govern-

29. Most other classes of villagers were to be absorbed into Mutual Aid Teams, including former urban workers and poverty-stricken people who had fled the cities before land reform and who had received a share of land, vagabonds or itinerants who were willing to work and be reformed, former KMT or warlord officers and soldiers, reformed bandits, former bureaucrats and *pao* chiefs, members of reactionary parties or leagues, and members of Taoist sects, if they repented after liberation and no longer took part in counterrevolutionary activity. All these people might join, with the consent of the other team members, and they were entitled to all the rights and privileges of ordinary members. This discussion of class policy for MATs is based heavily on "Questions and Answers about Several Labor Mutual Aid Policy Problems," in *Reference Material . . .* [330], pp. 15–20. See also "Decisions on Mutual Aid and Cooperation . . ." [495], *passim.*

ment leadership. Their internal organization was to become more highly structured and the division of labor was to be more rational and efficient, as well as fair. Finally, they were to follow a strict class policy in order to conform to the Party's principles for the transition to socialism, restraining the growth of the "rich peasant economy," while at the same time remaining flexible and inclusive enough to make a broad and positive impact on the development of agricultural production. The following sections will now explore various obstacles encountered in the effort to create the Mutual Aid Teams of Hunan and Hupei in this image.

WORKPOINTS

Within the Mutual Aid Team, each household retained full and private ownership of its land and of all that its land could produce. The operation of teams involved no transfers of ownership or wealth. On the contrary, households with more fertile land or with better irrigation systems were expected to produce and consume more than other less fortunate households in the team. The purpose of the teams was merely to raise the productivity and thus the security of each member household, and to help it avoid incurring new indebtedness by sharing and using more efficiently the available means of production. In theory, if one team member worked as much on other members' land as they worked on his, they would owe each other nothing in the end, and each household would keep what it harvested. In reality, however, some households required more assistance from other members than they could return in kind; others had oxen and tools to loan but could not use efficiently a commensurate amount of labor by others in repayment. Furthermore, one day's work by one peasant was not always equivalent to one day's work by another, due to differences in skill, experience, health, and attitude. While it may have been feasible and even functional to overlook such imbalances in the quality of different villagers' work in the context of traditional temporary mutual aid arrangements, they could not be tolerated in long-term cooperation without gross unfairness and resulting friction and disillusionment. It was absolutely necessary, if Mutual Aid Teams were to be kept going, that a more flexible means of calculating labor exchanges to take account of these disparities among members be brought into general use. Therefore, while seasonal teams were officially permitted to preserve the most simplistic traditional day-for-day labor exchange practices, the year-round or permanent Mutual Aid Teams were each to devise a more sensitive workpoint system of its own to facilitate fair and accurate exchanges among members.

It was around these workpoint systems and other workpoint-related issues that most of the internal politics of teams revolved. Whereas mutual aid had generally previously been confined to a limited number of exchanges with traditionally agreed forms of repayment that would have involved a loss of face in cases of nonfulfillment, now in year-round teams there were to be scores of additional tasks taken on with no traditional exchange rates for guidance. Most peasants appear to have assumed that others would naturally try to cheat them, and even the more sophisticated workpoint systems adopted were subject to abuse by selfish members, so there was often interminable bickering and maneuvering over workpoint assignments within teams.

In most cases it fell to the team leader to decide how to settle disputes. And as these people had often been chosen for their knowledge of the land and not for their political and bargaining skills, the members were frequently dissatisfied. Families dropped out of teams, and quite often in the immediate post-land-reform period, whole teams collapsed. Political activists helped out with team affairs when they could, but since they were usually younger peasants, and away from the fields a good deal of the time anyway, their opinions on workpoint-related issues were not always well respected by other members. Because the teams were numerous and small in size, county and *hsiang* officials, who were in any case preoccupied with other tasks in 1952–53, could not have spread themselves thinly enough to provide adequate political and administrative leadership for all of them.

The workpoint systems finally devised for year-round Mutual Aid Teams varied considerably. Where labor power was scarce it naturally received a high valuation, but where it was plentiful land and implements counted for more. The number of oxen available, the need for certain sorts of skilled labor, the type of crop to be planted, all varied from village to village, and the assignment of values to different kinds of work (and of property) necessarily varied as well.[30] Generally speaking, however, there were five distinct but overlapping aspects to the work-

30. An excellent survey of workpoint systems in use in one Hupei county is contained in "Fundamental Systems of Agricultural Production Mutual Aid Teams in Yao-shui County," in *Reference Material* . . . [168], pp. 66–74. Much of the information in the following discussion is drawn from this survey.

point system of a well-organized Mutual Aid Team: (1) the system of evaluating and calculating work; (2) the system of recording work done and of settling accounts; (3) the wage standard, or more precisely the determination of the real value of a workpoint; (4) the exchange system applicable to draught animals and farm implements; and (5) the system for arranging and coordinating work to be done.[31] These five can be dealt with in turn.

Evaluation and Calculation of Work

There were several recognized systems of evaluating and calculating work. The first was to assign points according to days worked *(i jih chi)*. This was the traditional system to which most peasants were accustomed. If one man worked one day, he was credited with one *kung* (standard labor-day value, consisting of ten *kung-fen* or workpoints); if a woman or a child rated as one-half labor power worked one day, he or she was credited with one-half *kung*. No other distinctions were made concerning the comparative strength or technical abilities of team members. This system was frowned upon officially, since lazy and inept members could readily earn as much as hardworking and highly-skilled members. This would tend to discourage the better workers, and their resentment might eventually lead them to withdraw from the team unless the system were rectified. (As we shall see, the new government always preferred workpoint arrangements that included incentives for hard work and high productivity.) Teams were nevertheless permitted to adopt this calculation procedure in the beginning.

A second system involved dividing the day into parts *(i shih chi)*, with a specified number of workpoints *(kung-fen)* assigned for work during the different parts of the day. The division was usually into early morning, mid-morning, and afternoon, and the points distributed among the three periods would generally add up to ten for a full day's work. A team member was thus credited with the appropriate number of points for the part of the day worked. This method was considered to be more flexible than the first since it allowed tasks that only took part of a day to complete to be included in the mutual aid work. Apparently, several different variations of this system were quite popular in the first stage of year-round Mutual Aid Teams. They still, however, did not take into account

---

31. In Chinese terminology, these are: (1) *p'ing-kung, chi-kung chih-tu;* (2) *chi-kung, chieh-chang chih-tu;* (3) *kung-tzu piao-chun;* (4) *keng-niu, nung-chü hu-li huan-kung chih-tu;* and (5) *p'ai-kung chih-tu.*

differences in the quality of work performed by different members, and therefore offered no incentive for superior work.

A third system *(p'ing-fen huo-chi)* represented a significant departure since it assigned points not to time consumed but to tasks to be done. Every day the jobs to be done would be discussed by the members, and each job would be assigned a number of workpoints. Members would either volunteer for or be assigned to the different jobs for the day. After the work was completed, each member's performance would be appraised by the others. If the job had not been done satisfactorily that member would not be credited with all the workpoints specified for it; and if the job had been done exceptionally well, the member would be credited with bonus points. This was hailed as a "scientific method" greatly to be encouraged because it would raise "production enthusiasm" in the teams. In other words this method incorporated incentives for doing good work and disincentives for doing shoddy work, and in this respect it was superior to the other two. But it was also recognized that such a daily procedure was not only difficult to carry out— involving as it did a great deal of extra discussion, work, and trouble— but also potentially divisive. It might well make it necessary for all team members (including perhaps even those who had not that day engaged in any mutual aid work) to make the rounds from field to field together every evening, checking on the work of each of the others.

A fourth system *(ssu-fen huo-chi)* involved assigning points to the worker rather than to the work. This is the method apparently officially promoted for general use in advanced and mature Mutual Aid Teams, and it was said to have evolved in teams with prior experience in the *i shih chi* method. Typically, a standard minimum number of workpoints would be assigned to each working member of the team for a day of work, and then each day's work would be evaluated by the others and an adjustment in the actual points credited to the worker might then be made. Ten workpoints for a full day's work were usually to be assigned to a robust member, and unless an unusually sloppy job was done, that member could count on earning ten points for every day of mutual aid labor. A youth of sixteen might be assigned only seven workpoints for a full day's labor; and an old or weak member might be rated from three to eight points, depending on the extent of his or her infirmity as judged by the others. After each day's labor, the work of the members was to be evaluated, taking into consideration the length of time put in on the job, the technical skill that the worker brought to the task, and the apparent over-all quality of the work done. Points could either be added to or subtracted from the individual worker's standard minimum and then recorded.

There was a common variation of this system of which the government generally disapproved. In it, not only a member's strength and health but also his or her technical ability as judged by the other members was taken into consideration in assigning the individual a standard minimum number of workpoints for a day's work. Then, in evaluating the work each day, *only* the member's diligence and the time spent on the job were generally taken into account, a measure for quality having already been made. This would seem to be a perfectly reasonable system, and perhaps even a more subtle and fairer system than the original. But in practice, apparently, it led to several undesirable results. First, there must seldom if ever have been a peasant who was genuinely and clearly superior in all aspects of farm work. A farmer who could hoe a field quickly and thoroughly was not necessarily any better than others at carrying mud with the shoulder pole; nor was the master of the ox and plough necessarily also the best at transplanting rice. To rate a person higher than others because of a particular talent or skill was to overpay that individual for the days of work that did not require the use of that special skill. Inflated standard minimum figures for some members naturally caused resentment among other members and threatened the solidarity of the team.[32] Second, this system removed any incentive that might have existed for members to improve their technical skill and performance on the job. If they might earn extra points for trying to better their technique, it was considered far more likely that they would do so than if the matter of their technical capability had already been settled and could not change their income. These were serious drawbacks, and the first type of *ssu-fen huo-chi* was officially preferred. *Ssu-fen huo-chi* was definitely considered to be superior to *p'ing-fen huo-chi* because it was more settled and, it was said, better able to take special

---

32. It seems reasonable to suppose that a way out of this difficulty could have been found by rating each member for each job—the same peasant might then be assigned a standard minimum of five workpoints for a day of weaving fishnets, ten workpoints for a day of spreading fertilizer, and so on. Such a solution was evidently considered to be far too troublesome and complex by most peasants, however, because it does not appear to have been tried often. Such a procedure might have required trial runs and competitions that would have consumed valuable time, perhaps been inconclusive, and even led to quarrels and bitterness.

circumstances into account. It also provided a way to absorb all types of labor power into the team, including, for example, the labor power of children, women, and old people.[33]

A fifth common workpoint system was sometimes referred to as a "piecework" method *(i chien chi-kung)*. Under this system, a given task would be isolated, considered, and assigned a total number of workpoints. Then any group of team members wanting to work together on the job would undertake to complete it. No matter how many persons worked on the job and no matter how much time they consumed, the designated number of workpoints would be credited to the group when they completed the task, and they were to divide the points fairly among themselves. This system was considered especially appropriate for the busy seasons. It made the calculation of workpoints easier, and it clearly provided an incentive for members to work quickly and efficiently. In this respect it solved the most serious deficiency of the *i shih chi* method, by which members were paid primarily according to the amount of time they put in on a job. But it was emphasized that before a Mutual Aid Team decided to adopt this system, it should make sure that all its members really understood and wanted it. And then there should be careful supervision so that members would not let the quality of their work slip in their haste to earn more points. There is ample evidence from reports throughout the mutual aid movement that whenever the quality of work performed was not closely keyed to workpoints received, peasants tended to neglect quality in mutual aid projects, and this endangered overall productivity.

It should also be pointed out that these five systems did not by and large apply to the important matter of calculating women's labor in the Mutual Aid Teams, for which separate standards were usually devised. One fairly frequent practice seems to have been to assign women three or five points for a day's work on any project across the board where the normal rate for men was ten points. This system rested on the simple assumption made by many that no women's work could be of any great value. Sometimes local or county cadres would protest to the teams that this system was both unrealistic and unfair. It was not unusual for the team to respond by seeming to capitulate—nine or ten workpoints would be assigned to women for a day's work, exactly the same number as to an average male member. But when it was time to settle the ac-

33. For another account of *ssu-fen huo-chi* in Hupei, see *CCJP,* 14 Apr. 52 [376].

counts it turned out that each "workpoint" the women had earned was only worth one-half or one-third of the workpoints the men had earned. The women were being compensated at the same low rate as before, despite appearances to the contrary.[34]

The official goal was equal pay for equal work, but it was admitted that in practice this was rarely found. Although the matter was not pushed especially hard, some Mutual Aid Teams did evolve a sort of piecework system for women's subgroups within the team that was at least somewhat more equitable than the across the board assignation of low numbers of workpoints to women. In this system, the team was divided into several men's subgroups *(hsiao-tsu)* and women's subgroups. When assigning a task to a women's subgroup, the number of workpoints the group would receive for completion of the task was decided by gauging how many men's workpoints it would be worth. For example, if it would take thirteen good men one day to cut a certain amount of grain, then the women's group would receive and divide among themselves thirteen *kung* (130 *fen*) for doing the job, regardless of the length of time they consumed in doing it. This system was officially approved, since it was regarded as basically conforming to the principle of equal pay for equal work and since it helped give women a more vital role in Mutual Aid Teams. But it does not appear that even this system was adopted very widely. As with all the other workpoint systems sketched here, this was only a suggested guideline for teams to approximate and adapt to suit their own peculiarities.

Recording Work and Settling Accounts

There were also several different methods of recording work done and of settling accounts between members. The authorities promoted two distinct accounting systems: the account book method and the work token or chit method. For the book method it was recommended that there be two columns corresponding to each member's name, and that each day one of them would be used to record how many workpoints the individual member had earned and the other to record how many workpoints were owed to others for work done on the member's land. To settle accounts it was a simple matter of subtracting the smaller column total from the larger one, the remainder being either the number of points owed to the member or the number owed by the member to the rest.

34. See "Fundamental Systems . . . " in *Reference Material . . .* [168].

Uncomplicated as this may sound, it was evidently considered quite tortuous and troublesome by many team members and fledgling accountants.[35] There were a good many mathematical errors, and individual members were frequently uncertain as to how they stood vis-à-vis the others.

The chit method was more graphic and apparently more easily understood by peasants. All members were either supplied with or provided themselves with a number of tokens or chits in different denominations of workpoints—usually 10 *fen,* 4 *fen,* and 1 *fen.* Each day workers would receive the appropriate combination of tokens from the members for whom they had worked on that day. In settling accounts, those who held extra tokens were to be paid, and those who were short of tokens had to pay for this work. This method was considered simple, flexible, and economical. All the members were able to assess their own situation by merely glancing at their supply of tokens and determining whether they needed to work for more points.

In Mutual Aid Teams that had progressed beyond the concept of each day's work being for one or another individual member to the concept of work being for the team as a whole, the chit method was often preserved. But in these teams it was not the individual peasants who traded tokens between themselves but the team leader (or accountant) who passed them out to each member each day (or at stated periods) according to each member's work. When all the tokens had been passed out they would be recalled, a notation would be made of the total for each household at that point, and they would start handing out the tokens again. This illustrates an important shift in attitude toward labor exchange on the part of peasants, but one that CCP authorities curiously did little to popularize.[36]

Despite propaganda efforts to promote these standard techniques, instruction sessions in basic accounting for team leaders, and the dispatch of special accounting work teams to the villages, team leaders and accountants often lapsed into their own more haphazard procedures, since they neither had sufficient confidence in their hasty mathematical training nor quite appreciated the necessity for so many ledgers and apparent formalities. The standardization of accounting in the countryside was to remain a vexing problem for rural development cadres for many years.

---

35. *Ibid.*

36. *Ibid.* For an interesting comparison with a chit method in use in Fukien and its correlation with the real value of workpoints, see *FKJP,* 5 Mar. 52 [188].

The Wage Standard

Little appears to have been written during the Mutual Aid Team phase about methods or guidelines for determining the value of a workpoint. This was a matter each team had to settle for itself; it depended, in effect, on what members could afford to pay each other. But it was generally accepted that the real value of a day's labor should be standardized within the team and should not fall below the local pay for an equivalent day of hired labor. Thus, if a poor household encountered difficulty in repaying its workpoint obligations after the harvest, some postponement or other arrangement might be made, but it could not be permitted to pay for team labor at a lower rate than other member households.

The question of whether and how far the value of the workpoint should rise or fall with the fortunes of the team was a far more sensitive matter, however. For if real increases in output were normally absorbed into higher and higher values for workpoints, then households with considerable landholdings needing team labor but with no oxen or little manpower to be used in working off that labor might well find their incomes falling in relation to the incomes of other team households. Likewise, land-poor households possessing several able-bodied workers might find their incomes increasing proportionally rather more than their overall production increase would have indicated. Such a trend might have been intensified as Mutual Aid Teams matured and encompassed more and more types of labor, making it possible to earn workpoints by engaging in a wider variety of activities. In the leadership's terms, this would have aided poor peasant households at the expense of middle peasant households and could have destroyed team solidarity. For any dissatisfied middle peasant always retained the option of withdrawing from the team. And such withdrawals, if they were to occur on a large scale, could well have brought on the collapse of many teams and created an undesirable swing back toward independent farming.

The central authorities, therefore, did not wish to see workpoint valuations that favored some groups of team members at the expense of others. But since workpoint values were ultimately determined by the team members themselves—usually just before the main harvest—subdistrict and county levels were able to exercise only rather loose coordination in this area in the early years. There is no doubt that the local mismanagement of workpoint valuation, setting unfair restrictions on profitability for middle peasant members, did lead to many team collapses at first. But when teams were otherwise working well, even as members in different circumstances argued for rates of pay that would serve their own interests, they were usually constrained by the threats of others to withdraw. And since the withdrawal of a middle peasant household was more likely to have serious consequences for a team than the withdrawal of a poor peasant household, it is perhaps warranted to suppose that middle peasants most often came closer to getting their way on the workpoint value question.[37]

Sharing Draught Animals and Farm Implements

There were many different arrangements for sharing oxen and farm implements within Mutual Aid Teams. Some of these specifically involved workpoints and others did not. Both types, however, involved a determination of fair exchange of value, and for the sake of convenience both can be included in this discussion.

In some Mutual Aid Teams households requiring ox-power paid a sort of rent, in the form of grain and fodder, to the ox-owning household for the use of the animal. In others, the oxen were jointly owned by the team and all households were entitled to use them. Two main forms of joint ownership were widely practiced. In the first, it was possible for one team member to sell an ox to the team, which then owned it in common. The cost of fodder to keep the animal was divided up among the member households according to the amount of land they owned, which the ox presumably would have to plough. The team would engage a herd-boy or girl to graze the ox, and the child would receive workpoints for the task. Under this system all team members owned, paid for, and used the ox together.

A second system was for all member households to chip in and buy an ox in which all would then have a private share corresponding to the size of their contribution. The cost of fodder and the time needed to care for the animal were then apportioned among the member households according to the amount of land owned by each. Otherwise, one household could be put in charge of looking after the ox, and the others would contribute a certain amount toward herd-boy expenses, while the household looking after it would retain all manure. Although there may appear to be little difference between these two alternatives, the second system was greatly preferred by development cadres for use in Mutual Aid Teams because it retained the concept of private ownership of a share in the ox. It was feared, with apparent justification, that oxen considered to be owned by all would not properly be taken care of by any member. The

---

37. This conclusion is supported by some of the evidence in *CCJP*, 14 Apr. 52 [376].

private share system was better suited to the private ownership assumptions that still underlay mutual aid, and it was better for the health of the oxen.[38] The first type of joint ownership system was therefore generally advocated only for use in cooperatives, not in teams.

Of course, where oxen were not jointly owned, one member household could still pay for the use of another's ox with its own labor. Generally, one day's ox labor was still taken as equivalent to two days' human labor. Sometimes, however, borrowing an ox meant borrowing the ox-owner as well. The owner would come along to do the required job with the ox, and sometimes also with a cart or plough or other implement. This seems to have been done in cases where the ox-owner feared that the borrower might not care for the ox properly while he had custody of it, or else that the borrower would not understand the ox's nature or know how to handle it. In these arrangements, one ox plus one man for one day would be equivalent to three *jen kung,* that is, three manpower days would have to be put in to repay the loan of the ox.

There were also arrangements under which an ox's work, like a man's work, was subject to scrutiny before it was assigned a manpower equivalent. Points would sometimes be assigned after examining the quality of the work done by the ox *(p'ing-fen).* In other cases an ox, like a man, would be assigned a minimum daily number of workpoints: twenty points for a healthy ox, ten points for an old ox, and so on. There is no reason to suppose that any of these methods were mutually exclusive; individual teams, especially as they grew in size through mergers, frequently employed some combination of these separate arrangements, depending on the preferences and problems of particular households.

As for the sharing of farm implements in the teams, roughly the same range of systems as for oxen could be found in use. One exception, however, is that most peasants were not accustomed to the notion of assigning workpoints to all the different farm implements, and it was therefore rarely done. Where it was tried, it often worked to the disadvantage of the poorer members.[39] Most often tools remained privately

38. *Ibid.*

39. "Fundamental Systems . . . " in *Reference Material* . . . [168]. Nevertheless there seems to be some evidence that the largest implements, such as water wheels and boats, were often assigned workpoints, at least when teams were newly set up. This may not, as we ordinarily might suppose, have been done at the insistence of the owners. On the contrary, it is sometimes hinted in reports such as this that nonowner peasants were frequently embarrassed and hesitant to use such important implements belonging to others without making some form of repayment. See also *CCJP,* 18 May 52 [251].

Mutual Aid Team members in Hsiao-kan County, Hupei, determining the compensation to be paid for a plough ox. (Hsinhua News Agency)

owned but were used by all members, the team paying for repairs and maintenance by levies on each household according to the amount of land it owned. Buying the implements of member households and making them team property was, as with oxen, discouraged. However, joint purchase of new, modern or very expensive implements was recommended. There appears to have been, as in traditional mutual aid arrangements, somewhat less fastidiousness about deriving equal exchange value where tools alone were concerned.

Coordinating the Work

The job of scheduling and arranging work (which in effect amounted to making a daily allotment or assignment of workpoints) was not particularly complex or difficult in small teams of three to five households. It was done very informally, to be sure. In the larger-scale permanent Mutual Aid Teams, however, some distinct procedures for arranging work were needed. Under one system, each household desiring mutual aid labor was to make this known at the general meeting the night before. There would then be an immediate discussion of the task to be done, how much labor it would require, and who should go to do it. All the participants would know as of then how much they were to earn (or pay) for the job. No individual was required to do mutual aid work every day if he or she did not need or want to work. But the team leader was supposed to make sure that some few people were not doing all the work while others tended to their own affairs, and that all members were in fact asking for assistance when they needed it, and only when they needed it.

During the busiest seasons, when peasants were all fearful lest their own fields be tended last and their harvests suffer, a different work arrangement system was sometimes adopted. Each household would announce, the night before, which plot of its land was most in need of work. The entire workforce of the Mutual Aid Team would then go to tend to all these plots in succession, the following day. That evening, each household would declare which of its plots was next most in need of attention, and the team workforce would proceed to those plots, and so on. By dividing the fields and doing them in rotation this way, no member household had to fear that it would suffer by being last.

There was, finally, a system that amounted to handling the team as if it were one large household when arranging work. The team leader would simply assign the members to the tasks needing to be done. For this system to be successful, the leader needed to have a complete understanding of conditions throughout the team, as well as the full trust and confidence of the members. It was not recommended for very large teams, or for those without considerable experience of working together collectively with more complex divisions of labor.

From this short survey of workpoint and workpoint-related systems in common use in Mutual Aid Teams it is readily apparent that the adoption of any combination of these methods of calculation and coordination was bound to help solve some of the truly fundamental operations problems confronting newly organized peasants. It also, however, was bound to set in motion a new set of potential conflicts that would have to be analyzed and solved. More or less perpetual readjustments and reassignments would have to be made to keep up with changing conditions and unforeseen events. Some members would inevitably volunteer for an eight-point weeding job only on mornings after it had rained; and unless they were to be permitted to cheat other members, refinements in the points assigned to weeding jobs on damp and on dry ground had to be introduced. Emerging internal conflicts such as these will be explored in the next section.

But first it should be emphasized that all these workpoint and workpoint-related systems were transitional; they were experimental and expected to pass through perennial (even seasonal) changes and modifications. Yet even where these systems functioned equitably they clearly made cooperation cumbersome. Peasants and team leaders had their first opportunity at this period to perform a simple cost-benefit analysis of their own organizational efforts, and many of them became critical of the size limitations and the financial limitations of team work. The appeal, in a few years' time, of the larger units and expanded working capital of semi-socialist cooperatives, and later collectives, no doubt had its origins for many peasants in the heavy investments of time and energy demanded by the mutual aid efffort and in its real but limited returns.

ANXIETIES, DEVIATIONS, AND OTHER PROBLEMS

As with land reform and the collection of the agricultural tax, Party and government leaders faced a formidable array of obstacles in putting their mutual aid plans into effect. The concept of mutual aid may have been familiar to most peasants, but that alone did not quiet all their fears about the formation and operation of permanent year-round Mutual Aid Teams. In some respects their fears were ultimately to be justified; but in others the fear itself was the greater trouble.

Perhaps the most common sort of anxiety involved the conviction that the compensation (in workpoints, in grain, or in money) received for team use of privately owned goods would not be sufficient to make up for the probable damages and the inconvenience suffered.[40] Peasants were simply loath to turn over their property for use by someone else. They were most often not assured of the nature of workpoint and other compensation arrangements before they were supposed to commit themselves to join. And even when the rates of compensation had been settled, there was no guarantee that they might not be changed within a year or two.

Official accounts of the period pointed out that poor peasants, as well as middle peasants, were reluctant to exchange complete sovereignty

40. See *HHNP*, 17 Mar. 54 [398]. This is one of many reports in which ox-owning and implement-owning members are said to be angered and dismayed because other members do not take proper care of their possessions.

over what they did possess for the promise or the hope of more. And poorer peasants, whose greatest contribution to the team was often the labor power they brought to it, frequently voiced the related fear that pay would not actually be distributed according to work,[41] and that ox-owning and implement-owning households would be granted favorable conditions in order to persuade them to join and to stay in the team. The households with ample labor power but with insufficient land also feared that once they had joined a Mutual Aid Team they would not be permitted to hire themselves out for labor on other peasants' land.[42] They worried that team work would keep them so busy that they would have no time for their own sideline occupations and so would lose that extra income. And they worried that the settling of accounts, even if based on a fair workpoint calculation system, might not be carried out in a timely fashion, and that they, who had the smallest savings to fall back upon, would be the ones to suffer. Poor peasants as well as middle peasants were fearful of locking themselves into arrangements where others would make frequent use of their services, while their own private or outside economic activities would have to be restrained.

This fear sometimes led peasants to form Mutual Aid Teams along lines that did not conform to the official designs. Specifically, there was a tendency for households in similar economic circumstances to band together to form teams. This phenomenon was referred to with the old phrase, "Soldiers go with soldiers; generals go with generals."[43] What it meant especially was that middle peasants who owned an ox or some important tools formed Mutual Aid Teams with other middle peasants who owned these things and left the poorer peasants to form teams among themselves.[44] Since the primary object of the teams was supposed to be to bring together farmers with complementary deficiencies and resources, the "soldiers and generals" trend was viewed as potentially very dangerous. When ox-owning households were not able to form their own special teams, they frequently tried to cut the losses they were expecting to sustain by selling their oxen before joining a team, so

41. *CCJP,* 11 Jun. 51 [379].

42. See *CCJP,* 13 Jun. 51 [187]; and also *JMJP,* 28 May 52 [199]. This was a question on which there was some official equivocation.

43. *"Ping tui ping; chiang tui chiang."* See *CCJP,* 19 May 52 [441].

44. Although this was of course frowned upon, it was not condemned with the same vigor as the practice of rich peasants forming "mutual aid teams" among themselves.

as to bring less common-use property into it.[45] Such maneuvers were obviously both contrary to the spirit of mutual aid and harmful to the cause of increasing agricultural production.

If the anxieties and misunderstandings of peasants sometimes distorted the original concept of mutual aid and the goals of the movement, the anxieties and misunderstandings of local cadres and activists were sometimes even more of an ill influence. As has been pointed out before, these cadres were under multiple and often conflicting pressures from their superiors as well as from the peasant masses they were supposed to serve. The directives and the leadership they were given on mutual aid from the county authorities were often ambiguous and sometimes confused. Furthermore, the cadres at the lowest levels were still at this time lacking in the experience and training necessary to enable them to implement policy directives accurately and efficiently. The land reform work teams had been dispersed. Village cadres were often left without much immediate guidance and supervision and without fully developed organizational linkages with the upper levels that would have permitted them to call for help when they needed it. At the same time, they were expected to oversee many new programs then being extended down to the villages. In the welter of demands for action these people quite often emphasized the wrong theme and failed to see the main point. One frustrated cadre in Hunan was quoted as asking, "Now we have to do water conservancy work, collect fertilizer, and also do Mutual Aid Team work. Which one of these, after all, is the central one?"[46] This man was criticized for separating mutual aid from production in his mind, but it is easy to sympathize with his confusion. In fact, until the first promulgation of the "General Line" (in late 1953), which unmistakably underlined the centrality of the mutual aid and cooperation movement for the future of the countryside, the relative importance to be assigned to the several new policies was certainly not yet made clear to all rural work personnel.

It is apparent, at any rate, that many village cadres vastly underesti-

45. See, e.g., *HHNP*, 8 Apr. 54 [181]. There were at this time strict laws against the slaughter of yellow oxen, water buffalo, horses, mules, and donkeys in the Central South, especially if they were young, female, pregnant, or capable of being used for stud. In effect, only old or sick animals could be slaughtered, and then only on the authorization of the subdistrict government. There were, however, no official limitations on the sale or trade of draught animals between peasants. See *CCJP*, 6 Jul. 51 [80].

46. *HHNP*, 15 Mar. 54 [103].

mated the importance of the Mutual Aid Team movement and their role in it. As late as 1954, for example, it was reported that in one Hunan village only one of six Party members had even joined a team, and that he paid scant attention to it. Of the eight Youth League members in the same village, only two were Mutual Aid Team members.[47] Some Party and Youth League members were evidently unwilling at first to believe that their own personal futures lay in such an unexalted sphere. They did not join teams because they were expecting to be assigned to more elevated tasks after land reform.[48]

In view of the pressures, the uncertain leadership, and the morale crisis among some cadres, then, it was inevitable that a number of mistakes and deviations from the official guidelines would be committed by cadres in the organization and operation of teams. Probably the most serious deviation was the familiar one of "commandism"—forcing peasants to join teams against their will. Coercion may have been applied more often to middle peasants,[49] but it was frequently used as a short-cut method to meet deadlines and quotas and to avoid the work of proper propaganda and education among the poor peasants too. Any kind of coercion or threat used to make peasants join Mutual Aid Teams was condemned because it violated the principle of voluntarism and mutual benefit that was supposed to be the basis for the movement. Nevertheless, numerous cases of commandism—some quite serious instances of intimidation and others only minor infractions—were re-

47. *HHNP*, 29 Mar. 54 [49]. The Party branch in question was in Dragon Arch Rapids Village, Peach River County. A similar report of cadre failure to join and lead MATs can be found in *HHNP*, 3 Apr. 54 [300]. This report also mentions a cadre (a demobilized soldier) who joined a team but became dissatisfied with farm work and ran off to faraway Mukden to look for a job there!

48. *HHNP*, 7 May 54 [190]. From this report it appears that once the Youth League members were convinced that their place was in the MATs, they became more avid in their promotion of them and more radical in their plans for their development than the mainstream of the Party and government. One cannot help but speculate that these young people, frustrated in their hopes for a distinguished career, were doing what they could to make their assigned jobs as progressive (and as impressive) as possible.

49. See *CCJP*, 11 Jul. 51 [372]. In some villages all middle peasants were forced to join teams, and in ploughing poor peasants were automatically given priority. In Shaoyang county, some village cadres forced all women to participate in teams and threatened to report them to the government if they would not. Instances such as these illustrate not only the tendency to commandism but also a recurrent tendency toward political extremism and radicalism among some lower-level cadres that was not always contained.

ported in the two provinces in connection with the establishment of teams.

There is considerable evidence that village cadres were under pressure to report that they had succeeded in establishing one or more Mutual Aid Teams in their area. This pressure seems to have come less from the center than from officials at the county and special district level. These middle-level officials were aware that counties demonstrating outstanding progress in the transition to socialism were likely to receive special assistance from the government in support of their good work. Extra fertilizer, expert technical assistance with local irrigation projects, and above all, more investment capital were all more likely to be made available to counties with greater numbers of Mutual Aid Teams in an effort to ensure (if not to manufacture) production victories for more progressive forms of agricultural organization. In the competition for scarce resources, middle-level cadres with the economic interests of their area in mind made it plain that village cadres were to come through with the longest possible lists of functioning teams that they could put together. This led not only to outbreaks of commandism among village cadres but also to several other deviant and peremptory approaches to the establishment of Mutual Aid Teams.

Some village cadres were holding competitions to see which one could set up the most Mutual Aid Teams.[50] Cadres frequently reported the existence of teams, complete with names of members, that were in reality not carrying out any mutual aid activities. This reporting procedure, they assured the peasants, was only for "official purposes."[51] As one Hunan provincial government directive angrily declared:

> The principle of voluntarism and mutual benefit is central. Last year some Mutual Aid Teams were set up by forcing people into them, or just enrolling people and putting down names whether willing or unwilling. This is formalistic, it brings trouble to the people, infringes the [interests of the] middle peasants, and violates the principle [of voluntarism and mutual benefit]. It must be prevented and corrected.[52]

It was admitted in this directive and in many other reports on the situation in the two provinces that even where teams had been voluntarily set up by the peasants, this had happened only because they had been

50. *Ibid*. Lo-t'ien county in Hupei is cited in particular.

51. *CCJP*, 19 May 52 [441]. This "formalistic" deviation, sometimes called *pao pan tai t'i* as during land reform, was reported in Ch'ang-te county, Hunan, and in six Hupei counties including Huang-kang, Lo-t'ien, and Kuang-chi.

52. *CCJP*, 8 Apr. 52 [394].

led on by cadres' promises of immediate generous loans forthcoming from the People's Bank. There can be no doubt that the Bank's promised preference to Mutual Aid Teams as opposed to independent farmers in granting government loans was usually a major factor in influencing peasants to join. But when the loans did not materialize, the teams frequently collapsed.

Some cadres, in their somewhat frantic attempts to make Mutual Aid Teams succeed and endure, seriously distorted official policy, making either arbitrary rulings or spineless concessions. For example, once they had joined, peasants were sometimes forbidden to withdraw from the team, contrary to stated policy.[53] At other times, middle peasants were cajoled and lured into teams; occasionally they were deliberately flattered into participation by being elected the team leader.[54]

Once Mutual Aid Teams were established, the lower- and middle-level cadres evidently turned their attention to making them appear to be as progressive as possible, once again for the benefit of their superiors who were in a position to allocate funds and recommend promotions. Since unprecedentedly high yields were considered a measure of a team's success and progressiveness, yields were routinely exaggerated. But by far the fastest short-cut to a high yield was to start with peasants who had relatively large portions of land, labor power, and other means of production. Therefore, many cadres at first excluded poor peasants from the teams,[55] taking only the relatively secure and the better-off households into the group. This was certainly one of the most ironical of the cadre deviations; and it was also one of the most common. Besides making their production figures appear to be outstanding, this deviation probably suited the team members involved. An economically homogeneous Mutual Aid Team with members of above-average wealth was least likely to suffer from the serious internal conflicts of interest that make cooperation difficult and a mixed blessing. However, such a team was also least likely to accomplish any of the useful exchanges of the means of production that were supposed to be its object.[56]

53. Members were supposed to be free to leave as long as they did not pull out just at the time of year that would be most detrimental to other members. See *JMJP,* 28 May 52 [199].

54. *HHNP,* 28 Apr. 54 [54]. This report concerns a Miao national minority village.

55. *CCJP,* 14 Apr. 52 [376].

56. Although this deviation was universally condemned by provincial and central authorities, it may not have been an altogether unwelcome development. The production reports of these exclusivist MATs gave them very encouraging figures and success

A host of other devices were employed by local cadres in the hope of casting their teams in a good light. Some cadres demanded very low workpoint compensation for oxen, for example.[57] This was meant to illustrate the progressiveness of the team and its attention to the "needs of the poor." Such excess of zeal was only to be rewarded with stern criticism for creating imbalances in the mutual benefit relationships within the team. In other places, cadres demanded that handicraftsmen who had joined Mutual Aid Teams be made to do agricultural labor whether they had any experience or not.[58] The hope, it seems, was that their contribution to farm labor would help produce a higher yield for the team and thereby enhance its claims to success.

Local cadres also took the blame for other problems and deviations they may not actually have been able to control. Sometimes team members who were owing workpoints simply refused to pay.[59] Or, during the busy season in some teams all members demanded that their fields be tended to ahead of others and threatened to abandon mutual aid to return to their own crops.[60] Other team members, once they had saved up a little money through the benefits of mutual aid, wanted to withdraw and set up a small business of their own or go off to the city to find a job.[61] Frequently the cadres' ability to come to grips with disturbances such as these was hampered by their own tenuous positions within the teams. Because cadres inevitably had to attend periodic meetings and conferences as well as perform duties not involving manual labor, there nearly

---

stories to use as publicity for mutual aid. As described below, propaganda about the successes and the material advantages of mutual aid taken from the experiences of model and advanced teams was considered to be one of the most effective means for convincing peasants to form their own teams and thus for advancing the entire movement.

57. *HHNP*, 28 Apr. 54 [54].

58. *CCJP*, 11 Jul. 51 [372].

59. *JMJP*, 21 Aug. 53 [277]. For an interesting comparison with the situation in Kiangsu, see *CFJP*, 11 Jul. 52 [143].

60. *HHNP*, 17 Apr. 54 [312].

61. *TKP*, 27 Dec. 53 [170]. This is the story of a man in Pao-an, Hunan, who joined an MAT, garnered a small surplus, and then sold his ox in order to have more capital with which to set up a little store in his house. He became so interested in his store that he eventually hired a long-term laborer to take over his duties in the MAT. He was offended when criticized for this by the other team members and decided to drop out of the team altogether. This type of situation was symptomatic of the kind of damage that might be done by the new class differentiations emerging in the villages. Of course, not all team dropouts made their exits in such comfortable circumstances. Especially after the natural disasters of 1954 there were many who abandoned their teams in utter poverty and rushed to the cities to look for work. See also *HHNP*, 26 May 54 [184].

always arose some debate within the teams about how many workpoints the cadres should earn for various jobs and how much time they should be permitted to spend away from production work. Some Mutual Aid Teams simply did not wish to have cadres as members since they would not be productive enough; other teams actively sought cadre members because of their prestige and the chance that cadres could be helpful in obtaining financial support from the government.[62] As a result, the local cadres themselves were not always in a position to influence team members to comply with government policies. Thus while internal organizational and morale problems such as those mentioned here may well have been predictable, with the resources available at the time they were certainly not all equally preventable.

SELF-INTEREST AND THE TRANSITION TO SOCIALISM

The movement to establish Mutual Aid Teams began in Hunan and Hupei even before land reform was completed. Some secure and progressive counties had set up a few model teams quite soon after liberation. But for many months after the completion of land reform the mutual aid and cooperation movement remained modest in scale and gradualist in tone. Even the most advanced counties were reported to be trying to set up only about 100 permanent teams and about 1,000 seasonal teams. Many of these teams were later reported to have collapsed or to have functioned only haphazardly.[63] As of early 1954, reports indicated that most counties had organized only somewhere between one-third and one-half of the eligible peasants into Mutual Aid Teams, but the situation was extremely uneven.[64] Occasionally, as with *Huangkang* special district, there were reports of close to 100 percent participa-

62. *CCJP*, 14 Apr. 52 [376].

63. *CCJP*, 16 Jul. 52 [97]; and *CCJP*, ? Jun. 52 [294]. Here it is reported that there were a total of 1,103 permanent MATs in the *hsien* and an estimated 1,500 seasonal teams. They averaged nine member households with about fourteen ablebodied males. Only 10 percent (117) of the teams, however, were described as working satisfactorily.

64. Dragon Arch Rapids Village reported only 33 percent of the population in MATs in March 1954. See *HHNP*, 29 Mar. 54 [49]. Four Hunan counties reported a total of 2,219 teams, but they only involved about 50 percent of the *hsiang* in the area. See *HHNP*, 15 Mar. 54 [103]. Lin-hsiang *hsien* probably reflected the situation well when it reported a total of 53 percent of eligible households in the entire *hsien* involved in mutual aid, but with certain progressive *hsiang* reaching a figure of 80 percent. See *HHNP*, 24 May 54 [259].

tion,[65] but when further described and analyzed it emerged that most of the "teams" there were practicing mutual aid no differently than they had before liberation, save that they had each chosen a team leader.

The general attitudes and assumptions expressed in the writings of the period were that the mutual aid phase of rural development would take several years to reach its peak. This view prevailed until the enunciation of the General Line in late 1953 and the nearly simultaneous introduction of the Unified Purchase and Marketing system, at which point the pace of the mutual aid and cooperation movement was tremendously accelerated. (See Table 20.)

With the Korean situation then stabilized and the possibility of a joint American-Formosan invasion becoming dimmer, the Chinese leadership was prepared in late 1953 to move ahead with the risk of heavy investment in industry. The Unified Purchase and Marketing system (discussed in some detail in the next chapter) was to be the primary vehicle for limiting rural consumption, making the peasantry self-sustaining, and capturing a surplus from agriculture for investment in industry. But for Unified Purchase to work, the peasantry had to be organized into units that were economically more efficient and politically more accessible to central planning. The Mutual Aid Team was to be this unit. Teams would help peasants improve yields on their small and vulnerable plots of land and would also be large and dependable enough units themselves to sign Unified Purchase contracts with the state-organized Supply and Marketing Cooperatives. Thus it became imperative that teams be established as widely and as quickly as possible in 1954.

The methods and techniques then employed to advance the mutual aid movement were essentially the same as those described for the land reform movement. Great reliance was placed on the "keypoint-to-area"[66] method. Promising villages were selected, and within them promising groups of peasants were brought together and set on their feet as functioning teams, often, as will become clear below, with considerable financial assistance from the People's Bank or a Supply and Marketing Co-op. Once they had achieved some success, apprentice team leaders and local cadres were trooped in from neighboring areas to

65. As of April 1953 the Huang-kang district quoted incomplete statistics indicating that in eleven *hsien* 92.9 percent of peasant households were organized into MATs of one sort or another. See *JMJP*, 11 Feb. 54 [310].

66. *Yu tien tao mien,* described in Chapter 2.

TABLE 20. Establishment of Mutual Aid Teams in Hunan, 1952–57

(a) Total Number of Teams

Unit	1952	1953	1954	1955	1956	1957
Seasonal teams	132,873	206,906	392,740	294,915	—	—
Year-round teams	19,556	40,791	221,797	275,396	—	—
All MATs	152,429	247,697	614,537	570,311	—	—

(b) Total Number of Member Households

Unit	1952	1953	1954	1955	1956	1957
Seasonal teams	824,412	1,400,062	2,604,455	2,212,418	—	—
Year-round teams	144,374	309,323	1,771,273	2,554,623	—	—
All MATs	968,786	1,709,385	4,375,728	4,767,041	—	—

(c) Member Households as % of Total Farming Households

Unit	1952	1953	1954	1955	1956	1957
All MATs	12.60	22.16	55.95	60.50	—	—

SOURCE: *Hunan Nung-yeh* [15], p. 69.
NOTE: The disappearance of teams in 1956 is the result of their conversion into production cooperatives.

study their methods, observe how they solved their problems, and generally "learn from their experience." In this way the model experience would be spread from the keypoint to the surrounding area; new Mutual Aid Teams would be formed, themselves becoming models and keypoints in a very short time, and so on.[67]

It is probably accurate to say that rather more emphasis was placed on the "keypoint-to-area" method during the mutual aid movement than during land reform and that a similar trend can be observed in the use of "models" and "model experiences."[68] A heavier use of models and keypoints may reflect, however, only the somewhat greater degree

67. See, e.g., *CCJP*, 19 May 52 [441]; and also *KJP*, 9 Oct. 54 [353].
68. For reports on a couple of good model MATs in Hupei, see *CCJP*, 14 Aug. 52 [349]; and *CCJP*, 9 Oct. 52 [43]. The first team reported an average per *mou* output of about 927 catties, which was said to be 48.1 percent higher than the average for the entire *hsiang*. The second reported 875 catties per *mou,* which represented a 50.3 percent increase in productivity over the preceding year.

of administrative organization and coordination in 1954 than had been feasible in the countryside during the early days of land reform. Great publicity attended the successes of model teams—successes measured always in terms of increased productivity and increased income, as in the typical reports in Table 21. And as Table 22 shows, income increases were supposed to be comparatively much greater for the poorer team members.

As with land reform again, there was a rectification of Mutual Aid Teams following the main thrust of the movement. As usual, the movement had been impelled forward despite obvious unreadiness in many villages, and there emerged the normal complement of deviations, mistakes, and excesses committed, along the lines of those already described. The Party chose, as it had during land reform, to risk small disasters and distortions just in order to lay the groundwork of what was to be done. There was the intention, from the beginning, of returning to these teams after a few months to straighten out unrealistic workpoint systems, expel unqualified members, improve accounting methods, and so on. The overambitious thrust, followed by a deliberate mopping up and straightening out, remained characteristic of Chinese Communist rural workstyle. So institutionalized had the procedure become, in fact, that the rectification of Mutual Aid Teams was declared to be operating "from keypoint to area" in the very same way that the original movement was to have spread.[69] Once a team had undergone this rectification, in 1954, it was generally encouraged to expand its membership by taking in new independent farmers or by merging with another small team. In this way the momentum of the movement was to be preserved.

The propaganda for mutual aid that supplemented these organizational techniques is interesting for what it indicates about how peasants were actually motivated to join Mutual Aid Teams and to share their property. As with land reform and again with agricultural taxation, the main approach to the peasants was to point out to them again and again what they personally were likely to gain by joining a team and acting in accord with government policy on mutual aid. They would have access to an ox, they would receive a loan from the government, they could collect and buy more fertilizer, they could plant earlier; in short, their

---

69. See *CCJP*, 16 Jul. 52 [97]; and also *HHNP*, 16 Apr. 54 [308]. For other interesting reports on the rectification of MATs, see *HHNP*, 3 Apr. 54 [300]; and *HHNP*, 29 Mar. 54 [49].

TABLE 21. Production in Mutual Aid Teams

Independent Farmers	Seasonal MATs		Year-round MATs	
	Average per capita production	*% Higher than independent farmers*	*Average per capita production*	*% Higher than independent farmers*
1,184 catties of primary grain	1,329	12	1,455	23

SOURCE: Su Hsing [31], p. 67.
NOTE: Based on a 1953 survey of 10 *hsiang* in Hunan, Hupei, and Kiangsi.

yield could be increased and the family income would rise. There is absolutely nothing mysterious about how the revolutionary government managed to get most peasants to form teams. The general idea of mutual aid was itself an authentic means of raising production, at least by a small increment. It was, if not a brilliant stroke or a technical breakthrough, at least a reasonable and practical idea for solving some pressing problems.

Peasants had always engaged in mutual aid for the purpose of improving their own livelihood. And as described in the next two chapters, government policy after 1953 merely augmented the incentive possibilities that were already present in the nature of mutual aid. By giving priority to Mutual Aid Teams as opposed to independent farmers in the granting of loans (often promising many more loans than they actually could give), and by extending preferential assistance to teams in the marketing of their crops through the Supply and Marketing Co-ops, central authorities set out to—and succeeded in—drawing many more peasants into team cooperation. The official line was quite explicit in its reliance on appeals to the peasants' own self-interest and in its assertion that a collective socialist spirit would ultimately be based on a combination of self-interestedness and political consciousness:

First, since every peasant has need of participating in a Mutual Aid Team, make the peasant see the advantages to participation. At the beginning, make him see the advantages to himself as an individual and then make him see that advantages gained by the peasants are also advantages for the nation . . . . Voluntarism is built on a foundation of selfish benefit to the individual and also on a foundation of mutual benefit. At the same time, voluntarism must be built on a foundation of consciousness. If consciousness is lacking, then there will certainly be losses to the people's individual benefit. If only selfish benefit is encompassed and mutual ben-

TABLE 22. Farm Household Income by Class and Production Unit
(In catties of grain)

Class	Independent Farmers' Average per Capita Income	Seasonal MATs		Year-round MATs		APCs	
		Average per Capita	% Higher than Independent Farmers	Average per Capita	% Higher than Independent Farmers	Average per Capita	% Higher than Independent Farmers
Poor peasants	955	1,126	17.90	1,295	35.60	1,401	46.70
Middle peasants	1,214	1,371	12.93	1,435	18.10	1,471	21.16
Upper middle peasants	1,634	1,655	1.28	1,644	0.61	1,745	6.79

SOURCE: Su Hsing [31], p. 82.
NOTE: Based on a 1953 survey of 10 *hsiang* in Hunan, Hupei, and Kiangsi. Note that even at this early date production co-ops were being compared favorably to teams.

efit is neglected, then it will not be easy to have confidence in the advantages of Mutual Aid Teams, and it will not be possible to get organized. That is, in getting organized, all will be afraid that they will suffer, and it will be impossible to have unity and mutual trust. Then they must certainly collapse. Therefore, if we do not have a peasantry with a certain amount of consciousness, we cannot make a good job of this kind of Mutual Aid Team.[70]

In this short disquisition, the argument is very clear. At the beginning there is the peasants' own self-interestedness, which can be used to motivate them to join a Mutual Aid Team. Once the team is in operation, individual selfishness must be tempered or there can be no cooperation. In this process the peasant's consciousness will be awakened to the possibilities for mutual benefit and the benefits of collective life. Once this stage is attained, it may be possible to establish socialism gradually. But in the beginning, self-interestedness is the motive that can be used to mobilize peasants. In accord with this theory, constant appeals to personal interests were in fact made during the height of the mutual aid movement. Peasants were reminded again and again, through simple exhortation and through the parade of good results from model and keypoint teams, of what they stood to gain by participating and (perhaps more powerfully as time went on) what they stood to lose if they failed to participate.

In one very important respect, therefore, the mutual aid movement closely resembled both land reform and the administration of the agricultural tax. It offered peasants an opportunity to act in accord with government policy while simultaneously pursuing their own interest and enhancing their own well-being. As with the redistribution of the land and the payment of taxes, there were some villagers who stood only to lose and could not expect any material gains from these campaigns. But official policy managed in all three cases to keep the numbers of these people comparatively small and to offer the great mass of peasants the chance to make a small personal gain by following the government's lead. This creation of an identity of interests between the masses of peasants and the mainstream of government policy doubtless accounts in large part for the relative success of all three campaigns.

From an administrative point of view, then, the period immediately following land reform in these two provinces was one of consolidation.

70. *CCJP,* 1 Jun. 52 [391].

It was a time for supplementary training and continued weeding out of rural cadres and activists. And it was an opportunity to oversee programs with considerable popular support and with a *laissez faire* tone, such as tax stabilization and the gradual introduction of Mutual Aid Teams. These helped reinforce the legitimacy and the capacity of the new administration.

From the point of view of village politics, however, there were some developments in this interim period that were far less welcome. As peasants warmed to the task of making good at independent farming in a generally favorable petty-capitalist economic environment, the determination of some of them to pursue class struggle was waning perceptibly. Not only were they glad to be free from the demands on their time that the mobilization meetings and struggle sessions had made during land reform, but also as they began to envision themselves getting better and better off in the coming years, many recent reform beneficiaries were having second thoughts about the long-term desirability of dictatorship by the poor in the village. The "rich peasant mentality" obviously was becoming more current and respectable, even among many of the not-yet-rich. This was a manifestation of a rural small-capitalist, private accumulation syndrome that central planners found increasingly disturbing. For there were still large numbers of other villagers living in deep poverty, who did not share in such happy prospects even after land reform, and who would, if they could, have demanded more expropriations and further levelling. Among them, strains of the old, radical, egalitarian, expropriationist syndrome—also now condemned by the dominant central policy—were once again being voiced in the villages. Between these two groups, both of which the Party had counted among the "revolutionary masses" united in class struggle against landlord exploiters, there opened a small fissure with the potential to become a yawning chasm of opposing political and economic interests. The dismemberment of the Party's carefully cultivated revolutionary coalition of classes in the countryside was looking imminent.

In response to these trends between the end of land reform and the end of 1953, central leaders were to conclude that gentle measures like progressive taxation and the gradual proliferation of mutual aid were too weak to be effective constraints on the "rich peasant economy." Not only would Mutual Aid Teams have to be spread and consolidated more quickly to assist the poor, but state intervention in other aspects of the rural economy would now be launched to restrict more decisively the advances of the better-off and to lay the groundwork for a more deliberate transition to socialism in the countryside. The chapters that follow detail the measures taken in 1954 and 1955 to accomplish this reversal of trends, and they illustrate that once more the center would rely on appeals to peasant self-interest, this time to gain compliance with its openly prosocialist aims.

PART 3

"THE GENERAL LINE"

Decision on a Strategy
of Rural Development

Men these days search for a way through the clouds,
But the cloud way is dark and without sign.
The mountains are high and often steep and rocky;
In the broadest valleys the sun seldom shines.
Green crests before you and behind,
White clouds to east and west —
Do you want to know where the cloud way lies?
There it is, in the midst of the Void!

HAN-SHAN, T'ang Dynasty

CHAPTER 5

Rural Trade and the Supply and Marketing Cooperatives

The information available to Chinese leaders about trends in the villages at the end of 1953 was not encouraging. Production was increasing but so was consumption. Peasants were eating more and not marketing enough to support the cities or the plans for national industrialization. Even more disturbing, increases in farm production appeared to be attributable largely to a vibrant, petty-capitalist boom psychology that had gripped the villages in the aftermath of land reform. Admittedly some of the leadership's own programs had helped coax into bloom the hardy flower of peasant entrepreneurship, giving villagers the confidence to return to the pursuit of their personal enrichment with businesslike determination. But business was almost too brisk and old assumptions about the fates of winners and losers were too readily resumed. In the midst of rural economic recovery it was perceived that some of the poor were being allowed to slip further into poverty, while some villagers who had come through land reform with comparatively more than others were pulling themselves even further ahead. Mutual aid was not comprehensive enough and not sufficiently well supported, financially or administratively, to make up the difference for poor peasants. The progressive tax only slowed by a little the progress of the fortunate. Some central leaders saw what they took to be the beginning of repolarization in the distribution of wealth even in the villages of the later liberated areas, a trend they were confident was well-documented for those parts of the country where land reform had been carried out earlier.[1]

1. Su Hsing [31], p. 32. See also T'ung Ta-lin [34], p. 6.

The center's reassessment of the postreform situation yielded quick action. In the fall of 1953 the "General Line for the Transition to Socialism" was announced, dispelling any doubts about the Party's intention to promote socialist transformation in agricultural production and in all rural economic relations. The General Line called for the gradual formation of rural cooperatives leading to full socialist collectivization. The first steps to hem in the "rich peasant economy" were to be taken immediately. Western students of the Chinese revolution have often compared it with the Soviet and have tended to emphasize and admire the extraordinary speed and the relative peacefulness of China's agricultural collectivization movement. In seeking explanations for the rapid growth of rural socialism, it is well to examine first the prior and equally rapid decline of rural capitalism. Once the new Chinese authorities had succeeded in effectively restraining petty capitalism in the countryside, it was perhaps not so extraordinary that socialist forms of organization could quickly come to flourish in its place.

This chapter and the next consider two major programs launched to reverse the undesirable petty capitalist trends in the villages and to create the conditions for establishing socialist farming cooperatives. The first of these programs was the rapid proliferation of a state-led cooperative marketing network that would allow the government to intervene more decisively in the marketing of staple food and major industrial crops. With enhanced control over commodity procurement, central planners would be better able to assure the level of supplies needed for national industrialization. They would be able to exert a much greater influence over both the rate of savings and the kinds of capital investment to be made in the countryside. With these two important types of leverage, the state-led trade network could play a crucial role in quickening the pace of socialist transformation. It would be able to deprive surplus-producing richer peasants of their major means of "getting rich" at the expense of the poor. State control of the rural market would hobble the hopes of the rich peasant class without direct expropriation, as it gave central authorities the opportunity and the wherewithal for the preferential support of Mutual Aid Teams and later of Agricultural Production Co-ops. For as we shall see, the state-led Supply and Marketing Co-ops (SMCs) were to write contracts and handle all their business so as to give peasants of various classes incentives to join in presocialist, semi-socialist, and fully socialist cooperatives.

The second program, vigorously promoted at the same time, was that of the People's Bank to support the work of Supply and Marketing Co-ops and to set up a Credit Co-op in every *hsiang,* making low-interest loans available and absorbing peasant savings. Government and cooperative loans not only cut down on the private moneylenders' business (thereby delivering another blow to rich peasants), but also, used selectively and with preference to poor peasants, Mutual Aid Teams, and Agricultural Production Co-ops, provided even more incentives for peasants to move into the cooperative economy.

These two programs were clearly quite successful, despite early financial and staff limitations. They did a great deal to restrain the petty-capitalist orientation abroad in the villages, and in the space of a year or two they helped bring many peasants to the verge of setting up their own farming co-ops.

While the small peasant economy and private trading and credit relations still flourished, central planners had not been in a position to offer peasants many direct incentives to move toward cooperation. But with the decision on the General Line and the subsequent direct state intervention in the village economy, it became possible for the center to manipulate the economic environments of peasants in such a way as to underscore the convergence of self-interest and state policy once again. As private traders and moneylenders were finding their businesses threatened, the improved ability of local cadres to sign contracts and give loans to peasants and co-ops directly served the needs of farmers for marketing security and for cash advances.

The new cooperative arrangements discussed here did offer poor peasants some chances for improved productivity and income increases, but even more attractive perhaps was the greater economic security they could provide in a time of rapidly shifting conditions. Government programs in the early transition to socialism could not continue to offer free land and oxen to poor peasants as during the excitement of land reform. But the insurance aspects embodied in these programs did prove to be of continuing significance to peasants who were still poor even after land reform.

The truth of the matter was that most peasants had precious little latitude or freedom in their private credit and marketing deals, and they turned out to be usually quite willing to trade what amounted to no more than a theoretical chance to make a killing for a few credible guarantees that they would not lose what they had. As the state and cooperative share of the rural economy was deliberately and rapidly expanded, more and more poor and middle peasants found that they could make deals at the co-op that, from a price or interest-bearing standpoint, were not bad, and that were often most advantageous from the point of view of supply security. Only the very small minority of large-surplus-producing richer peasants who had enjoyed the ability to wait out fluctuations in the private market were isolated in general opposition to cooperative trade and finance.

In China's protracted rural class struggle, it was only during the early days of rent reduction and land reform that real wealth was taken from the better-off and given directly to the poor. In the later reforms of the transition period discussed here, the wealth of the richer peasants was generally funneled first through some larger institution, such as a cooperative, in the form of investments, dues, or contributions. Or in many cases it would be more accurate to say that it was not real wealth that was redistributed by reform so much as opportunity — the opportunity to take a loan on favorable terms, or to buy an ox or a superior strain of seed. Most of these later reforms were essentially means of closing off opportunities available to richer peasants and opening up to poorer peasants opportunities for advancement that formerly had not been available to them.

EARLY EFFORTS AT
MARKET STABILIZATION AND CONTROL

As soon as it came to power in 1949, the new government exerted strenuous efforts through intervention in the domestic trading sector to halt inflation and stabilize the supplies of essential goods and commodities. Since the means for coordinated state intervention were not immediately available in the later liberated areas, the central finance and trade authorities had to create their own comprehensive commodity purchase and supply system to deal with manufacturers, rural private traders, and ultimately with peasant farmers. Their early efforts had yielded surprisingly quick general price stabilization immediately following liberation. But further expansion and consolidation of the rural state-led trade apparatus was slowed by the all-consuming task of completing agrarian reform.

The very implementation of the early social and economic reforms had often, in fact, initially deepened the supply crisis. Rent and interest reduction and land reform itself, which were intended to shatter only "feudal economic relationships" in the countryside, also necessarily dealt a heavy blow to the "capitalist economic relationships" that so often involved the same individuals and depended on their investment and risk capabilities. Landlords and rich peasants had so frequently invested in small commercial ventures servicing the crop-marketing and consumer demands of the local peasantry that the crippling of these two classes in the villages greatly endangered the trade network linking peasant villages to market towns and market towns to urban centers. The progressive tax also did much to soak up (or else to drive underground) private accumulated capital that could have been channeled into trade. And the persistent fears and hesitations of rich peasants in the face of the new restrictions deterred them from using their surplus capital in ways that might be regarded as exploitative.

In the Central South the government moved almost immediately to try to fill the commercial void and restore domestic trade. Provincial and municipal authorities attempted to convince urban traders to go down to the villages to sell items of daily use and buy rural products and handicrafts to sell in the cities.[2] But there were several difficulties with this approach right after liberation. City peddlers were reluctant to go off into the countryside alone for fear of bandits. With local tax procedures still unregulated, peddlers feared that if they moved from one district to another, setting out their wares in different market towns, they would be forced to pay the commerce tax several times over. Furthermore, despite the disapproval of the CSMAC, there was still a cumbersome system of safe-conduct passes and business credentials for traders in use in some districts. This system had been instituted immediately following liberation to help prevent unlawful trafficking by criminals and counter-revolutionaries disguised as peddlers, but it was also undoubtedly sometimes manipulated by local traders with a view to limiting outside competition. Even proper credentials were no guarantee that city-based peddlers would be free to conduct business without harassment. For they relied on high-volume, low-profit business, underselling local traders, to make their excursions into the hinterland worthwhile. There were several reports of official credentials being torn up by local tradesmen trying to frighten and drive out the competition. Thus many urban peddlers confined their activities to the market towns and fairs and dared not venture into the *hsiang*. Still others were deterred by haulage prob-

2. *CCJP*, 1 Jun. 51 [182]. See also *CCJP*, 10 Jul. 51 [210].

lems. Until the *jen min pi* (people's currency) was widely circulated, they frequently had to take payment in kind from peasants, which seriously cut down their mobility and therefore their profits. For all these reasons, the simple dispatch of peddlers and small traders to the countryside was both unsystematic and unreliable, and of course it did little to consolidate central control over domestic trade.

The first step toward a comprehensive solution came with the establishment of national specialized trading companies, organized by commodity or product (grain, salt, coal, cotton cloth, and so on) in March 1950. They were to play a decisive role in limiting speculation, stabilizing prices, and eventually expanding the nation's commercial network. State trading companies were organized and financed under the Ministry of Trade. They obtained their commodities from essentially three sources: (1) tax in kind, requisitioned from the Ministry of Finance;[3] (2) purchase contracts with state-run and with joint publicly/privately run manufacturing enterprises; and (3) purchase contracts with private industries and with peasants.[4] Their basic strategy was to purchase as much as possible across the nation at competitive prices and then to sell at prices set by the Ministry of Trade.[5] Through their control of large quantities of products in major centers all over China and through their centralized organization, they were capable of saturating most markets in the face of speculative storms and also of exerting powerful price leadership. Even as early as 1950, the state trading companies were estimated to handle a large share of the total national trade in several key commodities.[6] Within a few years they were to develop near monopolies in most important products, contributing much to bringing China's serious inflation under control.

The concentrated nature of prerevolutionary bureaucratic capitalist industrialization in China had allowed the new government to ac-

3. This was naturally an especially important source for the state grain company, but since it was possible to pay taxes in cash crops and other crops as well as grain, the Ministry of Finance had many different commodities on hand to supply the various state trading companies.

4. Hsia [461], pp. 34–35.

5. At this period, as Hsia has pointed out, the state trading companies generally included a profit of 3–7 percent in their wholesale prices. He concludes that this probably helped them in the effort to curb inflation since "the inclusion of normal profit exerts a stabilizing influence" by promoting the cooperation of private wholesale and retail merchants. *Ibid.*, p. 39.

6. *Ibid.*, p. 35.

complish a swift and effective nationalization of major industries in the period immediately following liberation in 1949. This in turn brought enormous, one-time-only profits to the center and gave it the resources to move, through its state trading companies, into the rural markets to isolate independent merchants.

Table 23 provides an idea of the quick expansion in state trading company purchases from private manufacturers in the early years, while Table 24 presents rough estimates of the growth of the state share of wholesale trade throughout the country.

As the state trading companies' share of the total national trade rapidly increased, they naturally required more and more purchasing stations in market towns everywhere. They also needed to establish links with retail merchants who would serve as outlets for their goods. At first

TABLE 23. Index of Value of State Trading Company Purchases from Private Industrial Suppliers, 1949–55

	Value of State-ordered Processed Merchandise from Private Industry	As % of Retail Value of Output of Private Industry
1949	100 (index)	11.9
1950	258.6	28.8
1951	532.6	42.7
1952	726.9	56.0
1953	999.1	61.8
1954	1000.9	78.5
1955	731.5	81.7

SOURCE: Ch'u Ch'ing et al. [7], p. 12.

NOTE: Over this period the numbers of fully private industrial enterprises of course declined dramatically.

TABLE 24. State and Private Shares of Total National Wholesale Trade, 1950–54

(as % of total wholesale trade)

	State-run and Cooperative Commerce	National Capitalist Commerce	Privately-run Commerce
1950	23.8	0.1	76.1
1952	63.2	0.5	36.3
1953	69.2	0.5	30.3
1954	89.3	0.5	10.2

SOURCE: Ch'u Ch'ing et al. [7], p. 13.

the individual state trading companies set up their own purchasing stations to deal directly with the peasants.[7] But they were unable to staff a sufficient number of stations and did not have the personnel to go among the peasants and propagandize their price policy. Nor did they have adequate control over their commissioned retailers, who were permitted to sell at a small profit over the list price but who did not always abide by the agreements or fulfill the contracts. Furthermore, since most farmers had more than one type of produce they wished to sell and more than one type of item they needed to buy, the numerous purchase and sale arrangements made by specialized product state trading companies were neither particularly efficient nor especially convenient. It was in order to fill the need for a unified marketing and retail establishment with a network reaching into the market towns that the rural Supply and Marketing Cooperatives were proliferated.

In 1949 there were only 20,133 Supply and Marketing Co-ops functioning in the whole country, most of them concentrated in older liberated areas and doing business with only one retail outlet per co-op. By 1952 the total number of co-ops had only risen to 32,788, but membership had grown from just over 10 million to more than 138 million.[8] These Supply and Marketing Co-ops had a total of over 99,000 retail outlets and handled 20.5 percent of all retail sales on rural markets in 1952.[9]

The first Supply and Marketing Co-ops in the Central South were set up on an experimental basis, financed largely by government loans and advances from the state trading companies. They relied heavily on leadership and assistance from the province governments and the state trading companies in opening up their business.[10] Despite their origins, however, they were not intended to be entirely the creatures of the state-

7. *CCJP*, 15 Aug. 51 [211]. See also *CCJP*, 15 Jun. 52 [443].

8. And share capital (which was by no means all their working capital) had risen from 11,580,000 *yüan* to 224,330,000 *yüan*. Ch'u Ch'ing et al. [7], p. 18.

9. The outlets were broken down as follows: 82,305 retail shops, 5,128 permanent stalls, and 11,736 mobile retail units. Co-op purchases in some commodities in 1952, expressed as a percentage of the total marketed volume, were impressive: about 50 percent of all grains, cured tobacco, tea, and domestic silkworm cocoons; over 80 percent of cotton with seeds; 70 percent of jute; and approximately 35 percent of rapeseed and wool. *Ibid.*

10. *CCJP* editorial, 4 Apr. 51 [390]; also *CCJP*, 26 Aug. 51 [280]. For some evidence that Hupei's earliest SMCs were composed mainly of wealthier peasants, see also *CCJP*, 12 May 51 [272].

run economy. It was said that rural trade co-ops in the old liberated areas had relied too much on the government for leadership and financing and had in reality become simple extensions of the state-run economy. The new Supply and Marketing Co-ops were supposed to assist the state trading companies but to concentrate more on serving their local area and to rely more on their peasant members for funding and for business initiative.[11] In theoretical terms the new Supply and Marketing Co-ops were to be "semi-socialist" in character:

> The Supply and Marketing Cooperative is semi-socialist in the sense that it organizes independent producers in such a way that capitalism does not arise, but it is not yet socialist in itself; it is in this that it differs from state-run economy. [The co-op is neither privatistic nor capitalistic because] the share capital belongs to the mass of co-op members; it is put in by each member equally, and its goal is to get consumer goods into consumers' hands more easily, to enable producers to buy tools and materials more easily while also receiving a reasonable price for their products. The purpose is not to make profits and dividends, nor to exploit others; on the contrary, it is to protect the interests of consumers and producers. But the goal of private commerce is to make profits and to exploit consumers and small producers. This is a difference in principle.[12]

As this paragraph indicates, the organization and functions of the Supply and Marketing Co-ops were conceived rather strictly so as to conform to the situation during the transition to socialism. As with the Mutual Aid Teams, and with the Credit Co-ops described below, the official operational rules and guidelines for Supply and Marketing Co-ops were as often broken and abandoned as they were observed. Still, it is worth examining briefly here the original ideal formulations, in order to assess more carefully the real problems, successes, and failures that later emerged.

ORGANIZATION AND FUNCTIONS OF SUPPLY AND MARKETING COOPERATIVES

Each peasant gained membership to the cooperative by paying a flat entry fee and purchasing one share. Each individual was to have equal

---

11. Li Jen-liu [23], p. 21.

12. *Ibid.*, p. 20. The discussion of the organizational details of SMCs that follows is derived in large part from this source.

rights based on that equal share payment *(p'ing ku p'ing ch'üan)*, and therefore entry was officially to be made with the individual, not the household, as the unit. The limit of one share to a member was also intended to ensure that all members enjoyed equal powers in the organization, but it was certainly one of the rules most flagrantly disregarded. When SMC cadres could find peasants willing to invest more than the cost of one share in the organization, they were glad to have the extra capital. The real price of a share varied greatly from co-op to co-op. The entry fee was usually only nominal, but the share price seems to have been substantial enough to have made it impossible for many peasants to join, and to have caused others to buy their shares in installments. Cooperative shares were nontransferable and could not be used as collateral in any outside transactions or be pawned. A member wishing to withdraw from the co-op was supposed to give notice at least one month before the annual financial statement; then the member's share money would be returned, with deductions if the co-op had suffered losses, or possibly with a small addition if it had made a profit.

The payment of dividends was not to be a primary goal of the cooperative, and the official procedure for making dividend payments in a profitable year was quite cumbersome. A vote of the full membership (often several thousand people) had to be taken, and if a majority voted for dividends, and if higher-level co-op authorities approved it, a dividend not to exceed 15 percent of the original share value might be paid to members. When a member died, his or her share could be cashed in and the money transferred to the legal heirs; or else, if the heirs were also co-op members, the share money could be transferred to their accounts. This, naturally, was one of the ways in which some members accumulated more shares than others.

The class policy for Supply and Marketing Co-ops seems to have been somewhat looser than for Mutual Aid Teams and elementary production cooperatives. Only members of the laboring masses were to be eligible, but rich peasants were not specifically excluded, and even reformed landlords were generally to be allowed to join although the co-op reserved the option of denying them the right to vote and hold office. By and large, it seems that rich peasants with extra capital and produce, carts and oxen, greater purchasing power, marketing knowledge, and connections with people in the market towns were welcomed by SMC cadres and members.

The internal management structure of a basic-level Supply and Marketing Co-op was supposed to be divided into three tiers. The highest authority, with the ability to make final decisions on all important matters, was to be the general meeting of all co-op members. But even in theory the general meeting was only to be convened about four times a year—more than four times only if emergencies arose. It was really the executive committee of the co-op, composed of from five to thirteen members, that was to handle the day-to-day business. The executive committee's functions were to carry out decisions of the general meeting and directives from higher-level Supply and Marketing Cooperatives, and to draw up the business and organizational plans of the co-op (to be voted on by the general meeting and then sent to the higher-level SMC for approval). The executive committee was responsible for carrying out all such approved plans. It also represented the Supply and Marketing Co-op in signing agreements and contracts, carried out propaganda and education of the members, appointed and dismissed co-op administrative workers and other employees, and handled all other matters relating to the co-op's organization, business, and finance. The executive committee was to report periodically to both the general meeting and to higher-level co-op officials.

A third organ, the supervisory council, was to consist of from five to nine persons who would oversee the work of the executive committee. This council was, in effect, a watchdog committee for the general membership, and recent executive committee members as well as persons having close relatives on the executive committee were barred from serving on it. All SMC office holders were supposed to be elected directly by the full membership; but once chosen, their names had to be submitted to the higher-level co-op for approval. The term of office for all positions was supposed to be only one year.

In the larger Supply and Marketing Co-ops there was to be a fourth management tier that probably, in effect, replaced the unwieldy general meeting. This was the co-op members' representative committee.[13] The representatives would be chosen from the Mutual Aid Teams belonging to the SMC, and they were to reflect members' opinions to the executive committee and report and propagandize the work of co-op leaders to the members of their Mutual Aid Teams. Where there were no Mutual Aid

13. *CCJP,* 9 Jun. 52 [367].

Teams or where not all co-op members belonged to a team, co-op members' small groups *(she-yüan hsiao-tsu)* were supposed to be formed to take their place in the co-op administrative hierarchy.

The administrative level at which the basic Supply and Marketing Co-ops were to be established was a matter of some ambiguity and debate. In some parts of the old liberated areas there had been a Supply and Marketing Co-op branch in every hamlet *(ts'un)*. In the Central South immediately after liberation, however, there were insufficient personnel available to staff a co-op in every *ts'un* or even in every *hsiang*. At first it was thought that SMCs could be set up in the traditional market towns *(chen)* generally serving five or six villages.[14] Peasants could then continue marketing their crops in the accustomed places. But in the first two years probably very few if any experimental Supply and Marketing Co-ops were established below the subdistrict *(ch'ü)* level, which contained several market towns. And in mid-1951, Teng Tzu-hui announced an official policy of setting up SMCs as widely as possible in areas that had finished land reform, but not below the *ch'ü* level. Once again, inadequate staff and cost cutting were given as the main reasons.[15]

This was not to mean, however, that peasants and Mutual Aid Teams would have to travel all the way to the subdistrict seat to buy and sell. According to Teng, the well-run Supply and Marketing Co-op would have several departments and branches across the district.[16] There would be, for instance, a retail shop at the *ch'ü* level, perhaps a small shop in each market town stocking staple items, and in some of the larger *hsiang* a retail "office" might be created—that is, one or two people could be deputized to take orders from peasants, relay them to the nearest shop, and arrange for an SMC peddler to deliver the ordered

14. Li Jen-liu [23], pp. 30–32.

15. *CCJP*, 18 Jun. 51 [344]. From Teng's report it is evident that this had become a serious issue and one over which lines had been drawn, with some cadres strongly advocating that SMCs take the market town as their primary base of operation. It should be noted that at precisely the same time as Teng's announcement of SMC policy, however, an order was issued for a reduction in the size of the administrative *hsiang* and the *ch'ü* in the entire Central South. The reduction in size meant an increase in the number of both; the number of *ch'ü* in Hunan was increased to about 900, and in Hupei to about 850, each *ch'ü* having approximately 20,000 to 30,000 residents. This may well represent a compromise—the SMCs were to remain at *ch'ü* level, but the *ch'ü* would become smaller and serve fewer market towns. See *CB* 131 [490]; and also Hofheinz [502], pp. 142–43.

16. See also *TKP*, 20 Nov. 53 [446].

items. The co-op would also have a marketing branch to set up purchasing stations for Mutual Aid Teams and peasants in some or even all of the *ch'ü* market towns. And it would have a production department operating small enterprises at convenient locations across the *ch'ü*. An oil-extracting station, a hemp factory, a cotton-spinning shop, a cotton gin, a lime kiln, an iron forge—any of these might be set up where they could be staffed and would best serve the population and respond to local commercial opportunities. And finally, as explained in more detail in the next chapter, Supply and Marketing Co-ops were encouraged to set up credit and loan departments to either supplement or substitute for a separate Credit Co-op in the area. In their credit and loan activities, Supply and Marketing Cooperatives could utilize their own share capital, money supplied by the People's Bank, or money from capital advances made to them by state trading companies.

Although encouraged to diversify their operations as much as possible to draw greater peasant participation, the primary functions of the basic-level SMCs were in trade. They were to purchase the agricultural produce, the native products, and the handicrafts of their members and market them either in their own retail shops, or by selling them to state trading companies, or else by barter or other trade agreements with other co-ops. They were also to purchase important means of production as well as items of daily use required by their members, usually from state trading companies and other SMCs, but also when necessary from private merchants, and then make those goods available to members at fair prices. They were to make transport and credit arrangements for members insofar as possible, and to assist them in the special processing of local produce for marketing. They were to accept deputations from higher level Supply and Marketing Co-ops and from state-run commercial organs to buy, sell, and make loans.

The independent farming household or the Mutual Aid Team often derived important material benefits from joining an active Supply and Marketing Cooperative. The co-op helped assure peasants a stable minimum price and a reliable market outlet for their major agricultural crops. It could supply them with raw materials for sideline occupations and handicrafts at competitive prices and then market their products for them. It could give them access to another source of short-term low-interest loans and make available superior tools and fertilizer. And if they belonged to a Mutual Aid Team, the SMC gave them preferential treatment in acquiring and paying for these things. Co-ops could also give some peasants a chance to earn a little extra money, since they naturally gave preference to members in hiring when they required extra labor power to transport or process goods. In this way the co-ops took up some of the slack when former landlords, rich peasants, and others were hiring fewer short-term laborers. As the SMCs expanded and the capabilities of private merchants diminished and became more unpredictable, the certainty of a market the co-op provided for its members became a more and more persuasive argument for independent farmers and Mutual Aid Teams to join.

As already suggested, the Supply and Marketing Co-ops were supposed to be sufficiently responsive to the particular demands of their members and sufficiently charged with initiative to avoid becoming mere extensions of the state trading companies. By the same token, however, they were consistently encouraged to regard themselves as the willing assistants of the state trading companies, simply taking up the business in geographical areas and in commodity areas where the state trading companies left off.[17] In reality, SMC cadres relied on the state trading companies for so much—for loans, for preference and price reductions on transport services, for assistance with accounting, record keeping, and pricing, for their purchasing power and their supplies of basic goods—that they had little choice but to respond to the leadership of state-run commerce if they were to stay in business.

This is not to say that conflicts did not develop between the two. State commerce departments in local areas were sometimes reluctant to utilize SMCs for purchase and supply work, preferring to rely on their old contacts and collaboration with the private merchant network. The co-ops, for their part, frequently found ways to make greater profits through by-passing or misleading state trade company officials.[18] In fact, SMC cadres, especially those at the lower levels, were regularly criticized for "profit thinking," for exerting themselves primarily to obtain a profit for their own unit rather than to serve the state-run economy and the longer-term interests of their members.[19] A natural propensity to try to keep

17. For important characterizations of the relationship between SMCs and state trading companies and for some detailed elaboration of their close liaison, see *TKP,* 18 Nov. 53 [88]; *JMJP,* 30 Nov. 53 [385]; *TKP,* 7 Dec. 53 [151]; and also *TKP,* 11 Dec. 53 [213].

18. *JMJP,* 18 Aug. 53 [238]; see also *Basic Information about Cooperative Economy* [1], p. 13.

19. For two typical criticisms of "profit thinking" made at quite different stages in the development of SMCs, see *CCJP,* 4 Jun. 52 [202]; and *CCJP,* 18 Dec. 55 [177]. For a

their organization in the black seems to have been difficult to restrain among basic-level co-op administrators. No doubt they were sometimes hoping to be able to make a small dividend payment to members so as to attract more of the peasants' resources into investments in the co-op. More commonly, however, profits were ploughed directly back into the Supply and Marketing Co-op itself, to strengthen and diversify its business operations.[20] Insufficient liaison between state trading companies and co-ops, sometimes spiced with mistrust of each other's motives, occasionally led the two into direct competition as the co-ops sought a wider market and a better price and the state commercial units sought monopoly control and price stability.[21]

In addition to frictions of this sort, a great many other problems cropped up as the Supply and Marketing Co-ops developed. First the three- or four-tiered democratic administrative structure outlined above was largely ignored in the actual formation of co-ops. Co-op cadres and employees were fairly universally chosen by superior-level co-op officials rather than elected. And once they had gained a little experience on the job it would certainly have been counterproductive to retire them after only one year's service. Jobs in SMC leadership required some skills, training, and ability that were in short supply in rural areas. State trading companies and *hsien* governments selected personnel and pulled together co-op staffs as best they could, leaving democratic controls and the fine points of administrative procedure to a later day. Also, in their haste to establish SMC units widely, entry into the co-op was often permitted with the household as the unit rather than with the prescribed individual as the unit; and there was apparently little effort made to keep the number of shares owned by all members actually equal. Many other concessions like these were routinely made.[22]

One of the more serious problems (or deviations) was a tendency among SMC organizers to favor rich peasants and well-to-do middle peasants in recruiting members and in distributing the benefits of mem-

---

suggestive discussion of "profit thinking" and its relationship to "departmentalism" and a deviant co-op purchasing procedure dubbed "systematic intake of goods," see also *TKP,* 11 Dec. 53 [213].

20. An engrossing exploration of the pros and cons of "profit thinking" can be found in Ouyang Shan's novel *Uncle Kao* [475], which tells the story of a Supply and Marketing Co-op in Shensi-Kansu-Ninghsia border region in 1941.

21. *JMJP* editorial, 21 Dec. 53 [42].

22. *CCJP,* 18 Jun. 51 [344].

bership such as loans of fertilizer and seed.[23] They were naturally afraid that it would not be easy to collect on loans or credits given to poor peasants, and they therefore preferred to make arrangements with better-off members. In seeking out good investment risks they sometimes passed over all SMC members and extended their credit to non-member farmers or even to private merchants. The discrimination against poor peasants occasionally created a situation in which almost all co-op members were rich peasants, upper middle peasants, and small trader households. Poor peasants were discouraged from joining the co-op and they derived little benefit from it. Co-ops exhibiting deviations of this serious a nature were eventually subject to stiff rectification.

Of course there were also some cases of simple corruption perpetrated by SMC cadres.[24] A number of the young peasants recruited into co-op work succumbed to temptation in handling stocks, invoices, and cash flow. A far more serious problem with cadres, however, was that of inducing them to take intelligent risks in drawing up their purchasing and marketing plans. In the early years, SMC administrators at the county and subdistrict levels were not under very great pressure to accept or fulfill quotas for the state trading companies. They made their own estimates and placed their own orders, and in doing so they evidently betrayed a strong tendency toward "conservatism," for which they were regularly criticized.

First, SMC cadres were extremely hesitant to make commitments to the state trading companies until just before the main harvest. The advance output estimates they received from Mutual Aid Teams were usually inflated, while those of independent peasants fell short of the truth. Trade personnel were reluctant to commit themselves until they could make their own assessments of the actual crop and then project the potential buying power of the peasants. Second, SMC cadres could not be sure that an unexpected surtax or special exaction for relief of a nearby disaster-stricken area, or else a vigorous campaign to get grain-surplus households to make low-interest loans to poorer households, might not dry up the pool of available free capital among their members and leave the co-op overextended, if they had been unwise enough to purchase too large a stock of supplies. For reasons such as these, SMC cadres would bide their time until late summer or autumn while the state trading com-

23. *JMJP,* 8 Jul. 52 [306].
24. *HHNP,* 6 Sep. 55 [402]; see also *CCJP,* 4 Jun. 52 [202].

panies, which could not be expected to do nearly all their business in just one season, hounded and cajoled the co-op agents to get them to make earlier stock purchases.[25]

The uncertainty about real peasant purchasing power was only one of the worries bedeviling SMC cadres. They also were agitated by doubt that what the state trading companies had for sale was what their members would really want to buy. They were preoccupied with trying to procure "brand name" products for sale to members. These, however, were in short supply and were generally distributed to consumers close to the place of manufacture in order to economize on transport costs. Co-op agents were reminded that national industrial output was still quite small and that 60–80 percent of consumer goods and means of production would have to be supplied by urban and rural handicrafts that did not carry a "brand name."[26] Government and state trading companies insisted that peasants would be satisfied with local handicraft products, but SMC cadres were apparently not so sanguine about the outcome of stocking large quantities of such items.[27]

Either because SMC cadres did not make sufficient effort to stock native products or because members declined to buy them, the apparent result was that peasants were not being induced to part with their surplus grain. Some peasants were simply eating more. In Hunan, for example, per capita grain consumption was reported to have risen from 433 catties in 1950 to 493 catties in 1952. And in 1953 it rose again to 513 catties (see Table 28). Others in the villages were keeping the grain and other crops left to them after taxes and hoping for the prices to go up. The government blamed rich peasants and merchants for hoarding and speculation, but even poor peasants who had only a little surplus were guilty of the same transgressions only on a smaller scale. Some of them were clearly motivated by the simple fear of revealing that they had a surplus and could afford to buy new things at the SMC store. A reassessment of each household's tax liability was due in only a year or two. Furthermore, most people were aware by then that full cooperativization was coming soon, but no one was exactly certain how it would be implemented.

25. *JMJP,* 19 Nov. 55 [302]; and also *HYHW,* 2 Aug. 56 [276].

26. *JMJP,* 17 Aug. 53 [366].

27. With reference to co-ops seeking "brand names," see the article on Ling-ling county [Hunan], *TKP,* 13 Oct. 55 (n.t.). For cases of co-ops that overstocked handicrafts products and encountered difficulty in getting rid of them, see *TKP,* 29 May 53 [99]; and *TKP,* 2 Aug. 55 [198]; also *HHNP,* 13 Aug. 55 [296].

Many still feared expropriation such as had been visited on the land-lords, and they continued to conceal what signs of wealth they could, hoping to keep themselves from "sticking out above other people." For others it was more a matter of not finding anything at the SMC store that they wanted more than their grain, despite reported rises in their buying power.[28]

The Supply and Marketing Co-ops and the state trading companies tried a number of ways of enlivening and enhancing rural trade and inducing peasants to sell more grain. One of the favored techniques employed by both was to hold a product exhibition to attract customers and demonstrate the range of goods available.[29] Party and government personnel were mobilized to urge peasants to attend the three- or four-day fair, sometimes visiting people at home to further propagandize the local SMC's upcoming extravaganza.[30] Exhibitions received official praise not only because they increased business but also because they were said to influence nonmember peasants to join co-ops, and members to purchase more shares.[31]

Another important technique for improving business was for SMCs to employ itinerant peddlers to sell to peasants and to relay their orders for more supplies to the co-op office.[32] Some of the peddlers were full-time SMC cadres and administrators. But the great majority were temporary employees of the co-op who had previous experience as private peddlers. All the goods were supplied through the co-op, but the ped-

28. After land reform, the buying power of peasants was reported to have risen all over the country, but not by the same amounts in different farming regions, and not, of course, by the same amounts for different classes. Ch'u Ch'ing et al. [7], pp. 35–36, report, on the basis of a survey of three districts in Kiangsi and Hunan, that in grain producing areas poor peasant buying power rose about twice as fast as that of middle peasants, but in special products areas the increases in middle peasant buying power greatly outstripped those of poor peasants.

29. State trading companies sent representative samples of their products at attractive prices on tours from *hsien* to *hsien,* and local SMC leaders and deputies were invited to attend the exhibitions and place orders. When *hsien* and *ch'ü* co-ops held exhibitions of the manufactured and handicrafts goods they had available, they often borrowed money from the Bank to have a good stock on hand. For a report of a successful state trading company exhibition in Hupei, see *TKP,* 19 Dec. 53 [293].

30. *TKP,* 19 Dec. 53 [45].

31. *HNCSP,* 29 Jan. 54 [365].

32. There were a great many news reports printed about co-op peddlers during and after 1953. Two of the more informative ones are *TKP,* 24 Nov. 54 [364]; and *TKP,* 15 Dec. 54 [183].

dlers received a certain profit on their sales.[33] Because of this they were sometimes given the rather ostentatious title of "joint public/private peddler small groups." Peddling for the co-op became quite common. By the end of 1955 there were said to be 5,000 part-time SMC peddlers in operation in Hunan alone.[34] The co-op peddling system was praised for enabling peasants to make purchases and place orders without taking time away from workpoint-earning tasks. Except for villages in mountainous or otherwise remote areas, however, the heavy reliance on peddlers proved to be only a transitional phase. After the general establishment of Agricultural Production Cooperatives, the Supply and Marketing Co-ops tried to set up a shop for each APC, or at least for each *hsiang*, to handle local trade. Former peddlers were then often fully absorbed into the co-op as shop attendants and salespeople.

All these efforts yielded some good results in the Central South. Yet, well after the completion of land reform and well into the mutual aid movement, SMCs were handling the marketing and consumer needs of only a fraction of the total peasant population. In late 1953 most peasants still marketed their own crops in the traditional market towns, and they dealt with private merchants and traders. They continued to guard their surplus grain carefully. By 1953, however, central leaders were already committed to the general idea of a five-year plan emphasizing rapid industrial expansion. To support industrial growth and to feed the cities, they concluded that greater control over the supply of cash crops and grain would be indispensable. Despite achievements in general price stabilization and the regularization of domestic trade, the private sector of the economy was still capable of precipitating speculative flurries that could disrupt planning, and the peasants were not turning sufficient grain onto the general market to support the desired rate of economic growth. If peasants would not voluntarily trade their surplus grain for goods available through the Supply and Marketing Co-ops, they would have to be required to make the trade by a system of compulsory sales of grain to the state. In late 1953, such a system, called "Unified Purchase and Unified Supply," was introduced, and the Supply and Marketing Co-ops were made the primary organ for implementing it. They did this

33. In 1956 it was stated that in Hunan their profits ought to range between 2 and 8 percent, depending on the type of product. This may indicate that peddlers were offered small material incentives in the form of higher rates of commission to turn over some of the poorer-selling items. See *HNNM,* 10 May 56 [403].

34. *TKP,* 31 Oct. 55 [206].

job extraordinarily well, and in the process they consolidated and greatly expanded their own economic influence.

UNIFIED PURCHASE
AND SUPPLY OF GRAIN

The Unified Purchase and Supply order was probably the single most powerful step taken to restrain rural petty capitalism at this stage, because it quite simply eradicated the peasant's own control over the disposition—and most particularly, over the marketing—of the crop that was harvested.[35] Intelligent independent marketing had come to be the most important of only a few ways left to surplus-producing peasants to make a good private profit and raise family income. Land reform had sharply limited the profit to be made by renting out land; Mutual Aid Teams made it more difficult to make a profit with hired labor; as explained below, Credit Co-ops and low-interest government loans were, at the same time, making it harder to make much money by lending money; and now, sales quotas and set prices were to make it virtually impossible to do any better than anyone else in the marketplace.

This created conditions in which the only remaining way to increase income was to increase output. And this in turn made cooperation in agricultural production more attractive to peasants, insofar as cooperation might bring more public funding or make farming more efficient and therefore more productive. Unified Purchase and Supply in effect decisively closed off what was in most cases the last significant option

35. Technically, government acquisition of grain was handled through a system called "Planned Purchase and Planned Supply," a system later extended to cotton and oil-bearing crops but to no others. Unified Purchase and Unified Supply was a separate system applied to tea, tobacco, dates, silk, wool, jute, hemp, and several other crops. Under Unified Purchase there were no quotas as there were for grain. Peasants were simply required to offer these crops for sale to the SMC in the first instance. Any of the crop not purchased by the co-op the peasant was permitted to sell in the free market. Despite this important distinction, the two systems were obviously conflated in Chinese minds, and in fact the term "Unified Purchase of Grain" is encountered in local press and pamphlets far more frequently than the technically correct "Planned Purchase of Grain." The *Ta Kung Pao* editorial of 1 March 54 even went so far as to say that Unified Purchase and Supply was a shorthand name for Planned Purchase and Supply. Following the dominant practice in the Chinese sources, therefore, references here are to "Unified Purchase and Unified Supply of Grain." I have concentrated here on the various grains since they were, overall, the most important crop. For some useful comments on purchase policy for other crops, see Perkins [477], pp. 48–55.

available to peasants for getting rich through independent action, and consequently it made cooperativization, when it came, much less of a sacrifice than it would otherwise have been.

From the point of view of village politics, the success of Unified Purchase went a long way toward diminishing the major outstanding differences in interest between middle peasants and poorer peasants, and thus it helped reestablish a basis for class unity in the coming confrontation with rich peasants. In this way it helped create a broad village constituency for rapid collectivization. The introduction of Unified Purchase and Supply is one of the clearest examples of a central decision taken deliberately to restructure the economic and thus the political environment at the basic level, so as to remove some of the obstacles to socialist transformation.

Terms of the Order and Rationale

The order putting Unified Purchase and Supply of grain into effect was issued on November 19, 1953, although it would not be printed in the *People's Daily* until March 1, 1954.[36] It was signed by Premier Chou En-lai, and it quite simply decreed that peasants must sell their surplus grain in amounts, kinds, and at prices set by the government.[37] Any grain remaining in peasants' hands (after payment of taxes and after sales under Unified Purchase), which was not needed for family consumption, for fodder, or for seed, could be saved, eaten, sold to the Supply and Marketing Co-op, traded on government markets that were to be established, or even exchanged in small amounts within the village for other goods. That is, only a limited and carefully supervised private market in grain was to be allowed to operate in rural areas.

The directive went on to say that the total amounts of grain purchased and supplied (that is, made available for sale to grain-short peasant households) would be determined in accord with the needs of the country, the people, and the food situation in the villages. The large administrative areas would each receive quotas, based on the state plan, from the GAC Finance and Economics Committee. The quotas for province, special district, and *hsien* would all be determined at the next highest administrative level above them. The quotas for subdistrict and for *hsiang* (or *ts'un*) were to be determined by the county. These quotas were to be

36. *JMJP,* 1 Mar. 54 [295].

37. Surplus grain was at this point defined as "that grain which one cannot eat up oneself and sooner or later will want to sell." See *CKCNP,* 23 Oct. 54 [432].

passed down and announced to the people who were then to be "led in democratic discussion about them." Small adjustments in the quotas at the local level were evidently permitted. Lower-level cadres suggested alterations to their superiors, who passed them to provincial officials, who finally drew up a revised draft plan to be sent to the large administrative area officials for approval. It was stipulated (Article IV) that the price paid to peasants for their grain was generally to be the local market price.

In the cities, employees of government organs, other organizations, schools, and enterprises were to be supplied with grain through their place of work. The general urban populace would be issued with grain ration cards, or else grain receipts or other accounts would be kept of how much each household purchased for consumption. Urban residents who, after buying state grain, had either a surplus or a deficit, or who because of their personal eating habits wished to exchange one kind of grain for another, were permitted to sell grain at designated state grain shops and Supply and Marketing Co-ops or to buy or sell grain on government-established grain markets. In market towns, cash crop areas, disaster areas, and other villages where people were not able to supply their own need for grain, the grain authorities committed themselves to making sufficient quantities available for sale. Restaurants, bakeries, hotels, trains, and boats needing grain for guests and patrons, and other industries and enterprises requiring grain for their business, were to be assigned a quota, based on their past use of grain, and that amount would be made available to them for purchase. They were forbidden to buy any other grain supplies privately. Meanwhile, all grain trading and processing that was state-run, local-government-run, or joint publicly/privately operated, and all co-op grain shops and factories were put under the direct supervision of the local government's grain department.

All private grain merchants were positively to cease dealing in grain. They could only be deputized by the government grain department to supply grain (that is, to act as distribution stations) under close state supervision and control. All privately run grain mills for husking and grinding and all grain processing factories were expressly prohibited from purchasing their own raw materials and selling their own products. They could only operate when deputized by the government grain department or when under government supervision and management.

They would have to charge prices set by the government, and their products would have to meet government standards.

The purposes of this radical new policy, as stated in the order, were to guarantee the availability of grain needed for both consumption and national construction, to stabilize the price of grain across the country, to eliminate speculation in grain, and to "consolidate the worker-peasant alliance." When the order was published, it was admitted that there had been serious problems in purchasing all the grain that was needed in 1953. In October of that year, the amount of grain sold by the state was 38.42 percent greater than the amount purchased, a very bad situation for fall.[38] This was blamed primarily on private merchants and speculators who made the price of grain fluctuate greatly and caused the peasants to hold back their grain, but the real roots of the problem were seen as lying in the very nature of the small peasant economy, and Unified Purchase was explicitly intended not only to rectify the immediate situation but also to create the conditions for a quicker transition to socialism in the villages:

> There are spontaneous capitalist tendencies in the small peasant economy. Since land reform, as the rural economy has developed, these spontaneous capitalist tendencies have also developed. After a minority of peasants collect a little grain they gradually begin hoarding, hiring labor, making usurious loans, engaging in commerce on the side, and other such capitalist activities, thereby exploiting others. Also in the villages are some households lacking grain that have no choice but to take loans and sell their land or animals. If this condition persists, the inevitable outcome must be the dead end of capitalism, where a minority prosper while the great majority become poor and bankrupt. The present government policy of Unified Purchase and Supply can, to a great extent, overcome the peasants' spontaneous capitalist tendencies and put an end to the division between rich and poor in the villages. It will enable the peasants to follow the socialist road of all prospering together.[39]

Unified Purchase and Supply of grain and other important crops was to help eliminate "spontaneous capitalist tendencies" among the peasants by unceremoniously eliminating "capitalism" in one stroke, as far as the commodities that peasants had an opportunity to control were concerned. It was also to help promote the socialization of agriculture by

38. *TKP* editorial, 1 Mar. 54 [68].   39. *HWJP,* 14 Apr. 54 [339].

removing one of the last important reasons why an independent peasant would choose to remain outside a Supply and Marketing Co-op or a Mutual Aid Team.

Implementation and Incentive Mechanisms

There can be no doubt that in terms of grain acquisitions the Unified Purchase and Supply system was immediately and resoundingly successful. Figures quickly began coming in testifying to the abrupt turnabout in the condition of government grain reserves. Government grain purchases in November 1953, the month Unified Purchase was begun, exceeded the October purchases by 83.51 percent. This was the highest monthly purchase level recorded in four years. And in December purchases were said to be 77.88 percent higher than in November.[40] The government estimated that it had purchased, overall, 80 percent more grain in 1953–54 than it had in 1952–53![41] Much of this grain was immediately made available for sale to urban consumers and grain-short farming households.[42]

The negative impact on private commercial activity was reported to have been impressive. The total co-op share of purchases in the rural market was declared to have risen from 57 percent in 1953 to about 70 percent in 1954. And on the supply side, the co-op share rose from 45.5 percent in 1953 to 66.2 percent.[43] Broken down by quarters, the combined effect on private commercial enterprise in rural areas was depicted as in Table 25.

Results as immediate and as positive as these indicate a remarkable degree of mass compliance with the Unified Purchase and Supply policy. Of course, black market trade in grain did occur in many areas, and there were numerous reports of illegal private trade in grain even after Unified Purchase was well under way.[44] All security organs, police, investigative committees, and activists were urged to seek out and put an end to illicit

40. *TKP* editorial, 1 Mar. 54 [68].

41. Yang Po [38], p. 37. Yang also gives slightly higher percentage increases for the months of November and December than the ones taken from *TKP* above.

42. As early as March 1954, it was announced that over 10,000 *hsiang* in Hunan had carried out "planned supply" for grain-short households. And in January, the amount of grain that had been supplied to cities in Hunan like Hsiang-t'an and Chu-chou was said to be more than 20 percent greater than the amount supplied at the same period in the previous year. *TKP*, 4 Mar. 54 [204].

43. Ch'u Ch'ing et al. [7], p. 20.

44. See, e.g., *JMJP*, 7 Mar. 54 [307].

TABLE 25. Decline in Private Rural Commercial Activity,
1953–54

	1st Quarter	*2nd Quarter*	*3rd Quarter*	*4th Quarter*
1953	55.6%	45%	51%	46.4%
1954	38.2	32.6	32.1	31.1

SOURCE: Ch'u Ch'ing et al. [7], p. 20.
NOTE: Figures in this table represent the % of total rural marketing activity handled
by private traders.

grain deals. Still, the enormous majority of peasants responded to the
new policy demands and sold their surplus grain at the SMC, in accord
with the law.

To appreciate some of the reasons why peasants were so quick to
respond positively to the new marketing policy, it should be realized
that, coming as it did in November, the Unified Purchase order had
something of the quality of an *ex post facto* law. Most grain merchants
and many better-off villagers had made grain deals with peasants in the
spring and summer. Usually they advanced a certain proportion of the
agreed purchase price of the crop to the tiller, on the understanding that
the grain would be turned over after the harvest in return for the remainder of the payment due. In November, before many merchants had
collected the grain, these arrangements were declared illegal, and the
merchants were branded as "unlawful grain speculators." When merchants came for the harvested grain, peasants could refuse to let them
have it, insisting that these private deals were no longer legal and carting
their grain off to the co-op for sale to the state. As for the advance the
merchant had given out earlier in the year, the peasant could be sure that
not much effort would be wasted on getting peasants to reimburse the
very people who were now being vilified as selfish and unpatriotic
capitalist exploiters of the poor. Where Supply and Marketing Co-op
authorities moved directly in on the business of private merchants, it
seems likely that peasants were eventually made to return at least part of
the advance money. But even in these cases, they were still likely to gain
by selling to the co-op since it was paying the market price for grain, or
close to it, while an agreement to "sell sprouts" to a merchant in the
spring generally worked out to a very low per catty price for the farmer.

Poor peasants who had been dealing with private merchants, therefore, had a considerable incentive to report their dealings to the Supply
and Marketing Co-op, denounce the merchants as exploiters, and sell all

their surplus grain to the co-op at the local fixed rate. As for merchants who protested the *ex post facto* nature of the new rules, they were most unlikely to receive a sympathetic hearing from local cadres who had grain purchase quotas to meet. Nor were the better-off peasants in the villages likely to take the merchants' part, first, because it would not have been wise to identify themselves with people currently under attack, and second, because the more grain poor peasants had in their hands the more readily the local quota could be reached without further pressure on themselves. Timing the introduction of Unified Purchase to coincide with the harvest, then, dealt a double blow to the grain dealers: it not only cut off all their future business but also tended to penalize them for speculative activity during the previous year.

Insofar as the private individuals purchasing grain from peasants had been middlemen and market speculators (as they were generally pictured in Chinese reports), the double blow they received was quite advantageous to the government in consolidating its control over the market. But insofar as they represented productive enterprises that required grain for their business operations, the effects were potentially dangerous to the local economy. The duck raising compounds of Hupei are a case in point.[45] These enterprises had regularly sent representatives out to "buy green sprouts" from poor peasants in the spring and to make private grain purchases from other peasants after the harvest to obtain feed for their ducks. As soon as Unified Purchase and Supply was announced, these businesses came under fire for their "illegal" grain purchase activities. Businesses like these did not fold because they were assigned a quota of grain they were to be permitted to buy from the state. But the higher prices they would have to pay for grain from the co-op plus the losses they sustained when poor peasants reneged on 1953 agreements must have cut down on profits and affected productivity for a time. Still, it was well worth some temporary setbacks in the output of private enterprises for the central authorities to be able to provide such compelling incentives to peasants to renounce their private contract arrangements and sell their grain through the co-op.[46]

45. *TKP,* 19 Nov. 53 [145].

46. Peasants were urged to reveal their own private arrangements with merchants and speculators as well as those of other peasants they knew and to help co-ops in propagandizing Unified Purchase by denouncing these arrangements and refusing to honor them. For some Hunan examples of how this worked, see *CKCNP,* 24 Nov. 53 [241]; and *JMJP,* 28 Nov. 53 [180].

There were still other incentives for peasants to comply with the new policy at this time. First, as already pointed out, the price offered at co-ops was generally keyed to the prevailing local market price.[47] This was true, of course, with the marked exception of areas of the country in which hoarding and speculation, bad weather, or other unusual circumstances had inflated the prevailing price of grains. Good local data on actual grain purchase prices paid to peasants under Unified Purchase is difficult to collect since the returns to farmers were usually rendered, in the local press, in terms of how many oxen or how much fertilizer a Mutual Aid Team could purchase with the money it received from grain sales. In the absence of firm local information on specific crops, however, it is possible to turn to aggregate figures to get an idea of the effect of Unified Purchase on peasant incomes.

In view of the much slower, less steady rise in prices peasants were having to pay for industrial and consumer goods, the Hunan price figures in Tables 26 and 27 suggest that the terms of trade after Unified Purchase moved somewhat in favor of agriculture. In press reports of the period this impression tends to be confirmed. Peasants were never portrayed as quarreling with the prices they were paid for grain, although they apparently frequently complained about the large quantities they were required to sell. There were reports of serious food shortages in some places where too much grain had been purchased and taken away.[48] And the overall figures for Hunan output and consumption at this time (see Table 28) do indicate an absolute drop in grain available to peasants after the implementation of the program. Hunan may be somewhat atypical in the extent of the drop, however, since the province was affected much more seriously than many others by the flooding in 1954.

In late 1953 and early 1954 there was clearly some tension over the

47. For a report that state prices paid to peasants for grain were raised "rationally and in a planned way" earlier in 1953, even before the full implementation of Unified Purchase in Hunan, see *Hunan Nung-yeh* [15], p. 98.

48. In some places purchase quotas were set too high, and administration of the system was so disorganized that some peasants actually suffered temporarily from hunger and deprivation. Especially the tendency of local cadres to stress purchasing while neglecting to arrange for supplies to grain-short households created a situation in which many peasants who had responded enthusiastically to Unified Purchase in the fall became anxious and discontented in the spring. The handling of the problem of excess purchasing and peasant discontent is discussed briefly below. A thorough study of achievements and excesses in the first years of Unified Purchase is contained in Bernstein [491].

TABLE 26. Hunan Price Index, 1950–55

	1950	1951	1952	1953	1954	1955
Index: purchase prices of agricultural products	100	112.60	110.91	123.27	119.27	120.23
Index: retail prices of industrial products	100	107.40	104.49	101.54	103.38	105.41

SOURCE: *Hunan Nung-yeh* [15], p. 99.

TABLE 27. Comparative Agricultural and Industrial Prices for Hunan

Years	Index: Purchase Prices of Agricultural Products	Index: Retail Prices of Industrial Products	Index: Rate of Exchange, Agricultural to Industrial Products	Index: Rate of Exchange, Industrial to Agricultural Products
Base: 1942–1948	100	100	100	100
1950	188.45	256.84	73.37	136.29
1955	227.64	266.17	85.52	116.93
Base: 1950	100	100	100	100
1955	120.23	105.41	114.05	87.67
1956	123.62	105.20	—	85.10

SOURCE: *Hunan Nung-yeh* [15], p. 99.
NOTE: This works out to a drop in the scissors difference of nearly 15 percent between 1950 and 1956.

high sales quotas village cadres were expected to fulfill. But at least as far as prices were concerned, the average peasant did not stand to lose by selling to the state. Moreover, peasants frequently found that dealing with the co-op could relieve them of some of their transport problems as well as their anxieties about going to market and what their luck there would be. If the price the government had set had not been close to the market price, it seems certain that broad peasant compliance with the Unified Purchase order would have been much more difficult to attain. The contrast, in this regard, with Soviet agricultural purchasing policy in the late 1920's is an important one.[49]

In addition to this, the Bank backed up the co-ops' efforts in Unified Purchase with preferential interest rates available to peasants making

49. The Soviet state procurement program operated at prices dramatically below market prices for grain in the analogous period before the main collectivization drive. See Lewin [467], pp. 183–184, 287; Jasny [465], pp. 224–225; and Dobb [457], p. 285.

TABLE 28. Hunan per Capita Grain Output and Consumption

	Before Liberation	Before Unified Purchase and Supply			After Unified Purchase and Supply				
	1936	1950	1951	1952	1953	1954	1955	1956	1957
Grain output (in 100 million catties)	—	194	166	206	206	185	225	207	225
Population (in 10,000s)	—	3,074	3,190	3,271	3,322	3,397	3,440	3,507	3,213
Average per capita usable grain (in catties)	476	—	—	—	558	537	567	565	594.5
Average per capita grain consumption (in catties)	—	433	441	493	513	494	516	519	501

SOURCE: *Hunan Nung-yeh* [15], p. 93.

deposits of money received by selling surplus grain to the state.[50] The rates were very attractive: 1.5 percent per month on deposits of one or two months; 2 percent per month on deposits of three to six months. Six months was to be the maximum term of deposits, and only money from grain sales was to be accepted. The Bank made an effort to coordinate with the SMC purchasing schedule in a given area, making it impossible to receive the preferential rate once the co-op had completed its purchasing. This may help account for the quickness of peasant response to Unified Purchase in November and December 1953.

While few peasants may have been in a position to leave their money for the full six months, the earlier they deposited some of it, the more they could earn in interest. Bank cadres were at first unable to propagandize and administer the preferential interest rates in every market town in the country, and so it was made a matter of policy for them to focus attention on the richer areas, and within them, on the richer peasants. This focus tended not only to maximize the Bank's working capital but also to assist the Unified Purchase program in areas where purchases were apt to be the largest. That is, the government concentrated material incentives for compliance in the areas where it was most vital that it be able to attain compliance, and it aimed those incentives primarily at individual peasants with the least natural incentive to comply. For it was the peasants producing a considerable surplus who could have afforded to keep some grain off the market in speculation, and these same more prosperous peasants therefore who had potentially the most to lose through Unified Purchase. The Bank thus helped to gain compliance with the new policy from middle peasants and rich peasants by softening the blow to them and offering them an alternative way to put their surplus capital to work.

Finally, the manner in which local cadres handled the task of setting up and operating government markets for the authorized exchange of grain in the villages seems also to have been partly responsible for the quick response of peasants to the government call to sell their surplus grain at the co-op. Basic-level markets were supposed to be set up on the very sites where grain markets had traditionally functioned before Unified Purchase.[51] Existing grain trade shops, offices, and warehouses

50. The Bank directive itself, dated 21 Nov. 53, is available in *Collected Finance Laws and Orders* [135], pp. 107–108. See also *CKCNP*, 23 Oct. 54 [432].

51. *JMJP*, 2 Mar. 54 [324]. See also *JMJP*, 18 May 54 [95].

were to be taken over for government markets as needed, with a view to making trade arrangements at least as convenient as they had been before. The government commerce department, the grain department, and the local Supply and Marketing Co-ops were supposed to share the responsibility of running and regulating these new grain markets. They were to select a certain number of cadres for training and instruction in keeping records, bringing parties together and regulating the scales and measures. These cadres were to have some limited power to set the price of grain in their market, and they were to make sure that only buyers and sellers, working people, and grain-short peasants entered the market. No dealers were permitted; careful records were to be kept of how much of their allotment grain-short households had purchased; and bakeries and other shops with permission to buy in the market were to be closely supervised in the amounts they took.[52]

In fact, however, local finance cadres appear to have been quite tardy in setting up these marketplaces and in propagandizing them. They were officially criticized for this since it inhibited rural trade and since it also gave many peasants the false impression that they were only permitted to sell grain to the state and that all private trade of any kind was illegal.[53] This was a false impression most useful to local cadres trying to meet a state purchase quota, however. If there were no government-run markets nearby and if peasants knew they were forbidden to deal with private traders, then they had no choice but to come to the Supply and Marketing Co-op with their grain even after they had fulfilled their quota of sales.

There is good reason to think that few state-run grain markets were in fact established in 1953 and early 1954 and that this was not simply due to staffing and training problems, but was a deliberate move to channel even greater trade through co-ops. As late as May 1954, for example, it was reported that there were only 108 state-run grain markets functioning in the whole of Hunan province, and that most of those had been established within the preceding thirty days.[54] It was at about this time, in preparation for the 1954 harvest, that state-run markets were finally widely established. By mid-June of that year, the total number of such markets in Hunan had already jumped to 500.[55] For the first six or seven months under Unified Purchase, however, most peasants not living close

52. *HHNP,* 14 May 54 [322].
53. *TKP,* 11 Apr. 54 [297]; and *TKP,* 28 May 54 [139].
54. *HHNP,* 30 May 54 [320].   55. *HHNP,* 18 Jun. 54 [420].

to cities appear to have had no sizable legal marketing alternative to the co-op.

This review of some of the conditions surrounding the implementation of Unified Purchase and decisions taken in support of it illustrates how material incentives for compliance offered to peasants, plus a (probably deliberate but temporary) distortion of official policy, were instrumental in bringing about the extremely rapid expansion of government grain acquisitions under the program. Poor peasants dealing with private merchants had an incentive for compliance because of the *ex post facto* nature of the law; wealthier peasants were given an incentive for compliance through preferential savings arrangements coordinated with the Bank; and all peasants were drawn into dealing with the Supply and Marketing Co-ops because of the temporary absence of the state-run common exchange markets. China's peasants, who had not failed to respond to material incentives offered by the central authorities in the past, were once again not to disappoint the policy planners. Government propaganda and education for the program, not surprisingly, put a heavy emphasis on the contribution peasants could expect Unified Purchase to make to their own material well-being. The following short extract is typical:

> Ever since 1952 my family has been getting richer every day. I was beginning to sell surplus grain and make loans at high interest.
>
> In 1953 our *hsiang* implemented Unified Purchase and Supply, and the *hsiang* government wanted me to sell more than 6,000 catties of grain to the state, which ruined our family's plans for developing in the capitalist direction. At that time, the thinking of everyone in the family was stubborn and impenetrable. It was only after repeated education by the leadership that we forced ourselves to sell 5,600 catties of surplus grain to the state.
>
> But actual conditions have, little by little, made me deeply understand that the Unified Purchase and Supply of grain policy is really good. First of all, after Unified Purchase I had more cash to invest in production so as to make production increase even faster. And, what is especially unforgettable for me, last year our family was badly hit by flood. There seemed no way we could possibly get back to production. At that time of crisis, the government sent over 3,000 catties of food grain and gave us an emergency loan of over 100 *yüan*. There was also seed, fodder, winter clothing, and so on. This spring we also borrowed over 280 catties of seed and took various kinds of agricultural loans amounting to over 40 *yüan*, and some fodder for the ox. This enabled our 17-member family to get on

with production calmly, to get over the disaster smoothly, and to reap a fine harvest this year. I very deeply feel that if the state did not take the grain, it would not be possible for something like this to happen. It is really true that father, mother, and self together are not as good as the state is. Only by submitting to state plans will the individual, and family happiness, have a reliable guarantee.[56]

The success of Unified Purchase, certainly one of the most radical policy departures taken in the early years, like so many other steps in village transformation preceding and following it, was to rest heavily on the center's ability to convince peasants that compliance with the program would increase either their own income, or their own security, or both.

CONTRACT SYSTEMS

In their earliest days in operation, Supply and Marketing Co-ops made a great variety of *ad hoc* arrangements and deals with their peasant members that gradually evolved into a number of contract systems of varying degrees of complexity and sophistication. All these contract forms cannot be discussed here, but some of them were heavily propagandized and widely put into use. They played unusually important roles in limiting rural capitalism, in promoting the growth of mutual aid and cooperation, in making broader agricultural production planning possible, as well as in increasing crop yields. These contract systems were important in the process of early village transformation, both because of how they functioned and because of how they were made attractive to the peasantry.

From 1949 through 1953, when Supply and Marketing Co-ops in the later liberated areas were first set up on a keypoint basis and were, after land reform, gradually extended to each *ch'ü*, the most common type of contract they were negotiating with peasants was known as the "advance purchase" contract *(yü kou)*. The pattern was extremely simple. The co-op agreed in the spring or summer, often before planting, to buy a certain amount of the peasant's crop at a stated price after it was harvested, and it advanced a certain proportion of the purchase price at the time of the agreement. The peasant at that time incurred no obligation except to deliver the stated amount of the crop to the co-op at the agreed

56. *HNCNP,* 16 Oct. 55 [418].

time and to guarantee that it met the minimum quality standards. The farmer then collected the remainder of the money and the terms of the contract were complete. In these early years, advance purchase contracts were made for all sorts of crops and sideline products, from rice to chicken eggs to medicinal herbs gathered in the hills and mountains.[57]

The advance deposit on the goods given out by the Supply and Marketing Co-op was the aspect of the arrangement that appealed to poor farmers. Agreements to buy and sell immature or as yet unplanted crops were not new to Chinese peasants. The practice of "selling green sprouts" to merchants or wealthier peasants for the purpose of receiving just such an advance deposit has already been referred to several times. The difference, however, was that peasants who agreed in the spring to sell their crop to another individual were usually driven to it by the insufficiency of the last crop to sustain the family until the next harvest. They mortgaged their future crop in order to keep the family going, and it is not surprising that given their own desperation, and reminded of the risks that the purchaser was also to assume with the agreement, these peasants were usually made to accept a very low price for what they would deliver. When they made the agreement with a co-op, on the other hand, they still might be driven to it out of desperation, but the price the co-op offered was not reduced to take advantage of the peasant's situation: it was the estimated market price at the time the farmer would normally have sold the crop. The incentive effect of what was in essence an interest-free loan made these simple advance purchase contracts usually very popular.

The precise percentage of the purchase price paid in advance varied significantly depending on the type of crop or other commodity, the

57. Pfeffer has commented, "For the most part, advance purchase contracts have dealt with crops that are most vital to the state, especially those which since 1953 and 1954 have been subject to unified purchase and sales by the state." Pfeffer [510], p. 110. The materials for Hunan and Hupei suggest that this generalization applies only for the period after 1953, when a marked preference for applying advance purchase contracts to grain, cotton, and oil-bearing plants can easily be documented. Before Unified Purchase, however, it is not evident that any such preferences were expressed in the implementation of the contracts, and it seems doubtful that there were any very definite rules about it. In fact, during and after land reform, there were evidently many areas where advance purchase contracts were valued more as a means of supporting sideline and handicrafts occupations than as a method of assisting the state grain or cotton companies. For an interesting account of the advantages of advance purchase contracts in marketing sideline products, see CKNP 1 (6) [166], pp. 103–111.

location, and the financial and class status of the contracting peasants. In general the advances probably ranged between one-tenth and one-third of the total price, with the larger amounts being available to peasants cultivating crops that required relatively greater capital investments.[58] But a great many other factors were to be taken into account in disbursing these incentive payments. It appears that the size of the advance was generally greater in new areas and smaller in old ones, greater in disaster areas and smaller in nondisaster areas, and greater in cash crop and other special crop areas and smaller in staple grain crop areas.[59] Furthermore, it was a matter of policy to "give a big advance to households in difficulty and give a small advance or none at all to wealthy households" signing contracts.[60] Above all, it was thought to be necessary to "avoid egalitarianism" in the distribution of cash advances.[61] As a matter of fact, rich peasants who signed these contracts with co-ops were officially barred from receiving any cash advance whatsoever. They were given instead a line of credit good for purchases through the co-op.[62]

Advance purchase contracts were overtly used to support and encourage mutual aid and cooperation. Individual peasant households were permitted to request advance purchase contract arrangements with the co-ops, but Mutual Aid Teams were the deliberate objects of great favoritism in this process. It was one of the stated purposes of advance purchase contracts to foster the growth of mutual aid and cooperation by giving peasants an incentive to join teams and co-ops or to establish them.[63] Mutual Aid Teams were therefore recruited to sign contracts, and they were routinely given proportionally larger advances than individual households.[64] From the co-op's point of view, preferential treatment for Mutual Aid Teams made good business sense as well as good ideological sense. Most teams could produce and sell more than individual households, and contracts with them therefore meant larger purchases and acquisitions with a minimum of paper work. Where there were not enough teams and Agricultural Production Co-ops, the Supply and Marketing Co-op sometimes concluded contracts with its own co-op

58. Reliable local figures on this are scarce, but *Hunan Nung-yeh* [15], p. 112, reports that in 1956 the advance deposits for fine tea were between 15 and 25 percent; between 20 and 40 percent for coarse tea; and 15 percent for ramie.
59. *JMJP*, 28 Mar. 54 [169].   60. *HHNP*, 19 Apr. 54 [252].
61. *HHNP*, 18 May 54 [435].   62. *Ibid.* See also *JMJP*, 28 Mar. 54 [169].
63. *HHNP*, 15 May 54 [51]. See also *Hunan Nung-yeh* [15], p. 112.
64. *JMJP*, 28 Mar. 54 [57].

Wuhan (Hupei), East Lake area Supply and Marketing Co-op signing a contract with T'ao Sung-po's Mutual Aid Team for purchase of wheat and supply of fertilizer. (Hsinhua News Agency)

members' small groups or with other residential groupings. Even these arrangements strengthened the drive toward collectivism, however, and there can be no doubt that advance purchase contracts with Supply and Marketing Co-ops were behind the formation and consolidation of many a village Mutual Aid Team.

With the introduction of Unified Purchase, renewed emphasis was placed on the importance of signing advance purchase contracts. By the time the policy was initiated in November 1953, it was too late for advance purchase to play any extra part in the purchase of the 1953 harvest. But in the spring of 1954, the Party, the state trading companies, the co-ops, and several government departments mobilized their forces to sign contracts with peasants for grain and other commodities under Unified Purchase. In Hunan, besides rice, this included wheat, oil-bearing vegetables and seeds, tea, ramie, and hogs, as well as cotton, silkworm cocoons, and wool.[65] Finance and trade cadres from the county were sent down to basic-level Supply and Marketing Co-ops to help with the

65. *HHNP,* 17 Apr. 54 [321]. See also *Hunan Nung-yeh* [15], p. 112.

advance purchase work, which was now clearly concentrated on the Unified Purchase commodities.

Along with the purchase quotas local co-op cadres received, there came even more specific ''advance purchase quotas'' for the amounts of certain commodities they should be trying to acquire through advance purchase agreements concluded before the harvest.[66] A great deal of money was funneled through local Supply and Marketing Co-ops and into peasant hands in the form of advance purchase contract deposits, and this commitment of funds was one more means to induce peasants to cooperate with the compulsory sales program.

The advance purchase contract system was, on the whole, more than moderately successful in 1954. In some areas of the Central South, over 90 percent of grain-growing peasants agreed to sell their surplus grain to the state through advance purchase arrangements in the spring of 1954, and the extra cash that this brought into peasant villages before the growing season enabled some of these areas to attempt double-cropping for the first time, to purchase more expensive implements, and to raise their expected yield.[67]

Still, several sorts of problems arose in advance purchase work that inhibited its thoroughness and its contribution to accurate state planning. Sometimes peasants and Mutual Aid Teams were reluctant to commit themselves to sell large amounts to the co-ops. They were afraid there would not be enough of the basic raw material left over for them to make from it the things they would need, and they doubted the co-op's ability to supply them with alternative finished products for purchase. Or else they were simply afraid that the co-op would not live up to its part of the bargain and, at market time, would cut the purchase price of their crop. Or else they suspected that the co-op might later set an unreasonable conversion price for rice to wheat.[68] In addition, many peasants did not themselves abide by the contract agreement. They would take the cash advance, but when the time came to sell to the co-op, if they could get a higher price from a private merchant, they would make another deal instead of keeping faith with the co-op.[69]

66. *HHNP,* 24 May 54 [285].

67. See the report of one Hunan county in *HHNP,* 21 May 54 [52].

68. Some of the legitimate as well as some less well-substantiated fears of peasants entering into advance purchase contracts are listed in *HHNP,* 21 May 54 [371].

69. This was especially true of the ''Unified Purchase'' commodities as opposed to grain. See n. 35 above. *HHNP,* 19 May 54 [66]. See also *HHNP,* 20 May 54 [144].

Peasants and Mutual Aid Teams frequently greatly overestimated the size of the crop they would have available to sell to the co-op in order to get a larger advance. When they could not live up to their promises, the purchase and supply plans of the co-op would be thrown into disarray. Sometimes, however, they were prone to underestimate their crop, still trying to avoid "revealing their wealth" and still hoping that hoarding might pay off in the end.[70] Acceptance of false crop estimates was partly the fault of *ch'ü* SMC cadres who would come down to the countryside, go to the *hsiang* government office, and talk to anyone who would come in, believing whatever they said and signing contracts with them on the spot. Supply and Marketing Co-op cadres evidently failed to do sufficient liaison work with village cadres and activists. Many co-op cadres failed to propagandize the characteristics of advance purchase contracts among the people, and some used very disorderly procedures in their work, not keeping adequate records of which peasants had and had not received advances. Others failed to see to it that cash advances were actually put to productive use by the recipients; and some cadres were even charged with embezzling co-op money in the general confusion.[71] Still, with all these problems, advance purchase contracts were most successfully proliferated in 1954, and they were a central factor in the early enforcement of Unified Purchase.

The other important contract system employed in rural areas during the transition period was known as the "combined contract" *(chieh-ho ho-t'ung)*. Like the advance purchase contract, it was introduced early in the newly liberated areas, but it did not become universal until after 1953. Unlike advance purchase, it seems never to have been employed between Supply and Marketing Co-ops and individual households. Mutual Aid Teams and Agricultural Production Cooperatives were usually the only parties eligible to sign combined contracts with the Supply and Marketing Co-op.[72]

Combined contracts were generally signed in the spring, arranging for the purchase and sale of crops just being planted. And the purchasing side — the Supply and Marketing Co-op — generally made an advance deposit on the crop, just as with an advance purchase contract. But the Mutual Aid Team in this type of agreement took on greater obligations and responsibilities than those undertaken in advance purchase ar-

70. *HHNP,* 29 May 54 [131].
71. *TKP,* 28 Jun. 54 [141].   72. *CCJP,* 19 Jul. 52 [386].

rangements. In particular, the team estimated its need for fertilizer, seed, tools, salt, and other items it would have to buy, gave these estimates to the co-op, and promised, as part of the contract, to purchase them from the co-op. Sometimes the Mutual Aid Team also made an advance deposit on its promised purchases. Under this system, both parties to the contract were obligated *both* to buy *and* to sell, whereas under advance purchase one party had been obligated only to buy, and the other only to sell.[73]

The advantages of combined contracts from the co-op's point of view were numerous and important. No longer would peasants be able to take the co-op's cash advance to a private merchant to satisfy their consumer requirements. Peasants, through their Mutual Aid Teams, would contract for the Supply and Marketing Co-op to supply virtually all the industrial products, handicrafts, and manufactured goods they would need. This not only increased co-op business and helped to further isolate independent merchants, it also supplied state trading companies (by way of their client Supply and Marketing Co-ops) with superior marketing information allowing them to make longer-range and more accurate plans for production and distribution.[74]

Before the implementation of Unified Purchase and Supply in Hunan and Hupei, combined contracts were introduced only on an experimental keypoint basis, and they do not appear to have become very popular. Mutual Aid Teams were then still few in number, and price fluctuations on the free market inclined the peasant to avoid any more long-range commitments to the co-op than were necessary. With Unified Purchase, however, peasants were required to sell their surpluses of seven or eight different crops at the co-op, and furthermore, the co-op became the only place at which they could legally buy some of the things they would need. Private merchants were feeling the strain; free market prices became less attractive; and the certainty of finding a profitable outlet for sideline products through private merchants began to diminish. It became, therefore, more and more reasonable for peasants seeking security to sell even their non-Unified Purchase crops to the co-op, especially

---

73. For Hunan some totals of advance deposits by both peasants and co-ops are available: for 1955, 21,630,000 *yüan* in advance payments to peasants and 19,160,000 *yüan* in advance receipts from peasants; for 1956, 36,450,000 *yüan* and 24,990,000 *yüan*, respectively. See *Hunan Nung-yeh* [15], p. 112. It seems likely, however, that many of these exchanges were made on paper only.

74. *HHNP,* 11 May 54 [157].

since a combined contract for those crops signed in the spring would give them a cash advance or a line of credit that could be used to buy fertilizer at the co-op.

Gradually, Mutual Aid Teams began committing themselves to doing all their trade with the SMCs. The Unified Purchase commodities were generally handled through advance purchase contracts, while nonstaple and sideline products were handled through combined contracts. The more Mutual Aid Teams promised to the co-op, of course, the larger the cash advance to which they were theoretically entitled. It should not be supposed, however, that because of combined contracts, larger and larger sums of money were coming into peasant hands. Although the evidence is sketchy, it appears that the amount of the cash advance was usually put toward the cost of the goods the team agreed to buy at the time the contract was signed. In most cases, very little cash went directly to peasants.[75]

The combination of advance purchase contracts and combined contracts deployed by government trade departments in the Chinese countryside was clearly not simply a mechanism for state acquisition of agricultural produce. It was also a way of putting strictures on the free market and rural capitalism as well as an inducement for peasants to join in mutual aid and cooperation. Before Unified Purchase, peasants were attracted to the advance purchase contracts by the cash advances and the favorable prices. Afterward they were attracted to combined contracts by the security they offered in a time when independent entrepre-

---

75. The "Three Link" contract, an interesting variant of the combined contract that appeared on and off in the Central South in the early 1950's, may have been something of an exception to this rule. Three Link contracts were apparently only signed with Agricultural Production Co-ops (APCs) and part of the cash advance was deposited in the local Credit Co-op instead of being applied to the cost of goods the peasants were purchasing. The Credit Co-op usually paid a low rate of interest to the SMC on the deposit, and it also charged interest on loans to individual APC production teams wishing to use some of the cash temporarily. It is unclear whether this procedure was meant as a concession to APC members who insisted that more cash be available in the spring after contracts were signed, or whether this was merely a way of helping peasants to solve some of their own supply problems that the SMC was not yet in a position to handle. If Three Link contracts had been widely employed it is probable that they would ultimately have proven unnecessarily costly for peasants and inhibiting to SMC growth. But they appear to have been tried only experimentally and to have yielded to the more standard combined contract system described here. See *JMJP,* 28 May 54 [261]. Later reports of Three Link contracts were made by Radio Wuhan, 17 Dec. 55 and 21 Feb. 56.

neurship was suffering and when old marketing alliances could no longer necessarily be taken for granted. Aside from the peasants, who did collect on the material incentives built into the contract systems, the most immediate beneficiary of the success of contracts was the hierarchy of Supply and Marketing Co-ops. Through its contracts and deals with the peasants, the local SMC gradually became a center of village life. In its activities there was often the clearest manifestation in the villages of government and policy, of the General Line, and even of socialism. And through its contracts with peasants, the co-op was able to extend its influence and, to an increasing degree, its control, in the sphere of agricultural planning, organization, and production.

THREE FIX

As already noted, the program for Unified Purchase and Supply of grain enjoyed immediate and undoubted successes. State purchases of grain rose dramatically and the central government's grain reserves were restored and expanded. By the end of 1954, in fact, there is some evidence central planners were concluding that purchases had exceeded desirable levels, that Unified Purchase had, in effect, been too successful.[76] The grain purchase quotas sent down from upper levels had absorbed so much surplus grain that a backlash of discontent and anxiety was emerging, and the silent threat of peasants to cut production deliberately in the coming year became a major concern of the central au-

---

76. It has been suggested that the extremely high level of government grain acquisition in 1954 was accomplished deliberately in anticipation of a possible need for greater central grain reserves resulting from the coming rapid cooperativization. See Vogel [486], p. 139. Other analysts, however, have concluded that excess purchasing was essentially an error attributable to insufficient available data on real grain production and consumption, and that with cooperativization approaching the government exhibited a desire to get more grain into peasant hands rather than into the overflowing government granaries. See, e.g., Perkins [477], p. 51. Still others attribute the excesses of 1954 to the "campaign approach to implementation" of Unified Purchase, which, in the great pressure it puts on local cadres, tends to excesses in whatever policy is at hand. See Bernstein [491], pp. 397–398. In view of the resistance and discontent they could be certain extreme exactions would elicit from the peasants, it seems unlikely that central planners deliberately intended to put such a strain on them just when the planners were most in need of peasant goodwill and cooperation. The too-high grain acquisitions probably resulted more from poor information and the burgeoning demands of the industrial sector of the economy than from leadership apprehensions about rural cooperativization.

thorities. There were reports from Hunan and Hupei that large numbers of peasants were deliberately neglecting to put fertilizer on their rice plots and to prepare them properly for cultivation.[77] Since the leadership was not prepared to tolerate a nationwide reduction in grain output, they moved swiftly to revise the state grain purchase procedure so as to include incentives for peasants to increase production and to allow somewhat greater flexibility in distributing the burden of compulsory sales at the local level. The revised state grain purchase program put into effect in 1955 was known as the Three Fix policy.[78]

The Three Fix directive was first published in the *People's Daily* on August 25, 1955,[79] but it had actually been released in March to local cadres for study and preparation. The order stipulated that all grain-producing households be placed in one of three categories: grain-surplus households, self-sufficient households, and grain-short households. (All peasant households not producing grain automatically fell into the

77. See, e.g., *CCJP*, 2 Jul. 55 [279]. Vogel [486], pp. 139–140, reports that Kwangtung peasants, by contrast, reacted by planting *more* land to grain so as to have sufficient rice left over for themselves after meeting the quotas. Hunan and Hupei peasants seem to have been less concerned about their obligation to meet a quota and more inclined to think that by planting nonstaple crops they might be classified as grain-short, or at the least, be relieved of some compulsory sales. Both types of peasant reaction, of course, threw production planning into disarray.

78. It should be noted that not all economists agree on the causes prompting the introduction of Three Fix, or on its effects. Hughes and Luard, for example, do not find evidence of excessive state purchasing in 1954; instead they speak of peasant hoarding and the 1954 floods, which they conclude resulted in a "serious food shortage" in 1955. Three Fix, as they interpret it, was a means "to tighten the system of planned purchase" rather than a means to give it greater flexibility and to relax the government's quota system. See Hughes and Luard [463], pp. 186–191. My reading of the local press, however, inclines me to believe that concern with peasant hoarding, so pronounced in 1953, faded markedly after Unified Purchase and was replaced by concern over the potential production cutbacks of peasants rebelling against an overly vigorous compulsory sales program. The 1954 floods certainly presented serious problems, but there is every indication that the government was already in a position to provide relief grain and put an end to temporary food shortages. In fact, the preoccupation with preventing food shortages arising from natural disasters may have been partly responsible for the specially heavy local exactions through Unified Purchase. Furthermore, the national grain data other economists have collected (see, e.g., Perkins [477], p. 248) clearly demonstrates a sharp drop in state purchases in the 1955–56 season after the introduction of Three Fix. Such figures tend to support the conclusion that Three Fix represented a relaxation of state grain demands rather than an attempt at greater rigor.

79. *JMJP*, 25 Aug. 55 [325].

grain-short category.) To facilitate this division, a standard of grain consumption per household (ration) was determined at the province level, taking into the calculations food grain, seed grain, and animal fodder. Any household that produced just enough to pay its taxes and to meet its own consumption requirements (according to the provincial standard) without any grain left over was considered to be self-sufficient, and was neither required to sell nor permitted to buy any extra grain. Grain-short households were to be assigned an amount of grain they were entitled to purchase to make up for their deficit. And grain-surplus households were to be assigned an amount of grain they were required to sell to the co-op.

To help determine the status of each household, a normal annual yield figure for its grain crop, similar to the one used for tax purposes, was computed on the basis of the quantity and quality of its land, its tools, draught animals, and so on. This normal annual yield figure was one of the three fixed figures: fixed yield, fixed purchase, and fixed supply. Once set for 1955, the household's normal annual yield could not be changed for three years. This, as with the fixed normal annual yield of the agricultural tax, was intended to provide an incentive for the peasant to increase production. For, as the grain-surplus or self-sufficient peasant household increased its output in the following three years, its required sales to the state would remain constant. Peasants were to be more or less free to do what they liked with this extra grain—save it, eat it, continue selling to the state, trade it on a government grain market, or use it to barter with other peasants in the village.[80]

The fixed normal annual yield also provided an incentive for grain-short households to increase their production, but the incentive was somewhat less generous for them. Each grain-short household was required to draw up a plan of its expected year-by-year production increase. Its compulsory sales quota was keyed to this plan and also increased from year to year. Only if the household exceeded its planned production increase would it have surplus grain left over that was not subject to compulsory sales. However, a further stipulation (Article X) offered some special hope to the grain-short household. Any improvement that grain-short peasants made in the tools or cultivation technology available to their use would *not* be taken into consideration in draw-

80. In reality, there seems often to have been considerable pressure on grain-surplus peasants to continue selling to the co-op, or else to make their extra grain available for low-interest loans through their Credit Co-op, MAT, or APC.

ing up a plan of their probable production increase over the three years. This provision clearly established an incentive for poor peasants to seek out mutual aid and cooperation arrangements that would enhance their available means of production. And this incentive must certainly be considered one of the sources of the unusually swift enthusiastic reaction of poor peasants in 1955 to the establishment of Agricultural Production Co-ops.

Although, as with taxation, there may appear to be no place for quotas in a system resting on the determination of each household's normal productivity, state-set purchase quotas were not eliminated by the Three Fix policy. In fact, quotas and guidelines came down to the local cadres to help them make appropriate estimates for all three of the fixed figures. After receiving these estimates, the *hsiang* cadres discussed and propagandized them, made tentative categorizations for each household, and reported the figures to the county for approval. Deviations from the quotas could not be great. Entire provinces were not permitted to deviate more than 3 percent from the centrally determined quotas without first obtaining higher-level agreement (Article XXXIV). In general, SMCs were ordered to purchase 80–90 percent of the surplus grain of grain-surplus households. The locally stipulated percentage was supposed to be the same for all grain-surplus households in a given village, except that rich peasant households could expect to be required to sell more (Article XIV). When the Three Fix policy was first carried out experimentally in Hupei, 95–100 percent of the surplus grain of landlords and rich peasants was required to be sold to the co-op, and this was considered to be correct.[81]

As far as the supply of grain to grain-short households was concerned, the amounts and percentages are less certain. The evidence indicates, however, that in 1955 the amount of grain a grain-short household was permitted to buy at the co-op still left it below the consumption level of the grain-surplus households in its area.[82] This at least seems to have been the case in grain-producing areas. Some special effort was made, in contrast, to see to the grain needs of households classified as grain-short only because they were cash crop and technical crop producers. But for the ordinary grain-producing areas, there was evidently a double stan-

81. *CCJP*, 21 Oct. 55 [343].
82. *HHNP*, 6 Nov. 55 [404]. See also *JMJP*, 7 Oct. 56 [384]. In section four it is ordered that the same consumption standard be applied to both types of households, and that the prevailing discrimination against grain-short families be eliminated.

dard for how large a grain ration was sufficient for a family's needs: more for grain-surplus households and less for grain-short households. All things considered, the optimal classification the ordinary peasant household might hope to receive at this time would be that of having a very small grain surplus.

Although this discriminatory practice was officially abandoned in 1956, it was probably intended to do two quite different jobs in 1955 when Three Fix was first introduced: first, to keep the borderline peasants honest by deterring them from pretending to be poorer than they were, and second, to give the truly grain-short family an extra incentive to try to increase its output. Of course, this procedure also had the added advantage of reducing the potential strain on government grain reserves. Grain-short households were supposed to be issued with a certificate stating how much grain they were allowed to buy, and when and where they would be permitted to buy it. The exact number of catties a family was supposed to have to eat for the year now became a matter of public knowledge.

The emphasis of the Three Fix policy was on establishing the tasks and expectations for each household and then leaving them at the same level for three years so that ordinary peasants would not have to worry that if their grain output increased they would only be required to sell more and more of it to the state. Peasants knew that the purchase quotas of 1953–54 were not frozen. The quotas were already very high, and it seemed reasonable to expect them to go higher. It was this expectation that prompted them to put their capital and effort into other crops and enterprises on which they still had hope of making a higher rate of profit than they could in grain. With the Three Fix policy of 1955, not only were the quotas reduced somewhat and tailored more closely to individual household situations, but also the compulsory sales were fixed for three years and peasants were assured that an increase in their grain output would not bring a loss. This was a direct, unmistakable move to undercut peasant anxieties and stabilize production in the next few years.[83]

83. It is perhaps curious that some similar arrangement involving a determination of normal annual yield was not included in Unified Purchase from the beginning. The reaction of the peasants to the arbitrary quotas of 1953 and 1954 was after all fairly predictable; and as we know from the examination of agricultural tax policy, the government had already had considerable success in sidestepping this sort of problem through the use of a fixed normal annual yield. Still, it is probably accurate to suppose

Despite its emphasis on stability, the Three Fix policy did have to make provision for some changes that were liable to occur. Grain-short households that experienced a bumper harvest were naturally to have a reduction in the amount of grain supplied to them for purchase (Article XXVIII). In case of serious or widespread disaster in one area, the state reserved the right to increase purchases in bumper harvest areas, but the increase was to be limited to 40 percent of the amount by which the family's actual harvest exceeded normal yield. In general, births, deaths, marriages, or increases and decreases in livestock during the three years were not to change the normal yield estimate unless their effect on the household's income was quite dramatic. A loss or gain in land, however, was automatic cause for making a revised estimate (Article XXX).

All these rules and stipulations were transmitted to local cadres at special meetings, training sessions, and conferences. In Hupei a record 600,000 cadres and activists were said to have been prepared to carry out the work in the villages.[84] As with most important rural programs, once Three Fix work was under way model experiences in experimental villages were quickly publicized to serve as guidelines for local cadres to approximate in their own areas. The following such figures for Ho-tso Village in Hupei are typical of the grain purchase levels sought by central authorities through the implementation of Three Fix:[85]

quality of village land	middle grade
actual annual production (wet land)	3,691,678 catties
fixed production figure (wet land)	3,580,928 catties (97% of actual output)
actual annual production (dry land)	923,533 catties

---

that central planners in 1953 and 1954 still had only fuzzy and inadequate productivity estimates for large parts of the later liberated areas. They were very likely correct in assuming that, at least in the beginning, tough quotas reinforced by the radical anti-rich-peasant tendencies of many local cadres would provide them with a much clearer idea of the real level of grain output since land reform. Then, also, it was in the fall of 1955 that the agricultural tax figures were scheduled to be revised for the first time since 1952. It was more efficient and more profitable to do both normal annual yield calculations at approximately the same time, and at a time immediately following a period of fairly stringent exactions.

84. *TKP*, 15 Oct. 55 [228].   85. *CCJP*, 21 Oct. 55 [343].

fixed production figure (dry land)	893,832 catties (96.6% of actual output)
amount of grain purchased	85% of actual surplus grain
grain remaining in village for consumption	538 catties per capita
total amount of grain purchased and collected in taxes	1,515,313 catties (33.5% of total actual output)

Naturally, Three Fix work did not always progress smoothly and produce model results such as these. The stiff quotas of 1953 and 1954 filled many local cadres with fear that the purchase level would be set too high, that too little grain would be left in the villagers' hands, and that they would be both criticized by superiors for not meeting the targets and criticized by peasants for demanding too much.[86] Individual peasants, for their part, deliberately misrepresented their actual output, making reports of their productivity that would maximize the grain left in their hands. They antagonized local cadres, especially those who had tended from the beginning to emphasize grain purchase and deemphasize grain supply in their areas.[87] In some areas, the tension between cadres and peasants remained as great as it had been in 1954. The mutual distrust of the period as far as grain purchase and supply were concerned is sharply highlighted in this passage from an official study of Three Fix policy:

> In the past, grain-short households feared that the government could not or would not supply the amounts of grain it said it would. Consequently they reported the largest possible deficit, thinking that if they actually needed 500 catties they should report a need of 1000 catties. *Ts'un* cadres of course realized the masses were lying, and those reporting a deficit of 1,000 catties were just supplied with 500 catties. By implementing Three Fix this contradiction can be solved.[88]

The contradiction, however, was not always immediately solved. Exasperated cadres berated peasants for continuing to lie in 1955 when government policy was becoming less demanding. Rough words often only hardened peasant resistance, however. As one Hupei peasant defiantly explained: "If the government trusts me and doesn't want to criticize, I make a report leaving my family with 2,100 catties. If the

---

86. *CCJP,* 31 Oct. 55 [411].   87. *CCJP,* 13 Oct. 55 [444].
88. Jen Fu-hsiang et al. [19], p. 19.

government doesn't trust me and wants to criticize, I make a report leaving my family with 2,300 catties."[89]

Despite the persistence of some hardcore resistance, 1955 Three Fix work enjoyed overall success. The main point—that there were to be somewhat relaxed quotas and a fixed purchase level for three years—was not missed by the mass of peasants. Before Three Fix Hunan peasants were reported to have made up a rhyme expressing their fears, which said, "If there is purchase and supply without end, then there will be no advantage in increasing production." *(Kou hsiao wu ti, ts'eng-ch'an wu yi.)* But after Three Fix the peasants punned that it had also "fixed" their hearts, that is, their hearts were now at ease. *(San-ting lien wo-men ti hsin yeh ting-hsia-lai-le.)* Looking back on the work of 1955, even local investigators tended to give it high marks. In the first wave of rectification following a new rural policy initiative, it was not unusual for investigators to declare 50–60 percent of the work to have been "half-cooked" and deficient to one degree or another. But preliminary reports from Hupei suggested that the early Three Fix determination of a normal annual production figure for each household had been incorrect only in about 10 percent of cases: 7–8 percent too high and 2–3 percent too low.[90]

Following the initial implementation of Three Fix in the villages, a routine rectification of all such small errors and miscalculations was to be expected. In late 1955 and early 1956, however, the rectification of Three Fix work was interrupted in the countryside. At that time, peasants and cadres were overtaken by the tremendous hurtling movement to establish Agricultural Production Co-ops (APCs), which temporarily absorbed all the time, energy, and anxiety of everyone concerned.

Three Fix arrangements were necessarily altered to fit the new circumstances created by cooperativization. In October 1956 a new set of Three Fix regulations governing grain purchases from Agricultural Production Co-ops was released.[91] The most important feature of these regulations was the requirement that the 1955 fixed figures for each member household—fixed yield, fixed purchase, and fixed supply—were to be combined into a total for the APC. Co-ops with an overall surplus would then be classified as grain-surplus co-ops; those with

89. *HPJP,* 7 Oct. 56 [268].   90. *HPJP,* 30 Sep. 56 [373].
91. *JMJP,* 7 Oct. 56 [384].

neither surplus nor deficit would be considered self-sufficient; and those without enough grain would be classified as grain-short co-ops. As this new classification would imply, grain purchasing was from then on to be carried out with the Agricultural Production Co-op rather than the household as the unit. It has already been pointed out that the original Three Fix regulations gave poor households an incentive to join Agricultural Production Co-ops since improvements in their available means of production were not to be taken into account in estimating their probable production increase for the following three years. Now, in the 1956 Three Fix regulations, we find an important incentive for grain-surplus or wealthier households to join APCs with poorer members. Averaging incomes with poorer members, in accord with the new regulations, would mean a lower overall rate of compulsory sales for wealthier households; that is, more surplus grain retained in their own hands within the framework of the elementary Agricultural Production Co-op. It could, therefore, definitely be in the interest of grain-surplus households to form co-ops with grain-short households, as opposed to seeking out other grain-surplus families or Mutual Aid Teams.

This incentive to grain-surplus households was reinforced by the 1956 cessation of discrimination against grain-short households in the level of planned grain consumption. Since the amount of grain supplied to grain-short households was now supposed to bring them up to the standard of consumption of grain-surplus households, wealthier families did not have to fear that their allotted grain ration would be reduced by joining an Agricultural Production Co-op with poor families, or that they would be called upon to make special contributions or loans to poorer families in their co-op. These complementary incentives to both poor and well-to-do families provide at least part of the explanation why elementary Agricultural Production Co-ops were so quickly established and contained a desirable, economically rational class mix.

These incentives to poor and well-to-do peasants may not seem terribly impressive. But it must be realized that in a situation where increases in personal income were becoming ever more closely circumscribed, these Three Fix regulations represented some of the few remaining legal and socially acceptable modes of securing and of advancing one's own financial position. There can be little doubt that Three Fix provisions that made it more reasonable for poorer and richer peasants to consider allying with one another did help to create the conditions in which elementary Agricultural Production Co-ops could emerge so speedily.

There were, however, limits on the extent to which combinations of poorer and wealthier peasants could be mutually beneficial under Three Fix grain purchasing policy. Technically, of course, there would be no advance purchase contracts for grain in 1955.[92] With the introduction of Three Fix procedures, advance purchase contracts lost their significance as a means for the state to ensure its grain purchase level. But the possibility of receiving advance payment from the government had not lost its significance to the peasant. And in fact there were provisions in the Three Fix regulations for grain-surplus households (in 1955) and for grain-surplus Agricultural Production Co-ops (in 1956) to receive advance deposits from the Supply and Marketing Co-op on the amount of grain that it was determined they should have to sell. Grain-short households and APCs not selling grain to the state were not eligible for these advances to put toward greater production the following year. They were at a disadvantage in this respect.[93] It was not advisable for wealthier peasants, then, to join an APC with so many poor families already involved that it was liable to be classified as grain-short. The preferred classification was probably still that of having a small grain surplus, even after cooperativization.

Clearly the divergent interests between richer and poorer peasants and the tensions between them were not completely overcome by the Three Fix arrangements, even if these arrangements did tend to create conditions under which cooperativization could be immediately mutually beneficial. Obviously the exact nature of alliances and splits within the village was to vary with a great many factors from place to place. And furthermore, the Three Fix regulations themselves were often not explained thoroughly and not implemented as they had been planned, so that peasants did not always react as it was intended they would. Still, it is clear that the center continued to mold its rural policies with considerable attention to detail and with the management of the continuing village class struggle in mind. It is also clear that rural cadres were able to

92. *TKP,* 23 Mar. 55 [438].

93. As emphasized in the following chapter, however, all APCs, both grain-short and grain-surplus, were given priority over independent households in the distribution of other loans from co-ops and from the Bank. Grain-short co-ops were, therefore, not without resources for development. The loan priority of APCs was, as with MATs before them, a simple but strong incentive for peasants of all financial situations to join.

administer the Three Fix system in the countryside in 1955 and to make it stick. And the implementation of this policy, whatever its imbalances and discrepancies, made some radical alterations in the economic configuration of rural villages, helping to create a situation in which cooperativization could be viewed as less and less objectionable by a significant portion of the peasantry.

CHAPTER 6

Rural Finance and the
Credit Cooperatives

With the announcement of the General Line there came one other major economic program that, coupled with state intervention in domestic trade, was to be crucial in restraining the "rich peasant economy" and influential in drawing peasants into cooperative enterprise. This was the rapid move by state and cooperative institutions, starting in late 1953, to control the rural money market. State and cooperative dominance in rural finance was to allow much wider granting of low-interest loans specifically to undercut rich peasant and merchant moneylenders' opportunities to engage in usurious exploitation of the poor. This constituted another important step in reversing the perceived trend toward repolarization in the distribution of wealth in the villages. In the granting of this expanded state-managed credit, however, it also became possible to give more direct preferential terms and treatment to Mutual Aid Teams, to Supply and Marketing Co-ops, and later to production co-ops too, so as to support even more effectively the key institutional elements in the transition to socialism. Great numbers of peasants were soon drawn into cooperatives in the simple pursuit of a better deal, thanks to these supporting favorable credit terms. Once again the leadership sought explicitly to link the peasant's personal welfare with the intent of central policy, and to demonstrate that individual peasant interests could and would overlap with the collective interest of a larger village grouping.

But before the announcement of the General Line, the initial expansion of this supporting state and cooperative financial activity had rather a slow start. To begin with, state investments in the agricultural sector were tiny compared with investments in industry in the first years after liberation. The funds available for loans to peasants were minimal. As illustrated here, the People's Bank had made some remarkable efforts in rural areas in the early years, but its work was continuously plagued by lack of experienced staff and by insufficient funding to do what was required. Rural finance workers received little publicity and less glory during this period.

It was not until the wide proliferation of the Supply and Marketing Co-ops that the spotlight was turned on the by then urgent need to provide a financial support network for their expanding activities in trade. Then the role of the Bank and the newly forming Credit Co-ops (CCs) began to receive new emphasis. For if Supply and Marketing Co-ops were to be able to sign the planned volume of advance purchase contracts and complete their commodity procurement work, clearly there were going to have to be some large sums of centrally managed money devoted to these tasks and funneled to them quickly. The immediate key steps in socialist transformation were going to be heavily dependent on a fair degree of planned management of the rural money supply and particularly on the ability of cadres to produce loans and investments when peasants responded to the incentives deliberately built into the various contract systems, and later built into policies like Three Fix.

Even after 1953, as the discussion here suggests, the rural finance network, although important, was to play a somewhat muted support role in rural transformation. Yet without its rapid development the Supply and Marketing Co-ops, with their Unified Purchase quotas and trade contracts that were so crucial in altering peasant perceptions of the cooperative economy, could not have succeeded.

THE EARLY RURAL CREDIT SITUATION

As with the old rural trading relations, the availability of credit in the villages had been undermined to some extent by the accomplishment of the new government's most important socioeconomic reforms following liberation. It was pointed out earlier that the completion of land reform and the implementation of the agricultural tax laws effected radical alterations in village credit relations, capital circulation, and investments in agriculture. Those individuals who had traditionally maintained credit relationships with poor peasants—landlords, wealthy peasants, and market town moneylenders—had been restricted in the rates of interest they might charge immediately following liberation, and then many of them had been deprived of most if not all their surplus assets. They were, at this period, generally unable (and unwilling) to loan useful sums of money or grain to poorer peasants. While the long-term benefits to Chinese peasants of the CCP's limitation of usury were to be enormous, the short-term benefits were often rather difficult for peasants to appreciate, since the apparent immediate effect was to dry up sources of credit and to make it even harder to take a loan at *any* rate of interest.

In an attempt to meet the credit needs of the peasantry during and immediately after land reform, the government had adopted a policy of encouraging private loan agreements between individuals in the villages and market towns. This policy was referred to as "free borrowing and lending," and it involved government assurances to creditors that peasants would be made to repay what they borrowed, and assurances to poor peasants that unreasonably high rates of interest would not be permitted to reemerge. The ideal of free borrowing and lending was seriously undercut, however, by the prevailing conditions in rural villages. Middle and rich peasants who could afford to make small loans to poorer villagers were quite simply afraid to do it. First, they were afraid that the debts would never be repaid. The entire thrust of government policies and the behavior of local cadres were so clearly biased in favor of the poor, and the memory of landlords' expropriation without compensation was so vivid in the minds of potential creditors, that most were evidently convinced that they were never likely to see their money again, not to mention regaining principal and interest. Second, they were afraid that despite official assurances their loan activities would be considered exploitative by local people, and that consequently their class status *(ch'eng fen)* might be raised. This, they worried, could eventually subject them to expropriation of their property or to greater exactions through taxes and "voluntary" contributions. As noted several times already, fear of revealing wealth was neither easily nor quickly overcome, and the concealment of land and other assets therefore persisted for months and years after land reform. Such concealment effectively reduced the available investment capital in the rural areas.[1]

The apprehensions and suspicions of potential moneylenders were

1. Accounts of the fears of middle and rich peasants concerning private loans can be found in Ko Lin [20], pp. 102–103; and for Hunan in particular, *CCJP*, 24 May 51 [290].

elevated by widespread reports of middle and rich peasants who had been browbeaten or coerced into making loans. In some places "free borrowing" had been interpreted to mean that poor peasants might freely borrow other people's things, whether they were willing or not. Pseudo-official groups of poor and hired peasants sometimes went into the homes of middle and rich peasants to "draw up accounts" *(suan chang)*. They would estimate the household's harvest, deduct an amount for food, taxes, and other expenses, and then "borrow" all the remainder.[2] Although contrary to official policy, such acts of coercion and intimidation evidently occurred frequently, and middle and rich peasants found themselves under pressure to loan out more than they wished on terms they did not like to people they considered poor credit risks.

Where poor peasants had not been bold enough to demand loans, or where there were no wealthier peasants to prevail upon, they unavoidably suffered from the unnatural credit vacuum. When they could not get a loan, they were forced to sell their possessions in order to obtain enough to tide them over the "spring famine" and to cultivate their land. Desperate poor peasants, unable to find anyone in the village to extend a loan, "sold green sprouts" for the advance deposit a merchant would pay them.[3] These advances enabled many poor households to survive the period of scarcity, but deals made under these conditions, with the merchant incurring the risks of possible natural disasters and insect pest infestations and with the peasant in a weak bargaining position, naturally yielded extremely low crop prices for the farmers.[4]

In a few of the cash crop areas, state trading companies concerned with the production of specific commodities issued loans to poor peasants (and others) to promote production of those crops, and thereby helped to ease the credit problems of some farmers.[5] But clearly such measures had only limited use, and the credit problem, touching peasants everywhere, required unified, nationwide action consistent with other government policies and with the long-range goals of economic recovery.

2. *CCJP,* 24 May 51 [176].
3. See, e.g., *CCJP,* 22 Jul. 52 [352]; and also *TKP,* 24 Nov. 53 [263].
4. One example from Hunan indicates that peasants selling green sprouts in 1952 received about 3,500 *yüan* per *tan* of rice, while the local market price in July of that year was about 10,000 *yüan* per *tan*. *CCJP,* 22 Jul. 52 [352].
5. See the report of the loan program of the Central South branch of the China Tea Company in *JMJP,* 2 Jun. 50 [79].

FIRST PROGRAMS
OF THE PEOPLE'S BANK

While land reform was being carried out, the People's Bank was extending its organization into rural areas and setting up as many offices at the county level as possible.[6] In June 1951 Nan Han-chen, the Bank's director, reported that 80 percent of all Bank branches were directly involved in some aspect of rural finance, and that 60 percent of all Bank cadres (some 100,000 people) were concentrating on rural finance work.[7] Before the revolution, Chinese banking and financial activity had been lopsidedly concentrated in urban areas. Most of the preliberation office workers who were absorbed into the staff of the new People's Bank were city dwellers who were repelled by the idea of being sent out to a small town to open a new branch office. Furthermore, a great many of them, having been retained in their jobs only because of the vital nature of their expertise and experience, were not regarded as politically reliable elements.[8] For dependable staffing of all the new rural branch offices, therefore, it was said to be necessary to "absorb a large number of poor and suffering intellectuals who are familiar with rural conditions and who have ties with the local people, as well as cadres who have sprung from the peasants."[9] The difficulties involved in finding and training people to fit these specifications cannot be overemphasized.

Nevertheless, the People's Bank outlined an ambitious program of

6. Technically, the Agricultural Cooperative Bank, established in July 1951, was to be in charge of state loans and investments in agriculture, fisheries, animal husbandry, irrigation, and the promotion of rural cooperatives. While this bank was consolidating its organization, however, the People's Bank was left to oversee rural finance, and from all appearances, the Agricultural Cooperative Bank never did get on its feet sufficiently to take over the supervision of credit and loan activity in rural areas. In early 1955 a successor, the Agricultural Bank of China, was officially constituted, and it finally relieved the People's Bank of the primary responsibility for rural finance work.

7. Nan Han-chen [278], p. 4.

8. Cadres in economic and finance departments took a particularly tough drubbing during the "Three Anti" campaign against corruption, waste, and bureaucracy. One early 1952 report from the Central South complained that banking and trade cadres and employees were so nervous and anxious about the possibility of becoming targets of the Three Anti movement that work was piling up, loans and goods were not being relayed to the peasants, and a kind of paralysis was overtaking rural finance work just at the time of year when it should have been most active. CCJP, 6 Apr. 52 [334].

9. CCJP editorial, 6 Jun. 51 [291].

savings and loan plans for peasants.[10] Although rural savings was ultimately to become a matter of great urgency during and immediately following land reform, heavier emphasis was placed on the Bank's loan programs and these were officially regarded as the "core" of rural finance work during the reconstruction period.[11] Loans to peasants could be given directly from a Bank branch office, through a Supply and Marketing Cooperative or through a Credit Cooperative. In fact, following land reform Supply and Marketing Co-ops were the most widely used, and as explained in the previous chapter, the channeling of funds through them contributed greatly to the organization and consolidation of the Supply and Marketing Co-ops. The co-op itself either chose specific member households to receive loans, or else it used the money to buy products for loan to members.[12]

Generally speaking, loans were divided into three categories: (1) production loans; (2) loans for the transportation and marketing of agricultural and sideline products; and (3) general purpose capital loans.

1. Production loans granted by the Bank after land reform can be divided into two broad types. First, there were long-term loans (one to three years) for the purchase of major pieces of agricultural equipment and technical improvements. These loans were intended almost exclusively for Mutual Aid Teams, Agricultural Production Co-ops, and government-run collective farms. They were often referred to as "special purpose" loans *(chuan k'uan chuan yung)* because they were granted on condition that they be used only to buy certain items or to carry out certain projects. In the Central South, special purpose loans were generally for fertilizer, irrigation projects (especially the digging of wells), pesticides and sprayers, livestock, and superior strains of seed.[13] These loans were most often extended in collaboration with and on the advice of concerned governmental departments such as Agri-

---

10. Another important aspect of the Bank's work that received much attention at this period was to offer a variety of insurance packages to peasants and Mutual Aid Teams for the protection of their crops and oxen. The types of insurance arrangements administered by the Bank and their work methods are extremely interesting and a thorough study of ox insurance in particular would certainly contribute to an understanding of village economics before socialization. This cannot be attempted here, but see the discussion of rural insurance in Ko Lin [20], pp. 83–101.

11. *China Finance,* 20 Feb. 53 [284], pp. 5–6.

12. Ko Lin [20], p. 62.   13. *CCJP,* 22 Jun. 52 [77].

culture and Forestry, Water Conservancy, and the local Cooperatives Committee, which had sent teams into the villages to assess the needs of possible recipients. Second, there were shorter-term smaller loans of fertilizer, seed, and tools to poor and hired peasants with production difficulties. Mutual Aid Teams received preference, but some independent peasants also qualified for these small loans.

2. Trade and transport loans usually went either to state trading companies or to local Supply and Marketing Co-ops to aid them in purchasing and distributing agricultural and sideline products. Loans under this heading were also made to private merchants and companies to promote trade, the object being to supplement but not to interfere with state-run commerce. Also, loans were granted to local organs of government, Supply and Marketing Co-ops, and state trading companies for the purpose of organizing product exhibitions and trade fairs at all levels, and to arrange conferences to negotiate trade contracts.

3. General purpose capital loans usually covered extremely small advances to individual households to solve what were referred to as temporary problems of "livelihood." Loans for clothing, medicine, house repairs, funerals, and weddings all came under this heading, as well as small sums to enable peasants to engage in sideline occupations. It even covered occasional loans to private merchants to help them stock items desired by local peasants. General purpose capital advances were also made to Mutual Aid Team member households having difficulty in meeting their financial obligations to their team, and to poor peasants who wanted to buy a share in a co-op but could not afford it.

As Tables 29 and 30 illustrate for Hunan, the bulk of these loans were financed by the province.

It was said that over the whole period of the First Five-Year Plan, about 50 percent of all agricultural loans given out by Hunan province went to peasants for annual production expenses, and this was broken down as follows:

used to buy goods and fertilizer 73,240,000 *yüan*
(about 6,600,000 *tan* of ammonium sulfate)
used to buy seed 8,500,000 *yüan*
(worth about 1,500,000 *tan* of seed)
used to buy fodder, medicine, tools, etc. 22,850,000 *yüan*

TABLE 29. Total Hunan Agricultural Loans, 1953–57

(In 1000 *yüan*)

Type of Loan	1953	1954	1955	1956	1957
State-administered agricultural and water conservation loans (total)	171	1,155	982	4,893	8,052
State-administered agricultural loans	81	1,143	502	4,242	6,977
State-administered water conservation loans	90	12	480	651	1,075
Agricultural production loans (total)	38,856	44,123			
Long-term agricultural production loans (total)	17,319	6,321			
Long-term agriculture	821	—			
Long-term water conservation	12,856	6,321			
Long-term fishing	52	—			
Long-term cattle breeding	3,590	—			
Short-term agricultural loans (total	20,368	32,186			
Ordinary agriculture	19,746	32,186			
Fishing	192	—			
Cattle breeding	430	—			
Credit Co-op loans	1,169	5,618			
Agricultural production loans (total)			69,597	200,721	128,424
APC loans			33,031	81,939	62,993
Animal husbandry			5	40	34
Fishing			113	299	219
Loans to members of APCs, fishing or animal husbandry co-ops, and to individuals			19,426	28,121	16,588
Loans to poor peasants joining co-ops			2,572	40,198	11,073
Credit Co-op loans			14,450	50,124	37,517
Total	39,027	45,278	70,579	205,614	136,476

SOURCE: *Hunan Nung-yeh* [15], p. 109.

NOTE: Earlier loan activity by the province had amounted to 4,340,000 *yüan* in 1950; 7,840,000 *yüan* in 1951; and 17,860,000 *yüan* in 1952.

TABLE 30. Total Hunan Agricultural Loan Repayments, 1953–57
(In 1000 *yüan*)

Type of Loan	1953	1954	1955	1956	1957
State-administered agricultural and water conservation loans (total)	353	910	1,652	2,996	8,685
State-administered agricultural loans	223	208	1,372	2,750	6,924
State-administered water conservation loans	130	702	280	246	1,761
Agricultural production loans (total)	34,837	30,691			
Long-term agricultural production loans (total)	13,023	4,803			
Long-term agriculture	702	—			
Long-term water conservation	9,737	4,803			
Long-term fishing	48	—			
Long-term cattle breeding	2,536	—			
Short-term agricultural loans (total)	20,569	21,371			
Ordinary agriculture	19,887	21,371			
Fishing	177	—			
Cattle breeding	505	—			
Credit Co-op loans	1,245	4,517			
Agricultural production loans (total)			58,084	91,177	136,448
APC loans			21,638	47,452	72,750
Animal husbandry			3	9	40
Fishing			82	137	249
Loans to members of APCs, fishing or animal husbandry co-ops, and to individuals			22,512	19,537	16,757
Loans to poor peasants joining co-ops			423	5,074	10,842
Credit Co-op loans			13,426	18,968	35,810
Total	35,190	31,601	59,736	94,173	145,133

SOURCE: *Hunan Nung-yeh* [15], p. 110.

The province total during the same period for basic construction loans to agriculture (including the purchase of cattle and the building and repair of waterworks) was about 72,460,000 *yüan*.[14]

In distributing these and all loans, Bank cadres and other concerned cadres were enjoined to follow certain interesting guidelines and principles. Although independent farmers were not entirely excluded from consideration, preference for loans was to go to peasants organized into Mutual Aid Teams or Supply and Marketing Co-ops. Money and goods available for loan were to be distributed on a keypoint basis in an effort to strengthen production and supply in certain geographical areas and in certain trades and crops.[15] The tendency to divide loan money equally or to try to give all needy peasants a little something was supposed to be

---

14. *Hunan Nung-yeh* [15], p. 108. This by no means, of course, reflected the total provincial investment in agricultural improvement. Straight investments were reported as in the table which follows. The water conservation investment as reported here went into eleven medium-sized reservoirs and field irrigation systems serving 284,590 *mou*. The meteorology investment went into 164 observatories and weather reporting stations of varying degrees of sophistication. And the agriculture figure included the establishment of three large experimental farms, three tractor stations, and forty-five new tree farms. (*Hunan Nung-yeh* [15], pp. 106–107.)

Hunan Provincial Investments Related to Agriculture (in 1,000 yüan)

	Farm recla- mation	Agri- culture	Water conser- vation	Meteor- ology	Forestry	Aquatic products	Total outlay
1952	—	2,213	2,685	—	560	29	5,487
1953 Total	—	5,258	22,901	—	729	16	28,904
[As % of 1952]		[237.60%]	[852.92%]		[130.18%]	[55.17%]	
1954 Total	—	8,879	75,895	192	757	90	85,813
[As % of 1952]		[401.22%]	[2826%]		[135.18%]	[310.34%]	
1955	—	19,089	21,632	269	921	43	41,954
1956	—	21,698	40,051	435	5,930	74	68,188
1957	1,014	11,743	25,881	501	6,707	960	45,792
Five-year total	1,014	66,667	186,360	1,397	15,044	1,183	271,665*

SOURCE: *Hunan Nung-yeh* [15], p. 106.
NOTES: Figures include ususal province (and some *hsiang* and *chen*) disbursements. A part of the 1954 water conservation outlay was financed with a central government loan.
*This is figure given in original source. Actual column total is 270,651.

15. *CCJP,* 27 Apr. 51 [165].

steadfastly avoided. Of course, loans were to go first to poor peasants and not to rich peasants or former landlords. But a loan was not to be regarded as relief for the poverty-stricken. In natural disaster areas the Bank issued specially designated relief grants and loans to the suffering. But the usual rural loan programs were to be administered with a view to increasing production, furthering the development of semi-socialist organizations and modes of production, and enhancing trade, especially exchanges between city and countryside. Bank loans, by and large, were not intended to tide over or to bail out peasants who were going under.[16]

These guidelines and principles notwithstanding, a good many mistakes and deviations emerged in the Bank's early rural loan work. The special purpose loans, for instance, appear to have been given far too much prominence in the beginning. Money was made available for certain types of projects, but peasants needing loans for other purposes were turned away. The financing of well construction, for example, was so overemphasized that peasants in areas with sufficient surface water were compelled to take loans to dig wells. Since the people undertaking these unnecessary well-digging projects were often inexperienced, many wells collapsed or were unusable because they never reached the water table.[17] Peasants who had been prevailed upon to take these loans naturally had difficulty in paying them back. This kind of failure, which would have seemed farcical had it not been so serious, was blamed on the fact that loan policy was determined at too high an administrative level—at province level—and that quotas of loans to be made for special purposes were handed down the chain of command and carried out blindly, with or without the support of the peasants involved.[18] Upper-level Bank officials, unable themselves to devise sufficiently imaginative and flexible procedures, still did not trust the judgment of local cadres as to the most efficient disposition of public loans. The result frequently was waste and confusion.

There were other problems as well. In many cases, local Bank employees and cadres either did not understand or did not want to understand official policy on loans to people of different class status. Since loans to very poor peasants or Mutual Aid Teams had less likelihood of being repaid than loans to better-off peasants and teams, poor peasants were routinely overlooked in favor of households with better-than-

16. *Ibid*. See also Ko Lin [20], p. 57.   17. *TKP*, 23 May 53 [298].
18. *China Finance*, 20 Feb. 53 [284].

average land, labor power, and other means of production. The proscription against loans to landlords and rich peasants was made particularly clear, and there were, therefore, relatively few reports of serious violations of that kind.[19] But quite often people of questionable class status received loans for trade or capital investment in some small enterprise that were strictly speaking within the bounds of official policy, but that were nonetheless not carried out in the spirit intended or with the most desirable goals in mind. Investments in small businesses and trade were generally favored by finance cadres, because the capital turnover was likely to be faster and the profitability greater than with agricultural production loans. Likewise, many loan administrators were reluctant to give out general purpose capital loans for solving problems of livelihood and raising the standard of living, and they put the available funds into what they considered more secure and profitable ventures.

Finance cadres were criticized for these and other policy distortions. Despite the wide use of mobile finance work teams moving from village to village and assessing credit requirements and possibilities, finance and banking cadres were accused of spending too much time in their offices in town, of failing to make concrete investigations of how loan money was actually used, and in some cases of not even ever coming face to face with loan recipients.[20] They were also charged with advancing far too much credit to certain Mutual Aid Teams, production co-ops, and state farms, creating serious problems of overextension and heavy indebtedness while at the same time making hardly any funds available to independent farmers with legitimate needs and with the ability to repay small loans. And along with these criticisms, there were a number of cases in which it was revealed that finance cadres had embezzled Bank money, or loaned it out themselves at high rates of interest, or invested it in some capitalist enterprise, or used it to buy land.[21]

If the reported performance of the Bank in agricultural loan work seemed to be less than an overwhelming success, it might be noted that there were at least two important attitudes, endorsed by the center, concerning state rural finance work that contributed to the Bank's making only moderate gains. First there was the explicit preference among Chinese planners for handling peasants' ready cash problems through

19. One typical report of this type of deviation is in *CCJP,* 22 Jun. 52 [77].
20. *China Finance,* 30 Nov. 51 [361], pp. 17–18.
21. Hsiang-t'an district in Hunan seems to have been singled out for criticism over cadre corruption. See *CCJP,* 22 Jun. 52 [77].

improvements in crop marketing and trade contracts,[22] as opposed to relying on credit and loan arrangements made directly with the Bank. It was held that more efficient and more unified marketing of peasants' produce would increase their income and therefore make it less urgent that they obtain loans. And furthermore, through the use of trade contracts with advance deposits awarded to the peasants in the spring, the temporary or seasonal cash or grain shortages poor peasants typically experienced could largely be averted. Thus a preponderant proportion of Bank money was used not for direct loans to poor peasants but to support rural trade through the state trading companies and Supply and Marketing Cooperatives. In cases where improved marketing made a significant contribution to peasant welfare, however, it was generally the Supply and Marketing Co-op that would get the credit. The crucial role of the Bank in supplying a low-interest loan to the co-op was generally treated as strictly supportive.

This approach to solving the cash difficulties of peasants was related to a second strain of thinking among Chinese leaders affecting the scope and nature of Bank loans in the countryside. It was believed that if production loans were too readily available, this would tend to make peasants dependent on government financial assistance and too prone to come running for help whenever they encountered the slightest difficulty. Chinese leaders were particularly sensitive to the possibility that peasants generally might tend to lose their sense of self-reliance if they found help forthcoming from the government. To what extent this fear was justified seems doubtful, but it certainly became a constant theme in the development of Bank loan policy. Given that, for the long term, the heaviest state investment was going to have to be directed toward the economy's industrial sector, it was considered imperative that an unduly high level of expectations, which could only lead to disappointment, not be created among the peasant population. For this reason as well, then, Bank loans extended directly to peasant producers seem to have been somewhat restrained.

While these two attitudes about loan policy may have been quite appropriate in terms of the overall development strategy the Chinese leadership was then evolving, and also in the face of the still very limited

22. See the discussion of advance purchase and other contracts in the previous chapter. The point about improved trade versus government loans is made most clearly by Nan Han-chen [278], p. 5.

amounts of capital available to the Bank for rural investment, they did tend to create an immediate situation in which rural credit and loan work was not as effective as it might have been. Insofar as available Bank loans fell short of the real needs in the countryside, then, peasants were still having either to go without or to make their own private credit arrangements. And when they could not obtain loans at the comparatively low interest rates officially permitted, they made secret agreements with richer peasants and moneylenders to pay the old higher rates. Although the People's Bank can certainly be credited with many accomplishments in rural finance work before the announcement of the General Line, its own staff and personnel inadequacies, its limited financial capability—plus a certain reluctance to use its resources in the countryside fully—left many credit problems and instances of usury relatively unchanged for many months following land reform.

CREDIT COOPERATIVES

The People's Bank was not the only organization handling the many aspects of rural finance. There were a variety of "credit organizations of the masses" in operation as well, and they were to become increasingly important as time went on. In fact there were three types of credit organizations officially considered progressive and useful in coping with the difficulties of arranging insurance, savings, and loans in the countryside: the credit mutual aid team, the credit department of a Supply and Marketing Cooperative, and the Credit Cooperative itself.

As the name credit mutual aid team implies, this was an organization smaller in scope and simpler in design than the Credit Cooperative. Credit mutual aid teams were often formed in conjunction with Mutual Aid Teams, although they generally embraced the membership of at least two or three Mutual Aid Teams in order to enable accumulation of a significant sum of working capital. Independent peasants were also generally encouraged to join, and a credit mutual aid team typically encompassed twenty to thirty member households.[23] In some of these the *tsu chang* acted more or less as a broker, merely bringing potential borrowing and lending parties together and perhaps also assisting at the negotiations or acting as guarantor of the loan. In other teams, shares were actually purchased, savings deposits made, and loans advanced in the

23. *TKP,* 12 Nov. 54 [309].

name of the team as a whole. These latter teams resembled Credit Co-ops in most essentials but were much smaller.[24] The main aim of the government was to assist credit teams in combining with one another and in transforming themselves into Credit Co-ops, since they were too small to mobilize the sums needed to solve important production problems. And also because they were so small and so numerous, they did not lend themselves as easily as Credit Co-ops to supervision and control by the Bank.

Another means of cooperating in savings and loans was to establish a new department in an already existing Supply and Marketing Co-op devoted specifically to local credit and finance work. This approach had the advantage of employing a staff and a peasant membership that was already organized. It was a type of cooperation in savings and loans that had been applauded in the old liberated areas,[25] and that even in the 1950's was said to be appropriate in areas where the population was relatively widely dispersed and where the Bank had not yet been extended very deeply into the countryside. But at this period the emphasis was on keeping the credit department's operations and account books quite separate from the commercial activities of the Supply and Marketing Co-op.[26] And the central leadership advocated that Supply and Marketing Co-op credit departments convert themselves into full-scale independent Credit Cooperatives as soon as that was feasible. It was argued that the work of the Supply and Marketing Cooperative by itself was already extremely complex and demanding, and that in general it was not advisable to add finance work on top of it.

Thus the preferred form of finance organization for the later liberated areas was the independent Credit Cooperative. As with all cooperatives, peasants gained entrance to the organization by purchasing a share in it. The Credit Co-op's primary functions were to accept savings deposits on which it paid interest and to extend loans on which it charged interest. It also, however, could be deputized to act as the Bank's agent in insurance, tax, and relief matters. As one official statement put it: "The Credit Cooperative is part of the socialist village financial system under the leadership of the Party and the government. It is, on the one hand, the financial organization of the masses themselves, and on the other hand,

24. Some further information on the operation of these teams is contained in Ko Lin [20], pp. 114–115.
25. Selden [482], p. 239.   26. *TKP*, 14 Nov. 54 [412].

it is a part of the National Bank's socialist network in the villages and is serving the socialist transformation of agriculture."[27]

The money a Credit Co-op earned by selling shares was generally very limited, and the bulk of its working capital had to be obtained from other sources. In most cases, these other sources were savings deposits made by members and cash loans extended by the Bank.[28] As a matter of policy, the Bank always tried to make generous loans available to new Credit Co-ops to help set them on their feet. And in line with this, the interest charged on Bank loans to Credit Co-ops was to be 10 percent lower even than that charged on loans to state-run enterprises.[29]

The new Credit Co-op member could not expect to earn much in the way of dividends on a share in the co-op. As a matter of fact, dividends were ideally not to be paid at all, but, as a concession or inducement to get peasants to join, a very small dividend was sometimes offered at the beginning.[30] The main advantages to be had in joining a Credit Co-op were in the favorable interest rates earned on savings deposits, the preferential consideration members would receive in applying for loans, and the lower rates of interest they would have to pay on those loans.

Most Credit Co-ops offered a variety of savings plans to farmers. There was first a current savings account plan under which the member could deposit and withdraw money at will, earning interest on the balance from the date of deposit to withdrawal. Then there were a series of fixed term savings accounts, usually three months, six months, and one year, with higher interest rates corresponding to the longer terms. Technically, of course, a member making a fixed term deposit could not withdraw the money until the term was completed, but it was evidently universally acknowledged that in case of calamity or disaster this rule would be waived and depositors would be given access to their savings.[31] Rates of interest offered on savings naturally varied from place to

27. *TKP,* 1 Nov. 54 [433]. Other good discussions of the organization and functions of Credit Cooperatives can be found in *Basic Information about Cooperative Economy* [1], pp. 38–44; and in Liang Ssu-kuang [24], pp. 18–22.

28. *TKP,* 8 Nov. 54 [350].

29. See "Unified Directive on National Bank Support . . . " in *Collected Finance Laws and Orders* [417], p. 161.

30. *CCJP,* 11 Jun. 52 [332].

31. *TKP,* 8 Nov. 54 [350]. The Bank itself offered even more savings plans than the usual Credit Co-op. Included among the alternatives were "fixed amount deposits" and "combined savings and loan accounts." See Ko Lin [20], pp. 79–81.

place. The rule of thumb to be followed, however, was that Credit Co-ops should offer interest rates on savings higher than those available to individual depositors at the People's Bank but lower than the rate that the Bank offered on deposits made by the Credit Co-op. This was intended to allow the co-op to make a small net gain on transactions, to cover its own costs, and also to help it attract more working capital.[32]

As for loans, Credit Co-ops generally offered the same gamut of loans available from the Bank—production loans, trade and transport loans, and "livelihood" and general purpose loans—but they were expected to concentrate on short-term loans, leaving the long-term credit arrangements to the Bank.[33] Generally the Credit Co-op was permitted to charge a slightly higher rate of interest on loans to members than the rate it had to pay on its own outstanding loans from the Bank.[34] (But of course, since the Credit Co-op received preferential rates from the Bank, the rate individual peasants had to pay on loans from a co-op was still lower than the rate they would have paid to the Bank.) The most important goal was for the Credit Co-op to offer loans at a lower rate of interest than that being charged in private loan agreements in the area, even where the local rates were not considered to be unusually high. The interest on a loan from a Credit Co-op was generally in the vicinity of 1–2 percent per month.[35]

As is evident from this outline of Credit Co-op activities, these co-ops were heavily influenced, if not dominated, by the Bank and its policies and operations. Since, especially at the beginning, a large proportion of the Credit Co-op's working capital was obtained on loan from the Bank, the uses it made of the money and the rates of interest it could offer and charge were all largely determined by its agreements with the Bank. This was consistent with the notion that the Bank should provide leadership in policy and procedure for the many co-ops to follow.[36] And furthermore, the Bank had a hand in the training and education of most

32. *HHNP,* 18 May 54 [428].

33. *TKP,* 6 Nov. 54 [105].

34. *HHNP,* 18 May 54 [428]. The prevailing policy on this matter was evidently not always the same. Compare *CCJP,* 11 Jun. 52 [332], where it is declared that co-ops should not charge higher interest on loans than the Bank was charging them.

35. See, however, *Organization, Development, and Experiences of Rural Credit Cooperatives* [27], p. 46, where it is reported that in the Central South the annual rate of interest charged by co-ops "generally did not exceed 30 percent." It is also said here that the general guideline for the interest rate paid on deposits is that it should not be more than 0.5 percent lower per month than the interest charged on loans.

36. *China Finance,* 27 Jul. 51 [338].

Credit Co-op cadres and employees. The usual procedure was for the Party Committee of a given administrative area to choose a number of likely activists to become accountants and Credit Co-op administrators. These candidates were sent to the nearest Bank branch office for short training courses or else to a nearby keypoint Credit Co-op in the process of being established under the supervision of Bank cadres.[37] After they had begun the work of their own local co-ops, the new accountants and administrators were required to report back to their instructors, and they were subject to spot checks and investigations by Bank work teams. Although the training courses may have been barely adequate and the checkups often only half-hearted, the guidelines and techniques laid down by the Bank were the only ones available for local Credit Co-op cadres to try to follow.

In addition to operating according to the Bank's officially approved methods and procedures, Credit Cooperatives had a number of other political and administrative ideals they were to try to attain. For example, official policy on the class composition of Credit Co-ops was quite strict and was given rather heavy emphasis. Rich peasants were adamantly to be refused membership:

> Rich peasants are exploiters; they use hired labor, and make usurious loans, and invest in commercial enterprises to exploit the peasants. The rich peasants do not want to follow the path of mutual aid and cooperation; they want to follow the capitalist road. They are the force of capitalism in the rural villages. Our goal in developing Credit Cooperatives is to unite and to aid the development of mutual aid and cooperation in agricultural production and to limit, strike a blow at, and [finally] destroy usury. Therefore, the dangerous contradiction between rich peasants and the Credit Cooperatives cannot be breached. Rich peasants must oppose and try to destroy the Credit Cooperatives. There are some rich peasants who want to get into the Credit Cooperatives. This is because they know that once inside it will be easier for them to sabotage the Credit Co-op. Thus, we only wish to struggle against rich peasants, and not let them enter our Credit Cooperatives.[38]

37. See *TKP*, 3 Nov. 54 [194]; and also *TKP*, 28 Jun. 54 [195].
38. *TKP*, 3 Nov. 54 [194]. See also *Basic Information about Cooperative Economy* [1], p. 43, for a discussion of rich peasants and the class policy of Credit Co-ops. The fact that rich peasants were not rigorously excluded from membership in SMCs but were supposed to be excluded from Credit Cooperatives is probably one of the reasons why the government did not give enthusiastic support to the formation of credit departments in SMCs, as described above.

Rich peasants were, nevertheless, to be permitted to make deposits in the Credit Co-op, even though they could not become members.[39] And there was some confusion about whether or not rich peasants might receive Credit Co-op loans, because although members were to receive priority in the granting of loans, nonmembers could sometimes apply for and receive loans. Especially when rich peasants were large depositors, there seems to have been some feeling on the part of Credit Co-op cadres that they should be allowed to take loans if they applied for them. There were also difficulties in adhering to the official class line intended to help unite the interests of poor and middle peasants. In some Credit Co-ops middle peasants were heavily favored while poor peasants were treated as an unwelcome "burden." In others, heavier demands were made on the middle peasants who received lower interest on their savings deposits, while poor peasants received extra benefits. Local cadres often did not seem to realize that one of the purposes of Credit Co-ops was definitely to promote greater unity and cooperation between poor and middle peasants by making the co-op's activities advantageous to both classes in the village. The center demanded reconciliation of conflicting interests between these two groups in the context of the early Credit and Marketing Co-ops, in order to prepare a more solid popular opposition to the alternative exploitation of the "rich peasant economy," and in order to make semi-socialist production cooperatives soon appear to both sides to be a logical and acceptable next step.

While reconciling conflicting class interests within the organization, Credit Co-op cadres were also expected to administer co-op business according to certain established "democratic" and "socialist" principles. Credit Co-ops were set up experimentally at various administrative levels, but it was finally the *hsiang* level that was favored in the later liberated areas. This meant that before 1956 Credit Co-op members might include a number of Mutual Aid Teams, one or two Agricultural Production Cooperatives, and a host of independent peasant households.[40] In order to maintain the proper relationship between all these types of members and the central Credit Co-op authorities, a three- or

39. *CCJP,* 11 Jun. 52 [332].

40. Technically, the unit of membership in a Credit Co-op was not the household but the individual peasant. At least in Hunan and Hupei, however, this point appears to have been disregarded, for the share purchasing unit is most often reported to have been a household, and where borrowers were not Mutual Aid Teams they were most often referred to as households. See, e.g., *HHNP,* 27 Apr. 54 [265].

four-tiered organizational format, paralleling in almost every detail the format prescribed for Supply and Marketing Cooperatives,[41] was to be established in each Credit Co-op. There is not a great deal of information available concerning the internal governing of Credit Co-ops, but officers and committee members were admittedly first chosen by local Party, government, and Bank representatives, and later their selection was simply ratified by an election in which all members could vote. Also, the provisions for members' supervision of Credit Co-op cadres' work seem usually to have been subordinated (where they operated at all) to supervision by upper-level Bank and co-op officials. These distortions of what was usually considered proper procedure for running democratic mass organizations are understandable since relatively few villagers could have received the training necessary to carry out finance work and serve in responsible Credit Co-op positions, and hardly any members could realistically be expected to have sufficient information and education actually to supervise co-op work.[42] Still, the prescribed democratic organizational patterns were taken seriously enough that Credit Co-op cadres were commonly faulted for failing to make easily understandable periodic accounts of co-op work open for members' inspection, for failing to keep close liaison with and heed the suggestions of co-op members' deputies, and for creating unnecessary bureaucratic procedures and structures within co-ops that interfered with the democratic or "mass line" style of work.[43]

The development of Credit Co-ops in the later liberated areas was not as steady and deliberate as the development of Mutual Aid Teams. Although quite soon after liberation a few Credit Co-ops were set up experimentally, the total numbers in operation remained modest through 1953. Then, with the enunciation of the General Line and the introduc-

41. See above, Chapter 5—the section entitled "Organization and Functions of SMCs."

42. See the pessimistic assessment of the quality of Credit Co-op personnel in *Organization, Development, and Experiences of Rural Credit Cooperatives* [27], p. 43, where it is estimated that 70 percent of co-ops are run by genuine activists who nevertheless have little experience with finance work and therefore persist in the attitude of relying on the Bank. The masses do not have a high opinion of these people, it says. Furthermore, 20 percent of co-ops were much too hastily set up, they have no core *(ku kan)*, suffer from impure organization, and even give loans to merchants and invest in private commerce. These Credit Co-ops, it says, make a very bad impression on peasants.

43. See, e.g., *TKP,* 6 Nov. 54 [105].

tion of Unified Purchase in late 1953, Credit Co-ops were set up extremely rapidly. Some totals for Hunan province are illustrative (see Table 31). Broken down into shorter periods of time, as in Table 32, it becomes clearer just how quickly after the announcement of Unified Purchase the rate of development of Credit Co-ops jumped upward.

The figures for Hupei, although smaller, indicate about the same pattern and pace of development. At the end of 1953 Hupei had only about 325 Credit Co-ops; one year later, there were 7,481; and at the end of 1955 the total stood at 9,530.[44] The stated goal of the government and the Bank was to set up one Credit Co-op for each *hsiang,* and this was accomplished, practically speaking, in both provinces toward the end of 1955. It was later reported that during the entire First Five-Year Plan period, Credit Co-ops spread across Hunan had loaned out approximately 197,790,000 *yüan,* and that about 80 percent of all farming households had received some sort of loan from a co-op at one time or another.[45]

In early 1954 a great many news stories had begun to appear critical of the fact that the development of Credit Co-ops had lagged behind the development of Mutual Aid Teams and Supply and Marketing Cooperatives.[46] These reports complained about the overly conservative policy of the past, which took as its slogan "steadily moving forward" *(wen-pu ch'ien-chin).* In reality, they said, this had amounted to "steadiness, but no forward movement."[47] As with most sharp policy shifts in China, the propagandists found it necessary not only to announce and promote the change but also to denounce and ridicule the past policy line and those who might potentially continue to cling to it. But this time criticisms of "conservative thinking" were not carried too far; there apparently was not much time for recriminations. It was simply rather urgently pointed out that during the transition period there were supposed to be three important forms of cooperation in the villages — cooperation in production, in supply and marketing, and in credit; that of these three, Credit Co-ops had so far been the weak link; and that it was necessary to take immediate steps to remedy the situation.[48]

44. Sources for these figures, in the order given, are as follows: *TKP,* 22 Nov. 53 [359]; *TKP,* 8 Dec. 54 [401]; and Radio Wuhan, 31 Jan. 56.
45. *Hunan Nung-yeh* [15], p. 111.
46. See, e.g., *JMJP,* 4 May 54 [47]; and *HHNP* editorial, 5 May 54 [128].
47. *HHNP,* 16 Apr. 54 [60].
48. *TKP,* 27 Mar. 54 [46]; and *TKP,* 23 Apr. 54 [383].

TABLE 31. Establishment and Operation of Hunan Credit Co-ops, 1951–57

(In 1000 yüan)

	No. of Co-ops	As % of All Hsiang	No. of Members Households	As % of All Households	Actual Share Capital	Deposits		Loans	
						Total	Remainder	Total	Remainder
1951	2		1,301		61	2	1.6	27	8.6
1952	384		121,674	1.5	217	740	171	913	350
1953	582	3.8	194,499	2.4	348	3,478	263	4,480	470
1954	11,644	75.8	3,487,128	44.2	6,644	29,565	9,088	32,359	9,640
1955	12,720	85.0	4,455,600	57.0	9,212	65,845	12,591	54,949	16,111
1956	2,987*	100	6,153,953	78.0	12,929	210,767	24,932	75,434	54,354
1957	3,020*	100	6,342,608		13,792	371,073	56,116	56,669	58,848

SOURCE: *Hunan Nung-yeh* [15], p. 111.

*These two figures are reported without explanation in the original source. A nationwide administrative streamlining in 1956 did bring on the merger of many *hsiang*, reducing the number by about one-third in most areas. *Hsiang* Credit Co-ops were also merged at this time and thus their total numbers also fell, but not by any means as drastically as these figures suggest. Compare Chen [454], p. 469. There may have been an error in transcription here.

TABLE 32. Development of Credit Cooperatives in
Hunan Province

Date (approx.)	Total Number of Credit Co-ops	Total Number of Credit MATs
1. 30 Sep. 53	551	4000
2. 31 Dec. 53	582	4438
3. 10 Mar. 54	1405	6431
4. 31 Mar. 54	1734	7733
5. 2 Jun. 54	4843	14664
6. 31 Dec. 54	11500+	4000+[a]
7. 31 Mar. 55	11600[b]	—

SOURCE: 1. Radio Ch'angsha, 18 Jan. 54. 2. *HHNP,* 17 Mar. 54
[387]. 3. *HHNP,* 8 Apr. 54 [179]. 4. Radio Ch'angsha, 13 Apr. 54.
5. *HHNP,* 2 Jun. 54 [89]. 6. *JMJP,* 4 Feb. 55 [203]. 7. *TKP,* 21 Apr. 55
[201].

[a]Large numbers of Credit MATs had merged to become Credit
Co-ops.

[b]Total membership: 3,600,000 households, or approximately 47%
of all peasant households in the province.

Clearly, the continued expansion of Supply and Marketing Co-op
business depended on greater access to Bank financing. The Credit
Co-ops were hastily set up in effect to act as Bank extensions and to meet
this need; but they were also needed to help reabsorb into approved
channels some of the greatly expanding state funds being pumped into
the countryside with the success of Unified Purchase. Peasants were
urged to buy shares and deposit their money in the Credit Co-ops, and
through their leadership over co-op affairs, central finance planners
would be able to recapture at least some control over free capital in the
countryside, preventing it from flowing into the hands of private merchants or into nonproductive peasant expenditures. But in their very
haste to set up Credit Co-ops so quickly, conditions were created for a
certain amount of disorganization and disappointment.

All types of local cadres and activists were brought in on the 1954
movement to propagandize Credit Co-ops among the masses. Work
teams and cadres sent down from county and district levels to help with
the formation of Mutual Aid Teams also carried instructions to create
Credit Co-ops.[49] So anxious were the central planners for quick results
that local cadres were informed that it was not necessary to set up credit
mutual aid teams first and then convert them gradually into Credit Co-
ops. Establishing Credit Co-ops was said to be simpler and easier

49. *HHNP,* 18 Jun. 54 [275].

than getting Mutual Aid Teams and Production Co-ops on their feet. Although on the one hand "blindly seeking after higher forms" was condemned, local cadres were on the other hand warned against mechanically following the principle of "first teams and then co-ops." Where conditions were comparatively good, they were to begin immediate work on the "higher form," the Credit Cooperative.[50]

Once the Credit Co-op began its work, the advantages of participation would become clear to peasants, it was argued, and more and more of them would want to join. Manifested here again in Credit Co-op work is the Chinese leadership's penchant for forging ahead dramatically in some aspect of rural policy, despite apparent cadre and peasant unpreparedness, with confidence that once established the new system would prove itself attractive and receive mass support. Part of this pattern or workstyle, as observed before, is to follow up with a general rectification of the work to iron out inconsistencies and correct the inevitable deviations. The Credit Cooperative movement was no exception in this regard.

Deviations committed during the whirlwind movement to establish Credit Co-ops ranged from corruption and commandism at one extreme, to excessive conservatism and paralysis at the other. The financial accounts of a great many new Credit Cooperatives were quickly in a mess because of the dearth of trained accountants and bookkeepers.[51] In some places, peasants were forced to join Credit Co-ops whether or not they wanted loans or had savings to deposit, by cadres who evidently had quotas to fulfill for numbers of co-ops to be established. One of the worst reports of this sort came from certain areas of Hupei that had suffered from recent natural disasters. Despite their straitened circumstances, the peasants in these areas were forced to buy shares in Credit Co-ops, and some even had to sell parts of their houses and other possessions to get enough to eat after they bought the unwanted shares.[52]

In other places cadres demonstrated a remarkable reluctance to take any risks whatsoever. They set up the form of a Credit Co-op, took in savings deposits and s' .e money, and then practically suspended operations, causing understandable dissatisfaction among the members. They were so afraid that poor peasants would not repay loans if they granted

50. *HHNP* editorial, 5 May 54 [128]. See also *JMJP,* 12 Sep. 54 [48]; and *TKP,* 15 Nov. 54 [360].
51. *TKP,* 25 Dec. 54 (n.t.).   52. *TKP,* 12 Jan. 55 [229].

them that just at the time when people were wanting to borrow they transferred most of their assets to savings deposits in the National Bank, making it impossible to expand their own business operations. They also often further restricted the flow of money by forbidding loans of more than three months' duration, limiting the maximum per loan to a small amount and stipulating that no additional loan could be taken until the first was fully repaid.[53] These overcautious Credit Co-ops were worse than a total absence of rural credit organization because they absorbed available free capital but did not put it to use for local production. Local peasants were quoted as having wryly likened these organized but non-functioning co-ops to an actor who strides boldly onto the stage but "doesn't sing the opera."[54]

These rueful villagers were still better off perhaps than some others whose Credit Co-op cadres had been too ambitious in their undertakings. Many co-ops quickly went bankrupt because their expenses outstripped their income and they were lending out money for nonproductive or even frivolous projects.[55] Some of the cadres involved became so ashamed or so frightened of what the members would say when they found out that they simply tried to avoid the issue by making themselves scarce. Members who had hoped to take loans and who were looking for an opportunity to talk to Credit Co-op cadres found them as elusive as ghosts and mockingly said of them, "When the sun shines they have no shadow, and when it rains they leave no tracks in the mud."[56]

A general rectification of Credit Co-ops was begun toward the end of 1954 and continued through the first half of 1955. It was concentrated mainly on bringing errant co-ops back under Bank supervision, setting up more circumspect procedures for the disbursement of funds, and further training and educating accountants and bookkeepers at all levels. In March 1955, the Bank announced a halt to the drive to set up Credit Co-ops. Citing corruption, misappropriation of funds, inefficiency, incompetence, and a lack of democratic controls and procedures in the new cooperatives, a period of consolidation was ordered.[57] Of primary importance at this time was the process of bringing all Credit Co-ops under closer control by local Bank branches and Party committees.

---

53. *HHNP,* 2 Jun. 54 [89].   54. *JMJP,* 31 May 55 [107].
55. For reports on some bankruptcies in Hunan, see *TKP,* 9 Mar. 55 [430].
56. *TKP,* 12 Jun. 55 [448].   57. See *TKP,* 4 Apr. 55 [192].

There was heavier emphasis on Party and government control over Credit Co-ops than over any other type of cooperative or organ in rural villages.

It is important to stress that the period of greatest growth of these co-ops coincided with the early implementation of the Unified Purchase system, and that the two movements were actually intimately related. Under the Unified Purchase program, peasants were required by law to sell their surpluses of grain and certain other commodities to the state. This put the government in the position of releasing enormous amounts of cash into the countryside at harvest times. Since the industrial and consumer goods on which peasants might have spent their cash were still severely limited in quantity, central planners were naturally concerned about the uses to which the money in the villages might be put. The greatest fear was that much of it would find its way into small private enterprises, the fruits of the "spontaneous capitalist tendencies" of the peasantry. It was, therefore, a part of the official central policy promoting rural savings for the support of national industrialization that a portion of the money paid out to peasants under Unified Purchase be reabsorbed in the form of savings deposits with the Bank and with local Credit Cooperatives.

On the last day of November 1953, the People's Bank issued a directive ordering preferential interest rates to be paid to peasants who deposited their money from the sale of surplus grain to the state in savings accounts. In the previous chapter this directive was viewed as creating one more incentive for peasants to comply with the system of compulsory sale of grain to the state. This, however, reveals but one dimension of the Bank savings program at the time. Here, viewing the directive in the context of rural finance work, it is clear that the program also established an incentive not to sell grain, but rather to save money. The Bank printed deposit slips in denominations of ¥10,000, ¥30,000, ¥50,000, and ¥100,000 and distributed them to the Supply and Marketing Cooperatives that were serving as grain purchasing stations under Unified Purchase. Peasants who came to sell their grain were given these deposit slips as part of the payment more or less automatically. The official target was for 10–20 percent of the purchase price of all grain bought from peasants to be recovered for the state and cooperative economy in the form of savings deposits. But we know that in many areas Bank and co-op cadres prevailed upon peasants to accept deposit slips as payment for a much larger portion of their grain. There is no doubt that the rate of rural savings rose dramatically after Unified Purchase began in November 1953.[58] The staggering growth of Credit Co-ops at precisely the same time was clearly precipitated by central determination to do even more to absorb free capital in the countryside and drastically increase the rate of rural savings for the support of urban industrialization. Although another function of Credit Co-ops was undeniably to give loans for rural construction, the timing of their great advance leads to the conclusion that they were then viewed primarily as an added means of promoting rural savings.

EVALUATING RURAL FINANCE WORK

During this period, the work of rural finance never took on the mass character and the aspects of popular participation that typified other rural programs and policies for the transition period. As far as mutual aid and cooperation in production and even in trade were concerned, there was apparently the feeling that native know-how and experience would be important components in doing things successfully. In savings and loan work, by contrast, there was a marked lack of confidence in the ability of peasants or even of *hsiang* cadres to handle problems independently and to come up with solutions that were both practical and in accord with the General Line. Even during and after the formation of Credit Co-ops, ostensibly mass organizations responsive to the initiatives of members, there was a tremendous preoccupation with the need for higher-level Bank, Credit Co-op, Party, and government cadres all to keep careful control over the activities of *hsiang* finance organs. And when mistakes or miscalculations were made within Credit Co-ops they were far more often blamed on the failure of upper-level cadres to exercise adequate control and supervision than on bad elements or wrong attitudes among members and employees.[59] Credit Co-ops were not mass organizations in the way they were set up or in the way they functioned to the degree

58. Starlight estimates that by the end of 1953 the total rural savings deposits in the People's Bank amounted to the equivalent of U.S. $99.82 million, almost a 200 percent increase within two months over the amount of rural savings accumulated during the previous four years. And he concludes that the rapid increase in rural savings deposits, in the People's Bank alone, changed the proportion of rural to total national savings from roughly 10 percent in the first week in November 1953 to 22 percent by the end of 1954. See Starlight [483], pp. 227–228.

59. See, e.g., *HHNP*, 18 Jun. 54 [258]; and for two other discussions of the Party's control over Credit Co-ops, see also *TKP*, 11 Nov. 54 [106]; and *TKP* editorial, 30 Sep. 55 [421].

that Mutual Aid Teams and Agricultural Production Co-ops were, or even to the degree that Supply and Marketing Co-ops were initially. They were far more unquestionably primarily the tools of government policy in the villages. It is perhaps partly for this reason that the Credit Co-ops give the impression of having been strangely detached from the process and politics of village transformation even though they were in fact intimately related to both.

After the formation of Agricultural Production Cooperatives all over the country and their ascension to the position of the primary organizational form for production and village life, the question arose as to whether or not finance work ought also to be subsumed into their functions and activities.[60] Some people strongly advocated mergers of the two kinds of co-ops. But the official insistence that Credit Co-ops retain their separate identities remained adamant. Money and special finance arrangements could only perform their seeding and nurturing functions if they could be employed selectively. Therefore, the Bank and higher Party and government officials had to keep Credit Co-ops distinct from and beyond the control of Agricultural Production Co-ops. Otherwise all APCs would have had an equal claim on the Bank and the credit organs. And selectivity and preferential treatment, the two discretionary options giving money its power as a force for change, would thereby have been lost to the leadership.

There were of course from the outset two strong types of material incentives for an ordinary peasant to want to join a Credit Co-op. First, a member could take a loan at a comparatively low rate of interest; and second, a member could safely invest money in savings and earn a modest return in interest. These two types of incentives are perhaps sufficient to explain why most peasants, despite the fears and hesitations mentioned, were willing to become involved in Credit Co-ops. In a time of rapidly changing village economic relations, the Credit Co-ops offered peasants a modest but secure return on their investments. And also, while peasants may have regretted the necessity of purchasing a share in the Credit Co-op, this payment entitled them to ask for an emergency loan if needed at a rate of interest that would not ruin them. Even with its drawbacks and inadequacies, co-op membership served as a kind of insurance for poor peasants. It decreased the likelihood that the family could be wiped out in a disaster.

Furthermore, however, these co-ops were helping to demonstrate that

60. *TKP* editorial, 21 Aug. 56 [281]; and see also *JMJP,* 17 Oct. 56 [414].

a reasonable rate of profit for the individual investor could actually be consistent with collective effort and an improvement in conditions for poorer peasants. The activities of Credit Co-ops and the Bank consequently put a great deal of pressure on rich peasants, first to reduce the rates of interest they charged on private loans, but later also to turn most of their surplus over to the local co-ops, accept the interest rates paid as their profit, and allow the capital to be used by the co-ops in the larger village interest. The legitimacy of private profit making was reaffirmed but became more and more tied to the question of whether the profitable deal in question had also served the public or collective good.

The activities of Credit Co-ops reinforced what, through Supply and Marketing Co-ops too, was emerging as the basic tenet of China's transition to socialism in the countryside: that private profits for peasants could be and should be made in cooperative ventures that produced income increases for them while simultaneously serving progressive social goals. By putting a floor under the poorest and placing a ceiling over the better-off, these two types of co-ops were in effect reducing the potential economic distance between these two groups in the villages. Then by leaving open to each group a way of continuing to improve their own livelihood gradually within the context of cooperation, they were reducing the political distance between them as well, and making it possible for both sides to see their own interests being served by a decision for full-scale cooperativization, even in production.

In this way the Credit Co-ops contributed to a gradual realignment in village power relations. Whereas middle and upper-middle peasants had before been enthusiastic about their chances in the free market and had therefore tended to shun entanglement with the poorer families in the villages, the contracts and credit agreements of the transition period were written so as to appeal to the great majority of both poor and middle peasants. They made cooperation more immediately attractive to both sides. There remained only a small minority of still better-off villagers — rich peasants — whose interests would undeniably be hurt by the formation of peasant co-ops and the collapse of the free money and commodities markets. The confrontation with them was coming soon.

CHAPTER 7

Collectivization

This chapter looks at selected aspects of the movement to establish Agricultural Production Co-ops and at the organization and structure of the co-ops themselves.[1] This movement, with its extraordinary speed and all-inclusiveness, is generally regarded as epitomizing the socialist transformation of the Chinese countryside. And there is certainly a sense in which it is valid to say that Agricultural Production Co-ops marked a point-of-no-return in rural development, since before their acceptance by the mass of peasants there had been no thoroughly reliable guarantees against the collapse of the revolution or serious social and political retrogression in the villages. But, as this narrative is intended to demonstrate, it would not be possible to understand the process of socialist transformation by looking only at the rapid establishment of the socialist production co-ops and collectives of 1955 and 1956. The whirlwind cooperativization movement accomplished then was but the culmination of years of change in the rural economic environment and of shifting political struggles in the villages. Before turning to an examination of the "high tide of socialism in the countryside," then, it is perhaps worth pausing to review some of the distance already traversed by 1955.

THE RURAL CONDITION IN 1955

Before liberation the standard goal of every Chinese peasant, both rich and poor, was to save enough money to buy more land. Most peasants planned, once they had acquired more land than they could farm

1. There were two kinds of production co-ops in China, elementary and advanced. Private property and rent remained prominent features within the elementary form,

alone with their sons, to hire laborers or to rent out some of the land to tenant farmers, to harvest more and more, acquire and use more fertilizer, and ultimately buy even more land. This was not the only way of getting rich in rural China, but it was probably the safest and most honorable since, if it succeeded, the farmer's heirs were guaranteed a valuable inheritance. As we have seen, the revolutionary government's land reform policy not only redistributed land ownership, it also stigmatized those peasants who persisted in the old plan of using their wealth to buy up other people's land or to employ tenant farmers and hired laborers. While these activities were not strictly speaking illegal, they were sharply limited, and peasants who continued them found themselves subject to heavy exactions through the tax laws, "voluntary" contributions, and other government programs aimed at preventing the accumulation of sizable amounts of land by a minority of villagers. The single traditionally most important route to wealth and security that a peasant family could hope to tread was, therefore, heavily blockaded by government policy at a very early point.

If the investment of surplus capital in land was by and large not going to be possible, peasants naturally turned to some of the other means of making a profit that were available in rural society. One of these was to lend money or grain to less well-off peasants at high interest rates. But as we have seen, government policy gradually squeezed out this option as well. Low-interest loans available through government and cooperative institutions undercut the moneylenders' trade little by little, while at the same time casting their private profiteering activity in an ever gloomier and more sinister light. Potential moneylenders were not left without any outlet whatsoever for their surplus capital, it is true. They were offered an opportunity to make a small profit on low-interest loans to poor peasants arranged through Credit Co-ops, or on savings deposits in government and cooperative savings institutions. Better-off peasants with money to loan were gradually denied the opportunity of making a killing and were offered, as a consolation, a chance to make a modest gain.

In a similar manner, another option open to peasants, to invest in market speculation and private enterprise, was also gradually closed off by government policy. Early government efforts at price stabilization, market control, and monopolization of certain agricultural commodities

---

while advanced co-ops almost eliminated private property and rent and were fully socialist in their internal relations. Since the "advanced co-ops" were in reality "collectives" the two terms are used interchangeably here.

limited, although they certainly did not completely destroy, the profitability of business investments and market speculation. Once again central authorities reinforced their policy of limiting peasants' individual capital gains with alternative arrangements offering them certain benefits. The advance purchase contracts with Supply and Marketing Coops, in particular, sweetened the bitter medicine of central policy and once more edged the profit-seeking peasant into general compliance.

The overall pattern followed by the revolutionary government in these various moves was the same. It put heavy restrictions on the private profit available to the peasant, but it did not eliminate private profit altogether. It made those profits contingent on cooperation with programs intended to advance both agricultural development and the transition to socialism. Such profits to peasants were modest but, nonetheless, still real and sufficient always to attract a majority and to alienate only a minority. Where farmers were not offered absolute increases in income, they received enhanced security in the everyday economic risks they had to take or in times of disaster. For the great majority of peasants who still lived dangerously close to bare subsistence, the insurance incentives contained in central policies were possibly the most compelling.

While the central planners were steadily closing off these alternative investment options previously open to better-off peasants, they were also attempting to convince peasants of the greater agricultural productivity attainable by Mutual Aid Teams and Agricultural Production Cooperatives. Team and co-op successes were loudly propagandized all across the later liberated areas; successful teams and co-ops always reported income increases and a higher standard of living for members. As time went on and income increases from land rent or from credit and marketing activities became almost impossible or illegal, income increases derived through production increases were receiving wide acclaim and active government support. It was not news to peasants, of course, that greater capital investment in agriculture would result in higher yields, but the obstacles had always been formidable. Now, however, the center was promising to give loans to co-ops, and the cooperative system seemed to offer real possibilities for greater capital concentration, enhanced labor efficiency, and more rational land use, which could all add up to better harvests. Furthermore, as already noted, the Three Fix policy supplied some immediate incentives for both poor and rich to think about joining an Agricultural Production Co-op. For all these reasons and because they had practically no other remaining investment possibilities likely to pay off in increased income, ordinary peasants were being edged into the decision to join and make the initial investment in an Agricultural Production Cooperative.

This is not to say that many peasants did not join co-ops out of an attraction to socialist principles and a desire to progress toward communism. And it is certain that many peasants joined because they had faith in the Communist Party, or felt loyalty to local cadres who had led them during land reform, or respected other activists in the villages who urged them or pressured them to do so. Yet it is also unmistakably clear that the central government's policies since land reform had created a situation in which it made good personal economic sense for most peasants to consider joining. Not only was joining an APC not necessarily harmful to the individual peasant's own interest by this time, but given the rather sudden absence of good alternative ways to try to make a profit, it was often probably the best move a peasant head of household could make for himself and his family.

THE DECISION

Given careful local regulation and sufficient time, incentive programs like those described in previous chapters might well have gradually attracted a great majority of both poor and better-off peasants voluntarily to form farming co-ops conforming more or less to central guidelines. The local cadres pressing various kinds of cooperative business deals and cooperative organizations obviously sensed that they were gaining the upper hand in village affairs. A few more years of reliable and reasonably profitable dealings in the state-led cooperative economy may have been all most peasants would have needed to have been led bit by bit into more fully socialist relations of production. This, however, was not the way in which production co-ops were widely established in the Chinese countryside, because central policymakers, who had long promised a slow and gradual socialization of agriculture, abruptly came to the decision in 1955 that the country could not afford to wait as long as that might take. There were at least two important reasons for this decision.

First, the rate of growth of agricultural production attained throughout the country since the completion of land reform had not met the expectations of central planners and was, in their view, seriously impeding the intended industrial growth during the period of the First Five-Year Plan. Using 1952 as the base year, the national target for the rate of growth in grain output had been 4.6 percent per annum (1953–57), while the actual rate achieved in 1953–54 was only 1.7 percent. For 1953 alone, a good production year relatively free of natural disasters and benefiting from the "heightened production enthusiasm" of the peasants following on the heels of land reform, the national increase in grain output over 1952 had been only 2.5 percent and cotton output had dropped by about 8 percent.[2]

For Hunan, as illustrated in Table 33 (as compared to Table 14 in Chapter 2), it is clear that the rate of growth in value of output of the various agricultural subsectors slowed considerably after the immediate postwar recovery period. And breaking down the growth rate by specific crops as in Table 34 shows that even granting the widespread natural disasters in the province in both 1954 and 1956, the rates for growth achieved over the whole First Five-Year Plan were generally disappointing.

The effects of lagging agricultural growth on other sectors of the national economy were immediately appreciated by Chinese planners. The national growth rate in industrial production of consumer goods was much higher than the growth rate in agriculture, but it dropped from 26.7 percent per annum in 1953 to 14.2 percent in 1954. In 1955 output of consumer goods actually fell. Likewise the growth rate in the producers' goods sector declined from 36.5 percent per annum in 1953 to 19.8 percent in 1954, and then to 14.5 percent in 1955.[3]

Central planners might have considered lowering their targets for industrial growth to bring them more in line with agriculture's performance. But there is little evidence that this was in fact given much thought. On the contrary, they became only more determined to raise agricultural output by any means, and they were hoping that a short-range spurt of investment in agriculture, for the express purpose of help-

2. See the discussion of agricultural growth rates in Walker [523], pp. 22–26. The decrease in cotton production was certainly due in part to the government's deliberate lowering of the cotton-grain price ratio and the elimination of advance purchases of cotton that year, but it must also be seen against an announced planned growth rate of 16 percent for cotton output. See Perkins [477], p. 37.

3. Perkins [477], p. 55. Perkins also cites natural recovery from wartime destruction and miscalculations in the rate of state investment in industry as partial explanations for the high rates of growth in 1953, suggesting that a fall-off in industrial growth after that year was to a certain degree predictable and unrelated to agricultural production. "Nevertheless," he concludes, "the main cause of the difficulties was agriculture, and the Chinese Communist leadership was well aware of this."

TABLE 33.   Hunan Annual Growth of Value of Output: Agriculture and Agricultural Sidelines, 1953–57

(In 10,000 yüan)

| | 1953 | 1954 | 1955 | 1956 | 1957 | As % of Gross Value of Output: Agriculture & Industry | |
						1952	1957
Agriculture	186,992.13	165,933.81	199,868.46	187,805.18	211,425.64	54.62	40.66
Forestry	3,755.83	3,749.85	5,734.31	8,383.84	11,971.25	1.38	2.30
Cattle breeding	29,689.52	27,619.67	23,666.78	28,322.81	53,896.64	9.08	10.36
Fishing	982.96	950.00	1,189.56	1,095.00	2,831.49	0.20	0.55
Sidelines	44,505.02	45,670.05	58,487.15	55,899.09	57,959.27	12.25	11.15
Total	265,925.46	243,923.38	288,946.26	281,505.92	338,084.29	77.53	65.02

SOURCE: *Hunan Nung-yeh* [15], p. 86.

TABLE 34. Hunan Production of Various Crops: 1953–57 Index
(1952 = 100)

	1953	1954	1955	1956	1957	*Average Growth Rate %*
All grains (including soybeans)	100.20	89.96	109.18	100.35	109.72	1.87
All grains (not including soybeans)	100.20	89.99	109.30	100.52	109.72	1.85
Rice (only)	100.40	89.84	108.18	100.57	105.64	1.10
Wheat (only)	90.44	83.65	119.19	119.63	106.48	1.25
Other miscellaneous grains (only)	118.78	104.69	113.21	117.14	144.71	7.67
Potatoes (only)	91.17	86.69	120.89	88.24	149.85	8.42
Soybeans (only)	100.50	85.54	92.27	76.12	123.85	4.36
Cotton	71.05	15.77	63.57	74.42	80.97	—
Jute	—	4.16	237.26	648.82	942.91	56.64
Ramie	111.67	98.69	91.47	94.33	112.21	2.33
Tobacco	87.39	75.07	90.56	70.87	92.84	—
Sugarcane	67.12	47.09	26.41	29.59	35.80	—
Peanuts	98.59	53.69	82.72	71.82	110.89	2.07
Oil bearing seeds	102.03	57.57	61.25	70.39	61.80	—
Sesame seed	148.30	102.93	223.78	228.21	201.32	15.02

SOURCE: *Hunan Nung-yeh* [15], p. 87.

ing to bring off quick cooperativization, would be sufficient to set it on a path of growth more consistent with the targets of the Five-Year Plan.

A great part of the rationale for farming co-ops, then, rested on their capacity to solve the problem of low agricultural productivity. The main argument was that the pooling of land would allow the achievement of certain economies of scale. Resources would be utilized more rationally and efficiently and producers would accumulate capital for reinvestment at a faster rate. Cooperative farming would increase the land under cultivation by eliminating boundary mounds, redundant animal pens, and so on, while at the same time allowing the introduction of more efficient cropping patterns. Whereas the individual peasant household, in order to meet all its needs, often had to use some of its land for rice, some for vegetables, and some for fodder, whether or not it had any land suitable for each of these crops, the co-op could allot its fields so that particular crops were grown only where the natural conditions were most favorable to them. Co-ops would also be able to mobilize underemployed peasants for new construction work and turn the idle hours of the slack seasons into time spent on the large-scale projects to improve co-op productivity that were impractical under a system of individual farming. In particular, large reservoirs, dams and embankments, and smaller irrigation ditches and wells could all be tackled by co-op labor teams. According to central theory and propaganda, as output increased, surplus capital would accumulate more rapidly and be available for investment in superior strains of seed, fertilizer, insecticide, more draught animals, and improved implements—all contributing to better and better harvests supporting national industrialization according to the plan.[4]

A second important reason for the abrupt central decision to hurry along the establishment of semi-socialist production co-ops, however, was continued concern with the class composition of rural villages, especially the stubborn persistence of wide disparities in wealth between classes. As the results of a 1955 survey of 16,199 households across the country show, the disparities remained considerable. (See Table 35.) Despite government policies and programs intended to support the poor and the very poor, public funds were limited and some peasants at the bottom of the scale were still regularly going bankrupt, selling their land, or going heavily into debt. Especially as greater state investment in industry was contemplated, Bank loans to poor peasants and public disaster relief could not be expected to keep increasing to prevent the poorest villagers from going under.

Furthermore, the information available to Chinese planners at the time indicated that continued repolarization in the distribution of wealth, amounting to a weakening of the middle peasant class in the villages, might be harmful not only to the progressive social goals of the revolution but to its production goals as well. Their ongoing investigations suggested that while poor peasant productivity per *mou* of cultivated land was typically significantly lower than middle peasant productivity, rich peasant output per *mou* was not very much greater than that achieved by middle peasants. A 1954 national survey yielded the figures reported in Table 36.

Findings such as these indicated that the much greater income of rich peasant households was not primarily attributable to superior cultivation techniques and a higher rate of productivity but merely to their greater

4. For some typical contemporary explanations of the advantages of co-ops in raising agricultural production and the importance of this with regard to national industrialization, see Hsüeh Mu-ch'iao et al. [462], pp. 123–124; Huang Nan-sen and Wang Ch'ing-chu [14], *passim; Basic Information about Cooperative Economy* [1], pp. 20 ff; and Fang Ch'ang [9], *passim.*

TABLE 35. Rural Household Income by Class, 1955

(In *yüan*)

	Gross Income		Net Income	
	Average per Household	Average per Capita	Average per Household	Average per Capita
Co-op member households	463.5	94.1	399.7	81.1
All independent farmers	498.2	106.4	374.8	80.0
Poor peasants	355.6	85.2	274.9	65.9
Middle peasants	545.1	111.0	408.3	83.1
Lower-middle peasants	484.0	105.0	367.3	79.6
Upper-middle peasants .	660.0	124.1	489.1	92.5
Rich peasants	633.7	126.1	458.0	91.2
Landlords	402.0	93.7	304.2	70.9
All households surveyed	487.4	102.9	379.3	80.1

SOURCE: Su Hsing [31], p. 81.

TABLE 36. Agricultural Income and Income per *Mou* by Class, 1954

	Average Household Agricultural Income (yüan)	Average Household Income per mou of Cultivated Land (yüan)
Co-op members	466.4	28.8
Poor and hired peasants	272.4	24.3
Middle peasants	479.7	27.1
Rich peasants	860.6	27.7
Former landlords	286.0	22.3
Overall average	420.6	26.6

SOURCE: T'ung Ta-lin [34], p. 23.

ownership of the means of production, especially land and labor. Therefore it was perceived that the natural tendency toward depletion of the middle peasant ranks, if unchecked, would help not only to vitiate the egalitarian thrust of land reform but also to impede progress in raising the overall agricultural growth rate. At the center it began to be argued that there was little to be gained (and perhaps a great deal to be lost) by delaying the wide establishment of APCs: the sooner they could be established, the better their chances of succeeding would be. And in 1955, according to the new central assessment of village conditions, great numbers of poor and lower-middle peasants, who together were calculated to comprise 70–80 percent of all peasants, were ready and eager to join in cooperative farming ventures.

Thus in 1955 the leadership abandoned gradualism and seemed ready to force the pace of rural collectivization dramatically. Had all the policies described above, to contain the "rich peasant economy" and promote a gradual transition to socialism, in fact failed then? In a sense perhaps they had; for in terms of agricultural productivity the discontinuities between central hopes and rural realities were revealed to be staggeringly disappointing. And in terms of village equality, mutual aid and progressive taxation had not been enough to hold the line.

Yet, from the point of view of peasant attitudes and the village politics of collectivization, those previous seasons of mutual aid, co-op contracts, and rural cadre consolidation had yielded shifts in the balance of power that were to be vital to the success of the new quick pace of change in the countryside. Most importantly those interim years had highlighted the opposition of interests within the villages between the great majority of still-poor and not very well-off middle peasants who had been attracted by the increased security that cooperation with state policy frequently offered them, and the minority of wealthier middle peasants and rich peasants who suffered and grumbled under all the new government's restrictions. Although to the poor peasant cooperation in mutual aid was often annoying and cumbersome, the government had shown itself willing to see poor peasant incomes rise if mutual aid brought a rise in output, and this was encouraging. Still, the productivity gains of mutual aid alone had usually been limited, since when the poor band together their available means of production remain inadequate. Only if they could get their collective hands on better land, tools, water sources, and oxen could they hope for the qualitative improvements in output that would bring large increases in personal income under central policy.

This then was the attraction of large-scale collectivization. For although official policy statements did a two-step on the question of rich peasant participation in production co-ops, peasants knew that village-wide joint farming associations of the poor would isolate rich peasants even more completely. They would have no serious alternative but to apply to join. If the state and the rest of the village were united against them, they would be unable to hire laborers, market their crops, or buy needed supplies. To avoid being frozen out completely, they would have to join the co-ops and bring with them their better means of production, putting their property at the disposal of the rest. It was to be a kind of final, peaceful expropriation. The village consensus for it had been forming in the new economic conditions taking shape since land reform. Those interim years and gradualist policies had provided an opportunity for peasants to experience and assess central methods and intentions. On the whole they had found it useful to cooperate with them; and on the whole they would continue to do so over the next two years. This government had built up some credit with the masses of poor peasants, even as it had moved to contain peasant "petty capitalism." Now it signaled them to seize control over the remainder of the village wealth and use it in a planned and integrated way to serve their own interests and the state's. Rich peasants were in no position to mobilize much opposition. They put up little resistance. China's collectivization was to be accomplished with amazing speed and with little violence.

As is well known, the speed of cooperativization achieved in the Chinese countryside was far more rapid than that initially advocated by the central planners and key political figures. In the official Central Committee resolution on the establishment of Agricultural Production Co-ops,[5] a goal of 35,800 co-ops in the entire country was set for the end of 1954. In January 1954 the goal was raised to 45,000 but by March the total number of APCs in operation already stood at about 96,000.[6] By June the national total had risen to 114,000; by September, to 230,000; by December, to 497,000; and in March 1955 it stood at 633,000. This encompassed 14.2 percent of all peasant households in China. In the autumn of 1955 the figures had already multiplied to embrace nearly one-third of all households, and then the pace of co-op growth really quickened, as the month by month figures in Table 37 demonstrate.

The development of cooperatives in Hunan and Hupei generally paralleled the national rate of advance. At the end of 1954, when Hunan for example still had less than 1 percent of peasant households in co-ops, targets for co-ops to be established in the remaining years of the First Five-Year Plan began to rise. But it was not until after Chairman Mao's famous address of July 31, 1955, advocating a far more ambitious cooperativization movement, that the targets began their sharp climb.[7] In early 1955 there had been about 13,000 experimental APCs in all of Hunan, but as the "high tide" approached, the province planned for 75,000 by spring 1956 (containing 20 percent of peasant households).

5. *CCPCC Resolution on Development of Agricultural Production Cooperatives* [2].
6. Walker [523], p. 17.   7. See, e.g., *HHNP,* 21 Aug. 55 [85].

TABLE 37. National Growth of Agricultural Production
Co-ops, 1955–56

Month	Number Households in Co-ops	% of Total Peasant Households
Oct. 1955	38,130,000	32.5
Nov. 1955	49,940,000	42.1
Dec. 1955	75,450,000	63.3
Jan. 1956	95,550,000	80.3
Feb. 1956	104,190,000	87.0
Mar. 1956	106,680,000	88.9
Apr. 1956	108,450,000	90.3
May 1956	110,130,000	91.2

SOURCE: T'ung Ta-lin [34], p. 1.
NOTE: Compare the figures given in Schran [480], p. 28.

These targets were, like the others, greatly surpassed in the time allotted.[8] The same was true of Hupei's new targets. With something over
14,000 co-ops functioning in the entire province in autumn 1955, they
planned for a total of 70,000 in a year's time.[9] But in fact, as early as
January 1956 it was reported that almost 75 percent of all Hupei's peasant households had already joined APCs![10]

Not only were co-ops formed at a startling rate, but they were also
extremely quickly converted from semi-socialist cooperatives to fully
socialist collectives, as the national totals in Table 38 illustrate.

The enormous speed with which advanced co-ops or collectives proliferated in the countryside is one of the most arresting characteristics of
the movement, especially since the formation of a collective required
peasants to give up entirely their private landownership rights, so recently won during land reform. In the following discussion, this phenomenon is explained partly in terms of a sudden jump in central loans
and other funding to promote full collectivization, and partly in terms of

8. See *HHNP* editorial, 23 Sep. 55 [431]. In fact, the *totals* for numbers of co-ops
functioning in Hunan in 1957 were actually lower, but this was because so many elementary co-ops quickly merged to form much larger advanced co-ops. At the end of 1956
Hunan reported 46,432 co-ops in all, of which only 97 were still of the elementary form.
Advanced co-ops then claimed membership of 97.15 percent of *all* farming households
in the province, whereas the figure for the end of the previous year had been only 0.01
percent! See *Hunan Nung-yeh* [15], p. 69.

9. *CCJP,* 10 Sep. 55 [63].

10. See *JMJP,* 6 Jan. 56; and also *CCJP,* 9 Jan. 56 [220]. For some further statistics
on co-op formation in Hunan and Hupei, see also *CCJP,* 26 Nov. 55 [216]; *HPJP,* 13 Oct.
56 [178]; and *HHNP,* 26 Oct. 56 [269].

TABLE 38. National Growth of Advanced Agricultural
Production Co-ops, 1956

Month	Number Households in Advanced APCs	% of Total Peasant Households
Jan. 1956	36,520,000	30.7
Feb. 1956	61,030,000	51.0
Mar. 1956	65,820,000	54.9
Apr. 1956	69,840,000	58.2
May 1956	74,720,000	61.8

SOURCE: T'ung Ta-lin [34], p. 2.

the many difficulties encountered by local cadres and peasants in trying
to make the semi-socialist elementary form of cooperation workable.
These difficulties, by their very complexity and intractability, contributed not to a political retrenchment or a move to abandon cooperative
farming, but, on the contrary, to the determination to proceed even more
quickly to advanced, fully socialist collective organizations.

ELEMENTARY AND ADVANCED CO-OPS

Elementary production cooperatives were regarded as "semi-
socialist in character."[11] Insofar as possible, co-op members were to
receive compensation according to the work they had done for the
cooperative. To this extent, the co-op would be run according to socialist
principles. But since ownership of the major means of production remained in private hands and these means of production were, in effect,
rented, loaned, or sold to the co-op for use by its members, part of the
compensation paid to members would be based on their contributions of
property and not on their work. To this extent, the cooperative would not
be run according to socialist principles.

The elementary production cooperative was organized with a chairman and an elected executive committee and supervisory council,
according to the same pattern described earlier for other types of cooperatives. The general meeting of the membership was theoretically the
ultimate authority on all matters, and members were divided into small

11. The intended organizational form of elementary co-ops is clearly outlined in
Model Regulations for an Agricultural Producers' Cooperative [473], see Article III. A
good account of most important characteristics of elementary co-ops can be found in Ho
Ch'eng [13].

groups that elected spokesmen or delegates for administrative purposes. Peasants[12] joined the co-ops by purchasing a share in it, but unlike the share payments for other types of co-ops, this amounted to a substantial contribution in cash or in goods.[13] Wealthier households paid more than poor ones, the amount being assessed according to the quantities of land and labor each was bringing into the cooperative. This does not mean, however, that poor households found the burden light. They frequently had to take loans from a Credit Cooperative to pay their share, agreeing to several years of repayment on the debt. To avoid going into debt, many new members sold their draught animals or farm tools to the co-op at the beginning, and had the money credited toward their purchase of a share. Share money could not be returned to members unless they withdrew from the cooperative. Whenever the co-op was in need of capital, it might request members to make further investments. They were expected to respond to the call for extra contributions, sometimes receiving a small amount of interest on them, and sometimes not.

Cooperative farming was to bring land and other major means of production under unified, planned management. Members, therefore, put their land at the disposal of the co-op, accepting a rent payment for its use.[14] Each member's land was evaluated in terms of its quantity and quality, and an estimate of its normal productivity was derived and used as the basis for determining the payment the cooperative would make for

12. Article XI of the *Model Regulations* . . . [473] specified that during its first few years the co-op should not admit rich peasants and former landlords as members. The rule was quite strict: "Former landlords whose status has been changed according to law, and rich peasants who have for many years given up exploitation may be admitted individually into the cooperative but only when the cooperative in question is firmly established, and when over three-quarters of the working peasants in that particular *hsiang* and county have joined cooperatives, and after a general meeting of members has examined their cases and approved their applications, and this decision has been examined and sanctioned by the county people's council." Even after they were admitted to membership, rich peasants and former landlords were not supposed to be allowed to hold any important posts in the co-op "for a certain period of time." For a further explanation of the danger of letting rich peasants join co-ops, see *Talking about Some Problems in the Class Policy for Agricultural Cooperativization* [32], pp. 16–19. But as elaborated below, this was one of the rules most consistently disregarded during the "high tide."

13. See the *Model Regulations* . . . [473], Articles XXXII–XXXVII.
14. See the *Model Regulations* . . . [473], Articles XVIII–XXXIII.

its use. The principle to be followed in setting the price for land was suitably vague:

> The income of the cooperative is created by the work of its members; it is not derived from their ownership of land. The amount paid in dividends on land must therefore be less than the amount paid for agricultural work, for in this way all members will be encouraged to take an active part in the work of the cooperative. In the early stages of the cooperative's growth, however, the dividends on land should not be set too low; a reasonable dividend will help to attract peasants who own more or better land into the cooperative and enable members who own land but are short of labor power to get a reasonable income. (Article XVIII)

The rent payment given to peasants for their land was supposed to be a fixed amount rather than a percentage of total co-op income. In areas where yields tended to be uncertain from year to year, however, a percentage system was to be allowed temporarily. But whether it was a flat rate or a percentage, it was definitely intended that compensation for land would be reduced once co-op income had risen sufficiently, and eventually it was to be eliminated altogether.

When land was pooled, the irrigation works serving it also came under cooperative management. The following section from the *Model Regulations* provides an idea of the complexities involved in determining an appropriate compensation rate on irrigation facilities:

> If these irrigation works have already been in existence long enough to raise the yield of his land before the owner joined the cooperative and thus enabled him to get a high dividend on his land after joining, the cooperative does not, as a rule, have to give the owner any special compensation. If, however, after being turned over to the cooperative, these works can be used to irrigate additional land, then the cooperative should pay the owner appropriate compensation in consideration of the benefits thus accruing and according to local practice. If these works are newly built and the owner has not yet derived proper benefit from them and if the cooperative has agreed to buy these works at his request, then the cooperative should pay appropriate compensation to the owner for the work done and expenses incurred and turn such works into its own property. (Article XXIV)

Payments to owners of irrigation works were to be made in installments stretching over several years, sometimes with and sometimes without interest.

Peking area small group training session for the transition from Mutual Aid Team to Agricultural Production Co-op. (Hsinhua News Agency)

Other important means of production such as draught animals, large tools, carts and junks, groves, orchards, large herds or flocks, and equipment for sideline production were also gradually to be put at the disposal of the cooperative, and various sorts of compensation systems could be worked out for their use. In the case of draught animals, for example, the owner might continue to own and rear them, charging the co-op the going rate for their use; or else the owner might continue to own them but give the co-op the responsibility for rearing them and the right to use them at will, accepting a fixed payment; or else the owner might sell them outright to the co-op, accepting payment in installments over several years. Under the first two systems there was much room for controversy and recrimination if an ox should die or be injured. Therefore, outright purchases of animals were considered best, once co-ops were well established. The schemes actually adopted by co-ops to compensate peasants for draught animals, tools, and so on were extremely diverse.

Co-op members retained ownership and management of their homes and courtyards, small tools, poultry, and pigs. They also were allowed to retain small private plots for growing vegetables or other cash crops. In elementary co-ops the size of the private plot allotted to each person was not supposed to exceed 5 percent of the average per capita land holding in the *hsiang*. Co-op authority, however, extended to include the stipulation that members could not choose not to labor for the co-op, and except in cases of illness or debilitation the co-op could require individual members to put in a given number of days of work, if that became necessary. The co-op also reserved a prior right to purchase certain resources (particularly natural fertilizer) from member households at fixed prices, and often with delayed payment.

After the major harvest, the co-op was to deduct from its gross income its production costs, taxes, and the rent payments due to various members for their land and other property. The co-op also took responsibility for selling its specified quota of grain and other crops to the Supply and Marketing Co-op under the terms of Unified Purchase. Also to be deducted was about 5 percent of the net income for the year, designated as the ''reserve fund.'' This was to be put toward capital construction for the cooperative, the purchase of draught animals, tools, irrigation projects, and so on, to increase production in the coming years. As co-op income rose, the reserve fund was to be increased gradually to about 10 percent. Another 1–2 percent was to be deducted and designated as the ''welfare fund.'' This money was to be used solely for supplementary benefits to widows, sick people, and so on, and for other amenities for co-op members.[15] What remained of the net income was then to be divided among the members according to their work.

The size of an elementary co-op varied widely from village to village and from time to time during the process of cooperativization. Usually, several co-ops were established in one *hsiang*, and at the end of 1955 the average size was generally between 27 and 32 households.[16] In the country as a whole, a co-op had the use of, on the average, 92.5 acres and 13 draught animals. The acreage in Hunan and Hupei would have been generally lower than this average—perhaps 65 acres for a fortunate co-op. The collectives, by contrast, were much larger, generally encompassing the land and people of an entire *hsiang*. During the socialist

15. For further explanations of the sources and uses of co-op reserve and welfare funds and for clarification on how they were supposed to be distinguished from share funds, see Yang Hui-hsien [37], *passim*.

16. Compare the estimates of Schran [480], p. 30, and Chao Kuo-chun [452].

high tide they sometimes grew to include two or three *hsiang*. But thereafter they quickly leveled off to an average of between 100 and 200 member households.

Except for their larger size, collectives closely resembled the elementary co-ops in most of their essential characteristics.[17] The most important difference was that the members of collectives turned over all their land, draught animals, large farm tools, and other important means of production to the collective ownership of the cooperative. Houses, yard animals, and private plots were still the property of individual households, but none of the major means of production any longer remained in private hands. Some compensation was paid to peasants for these assets, especially where something particularly valuable was involved or where the peasant household had made a large private investment on which it had not yet received a reasonable return. Payments were often spread out over several years, however, and in many cases it is evident that members were never truly compensated for their property. When rich peasants and former landlords became members, all their major means of production were to be turned over to the collective without compensation (Articles XXI and XXII). With the abolition of private ownership of the major means of production, members would no longer collect rents from other members and would be paid solely on the basis of their work for the collective.

The size of the welfare fund remained at about 2 percent of net income in collectives, but their rate of capital accumulation was to be higher. Eight percent of net annual income was to be put into the reserve fund (12 percent for collectives growing industrial crops). With all rent paying eliminated, it was thought that collectives would be able to make larger investments in basic capital construction and therefore raise their output faster than elementary co-ops.

MIDDLE PEASANTS AND POOR PEASANTS

The official policy line at this time for the formation of production cooperatives was to "rely on" the poor peasants and to "unite with" the middle peasants, especially the lower-middle peasants.[18] A second im-

17. See *Model Regulations for Advanced Agricultural Producers' Cooperatives* [472].

18. See, e.g., *HHNP*, 28 Aug. 55 [429]; *JMJP*, 13 Oct. 55 [362]; and *JMJP*, 3 Nov. 55 [53].

portant guideline to be followed was that co-ops should be formed only if it was probable that 90–95 percent of members would experience a rise in income as a result.[19] There were many difficulties involved in balancing the interests of middle peasant members against those of poor peasant members, while at the same time arranging for an improvement in the standard of living of nearly everyone, and these difficulties dominated the thoughts of cadres and members in the elementary co-ops.

Middle peasants, by definition, possessed more and better things than poor peasants. When they brought these things—land, draught animals, and tools—into an elementary cooperative, they were entitled to compensation for them. The crucial matter of deciding on a value and a rental payment for such items of property while also assigning a value to labor to be done for the cooperative was the source of seemingly unending suspicion and disagreement between poorer and better-off peasants. In theory, poor peasants were most anxious to participate in production co-ops because they had the most to gain by it. But poor peasants were by no means always in the majority in villages following land reform; middle peasants had become the numerically superior class after the agrarian reform movement was completed. They also frequently held positions of authority in the villages even greater than would have been indicated by their proportion of the population.[20] Since middle peasants naturally favored generous rents on the means of production they were bringing into the cooperative, since they often constituted a majority or at least a very substantial proportion of potential co-op members, and since their property and participation were probably going to be essential for the co-op to succeed, they were often able to attain promises of high compensation. Poor peasants then complained that the only reason their own land was not as valuable and productive as middle peasants' land was precisely because they had been poor and not able to work it most advantageously, and that once it came under co-op management it would surely produce a higher yield. They were frequently able to get the co-op to pay them rent based on the potential value of their land rather than on its actual output.

There were, in fact, four recognized methods of evaluating land when bringing it into an elementary co-op: (1) on the basis of its actual output,

19. See, e.g., *JMJP,* 23 Oct. 55 [406]. See also *JMJP,* 18 Sep. 55 [242].

20. See Wong [487], p. 176. See also *HHNP,* 28 Aug. 55 [429]. Here it is estimated that poor peasants in the Hsiang-t'an area of Hunan amount to 20–25 percent of the rural population, while middle peasants range between 35 percent and 50 percent.

as well as its quality, fertility, the difficulty of cultivating it, and so on, calculating what it would be likely to produce in an ordinary year and translating that into standard *mou;* (2) on the basis of the last year's actual output, converted into standard *mou;* (3) on the basis of the normal annual yield figure used for tax purposes; (4) on the basis of real *mou* — one *mou* counting as one *mou.*

The first method took account of the fact that the low-yield land of poorer peasants was likely to show improved output once it was farmed cooperatively. It therefore met their demands at the same time that it mollified upper-middle peasants and others who had made improvements on their land before entering the co-op.

The second method was said to make poorer peasants unhappy, because it did not take account of their difficulties and penalized them for the very inequalities they had labored under before cooperativization. The third method was regarded as generally unsatisfactory since the tax assessment rates were left fairly far below actual output figures. And the fourth method, since it made no allowance at all for the quality of the land, was considered very crude and likely to cause much dissatisfaction within the co-op.

A 1955 survey of thirty-two elementary co-ops in Hupei found that nearly 72 percent had used the first method of land evaluation; 28 percent had used the second and third methods; and none had used the fourth.[21]

If a high proportion of the co-op's income were to go for rent on private property, then capital accumulation for reinvestment would be severely limited.[22] And if rent payments were to be high, co-ops frequently tended to undervalue labor contributions so as to conserve collective funds. Yet if the compensation for a day's labor were set too low, members would make excuses not to work for the cooperative; they would tend to their private plots, do a little private trading, or go in for poultry and pig raising on a larger scale.

In many early co-ops, the rent paid for land and other means of production was in fact set too low. Sometimes this happened because the Three Fix productivity figures were used to calculate the value of the land. When the cadres were determining their liability to compulsory grain sales under the Three Fix policy earlier in 1955, many peasants had

21. Based on the account by Su Hsing [31], pp. 73–74.
22. *CCJP,* 22 Dec. 55 [163].

of course persisted in their attempts to conceal the full productivity of their land, hoping to be declared grain-short or just self-sufficient in grain. If the Three Fix estimates were later employed to evaluate property for co-ops, then land rents were set too low for the actual value of the land, but the peasants found it embarrassing to protest. Later on, when the co-op took over responsibility for meeting grain sales quotas, the actual output of members' land was generally recognized and the rents could be adjusted upward.[23]

Where land rent was set too low, middle peasants were likely to experience a drop in income during their first year of participation in the co-op. Adjustment in the rents paid out was necessary, then, if the co-op were to approach the official target of raising the incomes of nearly all members. Poor peasant households with many members but with few able-bodied laborers also suffered if land rent was set too low. These households had often received considerable land during land reform because of the number of mouths they had to feed. If the labor they could contribute to the co-op was not enough to sustain them, they had to depend on fair compensation for their land. Likewise, orphans, widows, and the sick would suffer if land rent was not high enough. A proper settlement of the land rent problem was, therefore, not always a simple matter of poor peasant members versus middle peasant members. In official reports, co-op rent payments were just as often faulted for being too high as for being too low. In most cases, the evaluation of land and labor for elementary co-ops was done very hastily and imprecisely and was formulated according to whatever pressures from members seemed strongest at the moment, so that later rectifications and readjustments were inevitable.

Often the original promises about land rent payments had to be revised in the face of natural disasters or other production difficulties, causing the per *mou* output to drop below earlier projections.[24] A cry to change the originally agreed upon rent payments was also often provoked by the entrance of new members. The co-op cadres and better-off members frequently tried to prevent poor peasants from joining from the beginning.[25] To stave off discrimination against poor peasants and to

23. *JMJP*, 23 Oct. 55 [406]. Here it is reported that a survey of 100 APCs in Hupei's Huang-kang county had set land rents at 10–30 percent below actual value.
24. *JMJP*, 12 Sep. 55 [138].
25. See *CCJP*, 16 Oct. 55 [249]; and *CCJP*, 10 Dec. 55 [93].

enable them to pay the land rent necessary to attract better-off peasants to join in cooperative farming with them, the government offered special loans to poor peasants through the Bank and the local Credit Co-ops.[26] The availability of such loans to poor APC members rose dramatically with the onset of the socialist high tide, as did the availability of all state loans for agriculture.

As Table 39 indicates, along with the trebling in the size of loans granted between 1955 and 1956 came a trebling of loans outstanding at the end of the year. Although this in part reflects a trend toward longer-term loans to co-ops to finance large construction projects, it was also the result of a deliberate delay in debt collection that enabled more co-ops to meet the criterion of raising the incomes of 90–95 percent of members in their first year. The comparable figures for Hunan are somewhat more severe, as shown in Table 40.

Government loans to co-ops were intended to supplement investments made by individual members and to help get fledgling co-ops off to a good start. Many new members were reluctant to invest any more than was required in what they inevitably regarded as a risky venture, however, and the increased availability of small government loans often served to get them temporarily off the hook. Co-op leaders applied for loans when they encountered difficulty in mobilizing their own members to invest.[27] Occasionally production loans were obtained for frivolous purposes or were used in direct disregard of government guidelines.[28] But by and large cadres requested loans when they could not convince members to contribute their personal savings or the money left over from the previous year's grain sales. They hoped that members would be motivated to contribute more the following year if, with the help of the loans, the co-op could prove itself to be profitable in the first few seasons.[29]

Although all members may have been equally reluctant to turn extra capital over to the co-op, the issue of investment tended to become a divisive one between poor and middle peasant members since it was

26. *TKP*, 5 Aug. 55 [400]. Loans to specially needy individuals and disaster victims at this period were issued at an interest rate of about 0.75 percent per month. Ordinary loans to individual poor peasants incurred interest of 1 percent per month. See *HHNP*, 16 Aug. 55 [331].

27. See, e.g., *HNCCP*, 1 Apr. 56 [147]; *HNCCP*, 1 Apr. 56 [160]; and *JMJP*, 3 Mar. 55 [273].

28. *HHNP*, 3 May 55 [262]; and *HNCSP*, 27 May 56 [317].

TABLE 39. Agricultural Loans Granted by the People's
Bank, 1950–56

| | Million yüan | Index (1950=100) | Loans Outstanding at End of Year | |
			Million yüan	Index (1950=100)
1950	212.4	100.0	94.9	100.0
1951	401.5	189.0	204.8	215.8
1952	1076.3	506.7	481.6	507.4
1953	1264.0	595.1	666.2	702.0
1954	840.6	395.7	782.7	824.7
1955	1004.1	472.7	1000.7	1054.5
1956	3387.1	1590.4	3029.5	3192.1

SOURCE: Corson [456], p. 114.
NOTE: These figures and those in Table 40 do not appear to have been adjusted for inflation, but since the rate was generally low to negligible over the
period, they probably represent fairly accurately the rise in real value of state
credit available in the countryside. See also Wong [487], p. 314.

middle peasants who had the more significant sums potentially or actually available. After the arguments over how to evaluate and compensate
land pooled in the cooperative, dissension among poor and middle peasants over how much each household was obliged to invest in addition to
the basic means of production was the second most persistent problem
the elementary co-ops had to face.[30] Middle peasants preferred to put
their extra cash into investments of direct benefit to themselves, such as
house repairs, or else to invest in small business deals. From their point
of view, with land, tools, and oxen already tied up in the cooperative, it
was foolhardy to put in their spare cash as well. But the co-ops could not
hope to improve their output compared to that of individual farmers
unless their members would invest everything in cooperative farming
that they would have invested individually. As time went on, therefore,
and the "high tide" grew in strength, the principle that those who possessed more should invest more in co-ops came to be accepted by local
co-op leaders and cadres.[31] Indeed, as the movement progressed, most
better-off co-op members found themselves under greater and greater
pressure to invest all their surplus capital in the production co-op. But in
the meantime government loans helped both to make up the deficits of
new co-ops and to make them appear to hesitating peasants more sturdy

29. See, e.g., *CCJP*, 30 Jan. 56 [437].
30. *JMJP*, 19 Apr. 55 [439]; also *JMJP*, 3 Mar. 55 [273]; and *JMJP*, 13 Oct. 55 [362].
31. See, e.g., *HNCCP*, 1 Apr. 56 [271].

TABLE 40. Hunan Agricultural Loans and Repayments, 1952–57

(In 1000 yüan)

	Highest Amount	Loans Made Over the Year	Amount Due	Amount Repaid	Amount Repaid As % of Highest Amt.	Amount Repaid As % of Amt. Due	Amount Not Repaid
1952	12,227	10,930		9,590	78.4		2,640
1953	31,374	28,730	25,400	21,370	68.1	84.1	10,000
1954	43,023	33,460	27,500	22,940	53.3	83.4	23,000
1955	64,671	41,000	40,000	31,000	48.0	77.5	31,800
1956	162,709	142,210	95,000	34,030	20.9	35.8	145,770
1957	190,426	44,656	140,000	61,900	32.5	44.2	137,088

SOURCE: *Hunan Nung-yeh* [15], p. 110.

NOTES: Actual loans made over the year were calculated by subtracting the amount for the previous year not yet repaid from the highest amount outstanding. But because monies repaid were quickly loaned out again, the totals do not precisely coincide. As noted at Table 39, these figures do not appear to have been adjusted for inflation, but since the rate of inflation was low over these years, they probably reflect real trends fairly accurately.

The figures for the highest amount outstanding were obtained by telegraph and telephone reports. For this reason they do not entirely coincide with the figures in previous tables and are offered only for reference. Most, but not officially all, of this funding went to the use of new APCs. Compare Tables 29 and 30 above.

and more likely to succeed. Even in these crucial years, state investments in agriculture were small compared to industry's share in the national budget. But its far-flung rural administrative network allowed the
center to distribute small loan incentives very widely to attract peasants
into production cooperation.

In early 1956 the central planning units began sending down higher
and higher output targets for the production co-ops to meet. To increase
their resources for the year's production effort, co-op leaders prevailed
upon better-off members to bring out into the open whatever funds they
had been hoarding. Under pressure, they also often disregarded government guidelines on the matter of accepting rich peasants into elementary co-ops, actively soliciting their participation. Even if only one or
two rich peasant households were brought into an elementary cooperative, their land, animals, and tools could greatly enlarge the totals available for cooperative use. Many rich peasants were in fact anxious to join
elementary co-ops at this time. With the extremely rapid expansion of
cooperatives all around them, they were quickly being deprived of the
hired laborers on whom they still depended to work their land. They also
knew that in the collectives (which, it was becoming ever clearer, would
soon be upon them) they would not be given any rent or other compensation for the property they turned over for general use. From their point of
view it was certainly preferable to join while the co-op was still at the
elementary stage and they would be entitled to rent on their land and a
fair price for their tools and oxen, like other members. In the cooperatives' quest for more and more investment capital and resources it was
evident that they must soon, with government support, absorb the property of rich peasants. Unless this was to be a simple expropriation in the
style of land reform, it was better for a rich peasant to join voluntarily
and to try at least for equal treatment with the other members. So, at any
rate, many rich peasants appear to have reasoned; and when they joined
elementary co-ops under these terms the same sorts of conflicts over land
rent and the rate of investment that occurred between middle and poor
peasant members naturally arose between rich peasants and other members. In the end, rich peasants who managed to join elementary cooperatives probably gained little from the maneuver. Promises to better-off
co-op members to pay certain land rents or to deliver other compensa-
tions in installments were routinely abrogated in the coming "high
tide."

Incessant squabbling over land rent payments and persistent dissatisfaction with the amount of rent money co-op leaders were able to induce wealthier members to channel back into the cooperative led many co-op cadres to favor a quick transition to the status of an advanced cooperative.[32] In advanced co-ops land rents would be abolished, and the often quite considerable portion of co-op assets that, once paid out, had been so difficult to retrieve from the landowning members for cooperative use would remain in the co-op where it could be employed to expand production.[33] Elimination of land rent would not only mean a higher possible rate of capital accumulation; it would also allow the co-op to increase the amount it paid out as labor compensation. This would strengthen the incentive for members to participate in labor for the cooperative, which should in turn have increased co-op productivity. The appeal of fully socialist collectives, in which continuing conflicts over land rent and investment could by and large be left behind, became more and more compelling, especially to cadres and poor members. It was largely in an effort to escape the financial complexities and the conflicting interests inherent in elementary co-op organization that so many quick transitions to advanced co-op status were made.

WORKPOINTS AND WORK MANAGEMENT

So far the problems in early cooperativization considered have been those associated with the nonsocialist aspects of elementary co-ops — private ownership and private investment. There were, however, many important problems emerging that derived from the socialist aspects of

32. One of the classic statements of this argument occurs in Ch'en K'o-chien and Kan Min-chung [3], pp. 6–16.

33. The percentage of an elementary co-op's total income that went for rent payments naturally varied enormously depending on the particular circumstances and the nature of the co-op's membership. A 1955 survey of ten elementary co-ops in one area showed that land rent payments ranged between 16.82 percent and 30.28 percent of all compensation paid out to members, while interest on investments in the co-op ranged from 2.96 percent to 8.54 percent of all monies paid out, and labor compensation from 62.94 percent to 78.08 percent. See Ch'ih Yüan-chi and Hsieh Hsüeh-shih [5], p. 6. From a survey of 26,005 elementary co-ops, Walker [523], pp. 40–41, estimates an average of 21.6 percent of *co-ops' total income* going out for rent on land, animals, and tools. The touring Indian delegation, however, found some land rents between 30 percent and 45 percent of *total crop yields* in co-ops in Liaoning and Szechwan respectively. See *Report of the Indian Delegation to China on Agrarian Cooperatives* [479], pp. 41–42. These estimates are unfortunately not strictly comparable.

early co-ops, specifically from the need to devise fair systems of paying members according to their work. Although in official theoretical discussions of the drawbacks of elementary cooperatives writers tended to concentrate on the evils of land rent, private ownership of the means of production, and other capitalist holdovers, it is apparent from newspaper reports of the period that imbalances in work compensation systems caused just as much dissatisfaction and dissension among members, and were just as much of an impediment to the consolidation and success of elementary cooperatives.

In Chapter 4, several different workpoint systems in use in Mutual Aid Teams were outlined. Of these, the *ssu-fen huo-chi* system was the one most favored by the government for year-round teams. This system involved the assignment of a standard minimum number of workpoints for a day's work to each peasant, based on the individual's strength and performance. At the end of the day all work was reviewed, and if it had been done satisfactorily each member received his or her own standard number of points; if the work was especially good or bad, points could be added or subtracted for the day. When elementary co-ops were formed, many retained *ssu-fen huo-chi* for calculating workpoints.[34] This was said to be advisable because Mutual Aid Team members were used to the method (and most had already been assigned a workpoint standard), and also because it was thought that *ssu-fen huo-chi* was the most sophisticated system to which co-op members who had not been Mutual Aid Team members could be expected to adapt easily. In practice, however, there were a number of serious objections to the way *ssu-fen huo-chi* operated in elementary co-ops.[35]

First, if the nightly reviews of work and assignments of points had been cumbersome in the Mutual Aid Teams, they were to become positively onerous in the much larger co-ops where many more members were engaged in cooperative labor much more frequently and in a far greater variety of tasks. The accounting work alone for this procedure was formidable. Second, even the elementary co-ops were supposed to be divided into production teams, and nightly work evaluations were generally to be done within the context of the small team. With each team in charge of evaluating its own performance, in ignorance of how rigorous or lax other teams were in evaluating themselves, and in com-

---

34. See *JMJP*, 19 Mar. 55 [174]; also *JMJP*, 4 Apr. 55 [189].
35. See Ho Ch'eng [13], pp. 49–50.

petition for a certain fixed amount of pay to be distributed at the end of the season, there was a strong tendency for teams always to assign themselves maximum points, regardless of the actual quality or difficulty of the work done. They were no doubt usually correct in assuming that other teams were doing the same.

This tended to devalue the workpoint. Women, old people, children, and others who were assigned low standard minimum points for a day's work consequently became even less enthusiastic about laboring for the co-op: it simply was not worth their time for the little they would earn. Resentments between teams began to fester, and with each member routinely assigned the full number of workpoints each day no matter how hard he or she worked, labor discipline declined and peasants competed for easy jobs and avoided difficult ones. As the size and the efficiency of the work force in the co-op diminished, production naturally suffered, the ultimate value of the workpoint therefore slipped again, and the situation only deteriorated further.

Another, better system of labor accounting was obviously required, and the elementary co-ops were urged to switch to some type of piece-work method *(an chien chi-kung)* as soon as practicable.[36] The adoption of a piecework system implied substituting the evaluation of jobs for the evaluation of workers. Co-ops set about separating tasks into categories and assigning them workpoints according to their difficulty and their seasonal urgency. Any individual member or group of members who volunteered for a job would receive all the workpoints allotted for it, as long as minimum quality standards of the work were met. As with any piecework system, workers had clear incentives for improving their speed and skill on the job. Furthermore, women and others who had previously been assigned low personal standard workpoint earnings could now hope to receive equal pay for equal output, even if it took them longer to accomplish. This brought more labor into the cooperative,[37] but since it was productive labor (and since the number of workpoints earned overall could not be indefinitely inflated as before), co-op members could expect both that production would rise and that the value of a workpoint would be reliable.

36. See *HHNP* editorial, 18 Nov. 55 [388]; and *CCJP,* 24 Apr. 55 [44].

37. One co-op in Hunan reported that in 1953 full labor power males did an average of 213 workdays for the co-op; in 1954 it was 220 workdays; and in 1955 it was 236 workdays. In addition, better work compensation and work management systems had steadily expanded the utilization of women's labor power in the co-op. In 1953 only about 20 percent of women worked for the co-op; but in 1955 over 80 percent of women were

The most popular variation of the piecework system in production co-ops was called *pao kung pao ch'an,* that is, "guaranteed work and guaranteed production." A certain production task, rated at a certain number of labor days, would be given to a production team, which promised to complete the task within a stipulated time period. As long as it completed the task on time and met the necessary quality standards, the team was awarded all the labor days for the job and then divided the points among its members according to how much labor each had contributed. If it did not complete the task on time and was holding up some other aspect of production work, the co-op might reduce the number of labor days awarded to the team. If the team did an especially good job or if it had to overcome unforeseen difficulties in getting the work done, the co-op might award additional workpoints. If the team finished on time but did not meet the quality standards expected, the co-op could require them to do the job over without compensation, or else it might simply reduce the workpoints awarded.[38]

This system was favored because it helped promote diligence and labor discipline. If one team member slacked off or worked poorly, other team members were likely to lose points, and they were prompted, therefore, to keep careful watch on one another and to assist one another in improving their skill and performance. Local reports make it plain, however, that there was frequent collusion among all members of a team to do fast, poor quality work in order to finish quickly and take on a new task to earn more points.[39] Only when co-ops employed a separate, careful system of check-ups on work performance were they able to depend on high quality work being done under *pao kung pao ch'an.* To avoid the nightly checkups on the work of teams, some co-ops began measuring quality of work in terms of ultimate productive output. A team might work any way it wished so long as it produced a stipulated amount of each crop in the end.[40] This, of course, presupposed a contract between

---

working. In 1953 their labor accounted for 16.82 percent of all labor done by co-op members. In 1955, this was up to 21.01 percent. See *HHNP,* 31 Mar. 56 [247]. Further examples of local successes in expanding women's participation in cooperative work by adopting more rational workpoint systems can also be found in *Happy and Prosperous Advanced Agricultural Production Cooperatives* [12], p. 2 and *passim.*

38. Ho Ch'eng [13], p. 53. See also Han Hsing [10], pp. 38–39.

39. *JMJP,* 19 Mar. 55 [174]; and *JMJP,* 4 Apr. 55 [189]. See also *HHNM,* 13 May 56 [146].

40. See Chou Ch'eng [6], p. 24; also *HPJP,* 21 Oct. 56 [348].

the co-op and the team with a duration of at least one full season, and with team work done always on the same specified plots of land. *Pao kung pao ch'an,* therefore, tended to be introduced at first by co-ops on a short-term basis, but was extended rapidly to cover longer and longer periods.[41]

As *pao kung pao ch'an* became a fixture of co-op work management, it customarily came to include a third guarantee—"guaranteed cost coverage" *(pao ch'eng-pen).*[42] This meant that the co-op promised to supply all the capital and equipment the team would require to reach the stipulated output. The agreement also frequently included specific incentives to the team to surpass the stated production level. It was then sometimes referred to as "three guarantees and one encouragement" *(san pao i chiang).*[43] The incentive payments often came to a considerable sum. In Hupei's Sheng-li Village, for example, it was decided that production teams exceeding the quota would receive 50–70 percent of the surplus for themselves, while teams failing to meet their quota would be penalized by 30 percent of the amount lacking, unless good reasons could be given for their failure.[44]

Although contracts with incentives such as these were heavily propagandized and advocated for wide use within co-ops, they were not intended to apply uniformly to all the different sorts of work co-op members would do. In both elementary and advanced co-ops, a variety of work calculation methods was generally used simultaneously. There might be a full-year contract system in operation for raising pigs, chickens, and ducks, for example, with only a seasonal contract system for raising fish or planting trees. Temporary work assignments for panning for gold or for short-term transport might also be obtained by individuals or groups on an *ad hoc* basis. A piecework system might be applied to certain sorting, drying, or packing jobs. Points could be awarded with households as the unit for jobs in which the family group remained the most effective or most relevant delineation of workers. And sometimes even the old *ssu-fen huo-chi* could be resorted to for tasks that were difficult to evaluate in advance.[45]

---

41. Ho Ch'eng [13], pp. 53–54. See also *CCJP,* 10 Apr. 56 [152].

42. Sometimes "guaranteed materials" *(pao ts'ai-liao).* See Han Hsing [10], p. 39; and *HNNM,* 13 Apr. 56 [442]. There is also a mention of "guaranteed materials" in *HNCSP,* 7 Jun. 56 [235].

43. See, e.g., *JMJP,* 9 Oct. 56 [67].   44. *CCJP,* 10 Apr. 56 [152].

45. *HNCSP,* 7 Jun. 56 [235]. See also *HNCSP,* 9 May 56 [270].

In theory, all these different work compensation schemes could co-exist and indeed be made to mesh usefully within one cooperative, so that members could effectively be prevented from cheating one another on work. For success in this tremendous undertaking, careful considera-tion of all the types of jobs to be done was most necessary, along with mindfulness of the interdependence of particular tasks and their fluctuat-ing seasonal urgency, a close estimate of the labor power actually avail-able and a strong set of priorities for its use, sufficient knowledge of local conditions and of agricultural work to foresee the many delays and difficulties that might arise, and finally a subtle ranking and allocation of jobs for each season that would not only serve the needs of the coopera-tive but also conform to the attitudes and traditional practices of the peasants. In most newly formed cooperatives, of course, these condi-tions did not exist.

For many co-op members, even *ssu-fen huo-chi* and the "labor day" were new concepts not easily accepted. In other cases, where co-ops were formed of several permanent Mutual Aid Teams with fairly sophis-ticated work compensation systems, reconciling and integrating the existing systems often seemed more difficult for co-op cadres than start-ing from scratch. In many co-ops, teams continued working quite inde-pendently, deciding on their own job priorities and assigning themselves workpoints using their own criteria. This naturally aggravated suspi-cions and hostilities within the cooperative. But where co-op-wide norms were established and applied, the quotas were usually so crude at first that they failed to make allowances for such vital factors as different fertility and irrigation conditions in different parts of the cooperative, so that the members often refused to do some jobs or only worked half-heartedly at them. If total production was thus threatened, so was the ultimate value of workpoints earned, and members grew only more and more uneasy.

In early 1956, when conversions to advanced cooperatives were being widely advocated and publicized, many co-op cadres evidently con-cluded that this would be one way of solving their workpoint dilemmas once and for all. With the confusing and divisive factor of land rent completely eliminated, it would be possible to give full attention to labor compensation. Furthermore, new production targets coming down to these cadres from the central planning units indicated that their co-ops would be expected to increase output extremely rapidly in the next few seasons. Increased production and no further need to deduct a large portion of the income for land rent could result in higher workpoint values, very attractive to members.

Most collectives were several times larger than elementary co-ops, and their basic work units likewise increased in size. They were called "brigades" now instead of "teams," and they often corresponded in size to an entire elementary co-op. With these enlarged work units to deploy, collective cadres seemed to think it feasible to sign contracts of the *pao kung pao ch'an* model. They broke down the production targets they received from county authorities and presented them to brigade leaders, asking them to sign a contract promising that they would achieve a certain total output quota. Brigade leaders were often reluctant to agree to the contracts at this time, fearing that they and their members might be penalized if they failed to meet them. But co-op cadres had to persuade or force them to agree to try. They promised there would be government loans, more fertilizer, an agronomist to teach them double-cropping, and so on. As for workpoints, in most cases there still had been no careful analysis and ranking of the tasks to be done, yet there were to be all sorts of new jobs, new time factors, and new implements introduced for which brigade leaders could hardly be expected to devise fair compensation systems without previous experience. The *pao kung pao ch'an* agreements made in 1956 were obviously much more closely keyed to the centrally determined quotas than they were to local workpoint calculations. Brigade leaders were left to muddle through as best they could that year in allocating workpoints and trying to provide work incentives for their members.

In the initial excitement over what the advanced cooperatives might be able to accomplish, many new collectives put their members to work on ambitious construction projects during the winter. Irrigation dams and reservoirs, roads, and new buildings were common choices. Workpoints were naturally awarded for labor on these projects, and during the slack season so many earned workpoints were accumulated by members that the ultimate worth of a co-op workpoint was inevitably greatly lowered because generally it would take several years before a profit could be realized on the manpower investment in these large-scale undertakings. They would not, for some time, produce greater cooperative income, yet they would have to be paid for with workpoint compensation. The danger was that during the busy season, peasants, realizing the low worth of the workpoint, would find more lucrative ways of spending their time than in work for the co-op. Sufficient peasant dissatisfaction with co-op earnings could even bring calls for disbandment.

As the restlessness grew, the seriousness of the problem was realized, and co-op cadres were ordered to discontinue work on projects that would not yield short-term benefits.[46] Where earned workpoints had already reached a dangerous level, co-op cadres were told to count some or all of them in the year (or years) in the future when profits from the project in question would be realized, and not to include them in the 1956 accounting year. This supported the value of the workpoint but naturally made peasants anxious about the likelihood that they would ever in fact be paid for the work they had done.

Such moves contributed to popular discontent with the coops, as did the actions of some cadres who carried the orders to economize on labor days to extremes. They declared some work "co-op administrative work," for which no labor days would be awarded after all. They put restrictions on the number of days women and partial labor power workers might work, or else let them go on working but reduced the number of workpoints they received. Other cadres set the quotas for jobs so high that members could not possibly fulfill them, or they set a maximum number of days that members could work, going so far as to introduce a rotational labor system so that some members would be required to "rest" on some days. And other cadres even cut back on necessary production activities and work in the fields, reducing the planned output targets and criticizing members who were eager to work for having a "workpoint mentality." None of this served to strengthen peasants' confidence in the wisdom of joining the co-op.

The initial application of certain workpoint systems in the larger unit of the advanced cooperative sometimes also created serious dissatisfaction with the projected income distribution across richer and poorer (or rather, more productive and less productive) brigades. As already illustrated, the concept of pay according to work was subject to several different interpretations, and more productive brigades with higher output quotas to meet were not content with earning workpoints of the same value that less productive brigades received for meeting lower targets. Since, under many of the new *pao kung pao ch'an* contracts, the criterion for judging work performed was to be the ultimate size of the crop harvested rather than, say, the amount of time put in on the job, the members of more productive brigades seemed to have a point when they insisted that their work was worth more and should be compensated at a

---

46. See, e.g., *JMJP*, 20 Apr. 56 [434]; and *HNCSP*, 27 May 56 [260]. A clear account of this same phenomenon can be found in Walker [524], pp. 403–404 and 429–430.

higher rate. They wanted more workpoints or lower quotas so that they could receive bigger incentive payments on the surpluses they produced. Production brigades with fewer workers or inferior land objected, of course, maintaining that the object of cooperativization had always been to spread out the benefits to be derived from the availability of superior means of production.

Perhaps in many cases this was more of an organizational problem than a workpoint problem. Some of the large advanced co-ops made up of more than one entire *hsiang* were disassembled later in 1956 so as to help reduce the friction between brigades. But 1956 was only the beginning of a long struggle over the administrative level at which workpoint accounting should be carried out in order both to achieve the hoped-for economies of scale in agricultural production, and to preserve effective incentives for peasants to work. Finding a proper balance on this issue was to continue to plague Chinese rural planners and cadres for years to come.

The cadres who had hoped that a transition from elementary co-op to collective would automatically obviate all their workpoint dilemmas and their problems in motivating members to work were certainly more often than not disappointed in 1956. The rapid move to fully socialist collectives focused attention on workpoints, to be sure, and it promoted the introduction of more sophisticated and more comprehensive work contracts within cooperatives. To function smoothly, however, workpoint systems and contracts still would require careful evaluation of tasks, adjustment of incentives, and consideration of members with special problems. The hard work this involved would ultimately have to be faced up to, and decisions once made would have to be revised to take account of changing conditions and the diversification and growth of co-ops. If there was one important lesson in the experience of 1956, it was that while advanced co-ops might eliminate certain obstacles to peasants' enthusiastic and wholehearted participation in collective labor, they did not in themselves represent a magic formula for future harmony and growth.

THE HIGH TIDE

As the "high tide of socialism" mounted in the countryside, there were many more serious problems arising for co-ops in addition to the ones of reconciling conflicting interests of members. There had been some talk in the earlier stages of carrying out cooperativization using keypoints and moving "from point to area," as had been the pattern for earlier movements.[47] But these orderly plans were soon overtaken by events, and cadres and peasants all over China were busily establishing cooperatives without benefit of preparatory work teams, clear local guidelines, or even much assistance from the county. Under these conditions, deviations of the "commandist" variety were most prone to occur. There were occasional reports of coercion in taking over people's property and drawing them into new cooperatives.[48] Various kinds of indirect pressures were brought to bear on peasants who expressed the wish to remain independent farmers. The co-op, for example, might complain that the insects from the private farmer's land were going to damage its crop and would suggest a swap of some pieces of land, offering something inferior in exchange for the independent peasant's own land. Or else the co-op might insist that the farmer would have to pay the co-op a certain amount in compensation for the damage done by "his" insects.

Independent peasants were often told that they would not be allowed to borrow co-op oxen or equipment, and when co-ops were planning new irrigation works independent peasants were frequently forced to allow their own land to be utilized as the co-op saw fit. Officially the authorities decried all pressuring and intimidation of private farmers, but the higher-level leadership's great favoritism toward cooperative organizations could hardly be missed by individual farmers, and it certainly did not augur well for their attempts to register complaints against co-op arrogance with the *hsiang* government. Peasants who were pressured to join co-ops against their will, once inside, sometimes took revenge in sabotage. Trees were cut down; oxen were slaughtered.[49]

Oxen, it seems, were often the first to feel the brunt of many types of co-op failures. Some co-op oxen died of overwork when peasants in pursuit of workpoints disregarded the animals' health. The *People's Daily* reported: "Co-op members are trying to earn as many workpoints as possible, and so they work the animals to death and spare themselves.

---

47. See, e.g., *JMJP*, 24 Aug. 55 [311]; and *HHNP*, 30 Aug. 55 [316].

48. See, e.g., *HPJP*, 7 Oct. 56 [427]; and *HPJP*, 13 Oct. 56 [178].

49. A rise in the price of timber in the south may have had more to do with cases of forest depletion in 1956 than fears or sabotage connected with collectivization. See *Forest Industry* no. 12 (1957) [40], pp. 52–53. (I am grateful to Lester Ross for bringing this source to my attention.)

They think, 'Earning a few more workpoints, that's my affair; if the livestock die from exhaustion, that's the co-op's problem. The death of one or two animals wouldn't ever affect me personally.' "[50]

Co-ops were supposed to have set limits on the amount of work each ox could be permitted to do in a given period of time. But they frequently seemed to fail altogether to plan for the care of animals when working out timetables and space allocations. After turning their oxen over to the co-op, peasants refused to keep them unless paid for the trouble, but the co-op cadres often did not remember to find alternative places for the animals. Similarly, when several elementary co-ops pooled their resources to become a collective, each one would deny responsibility for its oxen and expect the collective to care for them.[51] The care of oxen and other animals was generally regarded as unskilled and unimportant work. It was usually assigned to elderly people or to young children; it did not earn much in terms of workpoints, and consequently members did not exert themselves greatly on the job. Deaths and illnesses of animals directly attributable to inadequate care did increase markedly for a time after the onset of rapid collectivization.

Still, there were no massive losses of plough animals in the process of collectivization. In 1957, for example, Hunan province reported 3,057,394 head of oxen, a 13.48 percent increase over the estimated population of 1952, despite the fact that many had drowned in the 1954 floods.[52] And as far as hogs were concerned, the population increased over the period, in contrast to the slaughter that characterized Soviet collectivization. Hunan estimated just under 11 million head in 1957, a 59.5 percent increase over the 1952 estimate of just under 7 million. After collectivization, 83.7 percent of all peasant households in the province were said to be raising hogs, with an average of 1.34 per household.[53]

50. *JMJP* editorial, 17 May 56 [142].

51. See *HHNP,* 20 Oct. 56 [436].

52. *Hunan Nung-yeh* [15], p. 88. This ox population was by no means considered adequate for provincial needs, however. It was estimated that leaving out old and weak oxen, there were really only one million which could work up to par, and that added up to a plough burden of about 52 *mou* for each ox, which was obviously much too high. *Ibid.,* p. 269.

53. *Ibid.,* p. 88. Figures like these do not tell the whole story, however. Even official Chinese nationwide live hog estimates showed declines of several million head in 1954 and 1955. It is clear that some slaughter, some sabotage, poor tending, and fodder shortages caused a drop in the hog population during the collectivization years. Official

The poor care of oxen was only one symptom of a general lack of forethought and attention to detail in much of the work of APCs during the high tide. It was reflected again in the chaotic state of finance and accounting work in both elementary co-ops and collectives.[54] Even the simplest budgeting and bookkeeping procedures were often not applied.[55] Sometimes there were several individuals making purchases for the co-op, failing to note down the precise amounts in stock lists, forgetting to obtain receipts, or losing them. Incorrect notations and mathematical errors were so common that co-op leaders seem rarely to have had a good idea of the co-op resources available and obligations outstanding at any given moment.[56] Despite quick training courses and special *hsien* conferences, the necessary experience in handling such large sums was simply not available in the countryside. Furthermore, there was a tendency to regard finance work as of only secondary importance when compared to production.[57] Cashiers and accountants were under pressure to finish their book work quickly and return to the fields. The confusion in finance work was only magnified when several elementary co-ops combined to form a collective. In many cases the difficulties of integrating so many different systems into one seem to have overwhelmed co-op cashiers and accountants.[58] In the midst of such confu-

---

statistics assert that the losses were made up quickly in 1956–57. But Liu and Yeh [469], pp. 363–364, suspect that the figures given for 1957 are inflated. Even discounting for this, however, Liu and Yeh estimate that by the end of 1956 the total hog population was back to its highest precollectivization level. So, however severe the total losses were, the subsequent recovery was impressive. Still, peasants ate less pork in 1956 than they did in 1952, while all other consumption indicators rose. See Chen Nai-ruenn [454], p. 438. In the nation as a whole, by mid-1956, just over 83 percent of pigs were still privately owned by peasant households, and only about 16 percent were owned collectively. See Chen Nai-ruenn [454], p. 341.

54. See, e.g., *HNNM*, 19 Apr. 56 [186]; also *HHNP*, 25 Oct. 56 [333]. Here it is estimated that only 36 percent of APCs in Hunan had balanced their accounts as of mid-October.

55. See *HHNP*, 26 Oct. 56 [65]. Here it is reported that in Hunan's Hsiang-t'an, Heng-yang, and Shao-yang special districts, 70 percent of APCs were planning to switch to the "account book method" for keeping track of workpoints. This indicates that in their first several seasons in operation APCs continued to use chits or tokens for a major part of their financial accounting. See also *HNCSP*, 25 May 56 [257].

56. *JMJP*, 21 May 56 [351]; also *HHNP*, 24 Aug. 56 [340].

57. *NFJP* editorial, 19 May 56 [91]; also *HHNP*, 21 Oct. 56 [283]. See also *HHNP*, 25 Oct. 56 [333].

58. See, e.g., *HHNP*, 7 Feb. 56 [232]; and *HNCSP*, 7 May 56 [86].

sion it was inevitable not only that members' anxieties would increase but also that there would be a certain amount of pilfering and corruption. With the assistance of special investigative work teams and of further county and subdistrict training courses, the most important lapses in co-op accounting work were gradually set right. But throughout 1956 it is apparent that most co-ops had fallen in over their heads both externally in their financial dealings with the Bank, Credit Co-ops, Supply and Marketing Co-ops, and individual factories and shops, and in their control of internal work compensation records and payrolls.

In the effort to assist and guide new co-ops and collectives, county, province, and central planners were working overtime in 1956. The basic regulations governing co-ops made them responsible for integrating their own productive activities with the state plan and for fulfilling what tasks were set for them by the government. By all accounts, however, the 1956 plans that came down to the counties and thence to the individual cooperatives were arbitrary, inflexible, and far too ambitious. Co-op cadres evidently had little choice about accepting these targets, even when there was scant possibility that they could be reached. The situation was complicated by vaunted claims for certain technological innovations to be implemented widely for the first time in 1956. Of these, double-cropping, close-planting, and the introduction of the double-wheel, double-blade plough probably had the greatest impact.

Double-cropping, for example, requires careful planning and the smooth cooperation of all co-op members during the all-important busy periods when one crop is harvested and stored and the earth is prepared for another crop, which is then sown—all within a few days' time. The strain on manpower and draught animals is tremendous even when everything is proceeding well, and a miscalculation in timing by even a few days can result in a total loss of the crop. Because of inexperience and insufficiently fine planning, many co-ops first experimenting with double-cropping in 1956 suffered losses. Weather conditions in 1956 were also very bad in parts of the country, and this added to co-op setbacks.

The nearly farcical complication of the unwieldy Russian-inspired ploughs settling into the muddy fields of South China while oxen reared and shied, refusing to be yoked to them in teams, made it plain that the technological advances introduced with such high hopes in 1956 were to be far less miraculous in their results than many central planners and co-op cadres had expected. Although agricultural production registered a reasonable increase in 1956, the ambitious plan and the targets were generally not fulfilled.

There had been a remarkably optimistic air pervading the upper (and to some extent the lower) ranks of Chinese rural work personnel during the high tide: they were encouraged to believe that now that socialism had arrived nearly everything had become possible. By the middle of 1956, however, the seriousness of some of the errors began to be realized and the reassessment commenced. Moves were made to decentralize planning somewhat and to restore an active free market in certain commodities where the overly ambitious application of the unified marketing system had been unable to cope with demand. Genuine consultations with collectives about what and how much to plant gradually replaced the arbitrary quotas.

In the middle of 1956, the enthusiasm of the high tide was just beginning to wane, as the magnitude and complexity of co-op problems were penetrating the consciousness of planners at all levels. Following these realizations, there was to be a most interesting period of readjustment and experimentation with the nature of collective operations. This was superseded by the Great Leap decision to organize peasants into much larger communes, which itself was followed by a gradual return to smaller production and accounting units. Yet, by mid-1956, the crucial transition had already been made. A number of extremely important accomplishments were registered with the establishment of collectives, and these were never to be essentially altered despite later revisions.

First, the nationwide establishment of farming collectives, led by cadres and members of the Party and committed to work according to government plan, gave the central government much greater control over agricultural output. Within co-ops it became much more difficult for peasants to conceal wealth and misrepresent crop yields. This meant that agricultural taxation and Unified Purchase could be more thoroughly implemented, yielding more predictable revenue and commodities for distribution to industry and urban populations. Through the co-ops, peasant consumption could be effectively limited and regulated with greater accuracy so as to avoid unfair or uneven exactions while simultaneously obtaining planned, large quantities of grain, cotton, and other crops to support national industrialization.

To obtain co-op members' ready compliance and enthusiastic participation in agricultural production, it is evident that more subtle and balanced incentives and work compensation systems than those in use in

1956 were going to have to be devised. This, however, was mostly a matter of time and experience. The basic organizational framework that would provide the setting for motivating and mobilizing peasants and for regulating their activity was already achieved with collectivization in 1955–56.

Second, farming collectives provided the Chinese leadership with a responsible institutional structure through which to disseminate knowledge and materials to raise the level of agricultural technology in the countryside. New equipment, fertilizers, and methods could all be tried out in selected collectives, over larger areas where conditions were believed to be most suitable and under careful supervision by the still limited numbers of technical personnel available. Little of this would have been possible in conditions of continued private small ownership and production. Most independent peasants had neither the means nor the inclination to experiment with new technology on their own land; and if once they did manage to purchase and use some new material, it was automatically limited in efficiency, productivity, and return on investment by the very fact of small private ownership.

The Chinese are sometimes criticized for having had, during this period, too much faith in the economic and technical gains that could be achieved in agriculture simply through the institutional change involved in moving from private to cooperative cultivation. During the early cooperativization movement a certain amount of wishful thinking was allowed to dominate the propaganda about the production advances that could be made if peasants would only sign up to join co-ops. A reading of the official theoretical literature on cooperativization, however, leaves the impression that such overoptimistic promises for the immediate future were more than counterbalanced by a heavy strain of thought emphasizing the need not only for socialist reorganization but also for massive inputs of improved machinery and technology before Chinese farming could approach its potential.

Collectivization was deemed desirable not only because in itself it would achieve certain economies beneficial to production, but also because it would allow central planners to introduce these technological advancements in what they considered the most rational and advantageous manner, and as rapidly as they became available. With some resignation on the part of rural planners still learning their jobs, the errors they committed at first were accepted as preferable to the inefficiency and unpredictability of technological advancement in a poor, smallholder economy.

To summarize then, cooperativization created a responsive rural institutional structure that was of assistance to the government both in making extractions from the agricultural sector of the economy and in directing and managing inputs into the agricultural sector.

A third accomplishment of cooperativization, and one of equal importance with the others from the point of view of the leadership, was that it effectively achieved a new redistribution of wealth and security from richer to poorer villagers. Moreover, this more equitable distribution of income and basic security guarantees, unlike the initial land reform, was designed to be self-perpetuating. It should be emphasized that the decision to move to the advanced cooperative, taken in most cases so quickly once elementary co-ops had been formed and the truly better-off members were greatly outnumbered, spelled the end of the rich peasant class and the rich peasant economy. Regardless of the new incentive structures of the cooperative economy, rich peasants and most upper-middle peasants, who by this time were actually as prosperous as many rich peasant families classified at the time of land reform, were hardly joyful at the prospect. Their assets were now put at the disposal of the general village population, and their opportunities for advancement depended only on hard work along with the rest. But by this time what choice did they have in the face of pressures from cadres and other co-op members? If they had tried to continue independent farming, where would they have marketed their crops, bought their cotton cloth, or obtained a loan in an emergency? The co-op members, if they remained united, now had strong means available to them to freeze out recalcitrants. Many peasants who dropped out of co-ops or initially refused to join ended up coming back and asking to be allowed in.

Because of government policies siphoning off agricultural surpluses and diverting them into the industrial sector of the economy, the increases in income that co-op members experienced as a result of utilizing the property of better-off peasants were not as great as they no doubt had hoped. And it was generally to be a long time indeed before the entire population in a given village was to achieve a standard of living comparable to the former rich peasants of the area.

But great achievements were not claimed on that score. In 1956 Hunan divided its peasant population into three categories as follows: (1) About 25 percent of all households had a comparatively comfortable standard of living. For them, per capita annual consumption stood at about 573 catties of grain, 4.8 catties of cooking oil (including pork fat), 13 catties of meat, and 17.8 feet of cotton cloth. (2) About 62 percent of all households had an "ordinary" standard of living. For them, per capita annual consumption stood at about 550 catties of grain, 3.5 catties of cooking oil, 9.4 catties of meat, and 16.4 feet of cotton cloth. (3) About 13 percent of all households still lived a comparatively difficult life. For them, annual per capita consumption stood at about 468 catties of grain, 2.15 catties of cooking oil, 5.15 catties of meat, and 14.6 feet of cotton cloth.[59]

On the basis of calculations like these, the province made standard of living comparisons between 1956 and 1936 (the best prewar year). Average per capita net income for peasants in 1936 was estimated at 69.7 *yüan,* and at 83.2 (in constant *yüan*) for 1956. This is a rise of 19.4 percent—not quite 20 percent for a period of just 20 years.[60] As for consumption, the following estimates were made:[61]

	1936	1956
grain	476 catties	556 catties
cooking oil	3 catties	4.5 catties
meat	8.1 catties	9.6 catties
salt	8.8 catties	13.6 catties
cotton cloth	9.3 feet	16.6 feet

These are not tremendous claims. And obviously considerable income differentials remained. Some, of course, were retained as incentives to work. Others were the result of variations in land, weather, and other natural factors. Yet, most important are not the comparisons with the situation twenty years earlier but the fact that by and large a radical collectivization had been carried out without causing either an overall drop in peasant incomes or a drop in productivity, as compared with the years immediately preceding it.

Full collectivization, as explained here, had by no means put an end to all peasants' production and welfare problems. Nor did it put an end to class struggle and opposing individual interests. What it did do, by finally eliminating the last remnants of inequalities attributable to the prerevolutionary property system, was to create for the first time the possibility of reconciling the pursuit of private interest with the pursuit of a still nascent common interest. Although it would by no means always work out this way, it was now at least possible that an individual's profit making could be confined to activities the benefits of which could also be shared by the rest.

59. *Hunan Nung-yeh* [15], p. 70. 60. *Ibid.,* p. 71. 61. *Ibid.*

Co-op members in Wu-Yang County, Hupei, transplanting rice. (Hsinhua News Agency)

Collectivization, in itself, could not eliminate poverty or all inequality, but it did provide a basic guarantee of livelihood and a guarantee of the intention that the remaining disparities in wealth, at least within co-ops, should not be allowed to become indefinitely greater. The ratios and the mechanisms to regulate permissible disparities were by no means perfected in 1956. However, the principle that these disparities should be sharply limited, as well as the basic methods by which they would be limited, were firmly established in the Chinese countryside along with the collectives. The widespread acceptance of this principle, limiting the *purely* self-interested economic advancement of the individual farmer, marked an important turning point in Chinese social and political development; and although much work remained to be done, it signaled the completion of the early phase of the transformation of China's rural villages.

PART 4

CONCLUSION

I use what remedy is at hand to save the world.

HAN-SHAN, T'ang Dynasty

CHAPTER 8

Concluding Perspectives

The primary concern of this study has been to describe a number of integrated policies that formed the crucial elements in the CCP's early effort at rural socialist transformation. The intent of these policies, the problems encountered in implementing them, and the pains taken to reappraise and then reformulate them, all provide the context in which to explain and evaluate the successes, failures, and legacies of the early Chinese Communist approach to rural development. Throughout the narrative, a number of explanatory themes have tended to surface again and again. In this concluding chapter it is now possible to draw these themes out more systematically and to indicate how they modify some standard views of the dynamics and the significance of this period of China's economic and political development.

SEVEN ELEMENTS OF THE CCP'S SUCCESS IN RURAL TRANSFORMATION

Even with all the problems the CCP encountered, the frustrations and the shortcomings in their rural work, the period from 1949 to 1956 was manifestly one of impressive political victories. During these short years the Party launched and managed several major economic and social transformations in the countryside while sustaining popular support and avoiding serious losses in agricultural production. Even with the gradual slowdown in agricultural recovery toward the end of the period, by all indicators and by any standard of comparison—whether with other socialist revolutions or with later periods in China's own development—these were years of unusually rapid change and smooth success. The narrative here points to seven key elements in this successful CCP approach to rapid rural transformation.

Care in Policy Formulation

Clearly, China's new revolutionary government was not content with crude policy statements or unrefined, undifferentiated approaches to the solution of rural political and economic problems. A surprising degree of care was manifested in the crafting of rural policy guidelines. From the sensitive differentiation of classes in the Agrarian Reform Law, to the refinements of the agricultural tax directives, to the comprehensive guidelines for Credit Co-op finance administration, to the rapid readjustments of the Three Fix policy, central and provincial authorities displayed a degree of knowledge and care in rural policy formulation uncommon among Marxist governments so newly come to power.

The probable differential impact of a directive on each class in the countryside was manifestly a central concern during the process of policy planning. If policy implementation was to vary by region, major crop, season, and so on, this was usually spelled out in considerable detail. The aspects of organization and policy that might be flexibly applied or temporarily postponed were distinguished for cadres from those that should not. Central and provincial directives were, of course, often still not precise enough, and village cadres did not always grasp the relative significance of different provisions. Confusion, error, and exaggeration were hardly banished from rural administration, as the narrative here has shown. Still, the central orders governing the major structural changes in the countryside during these early years were remarkably sophisticated, synoptic in approach, and knowledgeably constructed to reduce to a minimum their own counterproductive effects.

Flexibility in Policy Implementation

A preference for policy formulations that were as realistic and comprehensive as possible was, however, tempered with openness to the likelihood that not all village situations would fit the rules. And this openness fostered the development of an administrative style that was consciously experimental, self-critical, and adaptive. The CCP's approach to rural change deliberately put a high value on administrative innovation and flexibility, with its explicit recognition of the inevitable limitations on the sensitivity of central policy directives. Most deadlines, quotas, and classifications were negotiable and subject to review. Regional meetings were always held to iron out problems in fitting major policy guidelines to local peculiarities. Rural cadres were encouraged to voice their doubts and objections to central programs where they seemed inappropriate. And policies tried and found immediately unworkable, inadequate, or unacceptable to the majority of peasants were quickly shelved or revised to satisfy serious objections. Although there were a few basic principles all were supposed to observe, such as the necessity of achieving mass mobilization and participation in rural transformation work, there was little dogmatism about method. The widely scattered and little-trained nature of their rural cadre force led the Party center to accept that there could be many different but adequate routes to desired policy goal in the villages.

The Swift and Bold Assault Followed by Rectification

Many other developing countries have used their weak rural administrative capacity as an excuse for postponing attempts at change and have preferred to wait the often indefinitely long period needed to train the large numbers of technicians and rural organizers who would be able, they hope, to carry out policy without error or omission. The CCP, however, almost always preferred not to wait, since waiting might have afforded recalcitrant rural dilemmas a chance to harden further and provided enemies of the revolution with time to regroup. They opted for making the best of what administrative personnel could be trained on the job, and they established and proliferated systems, organs, and bureaux only as they appeared to be needed and could be staffed.

Plans and quotas did most often exceed what it was feasible for the rural administrators to accomplish. But a genuine effort that fell short was just as often regarded as satisfactory, and mistakes committed in haste were generally believed to be amenable to *post hoc* rectification. The systematic rectification of rural work after each campaign became a fixture of the CCP approach to reform. This style of bold attack and later critical review made the Party vulnerable to many criticisms of its work. It also, however, served to keep the opposition in the villages more or less continually on the defensive during these years.

Cadre Recruitment

The recruitment of local people to do village work, rather than the adoption of a system of central selection and training, was a key element in the success of the CCP's administrative strategy. By the end of land reform, the great majority of village activists and cadres doing basic administrative tasks were themselves peasants. And their local roots and common ways certainly made them more readily acceptable and accountable to the people in the communities where they did their work. From the point of view of the central elite these rural activists, with their vision fixed at the level of their own villages, exhibited many serious shortcomings, as the discussion of all their declared "deviations" and "errors" in this study makes clear. However, having to deal with such raw types of community leaders at the bottom of the Party's own organization was regarded as useful in the effort to keep the Party from becoming alienated from rural realities. For these professionally rather naive, small-risk players at the bottom of the political pyramid did not yet balk at asking the awkward questions or at making the unwelcome complaints. Having to cope with their queries, arguments, objections, and suggestions helped keep the Party aware of village viewpoints and even more conscious of the need for flexible administration to satisfy the variety of village situations it confronted. The recruitment and on-the-job training of village activists to assume new political-administrative roles was really the necessary condition of each of the other three elements just listed. Without the work of these people and their reports on basic-level conditions, the center could not have planned policy so carefully, administered it so flexibly, or attempted such rapid change on so many fronts at once.

The Management of Class Struggle

Looked at from one important perspective, the main business of those making policy for rural transformation over these years was to smooth the way for continuous, progressively more inclusive redistributions of wealth and opportunity from the best-off to the worst-off in the villages. During land reform there was a direct redistribution of property, in which the landlord class sustained a sharp fall in both absolute and relative economic strength in the villages. And as detailed in the previous chapters, the transition to socialism also involved a redistribution: better-off middle and rich peasants, while they were not supposed to lose the direct benefit of their property and were therefore not supposed to suffer an absolute drop in economic welfare, were nonetheless to be deprived of their superior access to opportunities for economic advancement. Thus, over time, they experienced a fall in their relative economic strength in the villages that accompanied the parallel decline of rural capitalism.

It is important to underscore that, in both redistributions, the method of expropriation was to be *explicitly conflictual*. It was to be understood and acted out in terms of class struggle. Although the second redistribution was milder and less sudden, it was still viewed as the product of an antagonistic contradiction between a small, privileged minority whose interests were opposed to those of the broad masses of peasants.

The main strategy of the revolutionary government, then, was to promote and manage village political conflict along class lines— different class lines at different times—consistent with the degree of change that could simultaneously be effected in the economic environment of the peasantry. Most of the policies detailed in this study were designed and implemented as part of this strategy to sharpen the relevant class cleavages and to blunt others in the countryside.

For purposes of land reform, it was possible to use the class categories outlined along with the Agrarian Reform Law to isolate the small minority of landlords from the rest of the village population. In the transition period, however, it became necessary to create two new categories—upper-middle and lower-middle peasants—and to draw the line between them, isolating the larger (but still small) number of rich and upper-middle peasants in opposition to the poorer peasant masses on the question of forming co-ops. This proved to be a blurred and partly artificial line, but one meaningful enough to serve as the dynamic in the "high tide." Struggle and principled seizure were regarded as necessary elements in rural transformation, so that peasants would know their good fortune was made by themselves, not given to them by beneficent richer neighbors. There was to be no pretense, as there has been in some other socialist experiments, that all shared the same interests or that the co-ops obviated what conflicts there were.

At liberation, the Party confronted a wide variety of village polities in which its scheme of socioeconomic class divisions was not always readily recognized, and other political and economic interest cleavages involving family, lineage, religion, sex, age, locality, ethnic groups, and so on were regarded by villagers as the salient ones. Recognizing the existence of these cross-cutting tendencies, but unwilling to surrender to them and to the extreme complexity of prevailing village political relationships, the new leadership first strove to make its own class categories plain and relevant. Every villager was assigned to a class category.

Then, in the years following, the center expended most of its economic and political resources in the countryside in the effort to design policies, like those examined in this study, that would help guarantee that villagers' perceived real interests coincided with their designated class interests. That is, central policy did much to manipulate the economic environment of villagers in such a way that the lines of political interest cleavage and conflict paralleled as closely as possible the desired class lines. The leadership then deliberately underscored the issues that were class-based or could reasonably be described that way, to consolidate the economic structural changes they had put in place and to clarify the progressive shifts in the political power balance involving different groups in the villages. Thus the CCP was able to evolve a set of policies that, while explicitly conflictual and dramatically redistributive, nonetheless remained attuned to the perceived broad interests of the majority of peasants. And in this way they were able to rely heavily on the natural, self-interested energies of peasants to make village class struggle a reality.

Incentive Systems

Within this broad strategic conception of the CCP it is obvious that peasants were expected to act in all matters out of rational self-interest. This pattern of peasant choice — for or against the revolution — the Party expected to hold as much in the excited moments of revolutionary power seizure as in the arduous construction of socialist society. Chinese peasants were not expected to exhibit self-sacrificing altruism in their embrace of socialism. Nor were they expected to shed very quickly their age-old preoccupations and beliefs in favor of ideological attachment to Marxism-Leninism. They were, on the contrary, expected to be willing to cooperate with social and economic change insofar, and only insofar, as they were convinced that change might benefit themselves. Thus, as shown in the preceding chapters, the policies of socialist transformation, designed at the center to attract the peasantry, were virtually without exception intended to appeal to the perceived self-interest of the majority of villagers. The recurrent concern of this study to draw out and highlight the material incentives to peasants that were built into central policies for the rural transition to socialism has provided repeated illustration of this core conception of the CCP about the relationship of human motivation to social revolution.

The very consistency with which this approach to winning peasant cooperation was employed over these years is itself important to note. It is often supposed that the CCP leadership would have preferred to obtain mass compliance with its intentions through normative appeals, that is by moral-ideological argument and persuasion. As Skinner and Winckler have put the case in one influential formulation,[1] the Party holds that its members can and should persuade peasants to take actions that are contrary to their own interests (or merely neutral as far as their interests are concerned), just by convincing them that to take those actions would be "ideologically correct." If this kind of appeal fails to elicit the desired level of compliance, as in their analysis it often does, then the Party may turn to remunerative appeals (material incentives) for peasant compliance. These are considered very effective appeals, but since they are expensive to sustain, for more continuous or more perfect compliance with central demands the Party may have to resort to coercive measures against the masses. These measures are also regarded as involving certain costs, however, and the model predicts that once coercion succeeds in assuring a degree of compliance the Party will back off and return to normative appeals to consolidate the situation. Thus a cyclical application of the three kinds of pressures at the Party's command is postulated.

It is interesting how little relationship this kind of trichotomization of Party options has to the picture of rural politics that emerges in this study. The argument that peasants might be moralized and inspired into socialism would simply have been howled down during these years. Cadres who tried using rhetoric rather than reward might appear at first to have had some success thanks to accommodating peasants who preferred to seem to go along; but it was consistently maintained that their day of reckoning could not be far off. Cadres displaying this tendency were warned that they were departing from the mass line, that their theories about rural socialism did not coincide with village reality and peasant experience. Peasants, it was often repeated, were "practical people" whose values and inclinations were by no means naturally socialist. One day, the Party predicted, their old values and attitudes would be transformed and they would emerge as new socialist men and women. Propaganda, education, and persuasion would play a role in this transformation. But far more decisive, it was consistently argued, would be the peasants' discovery that socialism could mean prosperity for

1. Skinner and Winckler [517].

themselves.[2] Evenings spent lecturing peasants on Marxism precepts did not compare, in the Party's eyes, with time spent figuring out ways to increase team income.

Likewise with coercive measures against the masses; the Party was well aware of the backlash of discontent that would arise if these were employed in the absence of real economic benefits. The point of course is not that direct and indirect coercion were never used, for nearly all the chapters above consider cases of cadre "commandism" and peasant fear. The point is simply that the Party never accepted the use or threat of force against the mass of the peasantry as either legitimate or, in the long run, functional. Coercion was regarded as appropriate only for the control of class enemies. And even so, after land reform, rich peasants and others were cajoled and bought off with promises as often as they were "struggled against." Similarly, normative appeals for self-sacrifice and dedication to the collective interest were expected to find their best audience among cadres and activists in the villages, whose level of political consciousness was presumed to be higher than that of the broad masses. And again, even with cadres, as has been shown here, the Party often offered material incentives for speedy, enthusiastic work, expecting better results from this than from appeals to Party spirit and socialist values.

It should be clear that, in this formative period of contemporary Chinese politics, the rural situation was characterized by a mixture of the three elements isolated by Skinner and Winckler. All three appear to have been in operation simultaneously — not in any particular sequence, not necessarily in response to signals from higher levels, and not by any means in the same pattern or mix in all villages. But what the analysis here conveys is that while fear and force were sometimes decisive and ideological fervor may account for some bursts of activity, the heaviest element by far in the mixture of appeals to peasants to move toward socialism was the element of material self-interest woven by the Party into most of its policies for the period.

The Developing Central-Local Relationship

In the account provided here of the relative effectiveness of the Party and state center in implementing, modifying, and rectifying policy at the basic level in the countryside, it is clear that this was a period of considerable progress toward the unified control and political integration of

2. Shue [515].

the Chinese nation. In this respect it marked a most significant change after generations of ineffective dynastic rule, warlord fragmentation, and civil war. Still, it is also clear that during this period central control was far from absolute, and that there were limits on the degree of central penetration actually sought. This government seemed at times to possess a remarkable awareness of the damage it might do by attempting to hold the reins too tightly. A degree of latitude was deliberately granted to local communities and local leaders, reflecting the "mass line" revolutionary values that stressed the potential fallibility of the center. A limited amount of local detachment was considered desirable and the central-local relationship that was intended to develop was one of cooperation and consultation, with two-way channels of communication and with occasional opportunities for peasant communities both to influence basic policy lines and to protect themselves from potentially unwise central demands.

Merely approximate local compliance was usually acceptable, a high level of "deviation" from officially recommended methods was complained about but tolerated, a certain amount of leeway for local cadres was almost always written into guidelines, and potentially embarrassing questions were often not asked at all out of consideration for the problems of local cadres, or at least they were postponed for later review. As analyzed here, rural compliance with central decisions was generally high over these years, but in order to achieve these good results many concessions were made along the way to the real problems of cadres and to the many reservations of peasants. In the interests of faster progress and the cultivation of its local cadre force, the center demanded and expected neither total knowledge nor total control in the countryside.

For more perfect control, the Party might have tried putting outsiders into leadership positions in villages rather than relying on the recruitment of locals. This would undoubtedly have given rise to hostility on the part of villagers, but it would also have lessened the tendency of peasants and local cadres to enter together into plots and conspiracies of silence to deceive the center. Locally recruited leaders, with complex and emotion-laden ties to the people in their areas, found it hard to execute central policies perceived locally as harsh, unnecessary, or unfair. They also naturally tended to defend and pursue particularistic local interests with extra vigor inside the administration. Nonetheless, the localist transgressions of these people, which kept the center from more thoroughly penetrating most rural communities, were rather cheerfully tolerated at the center since the alternative of trying to crack open the secrets of each village was not considered practicable.

Indeed it often seemed as if the center relied precisely on the special ability of these local cadres to make private, locally acceptable deals and compromises with villagers for the very purpose of achieving more effective policy implementation. It was clearly perceived that more total central knowledge and control might have served to interrupt undesirable personal attachments in the villages, but that it would also probably have served to dissolve the existing networks of trust that could have been harnessed by the local cadre force for purposes of policy accommodation and implementation.

Thus, local cadres were, by and large, understood at the center to be partly apologists and partly partisans as far as the administration of affairs affecting their counties and villages was concerned. It was recognized that local cadres were caught, most of the time, in one or another contradiction between their duty to their superiors and their responsibilities to their village constituents. They were known to be advocates—magnifying their local difficulties to avoid central extractions, to get a special waiver or some emergency aid, or alternatively magnifying their local achievements to get more credit, some special assistance, or some other goods distributed through the hierarchy.

Peasants expected their cadres to misrepresent conditions somewhat, in order to protect the village against undesirable central demands for taxes, grain sales quotas, unpaid labor, and so on. In their more beneficent roles, traditional village elites had performed similar functions of deflecting imperial bureaucratic penetration into community affairs. Now, after liberation, as the center gradually took on the role of the provider of special scarce inputs, as well as the extractor of local resources, the localist aspects of a cadre's work came to include competition with other communities for distributable goods, along with protection of the community from unwanted demands.

Although disapproved of, the misrepresentations of local cadres were tolerated at higher levels in the expectation that *post hoc* rectifications would suffice to reveal the worst abuses. Yet in these early days, when the rectifications of cadres were still "open door"—that is, when they still involved mass participation and judgments on the crimes and punishments of local leaders—the wishes of the Party for cadre discipline remained in the final analysis subject to modification by the norms of local life and the values of the cadres' own peasant constituency.

In point of fact, village activists and cadres probably made the least impact on general policy during the earliest days of rent reduction and land reform. These were programs the Party already had long experience in handling. There was considerable confidence that the class dynamics of land revolution were well understood and fully manageable through Party policy. Recruitment of village activists in the new areas was required for implementation, of course; but, except in matters of local detail, their input into decision making was slight. With the announcement of the General Line for the transition to socialism, however, the new bureaucracy found itself administering a host of less familiar, less well-tried programs for team and co-op proliferation over still largely unknown territory. In this situation, there was naturally greater reliance on local cadre perceptions of program feasibility, desirability, pace, staffing, and other factors. Village cadres themselves had by that time acquired a degree of political experience. And it seems apparent that the beleaguered middle administrative levels often called their numerous week-long meetings with basic-level cadres as much to get from them ideas and information on how to proceed as to provide them with policy briefings and guidelines.

It is important to emphasize that the contribution of these local cadres to the decision making for socialist transformation was by no means usually conservative or obstructionist. On the contrary, it is clear that they often felt themselves manacled by the center's declared preference for step-by-step, slow and steady progress in socialist institution building. Village leader advocates of teams and co-ops knew they were in constant competition with influential rich peasant and other defenders of independent petty capitalism. They wished out loud for faster action, a freer hand, and more pronounced central backing in the struggle for peasant investment and allegiance. It was much easier for them to convince wavering peasants and to whip up enthusiasm in the context of an unambiguous national movement than it was always to be urging their villagers to take seemingly isolated and unusually progressive actions.

The "high tide" of collectivization, as is well known, was precipitated by Chairman Mao's July 1955 speech, in which he took a position probably not shared by most of the rest of the Peking political elite.[3] And yet in the provinces and rural counties they leapt at his words as the solution to their problems of rural investment capital seepage. It is evi-

3. Chang [450], pp. 14–15.

dent that at the bottom level there had been pressure for a top-level go-ahead to permit the quick, final expropriation of upper-middle and rich peasants they felt they needed to consolidate broad peasant support behind the co-ops and behind their own political leadership in the villages. Mao and the provincial leaders he summoned to his expanded session that summer read correctly the sentiment of many cadres at the village level. Even with all the headaches the ''high tide'' was to bring them, they clearly felt nonetheless that they could manage a swift and decisive transition much more successfully than a continuation of the phases and the ambiguities that had been preventing them from giving peasants the firm answers and assurances they demanded for cooperation.

Some analysts have regarded the ''high tide'' as a betrayal of the peasantry, which had been promised a gradual transition, and as a confirmation of the consummate power a single leader may possess willfully to throw life into disorder in a ''totalitarian'' system. As it is analyzed here, however, Mao accurately perceived the precariousness of the shifting balance of power in the villages. The peasant constituency for a swifter transition was clearly in place; the demand for it was voiced by a restless village cadre force. Mao merely advocated that the potential for swift action on behalf of the poorest be utilized, lest the moment be lost in overnice central conscientiousness to ''protect the small peasant economy.'' Still, his words might have gone unheeded or might have been covered over by elite rivals with a different understanding of the rural situation. The undignified speed of the ''high tide'' is not proof of what one visionary could do to disorient a whole national economy. It indicates rather that many cadres at the bottom found in Mao's go-ahead an answer, if only a temporary one, to their most vexing problems. And the middle-level rural administration, under the circumstances, had to abandon its preconceptions and gear itself up quickly to respond to the unexpected pace and demand. The development of the ''high tide'' is just one of the more dramatic examples of the dynamic central-local relations cultivated in this period. The forming vertical lines of bureaucratic hierarchy and command remained, at this time, cross-cut by the voices of local advocates. And the considerable leeway still allowed to local leaders made possible the development and articulation of popular trends, at times for and at times against the revolution, as it was being planned and administered from the center. During the ''high tide'' frustrated local leaders seized Mao's words and pushed the movement beyond even his intentions. At other times however, as the analysis here has shown, the coalescence of local doubts and hesitations served to delay progress toward socialism. On questions of policy implementation, to a considerable extent throughout this period, relations between central and local administrators remained fluid and conditional.

If each of these seven was an important element in the overall success of rural work during the period, each was also probably responsible for certain difficulties and drawbacks. The uncommon speed and boldness of the CCP's assault on rural institutions certainly led to some of the excesses and "deviations" reported, as did the reliance on untrained local recruits for Party work in the villages. The deliberate concentration on the management of rural class struggle sometimes meant a neglect or misunderstanding of the non-class-based social and political cleavages that were impeding progress toward socialist cooperation. And some of the incentive systems tended to backfire, setting forces in motion that undermined the desired relations of production in the transition period. Yet, despite its imperfections, it was a resilient political system that was developing around these seven elements, one capable of absorbing setbacks and mixed results on some of these fronts, adjusting to them swiftly, limiting the damage done by them, and maintaining an overall forward momentum.

IMPLICATIONS OF THE ANALYSIS

If this analysis of CCP rural success during these years is correct, then it should change some of the ways we have traditionally summarized and evaluated this formative period of contemporary Chinese politics.

The Nature of the Rural Revolution

First, according to this analysis, the revolutionary rural transformation in China could not be characterized as an essentially irrational outburst acted out by one generation but explicable only by reference to centuries of pent-up frustration. Nor should the rural transformation be regarded in terms of the sudden mass embrace of utopianism in the guise of Marxism-Leninism. Few peasants during these years would have claimed the Marxist vision as their own. Nor again can the revolutionary rural transformation be regarded as the sheer imposition by organized force of new values and systems on a feeble (or a defiant) old natural society. These familiar synopses of the rural revolutionary and peasant socialist experience lose much of their descriptive and analytic power when we consider, as we have here, such prosaic but persuasive devices as tax breaks, preferential contracts, low-interest loans, and workpoint assignments.

Of course this revolution did have its moments of blind rage. At times also it attempted a utopian leap and then came to a halt before its own visions. And at times rural people—different classes, different villages—were forced into step with change against their will. Yet the evidence of this study suggests that none of these aspects of rural revolution was actually at the heart of the matter of getting Chinese peasants to cooperate with change toward socialism. The heart of the matter is found instead in the numerous, deliberate appeals to peasants, on grounds of their own self-interest, to abandon petty-capitalist enterprise and to enter presocialist and then fully socialist institutions. The initial growth of these institutions in the countryside, as detailed here, served in turn to alter further the political and economic environment of peasants, leading them to reassess how best to pursue their own interests, and eventually leading them to redefine those interests partly at least in ways that could coincide with the interests of a larger collective.

The Ideology-Pragmatism Dichotomy

It is one of the conventions, in looking at the Chinese revolution and in analyzing postrevolutionary Chinese politics, to point out the "ideological" as opposed to the "pragmatic" strains in its development, and to treat the two as essentially and inevitably in contradiction. Entire theories of Chinese leadership factions have rested on this dichotomy, as does much of the standard periodization of political trends in China since 1949. In that context this study, with its focus on the Party's efforts to accommodate the day-to-day practical interests of the mass of peasants, might be read either as an argument that the Chinese communists are "pragmatists" after all, or at least that "pragmatists" were certainly in power from 1949 to 1956. Neither interpretation would be warranted, however. The point of this analysis has been, rather, to demonstrate just how empty the distinction between "ideology" and "pragmatism" in fact was during these years; how seriously the Party took its task of making its ideological goals and its practical goals interlock; and how generally, despite numerous obstacles, it was successful in this effort in the countryside.

Concern with ideological rectitude and concern with solving practical dilemmas may remain conceptually distinct, of course. But the content of the Chinese communist ideology of this period was so thoroughly suffused with finding practical solutions to the practical problems of peasants that to categorize the policymakers or administrators of the time as either "ideologues" or "pragmatists" would be quite meaningless. When "class struggle" means expropriating the wealth of a relative few and redistributing it among the majority who are poor, when "restricting rural capitalism" means halting inflation and lower interest rates on loans, and when "consolidating socialism" means more land and draft animal power available to poor peasants, then the potential contradictions between ideological and practical goals fade into insignificance.

Above all, to follow the mass line meant precisely to take the practical concerns of the mass of peasants and to reconceptualize them and find solutions for them in terms of the theory of the revolution, thus quite literally uniting theory with practice. The mass line concept was at the forefront of political work in the countryside during this period, and although it was by no means followed perfectly in every village, the overall effort to accomplish a unity of theory and practice in rural work made a meaningful separation of ideology and pragmatism in policy implementation hard to find at this time, whatever formalisms may have set in later.

The Idea of the Common Interest in Chinese Socialism

Socialism is generally associated with some notion of the common interest. And in considering the radical socialism that has developed in China, it is often observed that it has displayed a special tendency to seek to subordinate personal or small group interests to the pursuit of the common good. Yet little has been written in this study about the common interest. In "building socialism" in the countryside, it is unmistakably clear that Party work personnel spent far more time and effort on the task of defining and isolating a common class enemy than in promoting commitment to the myth of an overarching common interest.

Even in the establishment of cooperatives, a genuine sense of the common interest was something they obviously imagined would develop only gradually, and primarily through continuing class struggle. Their concept was to build on successive resolutions of conflict so that formerly competing individual and group interests came to overlap, and so that thereby a new common interest that could be appealed to would be created—a common interest that before had not existed and could not genuinely have been appealed to. In their vision, even into the socialist era, it was in the continuing class struggle, the uncomfortable but ultimately exhilarating necessity of taking sides or making principled choices and demands, that the seeds of sincere cooperation for wider social benefit would eventually be found.

This meant that even within co-ops latent divisive tendencies were not supposed to be camouflaged or papered over, but rather deliberately sought out and laid on the table for discussion. In this manner all arguments could be heard, the degree of hostility could be estimated, and the process of negotiation to reach a settlement accommodating divergent interests could be begun. A continuous process of drawing out and articulating dissatisfactions and conflicting interests, followed by a phase of persuasion, bargaining, and tentative settlement, was intended to characterize the internal operation of production co-ops. Within these basic units, the importance of allowing the conflict and bargaining process to play itself out more or less unimpeded by excessively progressive moral or political presuppositions was emphasized.[4] There was criticism for cadres who tried to stifle legitimately conflicting interests and to run co-ops on more utopian principles of self-sacrifice for the common good.

To acknowledge frankly the existing conflicts of interest in early socialist ventures was, of course, to risk failure and collapse. But the dominant voices from the center at this time were convinced that to attempt to disregard or explain away the conflicts would have done much more to guarantee failure. It also appears that they believed that the very process of conflict and accommodation would impart greater credibility to the project of collectivization by providing legitimate recognition to private interest while simultaneously leading the peasants gradually into forms of political and economic cooperation with potentially wider social horizons. In essence this had remained their formula for inducing village political and economic change throughout the early transition to socialism. And it stood in marked contrast to another development mode that, in an attempt to sidestep overt conflicts, might have relied instead on phony egalitarianism and insubstantial claims about the common interest.

4. Shue [516], p. 5.

LATER EROSIONS OF THE NECESSARY CONDITIONS
OF SUCCESSFUL CHANGE

If now we look beyond the seven specific elements in early CCP rural success outlined above, we can hypothesize four necessary conditions that underlay their convergence. The first condition was that there be a local-level and higher-level leadership consensus in favor of maintaining the deliberately conflictual approach to rural reform. This was a condition concerning basic strategy. The second necessary condition was that there be a degree of overall economic growth in the nation. This was a condition concerning the environment in which the political system operated. The third necessary condition was that the Party always have available a subtle and pertinent set of class categories for rural analysis. This was a condition concerning theory. And the fourth necessary condition was that a relatively open, straightforward, and consultative working relationship between cadres at the center and those in the localities be maintained. This was a condition concerning administration. All four of these conditions were generally met in the early years of 1949–56, but each was to fail at later periods, contributing to the CCP's later difficulties in maintaining the momentum of rural transformation. Here we may conclude by indicating briefly how they were to fail.

Leadership and Continuing Conflict

An approach to continuing rural development such as the one described here, resting on explicit articulation and confrontation of conflicting interests and drawing out the meaning and the settlement of conflicts in the terms of class struggle, could not be an easy path for national or local leaders to follow indefinitely. It called for both more patience and more trouble-shooting zeal than most cadres could summon. Not all basic-level cadres were able to tolerate the degree of dissension this approach demanded and still run collective enterprises fairly. Many found it too temptingly convenient, over time, to brush aside the complaints of individual members with platitudinous rhetoric meant to shame them out of selfishness.

Problems in the higher Party commitment to continuing this conflictual approach emerged as well. Just as Mao was elaborating the distinction between antagonistic and nonantagonistic contradictions in socialist society, an ideological contribution that was to allow continuing conflicts between self-interest and collective interest to be regarded as a matter of course even under socialism,[5] it seems that other leaders were having their doubts. Some, especially those at middle administrative levels, came to favor further consolidation of progressive collectivism by leaping over the petty bickering among teams and households and establishing the basic accounting unit over a much larger area. They seemed to want, by rural structural change alone, to bring a commonality of interests into being, without going through the arduous struggle of constructing it bit by bit through argument and compromise and growth. Proponents of this course were to have their chance during the Great Leap Forward, but as soon as that ill-fated movement fell into difficulty, they were vigorously opposed by others who saw this untimely leap toward the common interest as potentially so divisive, so prone to fragmentation, as to make the modest bridge toward socialism already constructed fly apart. They, like their more utopian opposition, began to eschew as dangerous the continuing petty squabbling and struggle of the explicitly conflictual mode used in the early years. They preferred to scale down the level of community conflict for the sake of orderly growth, by granting more consideration to the privatistic inclinations of peasants — and this for the sake of efficiency. The debate between these "two lines," each in its own way shying away from the challenge of continuing the unrelenting struggle of the conflictual mode described here, would persist and would heavily influence the political agenda through the Cultural Revolution and up to the present day.

Sustaining Economic Growth

We should not assume, however, that it was either cowardice or laziness that caused the proponents of each of the "two lines" to pull back from the mass participatory, overt conflict model of the early 1950's. Changing economic conditions probably played a role as well. A deliberately conflictual course of development that demanded, for its success, both improvements in the personal welfare of the great majority of peasants *and* improvements in public welfare seems, from the evidence of this study, to have worked unevenly but well enough in the era of postwar agricultural recovery and land reform windfalls—an era that lasted through the mid-1950's. But it was to prove much more challenging to maintain the balance between these two demands in the years to

5. Mao Tse-tung [470].

follow, when agricultural performance perversely continued to slip below expectations, but population grew and the standard of living in rural areas still remained agonizingly low despite rising consumption patterns. The political model stressing the management of class conflict and the gradual overlapping of self-interest and collective interest did produce gains both for the peasant majority and for the proponents of expanded state power, at a time when the national economic pie was itself expanding. When the economic situation entered a period of slow-down, however, and national priorities were being reassessed, the feasibility and the fruitfulness of continuing to rely on that political model for redistributing wealth and building socialism would also come into question. Those later called "utopians" and those later called "revisionists" were reacting to straitened national economic circumstances making the conflict-with-growth, true Maoist model of the early 1950's seem far les reliable and appropriate.

Relevant Class Analysis

In understanding and influencing politics at the village level, the Party, as explained here, had depended almost entirely on its class analysis. By itself assigning the categories, then skillfully shaping its rural policies to appeal differently to different groups, and by an occasional strategic redrawing of a major line of class cleavage, the new government was able to assist the dynamic of class struggle toward socialism with the outcomes described in this study.

But this political strategy entailed certain drawbacks and was to leave certain rural dilemmas festering outside the problem-solving capability of the new government. It afforded no meaningful place to other lines of stratification and differentiation in the villages besides class lines. Sex, age, lineage, religion, number of generations of residence in the community, and many other such lines of distinction and personal definition were set aside and treated at most as local complications that might be annoyingly obdurate but still essentially irrelevant in revolutionary politics. It is a tribute to the negotiating acumen of local cadres in the early years that it was so often possible to put aside these other village animosities and allegiances, at least temporarily, so that the management of the local class struggle might proceed. But when the transition to socialism was nearly completed in the late 1950's and these other non-class cleavages remained to be reckoned with, the local cadres were still left without a theoretical basis for understanding their predicaments and without much practical help from the center in handling these other local contradictions.

Furthermore, as time passed and family fortunes were altered by the redistributions of wealth and economic opportunity of the transition period, the class categories that were assigned with land reform became less and less accurate reflections of real economic status. There was official concern about class drift very soon after the completion of land reform. But except for the introduction of the new upper- and lower-middle peasant categories, family class assignments remained the same. With the further levelling entailed in collectivization, the rural cadres were presented with numerous peasant class anomalies in their political work.

Despite the progressive levelling of family incomes and the effective limitations land reform and collectivization imposed on the "exploiting classes," these classes of village dwellers were to remain suspect over the years to follow—automatic targets of political campaigns, under closer surveillance than others, and routinely deprived of certain rights and rewards. Where the old class labels of these families had come to coincide no longer with their actual political and economic potential in the community, it was to encourage cynicism on both sides that they were so perpetually used as local scapegoats in campaigns. The political rhetoric of the next decades remained the rhetoric of class struggle, and the targets of struggle often remained the very same rich peasant and landlord families first subdued in the transition period. Because they were so often already obviously reduced to political impotence in the community, the rhetoric of the campaigns frequently failed in its mass mobilization goals and tended to elicit instead bitterness among the persecuted and alienation among the masses, whose real problems seemed inevitably to be forced through categories of analysis that had long since lost their urgency and their power to yield solutions.

During the Cultural Revolution some steps were finally taken toward a more sophisticated revolutionary sociology. But even this rethinking barely touched most of the countryside. More recently, the leadership has indicated its intention to relax some old class labels. But for nearly twenty-five years rural cadres all over China had little choice but to distance themselves in practice and in attitude from a Party center that they must have perceived as tying them formalistically to an interpretive theory useful in the past, but now too unidimensional to be credited. The Party had to become less effective in managing class struggle over those years, as it allowed its theory of class to become so distant from reality.

Openness in Central-Local Relations

Finally, the degree of local independence, deliberately cultivated as a healthy factor in central-local relations in the early years, proved difficult to sustain in innocence. As time went on, even the greenest village-level cadres were to become campaign-wise and careful, making their attitudes, behavior and verbal policy assessments less purely reflective of peasant perceptions and therefore less informative to the center. And the relationships of mutual dependence they developed with their county and subdistrict superiors—partly cooperative and partly adversarial—became less candid and fresh. Village cadres tried to get assigned tasks done to the specifications of superiors who were in a position to make crucial choices affecting their own careers. They also, however, always tried to get the most from and give up the least possible to the center, in order to satisfy the villagers, whose cooperation they still required to get things done. Middle-level officials, for their part, depended on local cadres to meet their own composite quotas, and they were therefore generally inclined to allow them the rope they needed to maneuver. There was opportunity for considerable complicity to develop among the cadres at these different levels of administration. Over the years, over much of the countryside, the early functionality of this complicity in local protectionism was to congeal into a fairly institutionalized system of mutual misrepresentation.

Village and county cadres had become so adept at carrying on with their work and evading contradictions and confrontations with the center that by the time of the Great Leap Forward, when truly unreasonable demands came down, most preferred to continue the fiction of enthusiastic response and overfulfillment of quotas. Commune cadres competed with each other in fantastic claims of unprecedented crop yields and victories in social reform. County cadres concurred. While no official wished to be the one to break the balloon of illusion, the center readjusted its projections upward, to discover, only after much valuable time had been lost, just how far it had been permitted to stray from reality. Legitimate local protectionism had been distorted: what was earlier a network of gentlemen's agreements to block total central penetration and control had become a gigantic careerist conspiracy that denied the center virtually any accurate information at all.

Later in the early 1960's, leaders like Liu Shao-ch'i attempted to use the Socialist Education Movement as a means of punishing rural cadres for this pernicious localism and for their egregious lack of Party discipline.[6] They tried to carry out a severe rectification of local cadres on the basis of central Party norms and values not mediated as before by the supportive values of the peasant community. But Mao in particular opposed such a harsh, centralist rectification, preferring instead to direct the sharpest criticism to decision makers higher in the administration. Mao opposed the penetration of the peasant community that would have been entailed in a strict enforcement of central Party norms without regard to local attitudes, preferences, excuses, and perceived needs. A successful rectification of local cadres of that sort, he thought, would serve ultimately only to split off those activists who survived it from the peasant masses, thus mangling the roots the Party had struck among the people. Mao preferred merely to presume that the great majority of the cadres were ''good,'' to regard their localist ''deviations'' only as the product of the still not fully developed mass political consciousness. That is, he preferred to leave the peasant communities and the Party's roots intact, cohesive, a viable counterweight to the tendencies toward centralist authoritarianism that he saw growing up in reaction to the breakdowns of the Great Leap.

The Maoist vision did not decisively prevail, we know. The years of the Cultural Revolution and after have been marked by deep contradictions and ambivalences about the proper allegiances of local cadres and the political significance of local communities in the system. The cooperative but localist *modus vivendi* that was taking shape in the villages of the early 1950's has been lately championed in some widely propagandized Chinese models and parables; but also it seems to have suffered many incursions by the theorists and practitioners of centralism.

It was, perhaps, easier in the early 1950's to imagine a system in which both the center and the localities could share in a growing political authority. In the early period surveyed in this study, the competition for political power and authority between center and locality was not neces-

6. See Baum [449].

sarily zero-sum. The very scope of political power and authority itself appeared to be expanding then. With nationwide peace, economic recovery, a sharp halt to inflation and stabilization of taxation, the new government enjoyed greater legitimacy than any regime for generations. After so many years of cynicism and despair, the Chinese people seemed to turn with renewed hope in 1949 to the promise of legitimate political authority based on government by the people's party. The elimination of the most egregious types of corruption and economic exploitation, and the tone of reason and order and planning for national recovery in the new government's pronouncements all helped to restore the sense of reliability and unity of purpose that had been so tragically absent from Chinese political life for so long. In such times as these, the local activists who stepped in to fill the power vacuum at the village level were viewed as aids and extensions of the new central authority, not as rivals to it. They were bringing government and reform to the people, and it was natural to leave to their discretion much of the running of local affairs. Indeed, it was impossible to do otherwise at the time.

It was not until some years had passed, when the new government's first blush of success was fading, when economic realities were no longer so unmitigatedly bright and some hard choices had to be made, when in short the reserves of political authority were in danger of depletion, that these community leaders at the bottom, used to exercising their own judgment and running community affairs according to their own style, would come to be seen as uncertain links in the chain of command and even as active rivals to central state power. Then they would find themselves targeted for new, harsh rectifications; there would be repeated thrusts to pare down their prerogatives. The proper regulation of the relationship between central and local community authority would remain a question in the development of the Chinese political system over the years.

Village cadres had always walked a narrow path between the peasantry and the state, representing each to the other. They were the glue that held the two sides together. And for the majority of them, their most heroic days were the ones described in this study, when they were able to carry out their duties without for the most part betraying either side. Most peasant communities retained a certain core of imperviousness to central desires even as they were being led along the road to socialism.

Higher cadres and local cadres had demarcated their spheres of influence. And the art of politics and administration in those days consisted of finding ways to accommodate the problems and demands of both sides. These were the days that constituted the formative experiences of many local men and women who remain in positions of responsibility in the countryside even today. These are the days they hark back to when they discuss the way the system ought to work.

GLOSSARY

catty	1.1 pounds
chen	town, market town
ch'eng-fen	classification
hsiang	rural village
hsien	county
hu	household
kung-fen	workpoint
mou	one sixth of an acre; 15 *mou* = 1 *ha.*
Nung Tai Hui	Peasants' Deputies Committee (of a Peasant Association)
nung-yeh jen-k'ou	agricultural dependent
pao	ward (administrative subdivision in certain very populous *hsiang*)
pao chia	a household enumeration system serving tax, census, and social control functions in prerevolutionary China
pao kung pao ch'an	guaranteed work and guaranteed production (a form of co-op contract)
su k'u	speak bitterness
suan chang	to settle accounts
tan	110.23 pounds
tsu-chang	team leader (of a mutual aid team)
ts'un	hamlet
t'ung	a tree cultivated for its seeds, which yield an oil used as a drying agent in varnishes and paints

BIBLIOGRAPHY

I. BOOKS IN CHINESE

1. *Basic Information about Cooperative Economy (Ho-tso-she ching-chi chi-pen chih-shih).* Canton: Hua-nan jen-min ch'u-pan-she, 1954.
2. *CCPCC Resolution on Development of Agricultural Production Cooperatives (Chung-kuo kung-ch'an-tang chung-yang wei-yüan-hui kuan-yü fa-chan nung-yeh sheng-ch'an ho-tso-she ti chüeh-i).* Peking: Jen-min ch'u-pan-she, 1954.
3. Ch'en K'o-chien and Kan Min-chung. *The Objective Basis of the Rapid Attainment of Advanced Agricultural Cooperativization in China (Wo-kuo hsun-su shih-hsien kao-chi hsing-shih nung-yeh ho-tso-hua ti k'o-kuan i-chü).* Shanghai: Shang-hai jen-min ch'u-pan-she, 1956.
4. Ch'i Wu. *The Growth of a Revolutionary Base (I-ko ko-ming ken-chü-ti ti ch'eng ch'ang).* Peking: Jen-min ch'u-pan-she, 1958.
5. Ch'ih Yüan-chi and Hsieh Hsüeh-shih. *Problems in the Transition of APCs from the Elementary to the Advanced Form (Nung-yeh sheng-ch'an ho-tso-she yu ch'u-chi hsing-shih hsiang kao-chi hsing-shih kuo-tu ti wen-t'i).* Shanghai: Hsin chih-shih ch'u-pan-she, 1956.
6. Chou Ch'eng. *Fundamental Problems in the Labor Management of Advanced Cooperatives (Kao-chi she lao-tung kuan-li chung ti chi-pen wen-t'i).* Peking: T'ung-su tu-wu ch'u-pan-she, 1956.
7. Ch'u Ch'ing, Chu Chung-chien and Wang Chih-ming, eds. *Reorganization of China's Rural Market (Wo-kuo nung-ts'un shih-ch'ang ti kai-tsu).* Peking: Ts'ai-cheng ching-chi ch'u-pan-she, 1957.
8. *Collection of Important Land Reform Documents (T'u-ti kai-ko chung-yao wen-hsien hui-pien).* Peking: Jen-min ch'u-pan-she, 1951.
9. Fang Ch'ang. *The Relationship between Developing Agricultural Pro-*

duction and Developing Industrial Production (Fa-chan nung-yeh sheng-ch'an ho fa-chan kung-yeh sheng-ch'an ti kuan-hsi). Peking: Jen-min ch'u-pan-she, 1956.

10. Han Hsing. *Questions and Answers on Advanced Agricultural Production Cooperatives (Kao-chi nung-yeh sheng-ch'an ho-tso-she wen-ta).* Canton: Kuang-tung jen min ch'u-pan-she, 1956.

11. *Handbook for 1952 Agricultural Tax Work in the Central South (Chung-nan ch'ü 1952-nien nung-yeh-shui-shou kung-tso shou-ts'e).* Canton: Hua-nan jen-min ch'u-pan-she, 1952.

12. *Happy and Prosperous Advanced Agricultural Production Cooperatives (Hsing-fu ti kao-chi nung-yeh sheng-ch'an ho-tso-she).* Hankow: Hu-pei jen-min ch'u-pan-she, 1956.

13. Ho Ch'eng. *Discussion of the Draft Model Regulations for Agricultural Production Cooperatives (Nung-yeh sheng-ch'an ho-tso-she shih-fan chang-ch'eng ts'ao-an chiang-hua).* Wuhan: Hu-pei jen-min ch'u-pan-she, 1956.

14. Huang Nan-sen and Wang Ch'ing-shu. *On the Objective Foundation of the Cooperativization High Tide in China (Lun wo-kuo nung-yeh ho-tso-hua kao-chi ti k'o-kuan ken-yüan).* Shanghai: Shang-hai jen-min ch'u-pan-she, 1956.

15. *Hunan Agriculture (Hunan Nung-yeh).* Peking: Kao-teng chiao-yü ch'u-pan-she, 1959.

16. *Hunan Villages before and after Land Reform (T'u-ti kai-ko ch'ien-hou ti Hu-nan nung-ts'un).* Ch'angsha: Hu-nan t'ung-su tu-wu ch'u-pan-she, 1953.

17. *Investigation of Rural Village Conditions in Hunan (Hunan nung-ts'un ch'ing-k'uang tiao-ch'a).* Hankow: Chung-nan tsung-fen-tien, 1950.

18. *Investigations of the Rural Condition in Several Central South Provinces (Chung-nan ko-sheng nung-ts'un ch'ing-k'uang tiao-ch'a).* Hankow: Chung-nan tsung-fen-tien, 1950.

19. Jen Fu-hsiang et al. *Talks on Fixed Production, Fixed Purchase, and Fixed Supply of Grain Work (Liang-shih ting-ch'an ting-kou ting-hsiao kung-tso chiang-hua).* Shenyang: Liao-ning jen-min ch'u-pan-she, 1955.

20. Ko Lin. *Rural Finance Work (Nung-ts'un chin-jung kung-tso).* Shanghai: Chung-hua shu-chü, 1953.

21. *Land Reform Handbook (T'u-ti kai-ko shou-ts'e).* Hankow: Chung-nan tsung-fen-tien, 1950.

22. Li Ch'eng-jui. *History of the Agricultural Tax of the People's Republic of China (Chung-hua jen-min kung-ho-kuo nung-yeh-shui shih-kao).* Peking: Ts'ai-cheng ch'u-pan-she, 1959.

23. Li Jen-liu. *Supply and Marketing Cooperatives in the Midst of Development (Fa-chan chung ti kung-hsiao ho-tso-she)*. Shanghai: Chung-hua shu-chü, 1951.

24. Liang Ssu-kuang. *How to Run a Cooperative (Tsen-yang pan ho-tso-she)*. Shanghai, 1950.

25. Liao Yüan. *New China's Land Policy (Hsin Chung-kuo ti t'u-ti cheng-ts'e)*. Hong Kong: Nan-fang shu-tien, 1949.

26. *Mutual Aid and Cooperation in Agricultural Production (Nung-yeh sheng-ch'an hu-chu ho-tso)*. Peking: Hua-pei jen-min ch'u-pan-she, 1952.

27. *Organization, Development, and Experiences of Rural Credit Cooperatives (Nung-ts'un hsin-yung ho-tso ti tsu-chih fa-chan yü ching-yen)*. Peking: Ts'ai-cheng ching-chi ch'u-pan-she, 1954.

28. *Reference Materials on Problems of Land Reform (T'u-kai wen-t'i ts'an-k'ao tzu-liao)*. Vol. 1. Hankow: Chung-nan tsung-fen-tien, 1950.

29. *Simple Land Reform Policy Propaganda Materials (T'u-ti kai-ko cheng-ts'e t'ung-su hsüan-ch'uan tzu-liao)*. Hankow: Chung-nan tsung-fen-tien, 1950.

30. *Study Questions and Answers on Land Reform (T'u-ti kai-ko hsüeh-hsi wen-ta)*. Shanghai: Wen-kung, 1951.

31. Su Hsing. *The Socialist Road of China's Agriculture (Wo-kuo nung-yeh ti she-hui-chu-i tao-lu)*. Peking: Jen-min ch'u-pan-she, 1976.

32. *Talking about Some Problems in the Class Policy for Agricultural Cooperativization (T'an-t'an nung-yeh ho-tso-hua chieh-chi cheng-ts'e ti chi-ko wen-t'i)*. Peking: Chung-kuo ch'ing-nien ch'u-pan-she, 1956.

33. *Thirty Questions and Answers on Agricultural Tax Policy (Nung-yeh-shui cheng-ts'e wen-ta san-shih t'iao)*. Hankow: Chung-nan jen-min ch'u-pan-she, 1952.

34. T'ung Ta-lin. *The Basis of the Great Development of Agricultural Cooperativization (Nung-yeh ho-tso-hua ta fa-chan ti ken-chü)*. Peking: Jen-min ch'u-pan-she, 1956.

35. *Typical Experiences in Land Reform and Party Rectification (T'u-kai cheng-tang tien-hsing ching-yen)*. Hong Kong: Chung-kuo ch'u-pan-she, 1948.

36. Wu Tan-ko. *Problems of China's Agricultural Tax (Chung-kuo nung-yeh-shui wen-t'i)*. Shanghai: Li-hsin k'uai-chi t'u-shu yung-p'in, 1952.

37. Yang Hui-hsien. *How an Agricultural Production Cooperative Accumulates and Uses Public Capital Funds (Nung-yeh sheng-ch'an ho-tso-she tsen-yang chi-lei ho shih-yung kung-kung chi-chin)*. Peking: T'ung-su tu-wu ch'u-pan-she, 1956.

38. Yang Po. *State Commerce during the Transition Period (Kuo-chia kuo-tu shih-ch'i ti shang-yeh)*. Peking: Kung-jen ch'u-pan-she, 1956.
39. Yen Chung-p'ing. *Collection of Statistical Material on Contemporary Chinese Economic History (Chung-kuo chin-tai ching-chi shih t'ung-chi tzu-liao hsüan-chi)*. Peking: K'o-hsüeh ch'u-pan-she, 1955.

II. ARTICLES IN CHINESE
(from newspapers, periodicals, and collections)

40. "A Discussion of Timber Purchase Prices in the South" ("Nan-fang mu-ts'ai chia-ko wen-t'i ti shang-ch'ueh"). *Sen-lin Kung-yeh (Forest Industry)*, no. 12 (1957).
41. "A Few Things I Have Learned from Participating in Land Reform" ("Wo ts'an-chia t'u-kai ti chi-tien t'i-yen"). *CCJP,* 13 March 1951.
42. "A Good Method of Division of Labor and Cooperation between State-Run Business and Co-op Business" ("Kuo-ying shang-yeh ho ho-tso-she shang-yeh fen-kung ho-tso ti i-ko hao pan-fa"). *JMJP* editorial, 21 December 1953.
43. "A Letter from Lü Hai-yün's MAT Reports Success and a Rich Harvest" ("Lü Hai-yün hu-chu-tsu lai-hsin pao-kao feng-ch'an ch'eng-chi"). *CCJP,* 9 October 1952.
44. "A New Atmosphere after Implementing 'Guaranteed Work and Guaranteed Production' " ("Shih-hsing pao-kung pao-ch'an i-hou ti hsin ch'i-hsiang"). *CCJP,* 24 April 1955.
45. "A Presentation on the Manufactured Products Exhibition Conducted by the Heng-shan County [Hunan] SMC" ("Chieh-shao Heng-shan hsien kung-hsiao ho-tso-she chü-hsing ti kung-yeh-p'in chan-lan-hui"). *TKP,* 21 November 1953.
46. "Actively and Steadily Open Up Credit Cooperation" ("Chi-chi wen-pu k'ai-chan hsin-yung ho-tso"). *TKP,* 27 March 1954.
47. "Actively Develop Rural Credit Co-op Organization" ("Chi-chi fa-chan nung-ts'un hsin-yung ho-tso tsu-chih"). *JMJP,* 4 May 1954.
48. "Actively Develop Rural Credit Cooperation" ("Chi-chi fa-chan nung-ts'un hsin-yung ho-tso"). *JMJP,* 12 September 1954.
49. "Actively Lead Mutual Aid Teams and Push Production" ("Chi-chi ling-tao hu-chu-tsu t'ui-tung sheng-ch'an"). *HHNP,* 29 March 1954.
50. "Administrative Work of the Central Provisional People's Government in the Coming Year" ("Chung-yüan lin-shih jen-min cheng-fu chin-i-nien-lai ti shih-cheng kung-tso"). *CCJP,* 7 February 1950.
51. "Advance Purchase of Agricultural and Sideline Products Can Promote Rural Mutual Aid and Cooperation" ("Yü-kou nung-fu-yeh ch'an-p'in k'o-i ts'u-chin nung-ts'un hu-chu ho-tso"). *HHNP,* 15 May 1954.

52. "Advance Purchase of Early Rice in An-hsiang County Exceeds the Original Set Norm" ("An-hsiang hsien yü-kou tsao-ku ch'ao-kuo yüan-ting chih-piao"). *HHNP,* 21 May 1954.
53. "After Chairman Mao's Report Was Propagandized" ("Mao chu-hsi ti pao-kao ch'uan-lai i-hou"). *JMJP,* 3 November 1955.
54. "After Investigation and Summary, Problems of Mutual Benefit Solved and Unity of Poor and Middle Peasants Strengthened" ("Ching-kuo chien-ch'a tsung-chieh hou, chieh-chüeh hu-li wen-t'i, chia-ch'ang le p'in chung nung t'uan-chieh"). *HHNP,* 28 April 1954.
55. "After Preliminary Rectification and Education, the Consciousness of Hupei People's Militia Members Is Raised . . ." ("Ching-kuo ch'u-pu cheng-tun chiao-yü hou, pen-sheng min-ping chüeh-wu t'i-kao . . ."). *HPJP,* 29 November 1950.
56. "After the Enlarged Cadres' Meeting of Heng-yang (Hunan) and Three Other Counties, Land Reform Work Is Now Opening Up in Keypoints" ("Hu-nan Heng-yang teng ssu hsien k'uo kan hui hou, t'u-kai kung-tso cheng chung-tien k'ai-chan"). *CCJP,* 11 January 1951.
57. "Agriculture and Pastoral Products Will Be Purchased through Advanced Purchase Contracts" ("Chiang t'ung-kuo yü-kou ho-t'ung ts'ai-kou nung-mu-yeh ch'an-p'in"). *JMJP,* 28 March 1954.
58. "All Walks Representatives Congress Opens" ("Ko-chieh tai-piao hui k'ai-mu"). *CCJP,* 21 January 1950.
59. "Almost All Hunan Counties and Municipalities Have Convened Congresses of Representatives from All Walks of Life" ("Hu-nan ch'uan sheng ta-pu hsien shih p'u-pien chao-k'ai ko-chieh tai-piao hui"). *CCJP,* 23 June 1950.
60. "An-jen Fifth District [Hunan] Actively Develops Credit Co-op Organization" ("An-jen wu-ch'ü chi-chi fa-chan hsin-yung ho-tso tsu-chih"). *HHNP,* 16 April 1954.
61. "The Autumn Tax Quota Is in Large Part Fulfilled" ("Ch'iu-cheng jen-wu ta-pu wan-ch'eng"). *CCJP,* 6 February 1950.
62. "Bandit Insurrections in Han-shou and Wu-kang (Hunan) Immediately Suppressed . . ." ("Hu-nan Han-shou, Wu-kang fei-t'u pao-tung ching chi-shih chen-ya . . ."). *CCJP,* 16 May 1951.
63. "Before Next Autumn APCs Will Grow to 70,000" ("Ming-nien ch'iu-ch'ien nung-yeh-she chiang fa-chan tao ch'i-wan-ko"). *CCJP,* 10 September 1955.
64. "The Burden on the Peasantry in 1956: Conditions and Questions" ("1956-nien nung-min fu-tan ch'ing-k'uang ho wen-t'i"). *Ts'ai-cheng,* no. 8 (1957), pp. 3–5.
65. "Business Management Step by Step Getting onto the Right Track"

("Ching-ying kuan-li chu-pu tso-shang cheng-kuei"). *HHNP*, 26 October 1956.

66. "Business Must Certainly Be Conducted According to Contracts" ("I-ting yao an ho-t'ung pan-shih"). *HHNP*, 19 May 1954.

67. "Calculating Workpoints According to Money Earned Is Not a Good Method for Sideline Work" ("Fu-yeh lao-tung an ch'ien chi-fen pu shih hao pan-fa"). *JMJP*, 9 October 1956.

68. "Carrying Out the Unified Purchase and Supply of Grain Is an Important Measure for Implementing the General Line" ("Shih-hsing liang-shih ti chi-hua shou-kou ho chi-hua kung-ying shih kuan-ch'e tsung-lu-hsien ti chung-yao ts'o-shih"). *TKP* editorial, 1 March 1954.

69. "Causes of Deaths of Draught Oxen in Hupei Province and Methods of Protecting the Oxen" ("Hu-pei sheng keng-niu ssu-wang yüan-yin chi pao-hu keng-niu pan-fa"). *CCJP*, 24 April 1951.

70. "CCP Huang-kang [Hupei] Land Committee Calls a Meeting of County Cadres to Summarize Keypoint Land Reform Experiences" ("Chung-kung Huang-kang ti-wei chao-k'ai ko hsien kan-pu hui-i, tsung-chieh chung-tien t'u-kai ching-yen"). *CCJP*, 15 February 1951.

71. "CCP Huang-kang [Hupei] Land Committee Directs That the Work of Rural Youth League Establishment Be Developed" ("Chung-kung Huang-kang ti-wei chih-shih, k'ai-chan nung-ts'un chien-t'uan kung-tso"). *CCJP*, 26 April 1950.

72. "CCPCC Central China Bureau Decision Concerning Rectification of Cadres' Workstyle and Correcting the Mistake of Indiscriminate Beating and Killing in Rural Work" ("Chung-kung chung-yang hua-chung chü, kuan-yü cheng-tun kan-pu tso-feng, chiu-cheng hsiang-ts'un kung-tso chung luan-ta-luan-sha ts'o-wu ti chüeh-ting"). *CCJP*, 9 December 1949.

73. "CCPCC Central South Bureau Directive on Quickly Beginning the Rent and Interest Reduction Movement in Non-Land-Reform Areas . . ." ("Chung-kung chung-yang chung-nan-chü kuan-yü tsai wei t'u-ti kai-ko ch'ü, hsün-su k'ai-chan t'ui-tsu t'ui-ya yün-tung . . . ti chih-shih"). *CCJP*, 22 April 1951.

74. "Central South Education Department Promulgates a Directive Concerning Participation in Land Reform Work by Elementary and Middle School Students and Teachers" ("Kuan-yü chung hsiao hsüeh shih sheng ts'an-chia t'u-ti kung-tso, chung-nan chiao-yü-pu fa-ch'u chih-shih"). *HPJP*, 12 November 1950.

75. "The Central South Finance and Economics Committee Issues a Directive Concerning Land Investigation and Fixing Yield" ("Chung-nan ts'ai-cheng ching-chi wei-yüan-hui, fa-ch'u kuan-yü ch'a-t'ien ting-ch'an ti chih-shih"). *CCJP*, 13 July 1951.

76. "The Central South Finance Department Notifies Local Areas That They Are to Strengthen the Autumn Tax Reporting System . . ." ("Chung-nan ts'ai-cheng-pu t'ung-chih ko-ti chia-ch'iang ch'iu-cheng pao-kao chih-tu . . ."). *CCJP,* 14 October 1950.

77. "Central South Gives Out Ten Thousand Hundred Million Yüan in Agricultural Loans" ("Chung-nan fa-fang wan-i nung-yeh tai-k'uan"). *CCJP,* 22 June 1952.

78. "Central South Land Committee Issues Another Directive Forbidding Waste of the Fruits of Land Reform Struggle Belonging to the Masses" ("Chung-nan t'u-ti wei-yüan-hui tsai-tz'u fa-pu chih-shih, yen-chin lang-fei ch'ün-chung t'u-kai tou-cheng kuo-shih"). *CCJP,* 25 February 1951.

79. "Central South Loans Support Tea Production" ("Chung-nan tai-k'uan fu-chu ch'a-ch'an"). *JMJP,* 2 June 1950.

80. "Central South Provisional Regulations Prohibiting Slaughter of Draught Animals" ("Chung-nan ch'ü chin tsai keng-hsü chan-hsing t'iao-li"). *CCJP,* 6 July 1951.

81. "Central South Region Provisional Stipulations on the Control and Reform of Landlords" ("Chung-nan ch'ü kuan-chih, kai-tsao ti-chu chan-hsing kuei-ting"). *CCJP,* 20 August 1952.

82. "Centralized Training of Militia Cadres in Yao-shui and Ta-yeh Counties [Hupei]" ("Yao-shui Ta-yeh liang hsien chi hsün min-ping kan-pu"). *HPJP,* 23 November 1950.

83. "Ch'angsha Special District Rectifies Peasant Associations" ("Ch'ang-sha chuan-ch'ü cheng-tun nung-hsieh"). *CCJP,* 23 October 1950.

84. "Ch'ang-te, Ch'angsha, and Other Counties (Hunan) Rectify Peasant Associations, Organize and Educate Cadres by Summing Up Rent Reduction and Other Work" ("Hu-nan Ch'ang-te Ch'ang-sha teng hsien t'ung-kuo tsung-chieh chien-tsu teng hsiang kung-tso cheng-tun nung-hsieh tsu-chih chiao-yü kan-pu"). *CCJP,* 24 September 1950.

85. "Ch'ang-te Special District [Hunan] Revises Plans for Co-op Establishment" ("Ch'ang-te chuan-ch'ü hsiu-ting chien-she chi-hua"). *HHNP,* 21 August 1955.

86. "Ch'üan-t'ang Co-op Finance Management Work Has Gotten onto the Right Track" ("Ch'üan-t'ang she ts'ai-wu kuan-li kung-tso tso shang le cheng-kuei"). *HNCSP,* 7 May 1956.

87. "Classification Work Basically Completed in the Various Keypoint Experimental Land Reform Villages of Hsiang-yang County [Hupei]" ("Hsiang-yang hsien ko t'u-kai chung-tien shih-yen ts'un, hua-fen chieh-chi kung-tso ta-t'i chieh-shu"). *HPJP,* 22 November 1950.

88. "Close Relationship between State-run Commerce and Co-ops Powerfully Organizes Increased Merchandizing" ("Mi-ch'ieh kuo-ying

shang-yeh ho ho-tso-she kuan-hsi ta-li tsu-chih shang-p'in t'ui-hsiao''). *TKP*, 18 November 1953.

89. "Closely Uniting with Production, Actively Opening up Savings and Loan Operations . . ." ("Chin-mi chieh-ho sheng-ch'an, chi-chi k'ai-chan ts'un-k'uan fang-k'uan yeh-wu . . .").*HHNP*, 2 June 1954.

90. "Combine the Land Reform Movement with the Establishment of the People's Armed Might" ("Chieh-ho t'u-kai yün-tung chien-she jen-min wu-chuang"). *CCJP*, 26 February 1951.

91. "Completely Rectify Co-op Finance Management Work" ("Ch'ieh-shih cheng-tun ho-tso-she ti ts'ai-wu kuan-li kung-tso"). *NFJP* editorial, 19 May 1956.

92. "The Condition of Li Ch'eng-kuei's MAT and Some Problems" ("Li Ch'eng-kuei hu-chu-tsu ti ch'ing-k'uang ho wen-t'i"). *JMJP*, 5 July 1952.

93. "Conditions of Opening the Agricultural Cooperativization Movement in Ho-tso Village [Hupei]" ("Ho-tso hsiang nung-yeh ho-tso-hua yün-tung k'ai-chan ch'ing-k'uang"). *CCJP*, 10 December 1955.

94. "Conscientiously Implement Policy, Mobilize the Masses to Complete the Autumn Tax Collection Task" ("Jen-chen chih-hsing cheng-ts'e fa-tung ch'ün-chung wan-ch'eng ch'iu-cheng jen-wu"). *CCJP* editorial, 6 October 1950.

95. "Conscientiously Organize State-led Basic-level Rural Grain Markets" ("Jen-chen tsu-chih kuo-chia ling-tao ti nung-ts'un ch'u-chi liang-shih shih-ch'ang"). *JMJP*, 18 May 1954.

96. "Conscientiously Prevent and Correct Instances of Wasting the Fruits of Land Reform Struggle" ("Jen-chen fang-chih yü chiu-cheng lang-fei t'u-kai tou-cheng kuo-shih ti hsien-hsiang"). *CCJP* editorial, 8 January 1951.

97. "Conscientiously Rectify Labor Mutual Aid Organizations" ("Jen-chen cheng-tun lao-tung hu-chu tsu-chih"). *CCJP*, 16 July 1952.

98. "Continue Deep Mobilization of the Masses . . ." ("Chi-hsü shen-ju fa-tung ch'ün-chung . . ."). *CCJP*, 10 October 1952.

99. "Co-ops Should Actively Develop Marketing of Native Products" ("Ho-tso-she ying chi-chi k'ai-chan hsiao t'u-ch'an t'ui-hsiao kung-tso"). *TKP*, 29 May 1953.

100. "Correct Feelings of Indifference and Self-satisfaction among Cadres; Arduously and Deeply Mobilize the Peasant Masses" ("Chiu-cheng kan-pu ma-p'i tzu-man ch'ing-hsü, nan-k'u shen-ju fa-tung nung-min ch'ün-chung"). *CCJP*, 17 January 1951.

101. "Correct the Bureaucratist/Commandist Workstyle" ("Chiu-cheng kuan-liao chu-i ming-ling chu-i ti tso-feng"). *CCJP*, 17 June 1950.

102. "Correct [the Deviation of] Formalism in the Rent Reduction Movement" ("Chiu-cheng chien-tsu yün-tung chung ti hsing-shih chu-i"). *CCJP,* 22 April 1950.

103. "Correct the Phenomenon of Separating Mutual Aid and Cooperation from Production" ("Chiu-cheng hu-chu ho-tso yü sheng-ch'an fen-li hsien-hsiang"). *HHNP,* 15 March 1954.

104. "Corruption and Theft of Public Grain Discovered in Yung-shuan (Hunan)" ("Hu-nan Yung-shuan fa-hsien kung-liang pei t'an-wu t'ou-tao"). *CCJP,* 15 February 1951.

105. "Credit Co-ops Must Administer Loans According to Policy" ("Hsin-yung ho-tso-she pi-hsü ken-chü cheng-ts'e pan-li fang-k'uan"). *TKP,* 6 November 1954.

106. "Credit Co-ops Must Work under the Leadership of the Party and under the Direction and with the Help of the Bank" ("Hsin-yung-she yao tsai tang ti ling-tao ho yin-hang ti chih-tao pang-chu hsia chin-hsing kung-tso"). *TKP,* 11 November 1954.

107. "Credit Co-ops Should Actively Open Up Savings and Loan Business" ("Hsin-yung ho-tso-she ying-kai chi-chi k'ai-chan ts'un-k'uan fang-k'uan yeh-wu"). *JMJP,* 31 May 1955.

108. "CSMAC Announces Methods for Province and County to Follow in Confiscating and Redistributing Mountain Forests during Land Reform" ("Chung-nan chün-cheng wei-yüan-hui pan-pu, ko-sheng hsien tsai t'u-kai ch'i chung shan-lin mo-shou fen-p'ei pan-fa"). *HTJP,* 30 June 1951.

109. "CSMAC Announces Stipulations Concerning the Problems of Handling Land Distribution to Criminal Elements during Land Reform" ("Chung-nan chün-cheng wei-yüan-hui pan-pu, kuan-yü t'u-ti kai-ko chung ch'u-li fan-tsui fen-tzu fen-p'ei t'u-ti wen-t'i ti kuei-ting"). *CCJP,* 6 April 1952.

110. "CSMAC Announces Ways of Handling Ownership of Land, Houses, and Other Assets" ("Chung-nan chün-cheng wei-yüan-hui fa-pu, chung-nan ch'ü pan-fa t'u-ti fang ch'an so-yu cheng pan-fa"). *JMJP,* 22 August 1951.

111. "CSMAC Decrees That Democratic Parties and Persons Be Absorbed to Participate in Land Reform" ("Chung-nan chün-cheng wei-yüan-hui kuei-ting, hsi-shou min-chu tang-p'ai min-chu jen-shih ts'an-chia t'u-kai"). *CCJP,* 10 November 1950.

112. "The CSMAC Finance Department Convenes an Interim Conference on Agricultural Tax Work" ("Chung-nan chün-cheng wei-yüan-hui ts'ai-cheng-pu, chao-k'ai nung-yeh-shui kung-tso lin-shih hui-i"). *CCJP,* 28 August 1952.

113. "The CSMAC Issues a Directive on Summer Public Grain Collection Work" ("Chung-nan chün-cheng wei-yüan-hui fa-pu, hsia-chi cheng-shou kung-liang kung-tso chih-shih"). *CCJP*, 26 July 1951.

114. "CSMAC Issues Directive Establishing Land Committees at Several Levels to Manage and Lead Land Reform Work in the Region" ("Chung-nan chün-cheng wei-yüan-hui pan-pu chih-shih, chien-li ko chi t'u-ti wei-yüan-hui, ching-ch'ang chih-tao ko kai ti-ch'ü t'u-ti kai-ko kung-tso"). *CCJP*, 22 June 1950.

115. "CSMAC Orders that People's Tribunals Be Quickly Established and Put into Use in Land Reform Areas" ("Chung-nan chün-cheng wei-yüan-hui chih-shih tsai t'u-ti kai-ko ti-ch'ü, hsün-su chien-li yü yün-yung jen-min fa-t'ing"). *CCJP*, 18 January 1951.

116. "The CSMAC Orders Thorough Investigation of Tax Collection Treasuries and Public Grain" ("Chung-nan chün-cheng wei-yüan-hui fa-ch'u ming-ling, ch'e-ch'a shui-shou chin-k'u yü kung-liang"). *CCJP*, 14 January 1951.

117. "The CSMAC Promulgates a Directive about This Year's Agricultural Tax" ("Chung-nan chün-cheng wei-yüan-hui fa-pu kuan-yü chin-nien nung-yeh-shui chih-shih"). *CCJP*, 12 September 1950.

118. "CSMAC Publicizes Provisional Regulations for the Punishment and Rehabilitation of Lawbreaking Landlords" ("Chung-nan chün-cheng wei-yüan-hui kung-pu, ch'eng-chih pu-fa ti-chu chan-hsing t'iao-li"). *NFJP*, 21 November 1950.

119. "CSMAC Releases a Directive Concerning the Work of People's Tribunals" ("Chung-nan chün-cheng wei-yüan-hui fa-ch'u, kuan-yü jen-min fa-t'ing kung-tso ti chih-shih"). *CCJP*, 29 July 1951.

120. "CSMAC Supplementary Regulations Concerning the Differentiation of Class Status in the Countryside" ("Chung-nan chün-cheng wei-yüan-hui . . . kuan-yü hua-fen nung-ts'un chieh-chi ch'eng-fen ti pu-ch'ung kuei-ting"). *CCJP*, 29 October 1951.

121. "Decision of the CCPCC Central South Bureau Concerning Strengthening New Democratic Youth League Work" ("Chung-kung chung-yang chung-nan chü, kuan-yü chia-ch'iang hsin min-chu chu-i ch'ing-nien t'uan kung-tso ti chüeh-ting"). *CCJP*, 13 March 1950.

122. "Decision of the CCPCC Central South Bureau Concerning Study by On-duty Cadres" ("Chung-kung chung-yang chung-nan chü kuan-yü tsai-chih kan-pu hsüeh-hsi ti chüeh-ting"). *CCJP*, 18 January 1950.

123. "Decision of the CSMAC Regarding Thorough Implementation of the State Council's Directive on Agricultural Tax Collection Work" ("Chung-nan chün-cheng wei-yüan-hui kuan-yü kuan-ch'e chih-hsing cheng-wu-yüan nung-yeh shui-shou kung-tso chih-shih ti chüeh-ting"). *CCJP*, 9 August 1952.

124. "Decision of the State Council Concerning Unified Public Grain Collection Organ, Safety, and Dispatch" ("Cheng-wu-yüan kuan-yü t'ung-i kuo-chia kung-liang shou-chih, pao-kuan, tiao-tu ti chüeh-ting"). In *Collected Laws and Decrees of the Central People's Government* 1, pp. 254–256, 24 March 1950.

125. "Deeply Open up Study by On-duty Cadres" ("Shen-ju k'ai-chan tsai-chih kan-pu hsüeh-hsi"). *CCJP,* 17 April 1950.

126. "Detailed Instructions for the Implementation of Rent and Interest Reduction in Hupei Province" ("Hu-pei sheng chien-tsu chien-hsi shih-shih hsi-tse"). *CCJP,* 6 January 1950.

127. "Determine the Policy Line for Rural Youth League Establishment" ("Ch'üeh-ting nung-ts'un chien-t'uan fang-chen"). *CCJP,* 5 February 1950.

128. "Develop Rural Credit Co-op Enterprises Actively and with Planning" ("Chi-chi ti yu chi-hua ti fa-chan nung-ts'un hsin-yung ho-tso shih-yeh"). *HHNP* editorial, 5 May 1954.

129. "The Development of Liao Jen-fu's Mutual Aid Team" ("Liao Jen-fu hu-chu-tsu shih tsen-yang fa-chan ch'i-lai-ti"). *CCJP,* 10 October 1951.

130. "The Deviation of Peacefully Dividing Up the Land Emerges in Wu-ch'ang [Hupei] Experimental Land Reform Work" ("Wu-ch'ang t'u-kai shih-yen kung-tso fa-sheng ho-p'ing fen-t'ien p'ien-hsiang"). *HPJP,* 27 November 1950.

131. "Deviations Have Emerged in Some Areas in Giving Out Advances for Agricultural Produce" ("Pu-fen ti-ch'ü fa-fang nung ch'an-p'in yü-kou ting-chin ch'u-hsien p'ien-ch'a"). *HHNP,* 29 May 1954.

132. "Directive of the Hupei Province People's Government . . . Concerning the Work of Storing Grain Collected in the Autumn" ("Hu-pei sheng jen-min cheng-fu . . . kuan-yü ch'iu-cheng ju-k'u kung-tso ti chih-shih"). *CCJP,* 19 August 1951.

133. "Directive of the State Council Concerning Agricultural Tax Collection in Newly Liberated Areas" ("Cheng-wu-yüan kuan-yü hsin-chieh-fang-ch'ü cheng-shou nung-yeh-shui ti chih-shih"). In *Collected Laws and Decrees of the Central People's Government* 1, pp. 275–276, 8 September 1950.

134. "Directive of the State Council of the Central People's Government Concerning 1951 Agricultural Tax Collection Work" ("Chung-yang jen-min cheng-fu cheng-wu-yüan, kuan-yü i-chiu-wu-i-nien nung-yeh-shui-shou kung-tso ti chih-shih"). *CCJP,* 23 June 1951.

135. "Directive on Actively Beginning Preferential Treatment in Savings with Grain Sales in the Villages" ("Kuan-yü tsai nung-ts'un chi-chi k'ai-chan shou-liang yu-tai ch'u-hsü ti chih-shih"). In *Collected Finance*

Laws and Orders (1953) (Chin-jung fa-ling hui-pien). Peking: Ts'ai-cheng ching-chi ch'u-pan-she, 1955.

136. "Directive on Land Reform and Tax Collection in the Newly Liberated Areas" ("Kuan-yü hsin-chieh-fang-ch'ü t'u-ti kai-ko chi cheng-shou kung-liang ti chih-shih"). *JMJP,* 1 March 1950; and also in *Collected Laws and Decrees of the Central People's Government* 1, pp. 63–66, 28 February 1950.

137. "Discoveries of Graft and Theft of Public Grain Are Made in a Few Places in Hunan, Hupei, and Other Provinces" ("Hsiang, O teng sheng, ko-pieh ti-ch'ü, fa-hsien kung-liang pei t'an-wu t'ou-tao"). *CCJP,* 19 August 1950.

138. "Do a Good Job of Distributing the Autumn Harvest; Consolidate Agricultural Co-ops" ("Tso-hao ch'iu-shou fen-p'ei, kung-ku nung-yeh ho-tso-she"). *JMJP,* 12 September 1955.

139. "Do a Good Job of Organizing the Regulation of Rural Grain" ("Tso-hao tsu-chih nung-ts'un liang-shih t'iao-chi kung-tso"). *TKP,* 28 May 1954.

140. "Do a Good Job of Propaganda to Eliminate Peasants' Anxieties" ("Tso-hao hsüan-ch'uan ta-hsiao nung-min ku-lu"). *CCJP,* 9 January 1951.

141. "Do a Good Job of Purchasing Agricultural Produce on the Basis of Advance Purchase Contracts" ("Tsai yü-kou ho-t'ung chi-ch'u shang tso-hao nung ch'an-p'in shou-kou kung-tso"). *TKP,* 28 June 1954.

142. "Do a Good Job of Rearing All Co-op Draught Animals" ("Pa ho-tso-she ti keng-hsü ch'uan-to yang-hao"). *JMJP* editorial, 17 May 1956.

143. "Do a Good Job of Settling Accounts and Balancing Workpoints . . ." ("Tso-hao chieh-chang chao-kung kung-tso . . ."). *CFJP,* 11 July 1952.

144. "Do Not Scheme to Get Small Profits and Be Taken in by Speculators" ("Pu yao t'an-t'u hsiao-li shang t'ou-jen ti tang"). *HHNP,* 20 May 1954.

145. "Duck Compounds Must Be Prevented from Coming into the Villages and Practically Stealing Rice" ("Ya-p'eng hsia-hsiang ch'iang-kou tao-ku ying chih-chih"). *TKP,* 19 November 1953.

146. "East Is Red Co-op Thinks of Ways to Guarantee the Quality of Work" ("Tung fang hung she hsiang-ch'u pan-fa pao-cheng kung-fu chih-liang"). *HNNM,* 13 May 1956.

147. "Economize from Beginning to End to Solve Capital Difficulties" ("K'ai yüan chieh liu chieh-chüeh tzu-chin k'un-nan"). *HNCCP,* 1 April 1956.

148. "Educating Peasants to Strengthen Political Work in the Village Is a Serious Problem" ("Yen-chung ti wen-t'i shih chiao-yü nung-min

chia-ch'iang nung-ts'un chung ti cheng-chih kung-tso''). *CCJP*, 8 November 1951.

149. "Eliminate Taxation by Class and Make Assessments According to the Rates" ("'Fei-chih an-chi p'ai kung-liang, i-lu chi-cheng"). *CCJP*, 4 April 1952.

150. "Empiricism of Cadres in Several Parts of Hunan Harms Work" ("Hunan mou-hsieh ti-ch'ü kan-pu ching-yen chu-i sun-hai kung-tso"). *CCJP*, 31 December 1949.

151. "Enhance the Co-op's Role as an Assistant" ("Fa-hui ho-tso-she ti chu-shou tso-yung"). *TKP*, 7 December 1953.

152. "Experience of Sheng-li Village in Han-ch'iao District [Hupei] in Promoting Guaranteed Work and Guaranteed Production" ("Han-ch'iao ch'ü Sheng-li hsiang t'ui-hsing pao-kung pao-ch'an ti ching-yen"). *CCJP*, 10 April 1956.

153. "Experience of Ta-chih Special District [Hupei] in Convening Subdistrict and Village Peasants' Deputies Committees" ("Ta-chih chuan-ch'ü chao-k'ai ch'ü hsiang nung tai hui ti ching-yen"). *HPJP*, 5 December 1950.

154. "Experiences of Distributing the Fruits during Land Reform in Various Parts of Hupei" ("Hu-pei ko ti t'u-kai chung fen-p'ei kuo-shih ti ching-yen"). *CCJP*, 14 March 1951.

155. "Experimental Land Reform in Forty-seven Villages of Hunan's Ch'angsha, I-yang, and Four Other Special Districts" ("Hu-nan Ch'ang-sha I-yang teng liu chuan-ch'ü ssu-shih ch'i hsiang shih-yen t'u-kai"). *CCJP*, 16 October 1950.

156. "Experimental Methods of Investigating Land and Fixing Yield in the Central South" ("Chung-nan-ch'ü ch'a-t'ien ting-ch'an shih-hsing pan-fa"). *CCJP*, 28 March 1951.

157. "Extend Combined Contracts between SMCs and Both MATs and APCs" ("T'ui-kuang kung-hsiao-she yü hu-chu-tsu, nung-yeh-she chih chien ti chieh-ho ho-t'ung"). *HHNP*, 11 May 1954.

158. "Extremely Serious Atmosphere of Departing from the Masses in the Work of Building the Youth League in the Countryside" ("Nung-ts'un chien-t'uan kung-tso tang-chung, t'o-li ch'ün-chung tso-feng chi yen-chung"). *CCJP*, 15 October 1950.

159. "The Feudal Influence of Clans in the Villages" ("Tsung-tsu feng-chien shih-li tsai nung-ts'un"). *CCJP*, 15 December 1949.

160. "Firmly Grasp and Solve Capital Problems" ("Chua-chin chieh-chüeh tzu-chin wen-t'i"). *HNCCP*, 1 April 1956.

161. "Firmly Implement the Policy Line of Mobilizing Peasant Men and Women Together" ("Chien-ch'ih kuan-ch'e nan nü nung-min i-ch'i fa-tung ti fang-chen"). *HPJP*, 17 November 1950.

162. "Flower Bridge Village in Ch'angsha County [Hunan] Peacefully Divides Up the Land" ("Ch'ang-sha hsien Hua-ch'iao hsiang ho-p'ing fen-t'ien"). *HHNP*, 18 December 1950.

163. "'Four Evaluations' Work during Establishment and Expansion of Co-ops in Ho-tso Village [Hupei]" ("Ho-tso hsiang tsai chien-she k'uo-she chung ti 'ssu p'ing' kung-tso"). *CCJP*, 22 December 1955.

164. "The Fruits of Rent Reduction Must Be Used for Production" ("Chientsu kuo-shih pi-hsü yung-yü sheng-ch'an"). *CCJP*, 15 April 1950.

165. "The Function of Agricultural Loans Must Be Fully Exploited in the Patriotic Production Movement" ("Ai-kuo sheng-ch'an yün-tung chung pi-hsü ch'ung-fen fa-hui nung-tai ti tso-yung"). *CCJP*, 27 April 1951.

166. "The Function of the Contract System in Organizing the Marketing of Rural Sideline Products and Some Problems Needing Attention" ("Ho-t'ung-chih tsai tsu-chih nung-ts'un fu-yeh-ch'an hsiao shang ti tso-yung yü ying chu-i ti chi-ko wen-t'i"). *CKNP* 1 (6): 103–111.

167. "Fundamental Conditions and Preliminary Experience of 1949 Cadre Training in the Central South Region" ("Chung-nan ti-ch'ü i-chiu-ssu-chiu-nien hsün-lien kan-pu ti chi-pen ch'ing-k'uang yü ch'u-pu ching-yen"). *CCJP*, 4 January 1951.

168. "Fundamental Systems of Agricultural Production Mutual Aid Teams in Yao-shui County [Hupei]" ("Hu-pei Yao-shui hsien nung-yeh sheng-ch'an hu-chu-tsu ti chi-hsiang chi-pen chih-tu"). In *Reference Material on Agricultural Production Mutual Aid Teams (Nung-yeh sheng-ch'an hu-chu-tsu ts'an-k'ao tzu-liao)*, pp. 66–74. Peking: Chung-yang jen-min cheng-fu nung-yeh pu ch'u-pan, 1952.

169. "GAC Finance Committee Issues a Directive on Deputizing Co-ops to Make Advance Purchase of Agricultural Products" ("Cheng-wu-yüan ts'ai-ching wei-yüan-hui fa-ch'u chih-shih, wei-t'o ho-tso-she yü-kou nung ch'an-p'in"). *JMJP*, 28 March 1954.

170. "The General Line Illuminated My Vision" ("Tsung-lu-hsien chao-liang le wo ti yen-ching"). *TKP*, 27 December 1953.

171. "The General Line Lights the Way to Progress for Peasants in Mountain Areas . . ." ("Tsung-lu-hsien chao-yao shan-ti nung-min ch'ien-chin . . ."). *HHNP*, 2 June 1954.

172. "General Order of the CSMAC Announcing Regulations for Rent Reduction in the Central South Region" ("Chung-nan chün-cheng wei-yüan-hui t'ung-ling pan-pu chung-nan ch'ü chien-tsu t'iao-li"). *NFJP*, 21 September 1950.

173. "General Regulations for the Organization of Municipality, County, and Provincial Congresses of People's Representatives from All Walks of Life" ("Shih, hsien, sheng ko-chieh jen-min tai-piao hui-i tsu-chih t'ung-tse"). *CCJP*, 7 December 1949.

174. "Getting Onto the Right Track of Collective Operations" ("Tso-shang chi-t'i ching-ying kuei-tao"). *JMJP*, 19 March 1955.

175. "Go All Out, Mobilize the Masses to Open Up the Rent Reduction and Return Movement Even Faster" ("Fang-shou fa-tung ch'ün-chung chin-su k'ai-chan chien-tsu t'ui-tsu yün-tung"). *CCJP*, 15 March 1950.

176. "Gradual Restoration of Credit Relations in Hunan's Keypoint Districts and Villages" ("Hu-nan chung-tien ch'ü hsiang, chu-chien hui-fu chieh-tai kuan-hsi"). *CCJP*, 24 May 1951.

177. "Gradually Do a Good Job of Suburban Supply Work . . ." ("Chin-i-pu tso-hao chiao-ch'ü kung-hsiao kung-tso . . ."). *CCJP*, 18 December 1955.

178. "Half the Counties in Hupei Have Accomplished High Level Co-operativization" ("Hu-pei sheng nung-ts'un pan shu ti hsien i shih-hsien kao-chi nung-yeh ho-tso hua"). *HPJP*, 13 October 1956.

179. "Help Peasants Solve Difficulties, Support Spring Cultivation and Production" ("Pang-chu nung-min chieh-chüeh k'un-nan, chih-ch'ih ch'ün-keng sheng-ch'an"). *HHNP*, 8 April 1954.

180. "Heng-shan County [Hunan] Peasants Actively Prosecute Grain Speculators and Merchants" ("Hu-nan sheng Heng-shan hsien nung-min chi-chi chien-chü liang-shih t'ou-chi shang"). *JMJP*, 28 November 1953.

181. "Heng-yang County [Hunan] Calls a Meeting of Mutual Aid Team Leaders' Representatives . . ." ("Heng-yang hsien chao-k'ai hu-chu-tsu chang tai-piao hui-i . . ."). *HHNP*, 8 April 1954.

182. "Heng-yang (Hunan) Organizes Private Traders to Go Down to the Villages to Develop Urban-Rural Trade" ("Hu-nan Heng-yang tsu-chih ssu-shang hsia-hsiang fa-chan ch'eng-hsiang mao-i"). *CCJP*, 1 June 1951.

183. "Heng-yang [Hunan] Special District SMC Organizes a Large Number of Peddlers to Go Down to the Villages" ("Heng-yang chuan-ch'ü kung-hsiao she tsu-chih ta-p'i huo-lang-tan hsia-hsiang"). *TKP*, 15 December 1954.

184. "Ho Chang-sheng Is Happy in Agricultural Production Now" ("Ho Chang-sheng an-hsin nung-yeh sheng-ch'an an le"). *HHNP*, 26 May 1954.

185. "How Are Troops in the Hupei Military District to Carry Out the Transition to Work Brigades?" ("Hu-pei chun-ch'ü pu-tui shih tsen-yang chih-hsing kung-tso-tui-hua?"). *CCJP*, 25 January 1950.

186. "How Did Hung-feng Co-op Rectify Finance Work?" ("Hung-feng nung-yeh-she shih ju-ho cheng-tun ts'ai-wu kung-tso ti?"). *HNNM*, 19 April 1956.

187. "How Does White Deer Shop Village (Hunan) in I-yang Second District

Run Production MATs Well?'' (''Hu-nan I-yang erh-ch'ü Pai Lu P'u hsiang shih ju-ho kao-hao sheng ch'an hu-chu tsu?''). *CCJP,* 13 June 1951.

188. ''How Lin Shu-ying's Mutual Aid Team Uses Work Tokens'' (''Lin Shu-ying hu-chu-tsu tsen-yang shih-yung kung-p'iao''). *FKJP,* 5 March 1952.

189. ''How Several Huang-kang Special District [Hupei] APCs Are Improving Labor Organization and Labor Calculation'' (''Huang-kang chuan-ch'ü ko nung-yeh ho-tso-she shih tsen-yang kai-chin lao-tung chi-suan fang-fa ti''). *JMJP,* 4 April 1955.

190. ''How the Party Branch . . . Leads Youth League Members to Participate in the Mutual Aid and Cooperation Movement'' ('' . . . Chih-pu shih tsen-yang ling-tao t'uan-yüan ts' an-chia hu-chu ho-tso yün-tung ti''). *HHNP,* 7 May 1954.

191. ''How to Carry Out the Work of Liaison and Discussion of Agricultural Taxation . . . between Various Areas'' (''Tsen-yang chin-hsing ko ti-ch'ü chien nung-yeh shui . . . ti lien-ho p'ing-i kung-tso'').*TKP,* 25 March 1953.

192. ''How to Consolidate Credit Co-ops'' (''Ju-ho kung-ku hsin-yung ho-tso-she''). *TKP,* 4 April 1955.

193. ''How to Ensure That the Agricultural Production Level in New Areas Does Not Drop during the Period of Village Social Reform'' (''Tsai nung-ts'un she-hui kai-ko shih-ch'i, ju-ho pao-ch'ih hsin ch'ü nung-yeh sheng-ch'an shui-p'ing pu chih hsia-chiang''). *CCJP,* 29 November 1949.

194. ''How to Organize a Credit Cooperative'' (''Tsen-yang tsu-chih hsin-yung ho-tso-she''). *TKP,* 3 November 1954.

195. ''How to Solve the Difficulties of Too Many Co-ops and Not Enough Personnel, and of the Leadership Not Coming Down'' (''Tsen-yang chieh-chüeh she to jen shao ling-tao pu kuo-lai ti k'un-nan''). *TKP,* 28 June 1954.

196. ''How Were the Masses in Huang-p'i County Mobilized to Investigate Concealed Land During the Grain Tax Collection?'' (''Huang-p'i hsien cheng-liang chung tsen-yang fa-tung ch'ün-chung ch'a man-t'ien?''). *CCJP,* 21 October 1950.

197. ''Hsiang-t'an Convenes Second Session of Congress of Representatives from All Walks of Life'' (''Hsiang-t'an k'ai erh chieh ko-chieh tai-piao hui''). *CCJP,* 4 March 1950.

198. ''Hsin-chou County (Hupei) Eighth District Co-op Does a Thorough Merchandise Inventory'' (''Hu-pei Hsin-chou hsien pa ch'ü she ch'üan-mien k'ai-chan shang-p'in p'u-ch'a''). *TKP,* 2 August 1955.

199. "Hsü Ting-hsüeh's Mutual Aid Team in Yao-shui County (Hupei)" ("Hu-pei sheng Yao-shui hsien Hsü Ting-hsüeh hu-chu-tsu"). *JMJP,* 28 May 1952.
200. "Huang-kang [Hupei] Special District Land Reform Experimental Keypoint Village . . . " ("Huang-kang chuan-ch'ü t'u-kai chung-tien shih-yen ts'un . . . "). *HPJP,* 24 November 1950.
201. "Hunan Calls a Credit Co-op Work Conference . . . " ("Hu-nan chao-k'ai hsin-yung ho-tso kung-tso hui-i . . . "). *TKP,* 21 April 1955.
202. "Hunan Co-op . . . Criticizes Only Thinking of Profits . . . " ("Hu-nan ho-tso-she . . . p'i-p'an tan-ch'un kuan-li ssu-hsiang . . . "). *CCJP,* 4 June 1952.
203. "Hunan Establishes Over 10,000 Credit Co-ops" ("Hu-nan chien-li ch'i i-wan-to ko hsin-yung-she"). *JMJP,* 4 February 1955.
204. "Hunan, Kiangsu Implement Correct Price Policy and Guarantee the Interests of Grain Producers and Consumers" ("Hu-nan Kiang-su huan-ch'e cheng-ch'üeh ti chia-ke cheng-ts'e, pao-cheng le liang-shih sheng-ch'an-che hsiao-fei-che ti li-i"). *TKP,* 4 March 1954.
205. "Hunan Land Reform Movement Opening Even Further" ("Hu-nan t'u-kai yün-tung chin-i-pu k'ai-chan"). *CCJP,* 13 January 1951.
206. "Hunan Organizes Peddlers to Take Products Right to the Door" ("Hu-nan tsu-chih huo-lang-tan sung-huo tao men"). *TKP,* 31 October 1955.
207. "Hunan Peasants in the Midst of Battle" ("Chan-tou chung ti Hu-nan nung-min"). *CCJP,* 26 April 1951.
208. "Hunan Province Provisional Government Announces Restrictions on the Sale and Transfer of Land and Other Assets by Landlords and Rich Peasants" ("Hu-nan lin-shih sheng cheng-fu pu-kao, chin-chih ti fu pien mai t'ien ch'an"). *CCJP,* 5 March 1950.
209. "Hunan Provincial People's Government Report" ("Hu-nan sheng jen-min cheng-fu kung-tso pao-kao"). *CCJP,* 26 September 1950.
210. "Hunan State Commerce Organizes Trade Teams and Mobilizes Peddlers to Go Down to the Villages . . . " ("Hu-nan kuo-ying mao-i tsu-chih mao-i-tsu, fa-tung shang-fan hsia-hsiang . . ."). *CCJP,* 10 July 1951.
211. "Hunan State-run Grain Company and Other Departments Collect Early Grain in a Planned Way" ("Hu-nan kuo-ying liang-shih kung-ssu teng pu-men, yu chi-hua ti shou-kou tsao-ku"). *CCJP,* 15 August 1951.
212. "Hunan's Autumn Tax Collection Basically Complete" ("Hu-nan ch'iu-cheng chi-pen wan-ch'eng"). *CCJP,* 6 February 1950.
213. "Hunan's Co-ops Should Have a Close Relationship with State-run Commerce" ("Hu-nan ho-tso-she ying mi-ch'ieh ho kuo-ying shang-yeh ti kuan-hsi"). *TKP,* 11 December 1953.
214. "Hunan's . . . Hsin-min Village Used a Peasants' Deputies Conference

to Overcome Production Difficulties'' (''Hu-nan . . . Hsin-min hsiang, yün-yung nung-min tai-piao-hui k'o-fu le sheng-ch'an k'un-nan''). *CCJP*, 7 April 1951.

215. "Hung-shan County [Hupei] Land Reform Training Class . . ." ("Hung-shan hsien t'u-kai hsün-lien pan . . . "). *HPJP*, 12 November 1950.

216. "Hupei Agricultural Cooperativization Enters High Tide" ("Hu-pei nung-yeh ho-tso hua chin-ju kao-ch'ao"). *CCJP*, 26 November 1955.

217. "Hupei and Hunan Provincial Governments Call on All Areas . . ." ("Hu-pei Hu-nan sheng fu hao-chao ko ti . . . "). *CCJP*, 1 January 1950.

218. "Hupei Province Committee . . . Determines the New Tasks in Rural Village Work" ("Hu-pei sheng wei . . . ch'üeh-ting nung-ts'un kung-tso hsin jen-wu"). *CCJP*, 8 December 1949.

219. "Hupei Province Enlarges Land Reform Area" ("Hu-pei sheng k'uo-ta t'u-kai ti-ch'ü"). *CCJP*, 12 November 1950.

220. "Hupei Province Has Already Basically Accomplished Agricultural Cooperativization" ("Hu-pei sheng i chi-pen shih-hsien nung-yeh ho-tso-hua"). *CCJP*, 9 January 1956.

221. "Hupei Province Land Reform Areas . . ." ("Hu-pei sheng t'u-ti kai-ko ti-ch'ü . . . "). *CCJP*, 8 January 1951.

222. "Hupei Province Land Reform Movement . . ." ("Hu-pei sheng t'u-ti kai-ko yün-tung . . . "). *CCJP*, 17 April 1951.

223. "Hupei Province People's Government Transfers 20 Million Catties of Grain to Help Peasants' Spring Cultivation and Production" ("Hu-pei sheng jen-min cheng-fu po liang erh ch'ien wan chin, fu-chu nung-min ch'un ching sheng-ch'an"). *CCJP*, 22 January 1950.

224. "Hupei Provincial CCP Committee Calls a Joint Conference of County Committee Secretaries" ("Chung-kung Hu-pei sheng-wei chao-k'ai hsien-wei shu-chi lien-hsi hui-i"). *CCJP*, 31 May 1951.

225. "Hupei Provincial Government Directive on Reserving Some Land for Fishermen to Have Houses When Carrying Out Land Reform in Lake Areas" ("Hu-pei sheng cheng-fu chih-shih so-shu, tsai hu-ch'ü chin-hsing t'u-ti kai-ko ti shih-hou, ying kei yü-min cho-liu i-pu fang-wu chi-ti"). *CCJP*, 18 August 1951.

226. "Hupei Rent Reduction Is Opened Up Everywhere" ("Hu-pei chien-tsu ch'üan-mien chan-k'ai"). *CCJP*, 12 April 1950.

227. "Hupei Second Provincial All Walks Representatives Forum Opens" ("Hu-pei sheng ti erh tz'u ko-chieh tai-piao tso-t'an-hui k'ai-mu"). *CCJP*, 14 December 1949.

228. "Hupei 'Three Fix' Grain Work Is Ready to Begin" ("Hu-pei liang-shih 'san ting' kung-tso chi chiang chan-k'ai"). *TKP*, 15 October 1955.

229. "Ignoring the Principle of Voluntarism, There Are Serious Cases of Coercion and Commandism" ("Hu-shih tzu-yüan yüan-tse ts'un-tsai yen-chung ti ch'iang-p'o ming-ling hsien-hsiang"). *TKP*, 12 January 1955.

230. "Immediately Correct Egalitarian Thinking and the Workstyle of Doing Everything Oneself in the Distribution of Fruits" ("Li-chi chiu-cheng fen-p'ei kuo-shih chung ti p'ing-chun chu-i ssu-hsiang yü pao-pan tai-t'i tso-feng"). *CCJP*, 21 March 1951.

231. "Immediately Investigate and Settle the Confiscation and Redistribution of Mountain Forests and Irrigation Works in Land Reform" ("Li-chi chien-ch'a yü ch'u-li t'u-ti kai-ko chung shan-lin, shui-li chih mo-shou cheng-shou yü fen-p'ei kung-tso"). *CCJP* editorial, 6 July 1951.

232. "Immediately Set Up New Accounts" ("Chi-shih chien-li hsin chang"). *HHNP*, 7 February 1956.

233. "In Areas of Ch'angsha Special District (Hunan) Where Land Reform Is Completed, Review of Land Reform Is Carried Out and Victory Is Consolidated" ("Hu-nan Ch'ang-sha chuan-ch'ü t'u-kai chieh-shu ti-ch'ü, shih-hsing t'u-kai fu-ch'a kung-ku sheng-li"). *CCJP*, 4 March 1951.

234. "In Areas Where Land Reform Is Being Contracted the Reasons Should Be Clearly Explained to the Masses" ("Shou-so t'u-ti kai-ko ti-ch'ü, ying hsiang ch'ün-chung shuo-ming yüan-yin"). *CCJP*, 14 April 1951.

235. "In Excellent Order" ("Ching ching yu t'iao"). *HNCSP*, 7 June 1956.

236. "In 1950 Leading Comrades at All Levels Across the Country Must Pay Attention to Congresses of People's Representatives from All Walks of Life . . . " ("I-chiu-wu-ling-nien ch'üan-kuo ko-chi ling-tao t'ung-chih pi-hsü chung-shih ko-chieh jen-min tai-piao hui-i . . . "). *CCJP* editorial, 7 December 1949.

237. "In Some Areas of Hunan Province Mass Mobilization Is Neglected during Land Investigation and Fixing Yield" ("Hu-nan sheng yu hsieh ti-ch'ü, ch'a-t'ien ting-ch'an chung hu-shih fa-tung ch'ün-chung"). *CCJP*, 12 September 1952.

238. "In Some Areas of Hupei the Grain Department and the Co-op Department Must Immediately Correct the Phenomenon of Not Harmonizing Their Grain Purchase Work" ("Hu-pei sheng pu-fen ti-ch'ü liang-shih pu-men ho ho-tso-she pu-men, ying chi chiu-cheng kou-liang kung-tso chung ti pu hsieh-t'iao hsien-hsiang"). *JMJP*, 18 August 1953.

239. "In Various Parts of Hunan Province the Masses Are Mobilized to Reveal Large Amounts of Concealed Land . . . " ("Hu-nan sheng ko-ti . . . fa-tung ch'ün-chung ch'a-ch'u ta-liang man-t'ien"). *CCJP*, 30 October 1951.

240. "In Various Places in the Central South Peasants . . . Organize Mutual

Aid in Labor and Develop Production'' (''Chung-nan ch'ü ko-ti nung-min . . . tsu-chih lao-tung hu-chu fa-chan sheng-ch'an''). *CCJP*, 8 April 1952.

241. ''In Whose Hands Is It Good for the Grain to Be?'' (''Liang-shih tsai shei shou li hao?''). *CKCNP*, 24 November 1953.

242. ''Income of the Great Majority of Co-op Members Rises'' (''She-yüan shou-ju ta-pu ts'eng-chia''). *JMJP*, 18 September 1955.

243. ''Instances of Corruption and Waste of the Fruits of Land Reform Struggle Have Emerged'' (''Fa-sheng t'an-wu lang-fei t'u-kai tou-cheng kuo-shih hsien-hsiang''). *CCJP*, 29 January 1951.

244. ''Instances of Wasting the Fruits of Rent Reduction Have Emerged in Several Parts of Hunan'' (''Hu-nan ko-pieh ti-ch'ü, fa-hsien lang-fei chien-tsu kuo-shih hsien-hsiang''). *CCJP*, 15 April 1950.

245. ''Introduction to the Nature of Congresses of Representatives from All Walks of Life and of Peasants' Deputies, Their Tasks and Powers'' (''Ko-chieh tai-piao hui yü nung tai ti hsing-chih, jen-wu, chih-ch'üan chieh-shao''). *CCJP*, 9 April 1950.

246. ''Investigate and Correct Instances of Imbalance in Autumn Tax Collection'' (''Chien-ch'a chiu-cheng ch'iu-cheng-chung chi-ch'ing chi-chung hsien-hsiang''). *CCJP* editorial, 19 January 1950.

247. ''Investigation of Labor Power Utilization in Liao-yüan APC'' (''Liao-yüan nung-yeh-she lao-tung-li shih-yung ch'ing-k'uang tiao-ch'a''). *HHNP*, 31 March 1956.

248. ''Investigation of My Own Closed Door Thinking in Setting Up the League'' (''Chieh-ch'a wo tsai chien-t'uan chung ti kuan-men chu-i ssu-hsiang''). *CCJP*, 23 December 1949.

249. ''Investigation of the Agricultural Cooperativization Movement in Three Hupei Counties'' (''Hu-pei sheng san-ko hsien nung-yeh ho-tso-hua yün-tung ti tiao-ch'a''). *CCJP*, 16 October 1955.

250. ''Investigation of the Situation Regarding Temporary Mutual Aid Teams in Ch'ing-liang Village, Ch'angsha County [Hunan] . . . '' (''Ch'ang-sha hsien Ch'ing-liang hsiang lin-shih hu-chu-tsu ch'ing-k'uang ti tiao-ch'a . . . ''). *HHNP*, 14 April 1954.

251. ''Jen Kuei-fang's Mutual Aid Team in the Midst of Steady Progress'' (''Wen-pu ch'ien-chin chung ti Jen Kuei-fang hu-chu-tsu''). *CCJP*, 18 May 1952.

252. ''Just Starting the Work of Carrying Out Advance Purchase of Agricultural and Sideline Products'' (''Cheng chao-shou chin-hsing yü-kou nung fu ch'an-p'in kung-tso''). *HHNP*, 19 April 1954.

253. ''Land Reform Completed in Over 2,000 Hunan Villages'' (''Hu-nan erh ch'ien yü hsiang t'u-ti kai-ko chieh-shu''). *CCJP*, 20 April 1951.

254. ''Land Reform Must Include Leadership of the Broad Peasant Masses in

Class Struggle" ("T'u-ti kai-ko pi-hsü shih yu ling-tao ti kuang-ta nung-min ch'ün-chung ti chieh-chi tou-cheng"). *CCJP,* 24 August 1951.

255. "Lend Surplus Grain to Solve the Difficulties of Grain-short Households" ("Chieh-ch'u yü-liang chieh-chüeh ch'üeh-liang-hu ti k'un-nan"). *HHNP,* 19 April 1954.

256. "Li Pao-jen Sees a Tractor and Then Decides to Join an MAT" ("Li Pao-jen k'an le t'o-la-chi hou chüeh-hsin ts'an-chia hu-chu-tsu"). *HHNP,* 16 April 1954.

257. "Lien-meng Co-op Revises Its Finance Plan and Can Raise the Income of Over 95 Percent of Members" ("Lien-meng she hsiu-ting ts'ai-wu chi-hua, neng shih 95% i-shang ti she-yüan tseng-chia shou-ju"). *HNCSP,* 25 May 1956.

258. "Lin-hsiang County [Hunan] CCP Committee Strengthens Its Leadership of Credit Co-ops" ("Chung-kung Lin-hsiang hsien chia-ch'iang tui hsin-yung ho-tso ti ling-tao"). *HHNP,* 18 June 1954.

259. "Lin-hsiang County [Hunan] Strengthens Leadership of MATs" ("Lin-hsiang hsien chia-ch'iang tui hu-chu-tsu ti ling-tao"). *HHNP,* 24 May 1954.

260. "Liu Yü-ch'üan Who Runs the Co-op with Strict Economy" ("Chien-ch'ih ch'in-chien pan-she ti Liu Yü-ch'üan"). *HNCSP,* 27 May 1956.

261. "Lo-ch'ao Village APC in Yao-shui County (Hupei) Experimentally Implements 'Three Link' Contract" ("Hu-pei Yao-shui Lo-ch'iao hsiang ho-tso-she shih-pan 'san-lien-huan' ho-t'ung"). *JMJP,* 28 May 1954.

262. "Loans to APCs Should Be Used for Production within the Co-op, They Should Not Be Diverted to Private Use" ("Nung-yeh-she ti tai-k'uan ying yung-yü she nei sheng-ch'an, pu te i-tso ssu-yung"). *HHNP,* 3 May 1955.

263. "Loans to Serve Production Achieve Successes" ("Fang-k'uan wei sheng-ch'an fu-wu huo-te ch'eng-chi"). *TKP,* 24 November 1953.

264. "Looking at the Agrarian Reform Law with Reference to Village Conditions in the Central South Region" ("Ts'ung chung-nan ch'ü nung-ts'un ch'ing-k'uang k'an t'u-ti kai-ko fa"). *HHYP* 1 (3), November 1950: 45–57.

265. "The Lung-feng Village (Heng-shan, Hunan) Credit Mutual Aid Team Becomes a Credit Co-op" ("Heng-shan Lung-feng hsiang hsin-yung hu-chu-tsu chuan wei hsin-yung ho-tso-she"). *HHNP,* 27 April 1954.

266. "Majority of Areas in Hupei Province Have Entered the Stage of Investigating Land and Fixing Yield in Autumn Tax Collection Work" ("Hu-pei sheng ta-pu ti-ch'ü, ch'iu-cheng kung-tso chin-ju ch'a-t'ien p'ing-ch'an chieh-tuan"). *CCJP,* 11 October 1951.

267. "Make a Class Division, Explain Policy Clearly . . . " ("Hua-ch'ing

chieh-chi, chiang-ming cheng-ts'e . . . ''). *CCJP*, 24 December 1949.

268. ''Make Policy Penetrate Deeply, Overcome Empiricism and Do a Good Job of Grain Work'' (''Shen-ju kuan-ch'e cheng-ts'e, k'o-fu ching-yen chu-i, tso-hao liang-shih kung-tso''). *HPJP*, 7 October 1956.

269. ''Management and Control Getting Step by Step onto the Right Track'' (''Ching-ying kuan-li chu-pu tso shang cheng-kuei''). *HHNP*, 26 October 1956.

270. ''The Many-faceted Economy of Shuang-feng Advanced Co-op Employs 'Three Guarantees''' (''Shuang-feng kao-chi she ti to chung ching-chi shih-hsing san-pao''). *HNCSP*, 9 May 1956.

271. '' . . . Members of Two Co-ops Actively Investing in Them'' ('' . . . Liang she she-yüan chi-chi hsiang she t'ou-tzu''). *HNCCP*, 1 April 1956.

272. ''The Misapprehensions of Some Co-op Cadres in Hsiao-kan County (Hupei) with Regard to Cotton Fertilizer Loans Should Be Corrected Further'' (''Hu-pei Hsiao-kan hsien pu-fen ho-tso-she kan-pu, tui mien-fei tai-k'uan ti wu-chieh ying chia chiu-cheng''). *CCJP*, 12 May 1951.

273. ''Mobilize Co-op Members to Invest Actively to Expand Production'' (''Fa-tung she-yüan chi-chi t'ou-tzu k'uo-ta sheng-ch'an''). *JMJP*, 3 March 1955.

274. ''Mobilize Peasants to Act Themselves, Utilize Rent Reduction Persuasion General Meetings'' (''Fa-tung nung-min tzu-chi tung-shou, yün-yung chien-tsu shuo-li ta-hui''). *CCJP*, 23 December 1949.

275. ''Most Important Methods of Leading and Opening Up Credit Cooperation of the Hsiang-t'an Third District [Hunan] CCP Committee'' (''Chung-kung Hsiang-t'an san-ch'ü wei-yüan-hui ling-tao k'ai-chan hsin-yung ho-tso ti chu-yao tso-fa''). *HHNP*, 18 June 1954.

276. ''The Municipal SMC Organizes an Investigation Team'' (''Shih kung-hsiao ho-tso-she tsu-chih chien-ch'a tsu''). *HYHW*, 2 August 1956.

277. ''The Mutual Aid Teams in Nan-liang Village, Yao-shui County [Hupei] Conscientiously Carry Out the Settling of Accounts . . . '' (''Yao-shui hsien Nan-liang hsiang hu-chu-tsu jen-chen chin-hsing ch'ing-kung chieh-chang . . . ''). *JMJP*, 21 August 1953.

278. Nan Han-chen. ''The Great Significance and the Aim of Rural Finance Work'' (''Nung-ts'un chin-jung kung-tso ti chung-yao i-i ho nu-li fang-hsiang''). *Chung-kuo Chin-jung (China Finance)*, 1 (7), 24 June 1951: 2–10.

279. ''Nan-hu [Hupei] District People's Committee Calls a Meeting of Cadres from All *Hsiang* in the District'' (''Nan-hu ch'ü jen-min wei-yüan-hui chao-k'ai ch'üan ch'ü ko hsiang kan-pu hui-i''). *CCJP*, 2 July 1955.

280. ''Native Products Exchange Contracts Negotiated by Several District and

Municipality Co-ops in Hupei'' (''Hu-pei ko ch'ü (shih) ho-tso-she hu-ting chiao-i t'u-ch'an ho-tso hsieh-i''). *CCJP*, 26 August 1951.

281. ''The Necessity of the Existence of Credit Cooperatives'' (''Hsin-yung ho-tso-she yu ts'un-tsai ti pi-yao''). *TKP* editorial, 21 August 1956.

282. ''Neglecting Ideological Mobilization of Peasants and Seeking Only After Economic Gain Has Adversely Affected the Implementation of Land Reform . . . '' ('' . . . Hu-shih ts'ung ssu-hsiang shang fa-tung nung-min tan-tun chui-ch'iu ching-chi li-i, yin-hsiang le t'u-kai ti shun-li chin-hsing''). *CCJP*, 15 January 1951.

283. ''Never Again Will There Be a Confused Account!'' (''Pu-tsai i-pi hu-t'u chang le!''). *HHNP*, 21 October 1956.

284. ''1953 Agricultural Loan Work in Hunan'' (''Hu-nan sheng i-chiu-wu-san-nien ti nung-tai kung-tso''). *Chung-kuo Chin-jung (China Finance)*, 20 February 1953, pp. 5–6.

285. ''Ning-hsiang County [Hunan] Finance Committee Sends Capable Cadres to Penetrate the Basic Level and Help with the Work'' (''Ning-hsiang hsien ts'ai-wei p'ai te-li kan-pu shen-ju chi-ts'eng hsieh-chu kung-tso''). *HHNP*, 24 May 1954.

286. ''On the Commandist Workstyle and How It Endangers Revolutionary Work'' (''Lun ch'iang-p'o ming-ling tso-feng chi ch'i tui ko-ming kung-tso ti wei-hai''). *CCJP*, 1 December 1949.

287. ''On the Problem of Going All Out and Mobilizing the Masses in Land Reform'' (''Kuan-yü t'u-kai chung fang-shou fa-tung ch'ün-chung ti wen-t'i''). *HPJP*, 1 December 1950.

288. ''Once Land Reform Is Completed, Immediately Investigate and Summarize'' (''T'u-kai chieh-shu hou chi-shih chien-ch'a tsung-chieh''). *CCJP*, 12 February 1951.

289. ''One After Another, Thirty-six Counties in Hupei Convene Congresses of Representatives from All Walks of Life'' (''Hu-pei sheng san-shih-liu ko hsien, hsien hou k'ai ko-chieh tai-piao hui''). *CCJP*, 2 March 1950.

290. ''Open the Door to Free Borrowing and Lending'' (''Ta-k'ai tzu-yu chieh-tai chih-men''). *CCJP*, 24 May 1951.

291. ''Open Up Rural Finance . . . '' (''K'ai-chan nung-ts'un chin-jung . . . ''). *CCJP* editorial, 6 June 1951.

292. ''Open Up the Rent Return Movement to Get through the Spring Famine'' (''K'ai-chan t'ui-tsu yün-tung tu-kuo ch'un-huang''). *CCJP* editorial, 1 March 1950.

293. ''Opening Product Exhibitions Is a Good Way of Getting Close Relations between State-run Commerce and Co-ops'' (''Mi-ch'ieh kuo-ying shang-yeh ho ho-tso-she kuan-hsi k'ai shang-p'in chan-lan-hui shih i-chung hao pan-fa''). *TKP*, 19 December 1953.

294. ''Opinions on the Organization of Investigation and Rectification of

Mutual Aid Teams to Ling-ling County'' (''Ling-ling hsien tsu-chih lao-tung hu-chu-tsu ti tiao-ch'a ho cheng-tun ti i-chien''). *CCJP,* ? June 1952.

295. ''Order Concerning Implementation of Planned Purchase and Supply of Grain Issued by the GAC'' (''Chung-yang jen-min cheng-fu cheng-wu-yüan, fa-pu kuan-yü shih-hsing liang-shih ti chi-hua shou-kou ho chi-hua kung-ying ti ming-ling''). *JMJP,* 1 March 1954.

296. ''Organize Products Sources According to the Needs of the Masses'' (''Ken-chü ch'ün-chung hsü-yao tsu-chih huo-yüan''). *HHNP,* 13 August 1955.

297. ''Organize the Regulation of Rural Grain'' (''Yao tsu-chih nung-ts'un liang-shih t'iao-chi''). *TKP,* 11 April 1954.

298. ''Overcome Subjectivism in Agricultural Loan Work'' (''K'o-fu nung-yeh fang-k'uan kung-tso chung ti chu-kuan chu-i''). *TKP,* 23 May 1953.

299. ''Overcome the Deviation of Closed-Doorism: Prepare for the Complete Opening Up of the League'' (''K'o-fu kuan-men chu-i p'ien-hsiang, chun-pei t'uan ti wan-ch'üan kung-k'ai''). *CCJP,* 13 December 1949.

300. ''The Party Branch of Ch'ang-hsing Village in Shao-yang County [Hunan] Leads Mutual Aid and Cooperation with Success'' (''Shao-yang Ch'ang-hsing hsiang chih-pu ling-tao hu-chu ho-tso yu ch'eng-chi''). *HHNP,* 3 April 1954.

301. ''Pay Attention to Purifying and Strengthening Peasant Association Organizations in Areas of Hunan Where Land Reform Is Being Carried Out'' (''Hu-nan chin-hsing t'u-kai ti-ch'ü, chu-i cheng-tun chuang-ta nung-hsieh tsu-chih''). *CCJP,* 6 March 1951.

302. ''Peasants Bought Even More Goods'' (''Nung-min mai-tao le keng-to ti huo''). *JMJP,* 19 November 1955.

303. ''The Peasants' Deputies Committee of Ta-ming Village [Hupei]'' (''Ta-ming hsiang ti nung tai hui''). *HPJP,* 5 December 1950.

304. ''Peasants' Deputies Committees in Various Parts of Hunan'' (''Hu-nan ko-ti ti nung tai hui''). *CCJP,* 11 February 1950.

305. ''People of the Entire District Warmly Welcome Establishment of the CSMAC'' (''Chung-nan chün-cheng wei-yüan-hui ch'eng-li, ch'uan ch'ü jen-min je-lieh yung-hu''). *CCJP,* 5 February 1950.

306. ''People's Bank and Co-op Cadres in Ts'ao County [Hunan] Must Correct a Serious Rightist Mentality'' (''Ts'ao hsien jen-min yin-hang ho ho-tso-she kan-pu, ying chiu-cheng yen-chung ti yu-ch'ing ssu-hsiang''). *JMJP,* 8 July 1952.

307. ''Political Legal Departments Must Ensure That the Unified Purchase and Supply of Grain Policy Is Thoroughly Executed'' (''Cheng-fa pu-men ying pao-chang liang-shih t'ung-kou t'ung-hsiao cheng-ts'e kuan-ch'e chih-hsing''). *JMJP,* 7 March 1954.

308. "Preliminary Experience of the Party Branch of Heng-yüeh Village, Heng-shan County [Hunan] in Leading Agricultural Production Mutual Aid and Cooperation" ("Heng-shan Heng-yüeh hsiang chih-pu ling-tao nung-yeh sheng-ch'an hu-chu ho-tso ti ch'u-pu ching-yen"). *HHNP,* 16 April 1954.

309. "Preliminary Form of Credit Cooperation—the Credit Mutual Aid Team" ("Hsin-yung ho-tso ti ch'u-chi hsing-shih—hsin-yung hu-chu-tsu"). *TKP,* 12 November 1954.

310. "Preliminary Research into Problems of Temporary MATs" ("Tui-yü lin-shih hu-chu-tsu wen-t'i ti ch'u-pu yen-chiu"). *JMJP,* 11 February 1954.

311. "Preparatory Work for Establishing Co-ops in Seven Shop Village, Yao-shui County [Hupei]" ("Yao-shui hsien Ch'i-p'u hsiang chien-she ti chun-pei kung-tso"). *JMJP,* 24 August 1955.

312. "The Problem of Arranging Work and Fighting over Who Will Be First and Last within the Team Is Appropriately Solved" ("Shih-tang chieh-chüeh le tsu nei p'ai-kung cheng hsien hou ti wen-t'i"). *HHNP,* 17 April 1954.

313. "Problems in Study by Rural Work Cadres" ("Nung-ts'un kung-tso kan-pu hsüeh-hsi wen-t'i"). *CCJP,* 21 June 1950.

314. "Problems of Leading Land Reform at Present" ("Kuan-yü mu-ch'ien t'u-kai ti chih-tao wen-t'i"). *CCJP,* 17 January 1951.

315. "Problems of Raising Up Cadres and Opposing Sabotage in Land Reform" ("T'u-kai chung ti t'i-kao kan-pu ho fan p'o-huai wen-t'i"). *HHNP,* 20 December 1950.

316. "Production and Co-op Establishment Must Be Carried Out Closely Together" ("Chien-she yü sheng-ch'an pi-hsü chin-mi chieh-ho chin-hsing"). *HHNP,* 30 August 1955.

317. "Production Loan Money Should Not Be Used to Buy Pork" ("Pu ying-kai yung sheng-ch'an tai-k'uan mai chu-jou"). *HNCSP,* 27 May 1956.

318. "The Progress and Most Important Experiences in Land Reform Last Winter and This Spring in the Entire Central South Region, and Our Future Plans" ("Chung-nan ch'üan-ch'ü ch'ü-tung chin-ch'un t'u-ti kai-ko ti ching-kuo yu chu-yao ching-yen chi chin hou chi-hua"). *CCJP,* 18 April 1951.

319. "Province Decides to Enlarge the Land Reform Area" ("Pen-sheng chüeh-ting k'uo-ta t'u-kai ch'ü"). *HPJP,* 17 November 1950.

320. "The Province Is Now Establishing Basic-level Grain Markets" ("Pen-sheng cheng chien-li ch'u-chi liang-shih shih-ch'ang"). *HHNP,* 30 May 1954.

321. "The Provincial Finance Committee . . . Decides on Six Kinds of Agricultural and Sideline Products to Be Bought from the Peasants by Advance Purchase . . . " ("Sheng ts'ai-wei chüeh-ting hsiang

nung-min yü-kou liu chung nung-fu-yeh ch'an-p'in . . . ''). *HHNP*, 17 April 1954.

322. ''The Provincial Finance and Economics Committee Directs That State-run Grain Markets Be Established Quickly'' (''Sheng ts'ai-cheng ching-chi wei-yüan-hui chih-shih ko ti hsün-su chien-li kuo-chia kuan-li hsia ti liang-shih shih-ch'ang''). *HHNP*, 14 May 1954.

323. ''The Provincial Peasant Association Directs Various Districts to Establish an Organizational Framework of County and Subdistrict Peasant Associations'' (''Sheng nung-min hsieh-hui chih-shih ko ti, chien-li hsien ch'ü nung-min hsieh-hui tsu-chih chi-kou''). *HPJP*, 17 November 1950.

324. ''Provisional Methods for Operating Grain Markets Announced by the GAC'' (''Chung-yang jen-min cheng-fu cheng-wu-yüan, fa-pu liang-shih shih-ch'ang kuan-li chan-hsing pan-fa''). *JMJP*, 1 March 1954.

325. ''Provisional Methods of Unified Purchase and Supply of Grain in the Villages'' (''Nung-ts'un liang-shih t'ung-kou t'ung-hsiao chan-hsing pan-fa''). *JMJP*, 25 August 1955.

326. ''Provisional Regulations for the 1951 Agricultural Tax in Land Reform Areas of the Central South'' (''Chung-nan-ch'ü t'u-ti kai-ko ti-ch'ü i-chiu-wu-i-nien nung-yeh shui chan-hsing t'iao-li''). *CCJP*, 19 August 1951.

327. ''Provisional Regulations for the 1952 Agricultural Tax in Land Reform Areas of the Central South'' (''Chung-nan-ch'ü t'u-ti kai-ko ti-ch'ü i-chiu-wu-erh-nien nung-yeh-shui chan-hsing t'iao-li''). In *Handbook for 1952 Agricultural Tax Work in the Central South*, pp. 2–11. Canton, 1952.

328. ''Provisional Regulations for the 1952 Agricultural Tax in Non-land Reform Areas of the Central South'' (''Chung-nan-ch'ü wei t'u-ti kai-ko ti-ch'ü i-chiu-wu-erh-nien nung-yeh-shui chan-hsing t'iao-li''). In *Handbook for 1952 Agricultural Tax Work in the Central South*, pp. 12–22. Canton, 1952.

329. ''Provisional Regulations on Agricultural Tax in the Newly Liberated Areas'' (''Hsin-chieh-fang-ch'ü nung-yeh-shui chan-hsing t'iao-li''). In *Collected Laws and Decrees of the Central People's Government* 1, pp. 269–274.

330. ''Questions and Answers about Several Labor Mutual Aid Policy Problems'' (''Tui lao-tung hu-chu jo-kan cheng-ts'e wen-t'i ti chieh-ta''). In *Reference Material on Agricultural Production Mutual Aid Teams (Nung-yeh sheng-ch'an hu-chu-tsu ts'an-k'ao tzu-liao)*, pp. 15–20. Peking: Chung-yang jen-min cheng-fu nung-yeh pu ch'u-pan, 1952.

331. ''Questions and Answers on the Timely Collection of Agricultural

Debts'' (''Kuan-yü shou-hui tao-ch'i nung-yeh tai-k'uan wen-ta''). *HHNP,* 16 August 1955.

332. ''Questions Regarding the Organization of Village Credit Cooperatives'' (''Kuan-yü tsu-chih nung-ts'un hsin-yung ho-tso wen-t'i''). *CCJP,* 11 June 1952.

333. ''Quickly Assist APCs to Straighten Out Their Accounts'' (''Kan-k'uai pang-chu nung-yeh-she ch'ing-li chang-mu''). *HHNP,* 25 October 1956.

334. ''Quickly Give Out Agricultural Loans, Strengthen the Marketing and Supply of Local Products'' (''Hsün-su fa-fang nung-yeh tai-k'uan, chia-ch'iang t'u-ch'an kou-hsiao kung-tso''). *CCJP,* 6 April 1952.

335. ''Raise Up Peasant Activists through the Land Reform Movement'' (''T'ung-kuo t'u-ti kai-ko yün-tung p'ei-yang nung-min chi-chi fen-tzu''). *CCJP,* 1 March 1951.

336. ''The Reaction of the Various Classes in I-ch'ang [Hupei] to the Land Reform Law'' (''I-ch'ang ko chieh-ts'eng tui t'u-kai-fa ti fan-ying''). *HPJP,* 20 November 1950.

337. ''Rectify Cadres' Thought and Workstyle'' (''Cheng-tun kan-pu ssu-hsiang tso-feng''). *CCJP,* 17 June 1950.

338. ''The Relationship between Credit Co-ops and the Bank in Rural Finance Work'' (''Nung-ts'un chin-jung kung-tso chung yin-hang yü hsin-yung ho-tso ti kuan-hsi''). *Chung-kuo Chin-jung (China Finance),* 27 July 1951.

339. ''The Relationship between Unified Purchase and Supply of Grain and the Socialist Transformation of Agriculture'' (''Liang-shih t'ung-kou t'ung-hsiao yü nung-yeh she-hui chu-i kai-tsao ti kuan-hsi''). *HWJP,* 14 April 1954.

340. ''Relying on Co-op Members, the Accounts Have Been Clearly Straightened Out'' (''I-k'ao she-yüan ch'ing-li hao-le chang-mu''). *HHNP,* 24 August 1956.

341. ''Report of Chairman Li Hsien-nien at the Second Hupei All Walks Representatives' Forum'' (''Li Hsien-nien chu-hsi tsai Hu-pei sheng ti-erh-ts'u ko-chieh tai-piao tso-t'an-hui shang ti pao-kao''). *CCJP,* 6 January 1950.

342. ''Report of Hupei Provincial Government Vice Chairman Wang Jen-chung on Production and Famine Relief Work'' (''Hu-pei sheng fu Wang Jen-chung fu-chu-hsi, kuan-yü sheng-ch'an chiu-tsai kung-tso ti pao-kao''). *CCJP,* 19 January 1950.

343. ''Report of the Suburban Area 'Three Fix' Experimental Point Summarization Conference'' (''Chiao-ch'ü 'san-ting' shih-tien tsung-chieh hui-i ti tsung-chieh pao-kao''). *CCJP,* 21 October 1955.

344. " . . . Report of Vice Chairman Teng Tzu-hui at the Second Conference of Directors of Cooperative Bureaus of the Central South Region" (" . . . Teng Tzu-hui fu-chu-hsi, tsai chung-nan ti erh chieh ho-tso chü-chang hui-i shang ti pao-kao"). *CCJP*, 18 June 1951.

345. "Research on Using the Method of Combining Point with Area During Land Reform in Hupei" ("Hu-pei sheng t'u-kai chung yün-yung tien-mien chieh-ho fang-fa ti yen-chiu"). *CCJP*, 17 February 1951.

346. "Resolutely Support and Implement the CSMAC Decision . . . " ("Chien-chüeh yung-hu ho kuan-ch'e chung-nan chün-cheng wei-yüan-hui . . . ti chüeh-ting"). *CCJP*, 9 August 1952.

347. "Results of the Land Reform Movement over the Past Year" ("I nien lai t'u-ti kai-ko yün-tung ti ch'eng-kuo"). *CCJP*, 12 July 1951.

348. "Revise Work Quotas and Improve Labor Organization" ("Hsiu-kai lao-tung ting-o kai-chin lao-tung tsu-chih"). *HPJP*, 21 October 1956.

349. " . . . Rich Rice Harvest for Hsü Ting-hsüeh's MAT" (" . . . Hsü Ting-hsüeh hu-chu-tsu chung-tao feng-shou"). *CCJP*, 14 August 1952.

350. "Running a Good Savings Program Is the Best Means of Enlarging the Cash Loan Fund" ("Pan-hao ts'un-k'uan shih k'uo-ta fang-k'uan tzu-chin ti chu-yao lai-yüan"). *TKP*, 8 November 1954.

351. "Rural Capital Problems at Present as Seen in an Investigation of Eleven APCs" ("Ts'ung shih-i-ko nung-yeh ho-tso-she ti tiao-ch'a k'an tang-ch'ien nung-ts'un tzu-chin wen-t'i"). *JMJP*, 21 May 1956.

352. "Seize the Moment, Organize Credit Cooperation to Eliminate the Phenomenon of Selling Green Sprouts" ("Chua-chu shih-chi, tsu-chih hsin-yung ho-tso hsiao-mieh mai ch'ing-miao hsien-hsiang"). *CCJP*, 22 July 1952.

353. "Seize the Opportunity; Rectify Mutual Aid Teams" ("Chua-chin shih-shi, cheng-tun hu-chu-tsu"). *KJP*, 9 October 1954.

354. "Serious Instances of Farm Land Lying Fallow" ("Huang-wu t'ien ti hsien-hsiang yen-chung"). *CCJP*, 19 July 1951.

355. "Serious Occurrences of Deaths of Draught Oxen in Parts of Five Provinces" ("Wu sheng pu-fen ti-ch'ü, keng-niu ssu-wang hsien-hsiang yen-chung"). *CCJP*, 21 February 1951.

356. "Several Opinions about Agricultural Tax Collection Work after Cooperativization" ("Kuan-yü nung-yeh ho-tso-hua i-hou nung-yeh-shui cheng-shou kung-tso ti chi-tien i-chien"). *Ts'ai-cheng,* no. 3 (1957), pp. 16–18.

357. "Several Problems in Autumn Tax Grain Storage Work in Hupei" ("Hu-pei ch'iu-cheng ju-k'u kung-tso chung ti chi-ko wen-t'i"). *CCJP*, 14 September 1951.

358. "Shao-yang [Hunan] Fourth District Enlarged Cadres' Conference Summarizes Work and Investigates Cadres' Workstyle" ("Shao-yang

ssu ch'ü k'uo-ta kan-pu hui tsung-chieh kung-tso chien-ch'a kan-pu tso-feng''). *CCJP*, 17 June 1950.

359. "Significant Successes of Rural Credit Co-op Organization in Various Parts of Hupei'' (''Hu-pei ko ti nung-ts'un hsin-yung ho-tso tsu-chih ch'eng-chi hsien-chu''). *TKP*, 22 November 1953.

360. "Simultaneously Developing, Propagandizing, and Doing Business Is a Good Way of Establishing Credit Co-ops'' ('''Pien hsüan-ch'uan, pien ying-yeh, pien fa-chan' shih chien-li hsin-yung-she ti i-ko hao pan-fa''). *TKP*, 15 November 1954.

361. "The Situation and Problems in Rural Finance Work at Present'' (''Mu-ch'ien nung-ts'un chin-jung kung-tso chung ti ch'ing-k'uang ho wen-t'i''). *Chung-kuo Chin-jung (China Finance)*, 30 November 1951, pp. 17–18.

362. "The Situations of the Various Class Strata in the Ch'i-mei Village [Hunan] Cooperativization Movement'' (''Ch'i-mei hsiang ho-tso-hua yün-tung chung ko chieh-ts'eng ti tung-t'ai''). *JMJP*, 13 October 1955.

363. "Small Granaries Are Eliminated in Hupei's Yao-shui County'' (''Hu-pei sheng Yao-shui hsien hsiao-mieh le hsiao ts'ang-k'u hsien-hsiang''). *CCJP*, 13 June 1951.

364. "SMCs All over Hunan Organize Peddlers to Take Products Down to the Villages'' (''Hu-nan ko-ti kung-hsiao ho-tso-she tsu-chih huo-lang-tan sung-huo hsia-hsiang''). *TKP*, 24 November 1954.

365. "SMCs in Liu-yang and P'ing-kiang [Hunan] Continue to Expand Membership'' (''Liu-yang, P'ing-kiang kung-hsiao she chi-hsü fa-chan she-yüan''). *HNCSP*, 29 January 1954.

366. "SMCs Should Intensify Organization of Sources of Local Handicrafts Products'' (''Kung-hsiao ho-tso-she ying-kai chia-chin tsu-chih ti-fang shou-kung-yeh-huo yüan''). *JMJP*, 17 August 1953.

367. "So As to Receive Even Better the Leadership of the State-run Economy . . . '' (''Wei le keng-hao ti chieh-shou kuo-ying ching-chi ti ling-tao . . . ''). *CCJP*, 9 June 1952.

368. "Some Areas of Hsiang-hsiang and Ning-hsiang Begin to Mobilize Women to Participate in Land Reform . . . '' (''Hsiang-hsiang Ning-hsiang teng ti pu-fen ti-ch'ü, ch'u-pu fa-tung fu-nü ts'an-chia t'u-ti kai-ko . . . ''). *HHNP*, 28 December 1950.

369. "Some Distortions of the Peasants' Deputies Committees in Hsin-yang District'' (''Hsin-yang fen-ch'ü nung tai hui ti chi-ko p'ien-hsiang''). *CCJP*, 24 February 1950.

370. "Some Experiences in Calling a Meeting of Poor and Hired Peasants' Deputies in Sheng-li Village, Huang-p'i County [Hupei]'' (''Huang-p'i hsien Sheng-li hsiang chao-k'ai p'in ku nung tai-piao-hui ti chi tien t'i-yen''). *CCJP*, 6 January 1951.

371. "Some Important Problems Which Must Be Solved in Advance Purchase of Agricultural and Sideline Products" ("Nung-fu-yeh ch'an-p'in yü-kou chung pi-hsü chieh-chüeh ti chi-ko chu-yao wen-t'i"). *HHNP,* 21 May 1954.

372. "Some Local Cadres in Hupei and Hunan Have Forced the Peasants to Organize MATs" ("Hu-pei Hu-nan liang sheng yu hsieh ti-fang kan-pu, ch'iang-p'o nung-min tsu-chih hu-chu-tsu"). *CCJP,* 11 July 1951.

373. "Some Points of Information on Experimental Point Grain Tax, Purchase, and Supply Work" ("Liang-shih cheng, kou, hsiao shih-tien kung-tso ti chi tien t'i-hui"). *HPJP,* 30 September 1956.

374. "Some Problems in Changing Over from Land Reform to Production" ("T'u-ti kai-ko chuan-ju sheng-ch'an ti chi-ko wen-t'i"). *CCJP,* 27 May 1951.

375. "Some Problems in Developing from Point to Area during the Land Reform Movement in Hupei" ("Hu-pei t'u-kai yün-tung chung, yu tien hsiang mien chan-k'ai chung ti chi-ko wen-t'i"). *CCJP,* 20 February 1951.

376. "Some Problems in Opening the Labor Mutual Aid Movement in Huang-kang Special District [Hupei]" ("Huang-kang chuan-ch'ü k'ai-chan lao-tung hu-chu yün-tung chung ti chi-ko wen-t'i"). *CCJP,* 14 April 1952.

377. "Some Problems in Women's Work in Hsin-yang Special District at Present" ("Mu-ch'ien Hsin-yang chuan-ch'ü fu-nü kung-tso chung ti chi-ko wen-t'i"). *CCJP,* 24 September 1950.

378. "Some Problems in Wu-yang Special District Keypoint Land Reform" ("Wu-yang chuan-ch'ü chung-tien t'u-kai chung ti chi-tien t'i-yen"). *CCJP,* 13 January 1951.

379. "Some Questions in Organizing Production Mutual Aid Teams" ("Tsu-chih sheng-ch'an hu-chu-tsu ti chi-ko wen-t'i"). *CCJP,* 11 June 1951.

380. "Some Questions Regarding the Organization of MATs" ("Kuan-yü tsu-chih hu-chu-tsu ti chi-ko wen-t'i"). *CCJP,* 11 July 1951.

381. "Some Regulations of the CSMAC Concerning Actual Procedures for the Agrarian Reform Law" ("Chung-nan chün-cheng wei-yüan-hui . . . kuan-yü t'u-ti kai-ko fa shih-shih pan-fa ti jo-kan kuei-ting"). *CCJP,* 2 November 1950.

382. "Southern Peak Village in Yao-shui County (Hupei) Deeply Mobilizes the Peasants to Democratically Discuss and Rationally Distribute the Fruits of Land Reform Struggle" ("Hu-pei Yao-shui hsien Nan-yüeh hsiang t'u-kai chung, shen-ju fa-tung nung-min min-chu p'ing-i, ho-li fen-p'ei t'u-kai tou-cheng kuo-shih"). *CCJP,* 15 February 1951.

383. "Spread Rural Credit Cooperation Even More Universally" ("Keng p'u-pien ti k'ai-chan nung-ts'un hsin-yung ho-tso"). *TKP,* 23 April 1954.

384. "State Council Provisions for Unified Purchase and Supply of Grain with APCs" ("Kuo-wu-yüan kuan-yü nung-yeh sheng-ch'an ho-tso-she liang-shih t'ung-kou t'ung-hsiao ti kuei-ting"). *JMJP*, 7 October 1956.

385. "State-run Commerce Departments in Yao-shui and Hsiao-kan (Hupei) Help Co-ops Open and Expand Business" ("Hu-pei Yao-shui Hsiao-kan kuo-ying shang-yeh pu-men, pang-chu ho-tso-she k'ai-chan yeh-wu"). *JMJP*, 30 November 1953.

386. "Steadily Extend 'Combined Contracts' between MATs and SMCs" ("Wen-pu t'ui-kuang hu-chu-tsu yü ho-tso-she ti 'chieh-ho ho-t'ung'"). *CCJP*, 19 July 1952.

387. "Steadily Increasing Organization of Credit Mutual Aid and Cooperation in the Province" ("Pen-sheng hsin-yung hu-chu ho-tso tsu-chih jih-i fa-chan"). *HHNP*, 17 March 1954.

388. "Step by Step Improve Current APC Business Management Work" ("Chin-i-pu kai-shan hsien-yu nung-yeh-she ti ching-ying kuan-li kung-tso"). *HHNP* editorial, 18 November 1955.

389. "Stipulations of the Finance Department Concerning Standards for Determining Land Area and Normal Annual Yield for Agricultural Tax" ("Ts'ai-cheng-pu kuan-yü nung-yeh-shui t'u-ti mien-chi chi ch'ang nien ying-ch'an-liang ting-ting piao-chun ti kuei-ting"). *Collected Laws and Decrees of the Central People's Government* 1, p. 277, 16 September 1950.

390. "Strengthen Co-ops, Organize Purchase and Supply of Native Products and Mountain Products" ("Chia-ch'iang ho-tso-she tsu-chih t'u-ch'an shan-huo kou-hsiao kung-tso"). *CCJP* editorial, 4 April 1951.

391. "Strengthen the Leadership of the Party Over Agricultural Production Mutual Aid Teams" ("Chia-ch'iang tang tui nung-yeh sheng-ch'an hu-chu-tsu ti ling-tao"). *CCJP*, 1 June 1952.

392. "Strengthen the Unity of *Ch'ü* Cadres and Granary Cadres and Do Grain Collection and Storage Work Well" ("Chia-ch'iang ch'ü, ts'ang kan-pu t'uan-chieh kao hao shou-liang ju-k'u kung-tso"). *HPJP*, 16 November 1950.

393. "Strengthen Theoretical and Policy Study; Open Up a Campaign for Study Among On-duty Cadres" ("Chia-ch'iang li-lun cheng-ts'e hsüeh-hsi, k'ai-chan tsai-chih kan-pu hsüeh-hsi yün-tung!"). *CCJP* editorial, 18 January 1950.

394. "Strenuously Develop Labor Mutual Aid Organization" ("Ta-li fa-chan lao-tung hu-chu tsu-chih"). *CCJP*, 8 April 1952.

395. "The Struggle to Complete the Plan for Land Reform This Winter and Spring" ("Wei wan-ch'eng chin tung ming ch'ün t'u-ti kai-ko chi-hua erh tou-cheng"). *CCJP*, 12 October 1950.

396. "Subdistrict and Village Peasants' Deputies Meetings Are Convened in All Counties Throughout the I-chang District (Hupei)" ("Hu-pei

I-ch'ang fen ch'ü ko hsien p'u-pien chao-k'ai ch'ü hsiang nung tai hui''). *CCJP*, 15 December 1949.

397. "Sum Up the Lessons of Experience; Gradually Overcome the Bad Workstyle of Doing Everything Oneself'' (''Tsung-chieh ching-yen chiao-hsün, chin-i-pu k'o-fu pao-pan tai-t'i ti pu-liang tso-feng''). *CCJP*, 20 April 1951.

398. "Summarize Production Work; Augment Mutual Aid and Cooperation Organization'' (''Tsung-chieh sheng-ch'an kung-tso, t'i-kao hu-chu ho-tso tsu-chih''). *HHNP*, 17 March 1954.

399. "Summary of Last Year's Agricultural Tax Work and Our Hopes for This Year'' (''Ch'ü-nien nung-yeh-shui kung-tso tsung-chieh ho chin-nien ti yao-ch'iu''). *CCJP*, 22 July 1952.

400. "Sweet Rain'' (''Kan-yü''). *TKP*, 5 August 1955.

401. "Swift Development of Credit Co-ops in Various Parts of Hupei Province'' (''Hu-pei sheng ko ti hsin-yung ho-tso-she fa-chan hsün-su''). *TKP*, 8 December 1954.

402. "Taking Goods Down to the Village'' (''Sung-huo hsia-hsiang''). *HHNP*, 6 September 1955.

403. "The Tasks Put before SMCs'' (''Pai-tsai kung-hsiao-she mien-ch'ien ti jen-wu''). *HNNM*, 10 May 1956.

404. "There Is Now More Free Grain Than Last Year'' (''Tzu-yu liang pi ch'ü-nien to le''). *HHNP*, 6 November 1955.

405. "Third Discussion of the Rent Reduction and Return Movement'' (''San lun chien-tsu t'ui-tsu yün-tung''). *CCJP* editorial, 10 March 1950.

406. "Thoroughly Implement the Policy of Mutual Benefit . . . '' (''Kuan-ch'e chih-hsing hu-li cheng-ts'e . . . ''). *JMJP*, 23 October 1955.

407. "Thoroughly Mobilize the Masses, Stop Landlords and Rich Peasants from Transferring and Concealing Property and Grain'' (''Ch'ung-fen fa-tung ch'ün-chung, ta-p'o ti-chu fu-nung chuan-i yin-pi ts'ai-liang''). *CCJP*, 26 February 1950.

408. "Thoroughly Propagandize the Land Reform Law'' (''Shen-ju hsüan-ch'uan t'u-ti fa''). *CCJP*, 15 October 1950.

409. "Thoroughly Utilize Peasants' Deputies Committees . . . '' (''Ch'ung-fen yün-yung nung-min tai-piao hui-i . . . ''). *CCJP* editorial, 21 March 1950.

410. "Thoroughly Utilize Peasants' Deputies Committees to Promote Work . . . '' (''Ch'ung-fen yün-yung nung tai hui t'ui-tung kung-tso . . . ''). *CCJP*, 27 November 1949.

411. " 'Three Fix' Grain Work Opens Smoothly in Nine Heroes Village, Nan-hu District [Hupei]'' (''Nan-hu ch'ü Chiu-fu hsiang liang-shih 'san ting' kung-tso hsun-li k'ai-chan''). *CCJP*, 31 October 1955.

412. "Transitional Form of Credit Cooperative—the Credit Department''

("Hsin-yung ho-tso-she ti kuo-tu hsing-shih—hsin-yung pu"). *TKP*, 14 November 1954.

413. Tu Jun-sheng. "Some Problems in Leading Land Reform at Present" ("Tang-ch'ien t'u-ti kai-ko chih-tao chung ti chi-ko wen-t'i"). *HPJP*, 4 December 1950.

414. "Two Factors in the Solution of Rural Capital Problems" ("Chien-chüeh nung-ts'un tzu-chin wen-t'i ti liang ko huan-chieh"). *JMJP*, 17 October 1956.

415. "Two Hupei Counties Call Enlarged Cadres' Conferences One after the Other to Rectify Cadres' Thought and Workstyle" ("Hu-pei . . . liang hsien hsien-hou k'ai k'uo-ta kan-pu hui, cheng-tun kan-pu ssu-hsiang tso-feng"). *CCJP*, 22 February 1950.

416. "Understand Clearly the Promising Future of Village Work" ("Jen-ch'ing nung-ts'un kung-tso ti yüan-ta ch'ien-t'u"). *CCJP*, 16 August 1951.

417. "Unified Directive on National Bank Support for Cooperatives" ("Kuan-yü kuo-chia yin-hang fu-chu ho-tso-she ti lien-ho chih-shih"). In *Collected Finance Laws and Orders (1949–1952) (Chin-jung fa-ling hui-pien)*, p. 161. Peking: Ts'ai-cheng ching-chi ch'u-pan-she, 1956.

418. "Unified Purchase and Supply of Grain Is Really Good" ("Liang-shih t'ung-kou t'ung-hsiao chen-cheng hao"). *HNCNP*, 16 October 1955.

419. "Use the Peasants' Deputies and Exceed the [Grain] Tax Quota . . . " ("Yün-yung nung-tai ch'ao-kuo jen-wu . . . "). *CCJP*, 13 December 1949.

420. "Various Places in the Province Continue to Establish State Grain Markets" ("Pen-sheng ko ti chi-hsü chien-li kuo-chia liang-shih shih-ch'ang"). *HHNP*, 18 June 1954.

421. "Various Places Must Strengthen Leadership of Harvest Season Rural Finance Work" ("Ko ti pi-hsü chia-ch'iang ling-tao wang-chi nung-ts'un chin-jung kung-tso"). *TKP* editorial, 30 September 1955.

422. "Vice Chairman Teng Points Out the Policy Line for Land Reform during a Regular Administrative Meeting of the MAC" ("Chün-cheng wei-yüan-hui hsing-cheng li-hui, Teng fu-chu-hsi chih-shih t'u-kai fang-chen"). *CCJP*, 8 January 1951.

423. "Victoriously Complete the Autumn Tax Collection Task on the Basis of Fully Concluding Land Investigation and Fixing Yield" ("Tsai yüan-man chieh-shu ch'a-t'ien ting-ch'an ti chi-ch'u shang, sheng-li wan-ch'eng ch'iu-chi nung-yeh-shui cheng-shou jen-wu"). *CCJP* editorial, 24 October 1952.

424. "Village Cadres Cannot Become Proud or Relax" ("Nung-ts'un kan-pu pu-neng chiao-ao sung-chin"). *CCJP*, 2 August 1951.

425. "Village Reform Must Proceed Together with Recovery and Development of Agricultural Production" ("Nung-ts'un kai-ko yao yü hui-fu ho fa-chan nung-yeh sheng-ch'an hsiang chieh-ho"). *CCJP*, 1 December 1949.

426. "Villages of the Central South Region Begin Rectification of Peasant Associations" ("Chung-nan ch'ü nung-ts'un k'ai-chan cheng-tun nung-min hsieh-hui"). *CCJP*, 19 September 1950.

427. "Voluntarily, Voluntarily, and again Voluntarily!" ("Tzu-yüan, tzu-yüan, tsai tzu-yüan!"). *HPJP*, 7 October 1956.

428. "The Way the Hsia Lü Lo Village [Hunan] Credit Co-op Carries on and Oversees Its Business" ("Hsia Lü Lo hsiang hsin-yung-she tsen-yang chin-hsing ching-ying kuan-li ti"). *HHNP*, 18 May 1954.

429. "We Must Definitely Rely on the Poor Peasants in the Cooperativization Movement" ("Tsai ho-tso-hua yün-tung chung pi-hsü chien-chüeh i-k'ao p'in-nung"). *HHNP*, 28 August 1955.

430. "We Should Not Let Credit Co-ops Lose Money" ("Pu ying-kai jang hsin-yung ho-tso-she k'ui-pen"). *TKP*, 9 March 1955.

431. "Welcome the High Tide of the Socialist Mass Movement . . ." ("Ying-chieh she-hui chu-i ch'ün-chung yün-tung kao-ch'ao . . ."). *HHNP* editorial, 23 September 1955.

432. "What Are the Advantages of Unified Purchase and Unified Supply of Grain?" ("Shih-hsing liang-shih t'ung-kou t'ung-hsiao yu shen-ma hao-ch'u?"). *CKCNP*, 23 October 1954.

433. "What Is a Credit Cooperative?" ("Shen-ma chiao-tso hsin-yung ho-tso-she?"). *TKP*, 1 November 1954.

434. "What Then Does It Mean to Economize on Labor Days?" ("Tsen-yang ts'ai shih chieh-yüeh lao-tung jih?"). *JMJP*, 20 April 1956.

435. "What Things Should Be Taken into Account When Carrying Out Advance Purchase of Agricultural and Sideline Products?" ("Chin-hsing nung-fu-yeh ch'an-p'in yü-kou shih ying chu-i hsieh shen-ma?"). *HHNP*, 18 May 1954.

436. "When Old and New Co-ops Combine There Should Be Attention to the Care of Draught Oxen" ("Hsin, lao she chiao-chieh shih yao chu-i keng-niu hu-yang"). *HHNP*, 20 October 1956.

437. "When the Co-op Was Well Run Then There Was Something to Rely On" ("Pan hao le ho-tso-she, chiu yu le i-k'ao"). *CCJP*, 30 January 1956.

438. "Why Is the State Not Making Advance Purchases of Grain This Year?" ("Kuo-chia chin-nien wei-shen-ma pu yü-kou liang-shih?"). *TKP*, 23 March 1955.

439. "Will Middle Peasants Who Invest in Co-ops Suffer Losses?"

("Chung-nung tsai she li t'ou-tzu hui pu hui ch'ih-k'uei?"). *JMJP*, 19 April 1955.

440. "Work and Tasks of the Central South Region in 1950" ("Chung-nan ch'ü i-chiu-wu-ling-nien ti kung-tso jen-wu"). *CCJP*, 16 February 1950.

441. "The Work for a Rich Harvest and the Mutual Aid Movement in Hunan's Villages" ("Hu-nan nung-ts'un ti feng-ch'an kung-tso ho hu-chu yün-tung"). *CCJP*, 19 May 1952.

442. "Work Organization Methods of East Is Red Co-op's Production Brigades" ("Tung fang hung nung-yeh she sheng-ch'an-tui an-p'ai sheng-ch'an ti fang-fa"). *HNNM*, 13 April 1956.

443. "Wuhan Branch of China Grain Company . . . Is Separated from the Masses" ("Chung-kuo liang-shih kung-ssu Wu-han shih kung-ssu . . . t'o-li ch'ün-chung"). *CCJP*, 15 June 1952.

444. "Wuhan Municipal CCP Committee Co-op Department Calls a Meeting on 'Three Fix' Grain Work" ("Chung-kung Wu-han-shih-wei ho-tso-pu chao-k'ai liang-shih 'san ting' kung-tso hui-i"). *CCJP*, 13 October 1955.

445. "Yao Nationality Peasants . . . Obtain a Rich Harvest with the Help of a Mutual Aid Team" ("Yao-tsu nung-min . . . tsai hu-chu-tsu pang-chu hsia te tao feng-shou"). *JMJP*, 27 October 1953.

446. "*Yao-shui* Co-op (Hupei) Establishes More Purchasing Stations Overflowing with Consumer Goods" ("Hu-pei Yao-shui ho-tso-she ts'eng she shou-kou tien ch'ung-shih kung-ying wu-tzu"). *TKP*, 20 November 1953.

447. "You Cannot Treat Holding Meetings as the Only Method of Mobilizing Peasants" ("Pu-neng pa k'ai-hui tang-ch'eng fa-tung nung-min ti wei-i fang-fa"). *CCJP*, 8 January 1951.

448. "Yu-lung Village [Hunan] Credit Co-op before and after Rectification" ("Yu-lung hsiang hsin-yung ho-tso-she cheng-tun ch'ien-hou"). *TKP*, 12 June 1955.

III. BOOKS IN ENGLISH

449. Baum, Richard. *Prelude to Revolution*. New York: Columbia University Press, 1975.

450. Chang, Parris. *Power and Policy in China*. University Park: Pennsylvania State University Press, 1978.

451. Chao Kuo-chun. *Agrarian Policies of Mainland China: A Documentary Study (1949–1956)*. Cambridge, Mass.: Harvard University Press, 1957.

452. Chao Kuo-chun. *Agricultural Development and Problems in China To-day.* New York: Institute of Pacific Relations, 1958.

453. Chekhutov, A. I. *The Tax System in the PRC (Nalogovaia sistema kitais-koi narodnoi respubliki).* Moscow: 1962. (Translated by JPRS 2227-N.)

454. Chen Nai-ruenn. *Chinese Economic Statistics.* Chicago: Aldine Publishing Company, 1967.

455. Chou Li-po. *Great Changes in a Mountain Village.* Peking: Foreign Languages Press, 1961.

456. Corson, William R. "An Examination of Banking, Monetary, and Credit Practices in Communist China, 1949–57." Ph.D. dissertation, American University, 1969.

457. Dobb, Maurice. *Soviet Economic Development Since 1917.* New York: International Publishers, 1966.

458. Ecklund, George N. *Financing the Chinese Government Budget: Mainland China 1950–1959.* Edinburgh: Edinburgh University Press, 1966.

459. *Economic Geography of Central China (Hua chung ti-ch'u ching-chi ti-li).* Peking: 1958. (Translated by JPRS 2227-N.)

460. Hinton, William. *Fanshen.* New York: Vintage Books, 1966.

461. Hsia, Ronald. *Price Control in Communist China.* New York: Institute of Pacific Relations, 1953.

462. Hsüeh Mu-ch'iao, Su Hsing, and Lin Tse-li. *The Socialist Transformation of the National Economy in China.* Peking: Foreign Languages Press, 1960.

463. Hughes, T. J. and D. E. T. Luard. *The Economic Development of Communist China 1949–1960.* London: Oxford University Press, 1959.

464. Huntington, Samuel P. *Political Order in Changing Societies.* New Haven, Conn.: Yale University Press, 1968.

465. Jasny, Naum. *The Socialized Agriculture of the USSR.* Stanford, Ca.: Stanford University Press, 1949.

466. Korkunov, I. et al. *Socialist Transformation of Agriculture in the Chinese People's Republic (1949–1957).* Moscow: 1960. (Translated by JPRS 4255.)

467. Lewin, Moshe. *Russian Peasants and Soviet Power.* Evanston, Ill.: Northwestern University Press, 1968.

468. Lippit, Victor. *Land Reform and Economic Development in China.* White Plains, N.Y.: International Arts and Sciences Press, 1974.

469. Liu Ta-chung and Kung-chia Yeh. *The Economy of the Chinese Mainland.* Princeton, N.J.: Princeton University Press, 1965.

470. Mao Tse-tung. *On the Correct Handling of Contradictions Among the People.* Peking: Foreign Languages Press, 1957.

471. Meisner, Maurice. *Mao's China*. New York: The Free Press, 1977.
472. *Model Regulations for Advanced Agricultural Producers' Cooperatives*. Peking: Foreign Languages Press, 1956.
473. *Model Regulations for an Agricultural Producers' Cooperative*. Peking: Foreign Languages Press, 1956.
474. *Mutual Aid and Cooperation in China's Agricultural Production*. Peking: Foreign Languages Press, 1953.
475. Ouyang Shan. *Uncle Kao*. Peking: Foreign Languages Press, 1957.
476. Pepper, Suzanne. *Civil War in China*. Berkeley, Ca.: University of California Press, 1978.
477. Perkins, Dwight. *Market Control and Planning in Communist China*. Cambridge, Mass.: Harvard University Press, 1966.
478. Phillips, Ralph W., Johnson, Ray G., and Moyer, Raymond T. *Livestock of China*. Washington, D.C.: U.S. Government Printing Office, 1945.
479. *Report of the Indian Delegation to China on Agrarian Cooperatives*. New Delhi: Government of India Planning Commission, 1957.
480. Schran, Peter. *The Development of Chinese Agriculture, 1950–1959*. Urbana: University of Illinois Press, 1969.
481. Schurmann, Franz. *Ideology and Organization in Communist China*. Berkeley, Ca.: University of California Press, 1966.
482. Selden, Mark. *The Yenan Way in Revolutionary China*. Cambridge, Mass.: Harvard University Press, 1971.
483. Starlight, Lawrence Lee. "Monetary and Fiscal Policies in Communist China, 1949–54." Ph.D. dissertation, Harvard University, 1956.
484. Stavis, Benedict. *The Politics of Agricultural Mechanization in China*. Ithaca, N.Y.: Cornell University Press, 1978.
485. Ting Ling. *The Sun Shines over the Sankan River*. Peking: Foreign Languages Press, 1954.
486. Vogel, Ezra F. *Canton under Communism*. Cambridge, Mass.: Harvard University Press, 1969.
487. Wong, John. *Land Reform in the People's Republic of China*. New York: Praeger Publishing Company, 1973.

IV. ARTICLES IN ENGLISH

488. "Absentee Landlords to Declare Possessions." *SWB* 83: 36.
489. *The Agrarian Reform Law of the People's Republic of China* (Adopted by the CPG GAC, 28 June 1950). *CB* 42: 2–9.
490. "Administrative Organization in Central South China." *CB* 131.
491. Bernstein, Thomas P. "Cadre and Peasant Behavior under Conditions of Insecurity and Deprivation: The Grain Supply Crisis of the Spring of

1955.'' In A. Doak Barnett, ed., *Chinese Communist Politics in Action*, pp. 365–399. Seattle, Wash.: University of Washington Press, 1969.

492. Bernstein, Thomas P. "Keeping the Revolution Going: Problems of Village Leadership after Land Reform." In John Wilson Lewis, ed., *Party Leadership and Revolutionary Power in China*, pp. 239–267. Cambridge: Cambridge University Press, 1970.

493. Bernstein, Thomas P. "Leadership and Mass Mobilisation in the Soviet and Chinese Collectivisation Campaigns of 1929–30 and 1955–56: A Comparison." *China Quarterly* 31 (1967): 1–47.

494. "Decisions Concerning the Differentiation of Class Status in the Countryside" (Adopted by the CPG GAC, 4 August 1950). *CB* 42: 12–20.

495. "Decisions on Mutual Aid and Cooperation in Agricultural Production Adopted by the Central Committee of the Communist Party of China." In *Mutual Aid and Cooperation in China's Agricultural Production*. Peking: Foreign Languages Press, 1953.

496. "Extension of Land Reform in Central South China." *FBIS* (Wuhan), 29 November 1950.

497. "Extension of Land Reform in Central South China." (NCNA, 29 November 1950), *SWB* 86: 61.

498. "Extension of Program in Kwangtung." (NCNA, 12 December 1950), *SWB* 87: 27.

499. "GAC Directive on Collection of Agricultural Tax." *SCMP*, 359 (1952): 9–13.

500. "General Regulations Governing the Organization of Conference of Representatives of the People of the *Hsiang* (Administrative *Ts'un*) Level" (Passed 8 December 1950). *CB* 144 (1951): 11–12.

501. "High Proportion of New Members." (NCNA, 1 July 1950), *SWB* 64:47.

502. Hofheinz, Roy M. "Rural Administration in Communist China." *China Quarterly* 11 (1961): 140–159.

503. "Improve the Collection of the Grain Tax." *SCMP* 213 (1951): 39–41.

504. Jao Shu-shih. "Experiences in East China Land Reform Experiments Summed Up." *SCMP* 39 (1950): 43–45.

505. "*Jen Min Jih Pao* Announces Rectification." (NCNA, 1 July 1950), *SWB* 64: 48.

506. "Land Reform in Hupei." (NCNA, 25 November 1950), *SWB* 85: 56.

507. Li Shu-te. "Agricultural Tax Work during the Last Ten Years." *Ts'ai-cheng* 19 (October 1959). Translated by JPRS No. 4162.

508. Lindsay, Michael. "The Taxation System of the Shansi-Chahar-Hopei Border Region, 1938–1945." *China Quarterly* 42 (1970): 1–15.

509. "Peasant Associations Grown to Powerful Size in the Country." (NCNA, Peking, 31 December 1950), *SCMP*, 40: 17–18.

510. Pfeffer, Richard M. "Contracts in China Revisited, with a Focus on Agriculture, 1949–63." *China Quarterly* 28 (1966): 106–129.
511. "Questions and Answers on 1952 Agricultural Tax." *SCMP* 385 (1952): 12–14. Translated from *JMJP,* 7 July 1952.
512. "Rent Reduction Completed in Central South China." (NCNA, Peking, 20 June 1950), *SWB* 62: 57.
513. Riskin, Carl. "Surplus and Stagnation in Modern China." In Dwight H. Perkins, ed., *China's Modern Economy in Historical Perspective,* pp. 49–84. Stanford, Ca.: Stanford University Press, 1975.
514. "Sabotage of Grain Collection." *SWB* 84: 58; and *FBIS* (Wuhan), 17 November 1950.
515. Shue, Vivienne. "Peasant Culture and Socialist Culture in China: On the Dynamics of Structure, Behavior, and Value Change in Socialist Systems." In G. Chu and F. L. K. Hsu, eds., *Moving a Mountain: Cultural Change in China.* Honolulu, University of Hawaii Press, 1979.
516. Shue, Vivienne. "The Politics of Cooperativization." (Paper delivered at the 1977 Annual Meeting of the Association for Asian Studies.)
517. Skinner, G. W. and E. A. Winckler. "Compliance Succession in Rural Communist China: A Cyclical Theory." In Amitai Etzioni, ed., *Complex Organizations: A Sociological Reader.* New York: Holt, Rinehart, and Winston, 1969.
518. "Strive for Completion of Collection of 1952 Agricultural Tax." *SCMP* 359 (1952): 13–14.
519. Teng Tzu-hui. "Basic Tasks and Policies in Rural Areas." In *Mutual Aid and Cooperation in China's Agricultural Production.* Peking: Foreign Languages Press, 1953.
520. Teng Tzu-hui. "Report on the Work of the CSMAC during the Past Half-Year." *CB* 39 (1950): 2–9.
521. Tu Jun-sheng. "Report on Agrarian Reform in Central South Region During the Past Half-Year." *CB* 39 (1950): 21–28.
522. "Twelve Thousand Bandits Liquidated in West Hunan." (NCNA, Hankow, 12 December 1950), *SCMP* 28: 15.
523. Walker, Kenneth R. "Collectivisation in Retrospect: the 'Socialist High Tide' of Autumn 1955–Spring 1956." *China Quarterly* 16 (1966): 1–43.
524. Walker, Kenneth R. "Organization of Agricultural Production." In Alexander Eckstein, Walter Galenson, and Ta-chung Liu, eds., *Economic Trends in Communist China,* pp. 397–458. Chicago: Aldine Publishing Company, 1968.

INDEX

Cadres *(continued)*
    peasants, 19, 142, 241; and rent
    reduction, 32; and SMCs, 204; and
    taxation, 129, 130; training of, 43,
    68, 130, 184f, 240, 263, 309, 311;
    and Unified Purchase, 224f;
    upper-level, 24, 272; workpoints for,
    183. *See also* "Commandism";
    "Deviations"; Work teams
"Capitalist tendencies," 4, 99, 182,
    190, 271. *See also* Private enterprise;
    "Rich peasant economy"
CCP. *See* Chinese Communist Party
Central People's Government
    Committee, 105
Central planning, 5; and APCs, 285;
    and control, 196, 268, 313, 315,
    328f; and credit policy, 257f;
    decentralization, 313; and
    industrialization, 145f; and private
    accumulation, 190; and rural
    savings, 271–272; and speculation,
    213; and technology, 312; and
    Unified Purchase, 184, 235. *See also*
    Central-local relations; Class policy;
    "Localism"; Policy planning
Central-local relations, 8, 39–40, 101,
    126, 235–236, 332, 337, 341–344.
    See also "Localism"; Policy
    implementation
Central South, 15; commercial areas,
    76–77; election of *hsiang* deputies,
    26; redistribution, 61; and land
    reform cadres, 67; and land reform,
    90; restoration of commerce, 199;
    and sabotage, 137; and SMCs, 202;
    and tax evasion, 127
Central South Military Affairs
    Commission, 56; and rent reduction,
    32; and rural commerce, 199; and
    taxation, 132
Chiang Kai-shek, 41
Chinese Communist Party, 1;
    recruitment, 26–27
Chou En-lai, 215
Class. *See* Gentry; Landlords; Middle

peasants; Poor peasants; Rich
    peasants. *See also* Redistribution
Class analysis, 7–8, 325f, 332,
    337–341; and Peasant Associations,
    23, 25. *See also* Class struggle
Class consciousness, 7, 76, 83. *See
    also* Class struggle; Conflict;
    "Speaking bitterness"
Class policy, 18, 43f, 274; and advance
    purchase contracts, 229; and
    collectivization, 215; and
    cooperativization, 282; and Credit
    Co-ops, 263f; and elementary
    co-ops, 288n; and land reform,
    47–56, 73–75, 92; and MATs, 158;
    and mutual aid, 147; and
    reclassification, 95–96; and SMCs,
    204; and taxation, 102, 115, 122. *See
    also* various Policy headings
Class struggle, 34; development and
    management of, 7, 29–30, 92, 108,
    120, 244, 274, 324–326, 331, 333;
    and land reform, 42f, 82–83; and
    MATs, 190; and taxation, 120, 142;
    as rhetoric, 340. *See also* Class
    policy
Collectives: income distribution within,
    307; organization of, 306; and rent
    payments, 300; and workpoints,
    306. *See also* Agricultural
    Production Co-ops
Collectivization: and Central planning,
    146; and compensation, 292–296;
    "high tide," 308–313, 331f; and
    industrialization, 146; and MATs,
    154; pace of, 196, 278–284, 300;
    and productivity, 281. *See also*
    Soviet experience
"Commandism," 34, 328; and
    collectivization, 309; and MATs,
    179f. *See also* "Deviations"
Committee of People's Deputies, 26
Conflict, 336–339; intravillage, 134,
    325. *See also* Class policy; Class
    struggle
Consumption, 195; regulation of,

Designer:	Wendy Calmenson
Compositor:	Viking Typographics
Printer:	Braun-Brumfield
Binder:	Braun-Brumfield
Text:	Times Roman
Display:	VIP Times Roman
Cloth:	Holliston Roxite B 53561
Paper:	50 lb. P&S Offset B-32